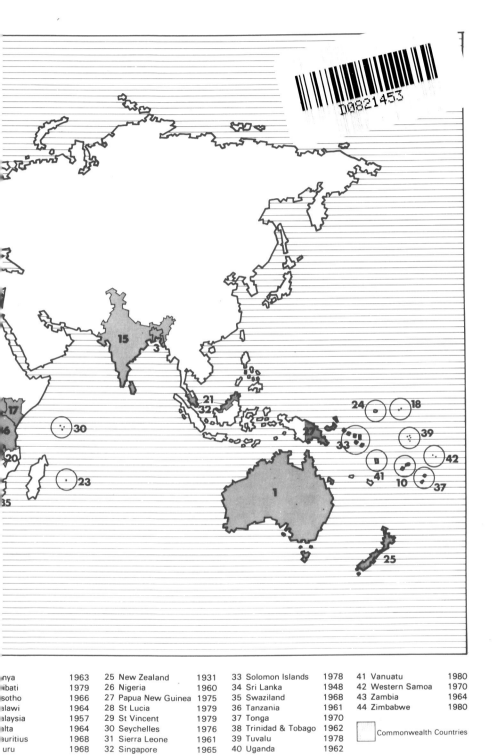

nya	1963	25 New Zealand	1931	33 Solomon Islands	1978	41 Vanuatu	1980
ibati	1979	26 Nigeria	1960	34 Sri Lanka	1948	42 Western Samoa	1970
sotho	1966	27 Papua New Guinea	1975	35 Swaziland	1968	43 Zambia	1964
alawi	1964	28 St Lucia	1979	36 Tanzania	1961	44 Zimbabwe	1980
alaysia	1957	29 St Vincent	1979	37 Tonga	1970		
alta	1964	30 Seychelles	1976	38 Trinidad & Tobago	1962	Commonwealth Countries	
auritius	1968	31 Sierra Leone	1961	39 Tuvalu	1978		
uru	1968	32 Singapore	1965	40 Uganda	1962		

Stitches in Time

Stitches in Time
The Commonwealth in World Politics

ARNOLD SMITH
with CLYDE SANGER

GENERAL PUBLISHING CO. LIMITED
DON MILLS, ONTARIO

© 1981
Arnold Smith with
Clyde Sanger
All rights reserved

FIRST PUBLISHED IN 1981 BY
General Publishing Co. Limited
30 Lesmill Road
Don Mills, Ontario

Canadian Cataloguing in Publication Data

Smith, Arnold, 1915-
   Stitches in time

ISBN 0-7736-0100-7

1. Smith, Arnold, 1915-   2. Diplomats -
Canada - Biography.   3. Commonwealth Secretariat -
Biography.   4. Commonwealth Secretariat - History.
5. Commonwealth of Nations - History - 20th century.
I. Sanger, Clyde.   II. Title.

FC626.S65A3   327.2'0924   C81-094664-5
F1034.3.S65A3

This book has been published with the help of a grant from the Social Sciences Federation of Canada using funds provided by the Social Sciences and Humanities Research Council of Canada.

Published in Great Britain by André Deutsch

First Printing
ISBN 0-7736-0100-7   Printed & bound in Canada

CONTENTS

CHRONOLOGY

of some world and Commonwealth events

1964 July   Commonwealth Heads of Government
                    Meeting (CHGM) in London approves
                    proposal to set up Secretariat.

1965 January   Senior Officials draft Agreed Memorandum
                    for Secretariat.
      June   CHGM in London, at which Arnold Smith
                    elected Secretary-General (SG).
      August   Singapore expelled from Malaysian
                    Federation. India-Pakistan war over
                    Kashmir, settled by Tashkent agreement.
      October   Health Ministers Meeting, Edinburgh.
      November   Ian Smith makes illegal declaration of
                    independence in Rhodesia. SG tours five
                    East African states.

1966 January   Special CHGM called in Lagos on Rhodesian
                    rebellion, launches Sanctions Committee
                    and training programme for Zimbabweans.
                    CHGM followed by 'majors' coup' in
                    Nigeria.
      February   Nkrumah overthrown by General Ankrah in
                    Ghana. Menzies retires as Australian
                    Prime Minister; Holt takes over.
      April   UN Security Council's 'Beira resolution' on oil
                    supplies to Rhodesia. Law Ministers
                    Meeting, London, calls for Legal Section.
      May   Guyana independence.
      June   Trade Ministers Meeting, London. Sherfield
                    Review Commission on Commonwealth
                    Organisations recommends Secretariat absorb
                    Education Liaison Unit and Economic
                    Committee.
      July   Gowon replaces Ironsi after second Nigerian
                    coup.

1966	September	CHGM in London dominated by Rhodesian issue. Botswana independence.
	October	Lesotho independence. SG's first visit to Asian Commonwealth countries.
	December	Wilson, Ian Smith hold talks aboard H.M.S. *Tiger*.
1967	February	SG visits Ayub Khan in Pakistan.
	April	SG to Australia, New Zealand and Canada.
	May	Senior planning officials' meeting, Nairobi, sets up Commonwealth technical assistance programme. Gowon's twelve-state decree in Nigeria. Ojukwu declares Biafra independent.
	June	East African Community treaty signed, Kampala.
	July	Canada's Centennial celebrations.
	September	Gibraltar referendum.
1968	February	Education Ministers Meeting, Lagos. UNCTAD-2, Delhi. British Ministers learn of oil companies' 'swap arrangement' to avoid Rhodesian sanctions.
	March	Mauritius independence.
	April	Pierre Trudeau takes over as Canadian Prime Minister.
	May	UN Security Council imposes comprehensive sanctions on Rhodesia. Nigerian peace talks, organised by Secretariat, in Kampala.
	September	Health Ministers Meeting, Kampala.
	October	Wilson, Ian Smith hold talks aboard H.M.S. *Fearless*.
	November	Nixon wins US Presidential elections.
	December	SG in Dublin, exploring Irish return to Commonwealth.
1969	January	CHGM, London. Issue of Nigerian war off-stage. Heads approve Legal Section for Secretariat.
	February	First meeting in Niamey on L'Agence de coopération culturelle et technique.

1969	May	SG on island-hopping tour of Caribbean, during crisis over regional cooperation. US preoccupied with Vietnam.
	September	Review of technical assistance programme, Barbados, sets stage for Commonwealth Fund for Technical Cooperation (CFTC).
	October	Caribbean Development Bank established. Pearson report, 'Partners in Development', issued.
	December	SG visits the Gambia, Sierra Leone ahead of their becoming republics in 1970-71.
1970	January	Nigerian war ends.
	February	SG tours Asian Commonwealth countries.
	March	Second Niamey conference establishes L'Agence.
	May	Western Samoa seeks Commonwealth membership.
	June	Tonga independence. Edward Heath wins British elections.
	July	British Government says it is considering selling arms to South Africa. Commonwealth Games, Edinburgh.
	September	Finance Ministers meet in Cyprus, approve plan for CFTC. Nasser dies. SG visits Yahya Khan in Pakistan.
	October	Fiji independence.
	November	De Gaulle dies. Cyclone in East Bengal.
	December	Awami League wins overall majority in Pakistan elections.
1971	January	Law Ministers Meeting, New Delhi. CHGM Singapore confronts issue of arms sales to South Africa, approves setting up of CFTC, Commonwealth information programme and youth studies. Idi Amin overthrows Obote.
	February	Education Ministers Meeting, Canberra.
	March	Pakistan army crushes students and other opposition in Dacca.
	April	CFTC established. Youth uprising in Sri Lanka.

1971	May	Pompidou-Heath meeting in Paris opens way for Britain in EEC.
	June	Senior officials meet in London to set up Export Market Development programme.
	July	Amin visits Israel and Britain.
	September	Finance Ministers meet in Nassau, ask Secretariat to prepare studies on implications of British entry into EEC.
	October	Health Ministers Meeting, Mauritius. On same journey SG visits Tanzania, Uganda over border dispute.
	November	Home signs Anglo-Rhodesian settlement proposals with Smith in Salisbury.
	December	Indian troops invade East Pakistan. Birth of Bangladesh.
1972	January	SG flies to Islamabad, but Bhutto withdraws Pakistan from Commonwealth. Pearce Commission arrives in Rhodesia.
	February	SG visits Bangladesh and four Asian countries to win support for its Commonwealth membership.
	March	Meetings of Commonwealth officials begin on African, Caribbean and Pacific (ACP) association with EEC.
	April	UNCTAD-3 in Santiago. Bangladesh accedes to Commonwealth.
	May	Pearce Report shows majority reject Rhodesian settlement.
	August	Amin expels Asians from Uganda on ninety days' notice.
	September	SG meets Leopold Senghor on ACP association issue.
	December	Whitlam's Labour Government takes over in Australia.
1973	January	Law Ministers Meeting, London. Youth Ministers approve CYP at Lusaka meeting.
	February	Organisation of African Unity (OAU) begins to take initiative on EEC association issue.

1973	March– April	SG visits New Zealand, Australia and Papua New Guinea. Special PNG programme set up in 1974.
	May	OAU 10th anniversary summit hears Amin perform, also endorses strategy for EEC association talks.
	August	CHGM Ottawa.
	October	ACP negotiations for EEC association begin in Brussels.
1974	January	Commonwealth Games, Christchurch. SG visits Hong Kong, New Zealand and Cook Islands.
	April	Coup in Portugal transforms southern African situation.
	May	SG helps initiate independence talks between Portugal and Mozambique liberation leaders.
	June	Education Ministers Meeting, Jamaica.
	July	Makarios flees Cyprus, after Sampson coup, and Turkish mainland troops invade.
	August	Nixon resigns after Watergate scandal.
	September	SG to Paris for first talks with new head of L'Agence.
	December	Zimbabwean leaders released, sign Lusaka unity declaration.
1975	February	Law Ministers Meeting, Lagos.
	March	Ministerial meeting on food production and rural development.
	May	CHGM Jamaica. Heads agree to training programme for Namibians, request studies on New International Economic Order. Shridath Ramphal elected SG.
	June	Mozambique independence. Arnold Smith retires as SG.

Note: Finance Ministers meet every September, Law Ministers every two years, Health and Education Ministers every three years.

ABBREVIATIONS

AAMS	Associated African and Malagasy States (to the EEC)
ACCT	L'Agence de Coopération Culturelle et Technique
ACP	African, Caribbean and Pacific states (EEC associates)
ACU	Association of Commonwealth Universities
ANC	African National Council (of Rhodesia; later the UANC)
ASEAN	Association of South East Asian Nations
BP	British Petroleum
CARICOM	Caribbean Community
CFTC	Commonwealth Fund for Technical Cooperation
CHGM	Commonwealth Heads of Government Meeting (also HGM)
CHGRM	Commonwealth Heads of Government Regional Meeting
CIDA	Canadian International Development Agency
CISGO	Commonwealth Interchange Study Group Organisation
CPA	Commonwealth Parliamentary Association
CRO	Commonwealth Relations Office (British)
CUSO	Canadian University Service Overseas
CZSF	Commonwealth Zimbabwe Scholarship Fund
ECA	Economic Commission for Africa (United Nations)
EDF	European Development Fund (for EEC associates)
EEC	European Economic Community
FCO	Foreign and Commonwealth Office (British; absorbed CRO)
FRELIMO	Front for the Liberation of Mozambique
GSP	Generalised System of Preferences (various offers by richer countries of tariff cuts for LDC manufactured and semi-manufactured exports)
IBRD	International Bank for Reconstruction and Development (alias the World Bank)
IMF	International Monetary Fund
LDC	Less Developed Countries

NGO	Non-Governmental Organisation
OAS	Organisation of American States
OAU	Organisation of African Unity
OCAM	Organisation Commune Africaine et Malagache (14 sub-Sahara francophone states, all also members of AAMS and the ACCT; see chapter 9)
ODM	Overseas Development Ministry (British)
PAIGC	Partido Africano da Independencia de Guinee e Cabo Verde (nationalist party of Guiné-Bissau)
RCS	Royal Commonwealth Society
SG	Secretary-General of the Commonwealth (also CSG)
SWAPO	South West Africa Peoples Organisation
TAG	Technical Assistance Group (of CFTC/Secretariat)
UDI	Unilateral Declaration of Independence (Rhodesia 1965)
UPC	Uganda People's Congress (Obote's party)
VSO	Voluntary Service Overseas (British)
ZANU	Zimbabwe African National Union (Mugabe's party)
ZAPU	Zimbabwe African Peoples Union (Nkomo's party)

Dedicated to my wife Eve
and to our children Alexandra, Stewart, and Matthew

FOREWORD

I have often thought that a visitor from another planet would marvel at the fragmentation of Earth's people, and would understand at once how important it is, in this age of proliferating atoms and threatened ecology, that we should work at building a global community. I believe he would also see that not to use the Commonwealth as one of the instruments for this purpose would be monumental folly. To him it would not appear in terms of the past, but as an instrument of great potential use in the development of habits of consultation and cooperation that transcend the limits of race, region and economic level.

That was the approach taken by Commonwealth leaders in 1964 when they decided that such central machinery as this informal association might need should be established in the hands of a new international body, not controlled by any one government, but placed under a Secretary-General elected by and responsible to them all. I had the good fortune to be elected to that post for its first two five-year terms.

This book tells the story of the growing uses of the Commonwealth and the development of its Secretariat since that 1964 decision. It describes events as I saw them from a central position and as one of the actors. It is based on a mass of contemporary documentation, much of it not yet available to researchers and, since detailed references to written sources which are classified can only be tantalising, I have avoided loading the text with notes.

Throughout my years as Secretary-General I dictated a diary, not daily but fairly regularly. During most of my meetings with heads of governments, ministers and other officials I was accompanied by one of my aides who wrote memoranda on the conversations for the files. There are also many other memoranda and minutes, and a mass of correspondence, circular and individual. These documents were built up in Marlborough House where the official files remain. My diaries and personal sets of documents are in Ottawa. The Dominion Archivist has asked and I have agreed that as soon as possible my papers will be deposited there with appropriate arrangements to govern access to them by interested researchers.

To examine and analyse these papers has been a daunting task. I have been fortunate in having the help and collaboration of Clyde Sanger, a former correspondent in Africa and elsewhere for *The Guardian* and *The Economist* of London, later an associate director at Canada's International Development Research Centre, and from 1977-79 Director of the Commonwealth Secretariat's Information Division. He has been invaluable as senior research assistant, and also a superb and sometimes ruthless editor. If the words of this book are largely my own, it is thanks to Clyde that they are contained in one volume and not two.

I am grateful to Alex Inglis for encouragement and advice before I got down to work on this task. I also want to thank Judith Lougheed, David Nobbs, Jack Sabine and Ruth Wahl, graduate students at Carleton University's Norman Paterson School of International Affairs, for indexing my papers and preparing summaries and guidelines to some of them; my secretary Carroll Parras, and Claire Paulin and Sally Cleary for typing, retyping, deciphering and transcribing; Carleton University and the Social Sciences and Humanities Research Council of Canada for making all this help possible; and the Department of External Affairs, especially its Historical Division and Dacre Cole, its Academic Relations Officer.

I want to thank the heads of Commonwealth governments for the opportunity they gave me to serve them and their peoples; and my colleagues from so many countries who joined me in that adventure. A particular word of gratitude is also due to the men and women of the news media who showed fairness, friendship and — when necessary — readiness to grasp new ideas, despite occasional efforts by a few officials to mislead or disparage.

Above all, I want to thank my wife, Eve. By insisting that some day I must document this story, she encouraged me to continue with my diary and with the collection of documents and clippings; and more recently she has commented, caustically when necessary, wisely always, on the various stages of this book. In the implementation of the job itself she played a vital part in the hospitality so important for its successful conduct, and by contributing in many ways to the creation of an 'esprit de corps' among Commonwealth groups, be they students, the wives of High Commissioners in London, or the leaders. At a farewell luncheon at our final Heads of Government Meeting in 1975 in Jamaica, one of the prime ministers' wives, presenting a gift to Eve from them all, spoke of her as their 'den mother'! It was also, we felt, a compliment to the nature of the Commonwealth.

Since my ten years as Secretary-General involved a shift in the nature and workings of the Commonwealth from residual but significant Anglo-centricity to full multilateralism, I wish to pay a final tribute. This is to Britain. As this book tells, there were sometimes problems with Whitehall officialdom; and the Oilgate scandal, of which I learnt only some years after leaving office, illustrates that perfidy could happen. But it is very much the exception. In my judgement the peoples of the little island of Britain have probably accomplished more for the social and political advancement of mankind than any other people: the development of English as an approximation to a world lingua franca, the development and spread of parliamentary democracy, the industrial revolution. Decolonisation involved some temporary ambivalence of attitude and outlook, but compared with other empires it was accomplished remarkably gracefully. A hundred years from now, I suggest, historians will consider the Commonwealth the greatest of all Britain's contributions to man's social and political history.

Arnold Smith

Stitches in Time

Chapter 1
HOW THE SECRETARIAT BEGAN
Surprise from the South

A visitor to the British Foreign Office, who is agile enough to spurn the elevator and walk up the broad staircase to the Secretary of State's offices, is treated to an artistic feast on the way. Covering the walls are several splendid murals, depicting Britannia in a variety of benevolent guises, painted in the high Victorian tradition. Britannia the bride, Britannia the peace-maker, and so on. The two that most delighted me, that used to stop me in mid-stride, from the first time I was calling there as Canadian Minister to Britain in the 1950s, were particularly gorgeous, Rubens-like murals labelled 'Britannia nutrix' and 'Britannia colonorum mater'. In the first she sat in a meadow with a white baby to her breast, while nearby a garlanded girl played the pipes, a black boy carried fruit on his head and an Indian youth stood in armour; in the second she was on the seashore in a diaphanous gown, waving farewell with her trident to six stalwart boys hoisting sail for distant lands. Britannia cared for them all, obviously; but I often wondered lightly whether the one she was nursing, and then sending across the seas, was meant to be Canada.

I remembered Britannia nutrix one Friday morning years later when I was back in London as adviser to Lester Pearson during the 1964 meeting of Commonwealth Prime Ministers. Sir Alec Douglas-Home had steered his seventeen fellow prime ministers and presidents adroitly through two days of talk on world politics. But the British prime minister feared explosions on the third day when the topic of Southern Rhodesia would come up under the general heading of 'Progress of British territories towards independence'; so he gave Duncan Sandys, his Commonwealth and Colonial Secretary, the task of opening the discussion with some soothing words.

Sandys' polished phrases fitted the scene: the long conference room at Marlborough House with glittering chandeliers hanging

1

from a gilt ceiling; portraits of three Queens gazing on us, and beyond the west windows the sunken garden where Queen Mary liked walking in her final years. Sandys gave an impressive account of Britain's process of decolonisation. It was, he said, now almost complete: 700 million people in twenty countries had achieved independence under British guidance. Britain had done this of her own will, not through any lack of power to continue her rule. She wished to give others the freedom she so much prized herself. His speech was pure Britannia nutrix, the proud mother who had nursed her infants to strength and independence.

But an African voice cut in from down the table. It was Dr Banda, whose Malawi had celebrated its independence only four days earlier.

'Now come, Mr Chairman, let's be frank with each other. You British have not been as pig-headed as other imperialists. You have recognised in time what is inevitable, and accepted it gracefully. That is your greatness, and we honour you for it. But it has not been all voluntary. There's been a significant element of persuasion, and many of us here have been among the persuaders.' He himself had been in prison – in Southern Rhodesia – for only thirteen months; others had been in British jails much longer. He went round the table, mentioning names and prison terms: Kwame Nkrumah, Jomo Kenyatta, Archbishop Makarios, and the Indian prime minister who had died only weeks before, Jawaharlal Nehru. Dr Banda ended: 'I wanted to make my point frankly. Frankness is the basis of our association.'

There was laughter around the room, but some of it was nervous laughter, because this was a barb as well as a good point. Mike Pearson turned it back into a joke. He liked being in 'inner circles', he said, and there seemed to be one forming here, of prison graduates. His record was more modest than some others: a week of being confined to barracks when he was a medical orderly attached to a British unit for a period in the First World War. But could he qualify? This time there was unalloyed laughter, and an end to the tension.

This atmosphere of frankness among world leaders, of informality and joking to help along a discussion of deep seriousness, was like a fresh breeze. In 1964, I was relatively new to Commonwealth affairs. Two difficult but fascinating years in London around the Suez period, which included a meeting in 1958 of Prime Ministers who were then so few that they met in the Cabinet room at Number 10 (I attended as one of John Diefenbaker's advisers); that, and a

2

week's visit to India in 1955 en route from Ottawa to become an International Truce Commissioner in Indo-China, was the sum of my direct acquaintance with Commonwealth countries other than Canada and Britain. Indirectly, I had appreciated the regular meetings held among Commonwealth heads of diplomatic missions in foreign capitals when I was ambassador in Cairo from 1958 and in Moscow in the early Sixties. Even during Khruschev's time Moscow was a secretive society, and the habit of comparing notes frankly with diplomatic colleagues from Asia and Africa, and learning how events appeared from their viewpoint, was very valuable. I came to the 1964 meeting with a flavour of the Commonwealth, but little more.

A newcomer could not help but be impressed by that week of talks in July 1964, and by the mixture of political leaders gathered for it. Ayub Khan, very much the Field Marshal but speaking with moderation as well as authority. Sir Robert Menzies, who had presided over a great domestic expansion of Australian society. Jomo Kenyatta, who on the second day was assaulted in the street by a hooligan shouting 'Mau Mau', and therefore absented himself from the meeting long enough to make a calming broadcast back to Kenya. Eric Williams, a powerful intellectual force from Trinidad. Others from Africa who had led their countries to independence: Kwame Nkrumah, Abubakar Tafawa Balewa, Julius Nyerere; and one of the most delightful of them all, Milton Obote, tremendously handsome with Nilotic bone structure and midnight-blue skin. Men who have led an independence movement and are in a sense the fathers of their country are often of bigger stature than most run-of-the-mill heads of government. Sitting there at Marlborough House with so many of them was like being at a meeting of governments where the United States was represented by George Washington.

It was impressive, too, to hear the half-day debate on economic affairs. Commonwealth countries had just played an important role at the first United Nations Conference on Trade and Development (UNCTAD) in Geneva: they had provided three of the five committee chairmen and other influential members. The meeting heard at first hand the problems of primary producers: how Ghana had increased its cocoa production by sixty percent since independence in 1957 and yet foreign exchange earnings remained stagnant because of falling prices; how Ceylon was suffering from worsening terms of trade in a year of general prosperity.

The debate foreshadowed many of the issues that became major global concerns in the next fifteen years. I remember telling a friend in London that, to my surprise, the Commonwealth was really an internal pressure group; in it the different sections of humanity were pressing each other to adjust to the others' needs. With its informal procedures and no set speeches, it was just what the world needed.

But the decision that made the 1964 meeting an historic one – and, in personal terms, ended by taking over my life for ten years – did not come out of any planned debate. Alec Home had five proposals ready and circulated for a discussion on 'The Commonwealth – the way ahead', that was set for Monday afternoon. But, before these were discussed, a quite different and more far-reaching idea had welled up in the speeches of African and Caribbean leaders, had been given some preliminary shape in a meeting of officials hastily called on the Saturday morning and had been endorsed by most of the leaders. This idea for a Commonwealth Secretariat, in fact, caught several countries (my own included) by surprise.

The British prime minister had given Canada, Australia and New Zealand details of his own schemes for future forms of Commonwealth cooperation a month earlier. The reason for his initiative was straightforward: he could see the Commonwealth coming under increasing strain in arguments about southern Africa with the newer members. 'Some are not the easiest of associates,' he wrote, 'and unless we can capture their enthusiasm now, the Commonwealth will cease to have much meaning.' So he wanted to place emphasis on practical ways in which it could be of service to its members. His reason for sounding out the older members was because he hoped they would not only join him in advocating, but would also contribute funds to, these five schemes: technical assistance in agricultural projects, capital aid for higher education, training in public administration, regional organisations for technical advice and the establishment of a Commonwealth Foundation to strengthen professional links.

It was Kwame Nkrumah, rather than Home, who first raised the idea of a Commonwealth Secretariat in July. Just as he believed that small and isolated African countries could only develop by forging unity among themselves, so he argued that the Commonwealth had to have a higher concept of its future role if it were to survive in world affairs. It was no longer an association of like-minded countries deriving their institutions from Britain; the main bond was respect

4

for each other's independence, and if it was to have any future strength its members needed to accept new obligations. The developing countries owed a duty to themselves to organise their own resources, while the richer countries had a duty to promote the development of the newer ones and, in particular, to ensure that terms of trade did not move against the poorer countries. His main thrust was for a unit that would help economic development. He proposed that the Commonwealth should set up in London what he called 'a central clearing house', with a primary function of preparing plans for trade, aid and development for circulation to all member governments.

Others added their ideas. Abubakar Tafawa Balewa thought the Commonwealth should have, not any rigid rules, but 'a set of guiding principles'. Milton Obote was probably the first to refer to a Commonwealth secretariat, which he thought could handle not only normal cooperation but also the work then being proposed for a 'conciliation committee' to mediate disputes among its members. Then Eric Williams followed by formally proposing that the meeting should consider the establishment of a Commonwealth Secretariat (it acquired a capital letter with his speech). His arguments were different from those of Nkrumah.

The weakness of the Commonwealth in international affairs, Dr Williams suggested, was that too many people thought of it as a club, congenial but disorganised. It needed formalizing with a set of efficient institutions to give proper value to the relationships. If there had been a Commonwealth Secretariat in 1964, the preparations for this meeting would have been more adequate, they could have had background papers on disarmament and several other subjects. In longer range, a Secretariat could have provided for prior consultation on many questions that had become crises: Malaysia's quarrel with Indonesia, for example, and Southern Rhodesia; Cyprus; and the boundary problems of what were then British Guiana and British Honduras (now Guyana and Belize). All these issues had been handed unilaterally, and he maintained that intra-Commonwealth consultations at an early stage would have been beneficial in every case. Finally, he proposed the establishment of a Commonwealth Fund for Development, with an associated programme of technical assistance drawing on the resources of all members.

For his part, Ayub Khan thought a Commonwealth Secretariat or clearing house should have an important part to play in helping economic development, by processing any schemes set up jointly by Commonwealth leaders and by embracing all the Commonwealth

5

agencies and committees then existing in London.

By the weekend in the middle of the meeting the movement for a secretariat from leaders of the newer countries was too strong for any delegation to ignore. Menzies gave it lukewarm support, recalling that he had on more than one occasion proposed such a body but refraining from any specific suggestions about what it might now do. The other prime ministers from the richer countries – Douglas-Home, Pearson and Keith Holyoake of New Zealand – kept quiet. But all the heads of government sent their senior officials into a Saturday morning meeting to sort out ideas on the subject. I went for Canada.

The truth was that these older countries were surprised at this sudden upsurge of interest among the newer countries in developing new Commonwealth machinery. Some of the ideas sounded to them highly impractical: the conciliation committee suggested by Ceylon's Mrs Bandaranaike and Sierra Leone's Albert Margai went no further. At the same time there was the feeling among the older countries, certainly Britain and Canada, that we might be reaching an encouraging turning point in the development of the Commonwealth.

The British officials had to accept that several of the reasons put forward for a secretariat reflected unfavourably on their own handling of relations, and administrative matters, in recent years. Among some officials in the Commonwealth Relations Office, in particular, there rankled a resentful feeling that a secretariat responsible to all governments would undermine their work, even threaten their raison d'être as a separate department from the Foreign Office. This was an attitude that lingered for years with some, but not all, of the senior CRO officials and caused many difficulties in the evolution of the Secretariat, as later chapters will show. On the other hand, there were splendid dividends for Sir Alec and his political colleagues from a meeting that produced bright new ideas about the Commonwealth. His government was obliged to call a general election within a few months, and the public prospect of a renewed rather than a collapsing Commonwealth was a valuable political windfall. The government was seeking to join the European Economic Community; Labour Party spokesmen were then claiming that this would betray and destroy the Commonwealth.

Canadians had to readjust their traditional thinking which for decades had involved opposing any schemes of closer union as carrying dangers of domination by London. Several times had such schemes been mooted, and Canadian prime ministers from Laurier to Mackenzie King had done their utmost to suppress them swiftly. The saga of the Imperial and Colonial Conferences from 1887 gave them ample grounds for their suspicions. Four of the first six conferences (those in 1887, 1897, 1902 and 1911) coincided with jubilees and coronations, complete with all the imperial trimmings. Joseph Chamberlain turned what was originally termed informal talks during the Diamond Jubilee celebrations of 1897 into five formal sessions at which he proposed an Imperial Council with executive and legislative powers over mainly commercial subjects. However, he retreated gracefully when the others would not accept the principle of representation by population – a formula for British dominance.

In 1907 the proposal for closer union came from a different quarter. Like Eric Williams a half-century later, the Australian prime minister Alfred Deakin was displeased with the inadequate preparations for the conference that had been made by the Colonial Office staff, who he thought were overwhelmed with work involving Britain's dependencies rather than the Dominions. He was as much a nationalist as Laurier, and believed as much in equal status with Britain; but he did not see this as incompatible with seeking safety for Australia in closer imperial union, a union of common policies and institutions. He proposed a secretariat, staffed by people knowledgeable about the Dominions and giving continuity between conferences; a secretariat independent of the Colonial Office and supervised by the British prime ministers. But Laurier was still opposed to any centralizing move, for fear it might erode Canadian self-government and offend francophone Quebec; he found allies, including Louis Botha, premier of the Transvaal. So an ineffectual compromise was agreed, and a tiny Dominions Division was set up inside the Colonial Office.

The pattern of attitudes altered little in the inter-war years. Australians remained keen on forms of 'closer union' that would relieve them of the anxieties of strategic isolation in the Far East. In the 1930s S. M. Bruce proposed a survey of the functions of a dozen inter-Imperial agencies, in the hope that it would provide support for the idea of a combined secretariat; but the Skelton Committee, headed by a Canadian, made only minor recommendations for change. Britain produced someone, in the person of Sir Maurice Hankey, who had a genius for creating ad hoc secretariats out of the staff of British Empire delegations at major conferences. A New Zealander by birth who had become Secretary both to the British Cabinet and to the Committee for Imperial Defence, he also took on the job of Secretary to successive Imperial Conferences. In the words of H. Duncan Hall, he 'acquired such prestige in the higher levels of government throughout the Commonwealth that from

1917 to the Second World War he was in effect the Secretary-General of the Commonwealth'.* Perhaps; but he never formed a continuing Secretariat. That this did not happen was due in part to steady opposition from Canada's Mackenzie King, who feared that any Commonwealth machinery would be 'Downing Street machinery.'

So there was a long tradition of caution, if not downright hostility, for a Canadian prime minister and his staff to overcome in 1964 when faced with proposals for a Commonwealth Secretariat.

On the strength of the statements of Nkrumah, Obote and Williams, I drafted a cable that was sent to Ottawa by Mike Pearson on July 9 and began a significant shifting of Canada's position. It summarized these speeches, reviewed the reasons for Canadian traditional antagonism to the idea of a Commonwealth Secretariat and added:

> 'On the other hand, for us to be in opposition to a proposal that emanates from some of the new and intensely nationalistic countries, and has the support of the UK and probably Australia and New Zealand, would be extremely difficult.'

Pearson added that, if the details were left to be worked out later by a special committee, there would be an opportunity to protect against attempts to expand it into 'an organisation of general scope or extensive activity'. His cable was phrased in guarded language, for it was going to External Affairs Minister Paul Martin, who then had little sympathy for such ideas. Pearson asked Martin to relay back whatever reactions the Cabinet gave on Monday.

Heads of government went off to Chequers, the historic country house of British prime ministers, to disport themselves for the weekend. Meanwhile, in a Marlborough House committee room on the Saturday morning, senior officials from fifteen countries met to clarify ideas on what the functions of a Secretariat might be and how it would be staffed. The representatives of Ceylon, Jamaica and several African countries put heavy emphasis on the Secretariat becoming a dissemination centre for both political and economic information about other Commonwealth countries and their problems in world affairs.

When I suggested that this sort of work – preparation of background papers before ministerial meetings and exchange of political information – could be done by the various countries' diplomatic services, I was firmly rebuked by Kenya's Duncan Ndegwa, Kenyatta's Cabinet Secretary. It was all very well, he said, for a Canadian to

---

* *'Commonwealth'* by H. Duncan Hall. Van Nostrand Reinhold Co. 1971, p. 587.

talk that way, but other countries could not afford missions all round the world. 'We need all the help we can get by doing things cooperatively.'

Others joined in. Jamaica's Arthur Brown pointed out that it had been extremely difficult to get information, for instance, about Malaysia's troubles with Indonesia. The Malaysian representative followed this up by saying his country had been forced to send a special team to African countries on this issue, because Malaysia had only one diplomatic mission in all of Africa, and that was based in Cairo.

I felt ashamed at having been stupidly insensitive, and admitted as much.

Several other questions were raised. Should the Secretariat be a clearing house for political information in cases where there were disputes between Commonwealth countries? Should it involve itself in political information work at all, or just concentrate on economic subjects? Should it absorb some (or even all) of the existing Commonwealth organisations, or try to coordinate their work, or assume new functions in fields not covered by these bodies? We could not possibly resolve these and several other questions in a morning. Instead, we all agreed to recommend to our prime ministers that a special committee of top officials meet later to go in detail into proposals about the functions of the new Secretariat. Its relationship with the Commonwealth Economic Committee and other liaison bodies already working in the economic, educational and cultural fields clearly needed careful consideration, but we agreed that the Secretariat would have to be of sufficient stature to allow it to stand in some sort of coordinating relationship with them.

We also agreed that the staff should be widely recruited from the public services of many Commonwealth countries, so that the Secretariat could be seen as completely impartial and at the service of all Commonwealth governments; at the same time, the numbers should be kept low, and the Secretariat should begin modestly with certain definite, if limited, tasks to undertake and with the understanding that success in these would lead to a broader scope of work. We agreed that Sir Burke Trend, Secretary to the British Cabinet and chairman of this meeting, should summarise these views of officials in a collective report to the prime ministers.

On the Sunday I worked with Gordon Robertson, who as Secretary of the Cabinet was Canada's top public servant, to prepare another cable that in tactful phrases gave a positive account of the officials' meeting. When Mike Pearson came back from the weekend retreat at Chequers, he read this second cable, sighed a little, and signed it. The two cables carried the day in Ottawa. On Tuesday a reply came from Paul Martin, which ended: 'I have read out your messages to our Cabinet colleagues. While they regard it as an unwelcome development, they recognise that Canada has to avoid a negative posture. Accordingly they concur.'

The prime ministers themselves accepted the idea of a committee of officials to work out details. They rounded off the final communiqué of the meeting with a paragraph supporting the concept, and saying that a Secretariat

> 'would be available, inter alia, to disseminate factual information to all Member countries on matters of common concern; to assist existing agencies, both official and unofficial, in the promotion of Commonwealth links in all fields; and to help to coordinate, in cooperation with the host country, the preparations for future meetings of Commonwealth Heads of Government and, where appropriate, for meetings of other Commonwealth Ministers.'

It would be, they went on, 'a visible symbol of the spirit of co-operation which animates the Commonwealth.'

This planning for a Secretariat stole the limelight from discussion of Alec Home's proposals for cooperation in agricultural development, education, administrative training and promotion of links between professional organizations, to which Canada had added the idea of cooperating in satellite communications. All these items were mentioned in the final communiqué, although with guardedly subjunctive tenses ('The Prime Ministers considered that . . . it *might* be desirable to establish a Commonwealth Foundation . . .'). In several cases they suggested these proposals merited 'further consideration'; but, until a Secretariat was established, there was no continuing machinery to carry this out. So logic pointed towards giving priority to the establishment of the Secretariat.

The subject of Southern Rhodesia will be covered in later chapters. I introduce it here only briefly because its shadow fell across the 1964 Prime Ministers Meeting, and made me realize some of the changes that were needed in Commonwealth relations between Britain and the other members.

Rather than use this Commonwealth meeting for a badly overdue exchange of views on contingency planning over Rhodesia, the British seemed intent to minimise discussion of the issue – apparently fearing that debate might provoke Ian Smith (who had taken over the prime ministership in Salisbury three months earlier) into unilateral independence. The provisional timetable drawn up by British officials would have placed the question near the end of the meeting and only in the context of its future membership of the Commonwealth. I disliked this evasiveness, and at the meeting of officials to approve the timetable I argued that the British could not claim at Commonwealth meetings that Southern Rhodesia was a British domestic affair and therefore should not be discussed, while at the United Nations they argued that it was self-governing and therefore Britain was not responsible for its policies of racial discrimination. Eventually we succeeded in winning for the Rhodesia problem a proper place on the agenda.

Pearson's speech on Southern Rhodesia had been prepared some weeks before, with the aim of outflanking the anticipated British argument that it was their domestic affair. One morning in Ottawa while shaving (often a good occasion for ideas to sprout), it occurred to me that we might draw an analogy between the racial situation in Southern Rhodesia, where Britain was doing little about the responsibilities she had, and the situation in British Guiana where she had sent two infantry battalions to prevent more race riots between those of African and of Asian origins; and that we might do this in the context of a proposal for a Commonwealth Declaration of Racial Equality, in which all member governments be asked to accept an express obligation to promote equal opportunity and non-discrimination among the various peoples in each country. Doug Hicks, an External Affairs officer with African experience, joined in drafting an action-oriented declaration that we thought had punch to it and yet could hardly be opposed by any democratic government.* We also drafted an accompanying speech for Mr

---

* The declaration read as follows:-

'Among the major issues of our age, one of the most important is race relations. It was agreed that the Commonwealth has a particular role to play in the search for solutions to the inter-racial problems which are threatening the orderly development of mankind in general and of many particular areas of the world today. The Commonwealth is itself an almost unique experiment in cooperation among peoples of several races and continents. Within their own borders many of its members have faced and are facing issues raised by the co-existence of differing cultures within a democratic society. The Prime Ministers affirmed their belief that, for all Commonwealth Governments, it should be an objective of policy to build in each country a structure of society which offers equal opportunity and non-discrimination for all its people, irrespective of race, colour, or creed. The Commonwealth should be able to exercise constructive leadership in the application of democratic principles in a way which will enable the people of each country of different racial and cultural groups to exist and develop as free and equal citizens.'

11

Pearson, to suggest that prime ministers might collectively adopt the declaration and then consider its application to the specific situations in Southern Rhodesia and British Guiana.

Pearson liked the idea, and used the speech at Marlborough House when he spoke first in the Monday morning session. Coming at the start of a fresh week, it met a positive response. It was, in fact, so well received by most other prime ministers that the declaration became the first substantive paragraph in their final communiqué. Its influence was apparent two months later, when Alec Home set out his Five Principles for a settlement on Southern Rhodesia. The declaration also helped establish that the domestic situation in Southern Rhodesia could, indeed must, be a matter for collective discussion by Commonwealth leaders if their meetings were to have honest meaning.

One week after the 1964 Prime Ministers Meeting, an article by Nora Beloff appeared in *The Observer* that surprised me. Carrying the headline 'Canadian as Mr Commonwealth?', it suggested that several African countries might put me forward as their candidate to head the new Secretariat. For several reasons at that time I was more interested in continuing my career in Canada than in taking on a job that was surrounded by uncertainties. When Britain's new Prime Minister, Harold Wilson, and his Commonwealth Secretary Arthur Bottomley visited Ottawa in December 1964, they asked Pearson to nominate me for the post. Several leaders from the Third World made the same suggestion. I was still opposed, and told Pearson why. It was not until March that I decided to try for the job.

Meanwhile, there was a good deal of discussion between capitals about the shape and scope of the Secretariat, and a British working paper and a Canadian background paper were widely circulated. In its main points the Canadian paper went some distance further than the British had gone, and it transpired, much further than the Australians then wished to go.

The Canadian background paper suggested that one of the best ways to spread informed understanding among Commonwealth members was for the Secretary-General to organize meetings of Commonwealth representatives, to discuss papers on political or economic subjects; these might be meetings of High Commissioners in London, or special meetings of experts or officials coming from national capitals which might take place in various regions of the Commonwealth. We also suggested that considerations of economy in staffing and of efficiency might lead to the merging with the Secretariat of most of the existing Commonwealth agencies that were based in London.

A senior CRO official visited Ottawa in mid-December, to follow up on the British paper. This had argued against any changes to the already existing Commonwealth Economic Committee and the Commonwealth Education Liaison Unit, and had also said that Britain would resist the idea of the Secretariat being active in the field of technical assistance either as a central processing point for Commonwealth inquiries or as a body that proposed some priorities for Commonwealth aid. But the matter that seemed to worry him most was the Canadian suggestion of periodic meetings of High Commissioners.

Reactions flowed in from various capitals. It was interesting to learn that Ghana, whose president had first proposed the Secretariat, envisaged a small organization of only some thirty staff. India was cautious about the Secretariat taking on any role in political or educational affairs, but thought it could serve economic, scientific and cultural developments. Most other reactions were positive, except some of those from Canberra. The Menzies government was worried that the Commonwealth would become organized and institutionalized, and thought the fabric of Commonwealth relationships could not stand any such burden. It wanted, at most, a low-powered Secretariat. Rather than a Secretary-General of the rank of a senior ambassador, Australia suggested someone 'less distinguished and more of an officer-in-charge of a common services organization'. The Secretariat should not do any such jobs as drafting communiqués for the prime ministers, and there should not be any centralizing of Commonwealth institutions under the Secretariat.

Forearmed with these reactions from other countries, and given the good advice of half-a-dozen 'elder statesmen' among Canadian officials with Commonwealth experience, I headed off to London in January 1965 to a meeting of senior officials from nineteen countries. Our job was to fill in the outline plans for both the Secretariat and the Commonwealth Foundation.

The starting point was a phrase that became almost a motto – 'Consultation is the lifeblood of the Commonwealth association'. It mixed respect for each country's independence with recognition of the benefits to be gained from learning the views of people from all quarters of the world. We agreed that the Secretariat therefore had a role (some would say, its main role) in promoting a fuller exchange of views and factual information in both economic affairs and

13

'international' (i.e. political) affairs. In both areas the Secretary-General could use his own initiative to prepare and circulate papers to governments, provided that they were not partisan. The Secretary-General should be given the duty of preparing papers on agenda items and other background papers for meetings of Prime Ministers, Finance Ministers and other ministers.

The officials who met that January in Marlborough House had only minor problems thus far. But there was considerable discussion about whether the Secretariat should ever acquire an executive role. A British draft was circulated which would have prevented this happening.* This was altered, in the document that by July became the Agreed Memorandum, to the phrase: 'The Secretariat should not arrogate to itself executive functions'. Nor has the Secretariat done so, but it has acquired executive functions in various areas by direction or consent of meetings of government ministers and by absorbing over the years some bodies, such as the Commonwealth Economic Committee, which already had an executive role – in trade promotion and other spheres.

This question of an executive role also arose when discussing Commonwealth development projects. It was agreed, under British pressure, that 'nothing should be done which might disturb the existing channels of economic and technical assistance to Member countries, or would duplicate the present bilateral and multi-lateral links'. The British wanted it then stated that 'the functions of the Secretariat in connection with *any* development projects [my emphasis] should be expert and advisory.' But the other officials narrowed this limitation down to apply only to the Commonwealth Development Projects floated by Sir Alec the previous July; and they added at my urging that the Secretariat could 'play a valuable part in assisting member governments, at their request, in advancing, and obtaining support for, development projects and technical assistance in a variety of fields on a multilateral Commonwealth basis, as appropriate'. This opened the way to many worthwhile initiatives and eventually to the Commonwealth Fund for Technical Cooperation.

The Secretariat's role in circulating material on dependent territories also provoked discussion. While it was generally agreed that the Secretariat might prepare papers on the constitutional advance of these territories and their progress towards independence, there was resistance to the view that the administering country (Britain in most cases, but Australia in the case of Papua New Guinea, and

---

* See Joe Garner, *The Commonwealth Office* (Hodder and Stoughton, 1978) page 352.

New Zealand for some islands) could object to the material and prevent its circulation. The compromise that found its way into the Agreed Memorandum was that the Secretariat 'might circulate to member Governments balanced papers . . . on the understanding that the responsible member Governments would always be closely consulted in the preparation of the papers.' With the issue of Southern Rhodesia already large on the horizon, this was an important distinction between consultation and censorship.

The officials rounded off their work by recommending that the Secretary-General be 'a man of high standing, equivalent in rank to Senior High Commissioner' and that he start with one Deputy Secretary-General responsible for economic affairs and development projects, and that a second might be added as work expanded. Both Deputies were to be elected by Heads of Government. Finally, they suggested that a small committee should review the relationship between the Secretariat and other Commonwealth organizations, a better procedure than the idea that was mooted earlier of having the Secretary-General sit with the heads of these bodies to determine their futures.

All these recommendations went to Heads of Government, and the only strongly negative reactions came from Menzies.

The Australian prime minister said that, while he had agreed in principle to a Secretariat, 'its functions and the nature and authority of its staff require a great deal of examination'. He did not want the Secretariat to have any executive authority that could cut across or diminish the authority of governments in national policies and he feared there was already 'some disposition to equate the position of the proposed Secretary-General (which seems a somewhat inflated title) with that of the Secretary-General of the United Nations'. Nor did he like the suggestion that the Secretariat might give expert advice on development projects, for 'the structure is already too elaborate'. He listed several other concerns, in typically sturdy style. But, despite this broadside, the recommendations in the officials' report were approved by Heads of Government as the Agreed Memorandum at their meeting in July 1965. The Secretariat was on its way.

Although encouraged by the outcome of the officials' meeting in January 1965, and its promising support for the concept of a renewed and modernized Commonwealth, I took two more months to decide that I wanted to be a candidate myself for Secretary-General.

But in March I was nominated by the Canadian Prime Minister and made what later served as an election speech to the Canadian Universities Society of Great Britain on 22 March. Copies of this speech, which had the title 'Canada, the Commonwealth and the World', were circulated to all Commonwealth governments and it helped advance my candidature, as did some discreet canvassing in various capitals by High Commissioners. In the speech I spoke of the crucial part Canada had played at several stages of the Commonwealth's evolution, from Confederation in 1867 to the acceptance of a republican India, and I also argued against exclusive blocs and continentalism in these words:

> '. . . Canada's historic invention of and attachment to the Commonwealth association, though it was largely a reaction to real or apprehended American pressure, was also in part based I think on a genuine and constructive vision that in the long term a satisfactory international environment for us must be more than continental. It was not merely defensive, but creative. That reaching out for overseas friends was a sound instinct. Ultimately, as we now know more clearly than earlier generations, our community of friendship must become global if humanity is not some day to blow itself up.'

It was a useful electioneering speech, and helped because there were several other candidates in the field. From New Zealand came the nomination of Alistair McIntosh, who had not only headed the Prime Minister's department for twenty years but as Secretary for External Affairs had built up a small but superb diplomatic service. Malaysia had proposed Charles Bennett, a New Zealand Maori who had been High Commissioner in Kuala Lumpur. Two first-rate Australians were nominated by African states: George Ivan Smith, who was U Thant's personal representative in ten countries of East and Central Africa, and Sir Robert Jackson who was United Nations economic adviser in Ghana. (He later became Deputy Secretary General of the UN.) But Menzies expressed disapproval of both and nominated Gonville Sextus Peiris, Director-General of External Affairs in Ceylon. The other candidates were Ghulam Ahmed, Pakistan's Ambassador in Washington, and S.C.A. Forster, head of Sierra Leone's Ministry of External Affairs.

Several of the candidates were old friends. I had known Robert Jackson since 1941, when he moved on from organizing the logistical side of the defences of Malta to a top job in wartime Cairo. Ahmed and Peiris I had known from meetings of officials. As for Alistair McIntosh, we had worked closely together in the planning for the

Secretariat and I would have been happy to see him in the job.

The question of how the selection of a Secretary-General was going to be made was constantly raised by British mandarins, and had not been settled. Fearful that McIntosh or I would be chosen, they kept emphasising that voting would be contrary to all Commonwealth traditions. Weeks before the Prime Ministers gathered in London in June 1965, Eric Williams requested that the matter be put in the hands of a nominating committee drawn from five countries which had had no direct or indirect role in nominating any of the candidates. Pearson objected to this suggestion at a meeting at Number 10 on the eve of the conference. Heads of Governments had been asked to nominate candidates, he pointed out, so why penalize those who complied? He thought a general discussion might lead to a consensus.

It was not to prove that simple. The meeting asked officials to recommend a procedure, and the British officials in particular made heavy weather of the task, at one point even suggesting there should be an interim appointment of a retired British colonial governor as acting Secretary-General for one year while further attention was given to procedure. So much attention had by then been given to procedure, so little to the selection itself in two days of talking by officials under British chairmanship in an upstairs committee room at Marlborough House that Canada's representative Gordon Robertson impatiently intervened to say they were wasting time with such talk: each official had instructions on which candidate his head of government wanted to support; write down that name on a slip of paper and let's have a ballot, he told the others. And that is what happened.

I was sitting behind Pearson in the plenary session at the time. The meeting adjourned for a coffee break, and Mike said I should stay outside when the Prime Ministers reassembled because the officials were going to report. Then the doors were opened and Harold Wilson, the chairman, asked me to come in and said: 'I'm glad to tell you that we've elected you Secretary-General. Do you accept?' And I said, 'Yes, I do.' No wasted words on either side.

On the day before the balloting, both Peiris and McIntosh had withdrawn. McIntosh had two reasons for doing so: his health was not good, for he had lost all hearing in one ear, and he also did not wish to split votes between us and jeopardize chances for both of us. Ahmed had withdrawn earlier; so the field had thinned. I received, I was told, eighteen of the twenty votes, including that of Britain. It was then made unanimous.

17

In the sunny courtyard of Marlborough House, at the end of that morning session, I was surrounded by a group of cameramen and journalists, who had just heard of my election. 'What do countries as diverse as Sierra Leone, India and Canada have in common?', one asked sceptically. 'We all need to learn to share a planet,' I replied, 'and we believe that using the Commonwealth can help.'

I had lunch with Mike Pearson and a small group of other heads of government. After some joking, Milton Obote proceeded to offer some serious advice. 'You will find in due course that you will need a flag and a symbol. When you do, don't ask heads of government to approve a design. We have enough to divide us, and problems enough on which we must think out an agreed solution. Decide what you can for yourself, and do it.' It was good advice and I never forgot it.

The tension of those few days ended with the humour London often provides. The Canadian delegation was staying at the Dorchester, and I had noticed that the hotel elevators had "sauna and massage" written alongside the basement button. Feeling a little massage would help me, I headed below – only to be stopped at the desk outside by a Cockney woman.

'This is jest fer lydies,' she said.

I raised my right hand with mock pomp and said: 'You must understand it says in the United Nations Charter there shall be no discrimination on grounds of race, religion, or sex.'

'Ow sir,' she answered, 'if we let gen'l'men in 'ere, we'd get the wrong koind of gen'l'men.'

She had, of course, the last word. And it was not to be the only time in those ten years when I found that grand declarations failed to carry the day.

Chapter 2
CRISES AT THE
OUTSET
Singapore, Kashmir, Rhodesia

I stayed on in London for a few days after the Heads of Government Meeting (HGM) in June 1965 to improve relations with some prime ministers and to begin recruitment of senior staff. I asked Harold Wilson for a political officer, explaining that I hoped this would ease Whitehall's apprehensions; and I sent a message to Colombo asking Peiris if he would seek election as Deputy Secretary-General in charge of economic affairs. I also made overtures to the Australian prime minister, and a mellowed Menzies promised a good young diplomat and seconded Michael Wilson who, with New Zealand's gift of Gerald Hensley, made an outstanding pair of special assistants.

In particular, I looked for an African who could be elected Deputy Secretary-General in charge of political affairs. Several suggested the name of Amishadai (Yaw) Adu, who had been the first head of Ghana's foreign service and then Secretary to the Cabinet and head of the civil service until differences with Nkrumah (he was one of the few men with the courage to give Nkrumah unpalatable advice, particularly over his habit of trying to subvert neighbouring states in the name of Panafricanism) led him to leave for Nairobi in 1962. Jomo Kenyatta, who knew his work as Secretary-General of the East African Common Services Organisation, said I could not find a better man, but doubted if Nkrumah would agree to his election. I decided to nominate Adu myself, but he made it a condition that I get Nkrumah's approval in advance. Nkrumah did in fact approve after calling Adu back to Accra for a day-long talk and impressing on him the importance Ghana attached to the job. Kenyatta was right: the Secretariat could not have had a better person, in its first five years of existence, to help give it steadiness and direction in the troubled politics of that time.

By then I was back in Ottawa, planning for the new job. I had asked Britain's Commonwealth Office to loan me an administrative officer to look after the hundreds of letters that would inevitably be addressed to the new Secretariat, until my return to London, and to consult me about anything important that arose.

Meanwhile, from Ottawa I carried on some intercontinental soundings about recruiting from other regions. But it was obvious that it would take several months at least for many of the kind of high-flyer officers I sought to be released by their governments and be ready to begin new work in London; so I persuaded the Canadian Department of External Affairs to loan me two Canadian diplomats for my first few months. One, Norman Berlis, was about to leave his post as High Commissioner in Tanzania to become Ambassador in Warsaw; the other, John Schioler, who was younger, also proved first-class. Their help in that first autumn was indispensable.

Before going to London I made a point of visiting New York to call on U Thant, the UN Secretary-General, and to have a meeting with the score of Commonwealth Permanent Representatives. These contacts, between the Commonwealth and the UN, were obviously going to be important, and they developed significantly in the years that followed.

It was a deceptively calm early morning when the *Queen Mary* docked at Southampton on 17 August 1965, bringing Eve and me to start the job of Secretary-General, and set up our new Commonwealth headquarters. A sea-crossing has always appealed to me as the ideal break between different jobs. Every time we had changed posts in my foreign service career – fourteen times in twenty-six years – it had meant shifting mental gears; when possible, we had changed continents by sea, giving time for the mind to straighten out before a new set of problems landed upon it.

Problems there were in plenty. Blair Fraser, writing in January 1966,* described me as 'living in the eye of the hurricane' ever since arriving the previous August. 'In the intervening six months he has looked sometimes like Jonah, sometimes like the boy on the burning deck, occasionally like Horatius at the bridge.' He was referring to the three crises that blew into a hurricane in those months: the expulsion of Singapore from the Malaysian Federation in August; the sharp outbreak of warfare between India and Pakistan in August-September; and the rising temper of Rhodesian politics which boiled over into rebellion and the unilateral declaration of

---

* *Maclean's Magazine*, Toronto, January 1966.

20

independence in November. Each crisis caused an urgent question mark to loom over the head of the infant Secretariat.

I shall therefore touch on each of them in turn.

On the train journey up from Southampton the British administrative officer who had been loaned to the Secretariat by the CRO, Don Abbey, rather shyly showed me a message. It was a telegram to me from the Malaysian Prime Minister, Tunku Abdul Rahman, reporting both Singapore's expulsion from Malaysia on 9 August and Malaysia's sponsorship of Singapore's application to become a separate member of the Commonwealth. Mentioning that he had also informed the British prime minister and some other Commonwealth heads of government of Singapore's desire to become a member, the Tunku requested that I take the matter up with all Commonwealth governments and coordinate responses.

My surprise that a message of such importance, received four days earlier, had not been telegraphed to me aboard ship was heightened the next day when I called on Sir Neil Pritchard, acting head of the CRO, for a general discussion and mentioned Singapore. I was intrigued that a young man sitting in with him immediately suggested that I leave the matter of membership application to the British since it was 'political' and verged on 'executive action'. Neil obviously recognised, I concluded, that such impertinence was best left to a junior third party. I told Neil that his colleague's suggestion was preposterous. I thought the Malaysian request to the Secretariat entirely proper, and I intended to circulate Singapore's application for membership forthwith to all Commonwealth heads of government. It was in Britain's interest, I added, that the newer countries should recognise that the Commonwealth was not a club owned and run by Britain, but one in which they all had equal participation; indeed, they had taken the initiative of proposing the establishment of the Secretariat partly to emphasise just this. I broadened the point by saying it was a key role of the Secretariat to coordinate the views of Commonwealth heads of government on *any* issue on which a collective decision was needed during intervals between their meetings.

It nevertheless took several months, and the example of two more countries' membership applications – Guyana and Botswana, which both became independent in 1966 – before it was universally accepted that it was the Secretariat's role to circulate formal proposals and coordinate replies from member governments on matters needing collective decisions. Arthur Bottomley, the British Commonwealth Secretary, moved into the act more circumspectly, expressing to me the view that Britain needed to coordinate responses over Singapore's application because various governments were having delicate discussions over the future of the naval and military base there. My response was that the Secretariat would not interfere with any discussions about the base; but on the separate question of Singapore's formal application for Commonwealth membership it was proper for me to act on Malaysia's request. Giving a local clubland analogy, I said that I had just been told of my election to the Athenaeum by the club's secretary, not by its oldest living member.

This little matter of procedure aside, an important substantive problem over Singapore's membership emerged. This was the antagonism of Pakistan. Ayub Khan's government began quarrelling with Malaysia in September after the Malaysian delegate spoke in the UN Security Council debate on the India-Pakistan fighting. A Pakistan protest note called the speech 'extraordinary behaviour on the part of a Moslem country'. After the Tunku replied on 26 September that 'Malaysia must regard her international ties as more important than her religious ties with other countries', Pakistan broke relations with 'the so-called state of Malaysia'. Although Singapore was by then separated from Malaysia, Pakistan's antagonism carried over and was, in fact, increased by hearing of a Singapore government comment that suggested sympathy with India in the Kashmir dispute: a comment that India and Singapore were caught in the nutcrackers between Pakistan and Indonesia. For their part, Malaysia and Singapore suspected that Pakistan was giving Indonesia's Sukarno some encouragement in his confrontation with Malaysia in Borneo.

Pakistan's first reaction to Singapore's application was not to reply at all, despite my reminders. After a month of hearing nothing, the Malaysians wired to ask me whether this silence would place any obstacle to Singapore's inclusion if all other countries supported it. There were, in fact, no rules on what constituted a consensus, and an impasse could have resulted. I was determined, throughout my period as Secretary-General, never to let consensus be defined in formal terms, and particularly not as involving a veto.

Fortunately, Pakistan's High Commissioner in London, Aga Hilaly, had been ambassador with me in Moscow and we had travelled together in Central Asia. He was a close friend. Through him I told the Pakistan leaders that, if they opposed Singapore's application, they would inevitably alienate important governments whose friendship they needed, including Australia, Britain and Canada. Lee Kuan Yew's prestige was at stake, and his domestic opponents were communists. Hilaly worked hard to sort out the problem in messages, both from himself and me, to his foreign minister, Zulfikar Ali Bhutto, and finally he intercepted Bhutto in Paris. In a telephone conversation from there Bhutto told me he could not support Singapore's admission but asked if he could abstain. I suggested he not use that term, since it implied a voting procedure, but that he simply say that Pakistan would not object if the others supported the application. He checked by telephone with President Ayub, who agreed to this formula; Hilaly put it in writing two days later.

So on 16 October, two months after the exercise began, I was able to announce, 'following consultations with Commonwealth Heads of Government. . . carried out at the request of the Government of Malaysia, who sponsored Singapore's application,' that the tiny city-state had been admitted as the twenty-second member of the Commonwealth. Months afterwards, I learnt from the Tunku and from Lee Kuan Yew the full story of why the break came. In brief, Singapore had been in and out of association with Malaya, or parts of it, more than once: in, during incorporation in the Straits Settlements with Malacca and Penang from 1826; out, as a Crown Colony from 1946 and selfgoverning from 1957; then in again when the Federation of Malaysia was formed in 1963 with Sabah and Sarawak. In the general elections for the Malaysian House of Representatives in September 1964, Lee's People's Action Party used the slogan of a 'Malaysian Malaysia.' The tacit implication was that all Malaysians were politically equal, and this alarmed those who did their ethnic arithmetic and realised that the predominantly Chinese population of Singapore (and activists in the PAP) came close to a majority when added to the thirty-five percent of Malaya's population who were also of Chinese origin. The long agreed convention in Malaya, by which Malay aristocrats ran politics and dominated the civil service, while the Chinese ran businesses, was threatened. More than that, although Lee was completely loyal to the Tunku personally, his brilliance gave him an obvious claim to becoming his successor. It was not a situation the Malay politicians behind the Tunku would tolerate.

When the expulsion was made, the lawyer in Lee wanted to protest at its unconstitutionality, but the statesman in him made him accept a *fait accompli*, realising (as he explained to me) that otherwise there would be riots to which many Chinese in Malaya and Malays in Singapore could have fallen victim. The Pakistan-Malay dispute taught me an important lesson in another field. It had been agreed, a year before, that the Colombo Plan meeting take place in late 1965 in Pakistan. The Malaysian Government told me that Pakistan was refusing to invite them since diplomatic relations had been broken. Attending the aid allocations conference mattered to Malaysia, of course, and they hoped I could do something. I managed, not without difficulty, to persuade Pakistan to back down and let Malaysia attend. But the lesson I drew – and it proved timely and important – was that all future invitations to attend Commonwealth meetings must be issued by the Secretary-General, not by the host government. This meant that Tanzania attended meetings of Commonwealth Law Ministers and Trade Ministers in Marlborough House in early 1966, although by then Nyerere had broken diplomatic relations with Britain over Rhodesia. I was able to persuade both Dar es Salaam and London that Marlborough House was an international headquarters, in which they would be at home, just as Cuba attended meetings at the UN in New York despite a lack of formal relations with the United States.

The sharpest outbreak of warfare for sixteen years between the two giants of the Commonwealth, Pakistan and India, took place in the middle months of 1965. By the time both sides obeyed repeated Security Council calls for a ceasefire on 23 September, a large tank battle had been fought after a Pakistan attack in southern Kashmir; Indian troops had attacked West Pakistan in three widely distant sectors; Pakistani warships had bombarded Dwarka, and their aircraft had tried to bomb Delhi and Bombay; and up to 10,000 people had been killed for the occupation of several square miles of each other's territory.

What was the Commonwealth to do about a dispute on such a scale? What could it do? The Nigerian prime minister raised with me the possibility of a Commonwealth peace mission. I saw little merit in this. The UN had been seized with the complexities of the Kashmir dispute for eighteen years; it had its own military observers on the borders; the issue had come regularly on the Security Council agenda; and in this 1965 crisis U Thant himself flew to Rawalpindi and Delhi in mid-September to urge a ceasefire. Even though the Council made no progress towards a troop withdrawal and other elements of a settlement in subsequent debates during

October, I thought it would be ludicrous for the brand-new Secretariat to try to take the play away from the UN with an attempt at mediation which neither combatant had invited.

Moreover, I knew the Indian prime minister was looking in other directions. When Bahadur Shastri had passed through Ottawa in June 1965, he made clear to Mike Pearson in my presence his worries about the build-up of Pakistan military strength with American supplies, and about Chinese intentions. He saw the skirmishing in the Rann of Kutch, which was then the trouble spot, as a preliminary to a larger attack in Kashmir. He was anxious for a settlement and prepared to make concessions; but this would be politically impossible for him, he told Pearson, unless he came under pressure from the Soviet Union and the United States, as well as Commonwealth countries.

In the end the combatants came to terms at a meeting under Alexei Kosygin's chairmanship in Tashkent in January 1966. As an old Muscovite (I had spent two periods of three years each there) I was personally delighted: it was the first time since 1917 that the Russians had tried to heal, rather than exacerbate, a dispute outside their own bloc. Later, there were people who said that the success of the Tashkent meeting was a severe blow to the prestige of the Commonwealth, in that an 'outside power' had stepped in. That is a petty view. The Commonwealth is only one of the available instruments of world politics, and sensible statesmen should choose whichever instrument is most appropriate for a particular action.

From conversations in London in late October with the British High Commissioners to India and Pakistan, John Freeman and Sir Morrice James, I gained an assessment of the strains the war had put on Commonwealth links. In India feelings had run strong against Britain after Harold Wilson made what he later admitted was a hasty judgement in publicly condemning India for an act of aggression. But there was a sensible distinction being made in Delhi between British links and Commonwealth ones. In Rawalpindi there was a different reaction, one of disappointment and puzzlement that the Secretariat had not tried to stir up a Commonwealth initiative during the fighting. Both countries, I was warned, might still decide to leave the Commonwealth in the next few months – but on a pretext external to their own dispute: they might decide to follow the lead of African states if these left the Commonwealth in protest against British mishandling of the Rhodesian situation.

These conversations confirmed me in my view that the Rhodesian crisis was then the most immediately explosive situation, and

25

also a situation in which the Secretariat could – indeed, must – act. It was important to move fast, to persuade African leaders to use the Commonwealth connection to bring about the desired results in Rhodesia, not to break these connections in dismay at British shortsightedness. If I failed there, the repercussions would spread also to Asia. So I pressed ahead with plans to tour five African states in early November.

When I flew to Entebbe in Uganda on 8 November 1965, it was my first time south of the Sahara. But I had formed some firm opinions from spending twenty months in charge of Canadian relations with African governments as assistant Under-Secretary of State for External Affairs in Ottawa, and from attending two Prime Ministers Meetings. One fundamental view was that for Britain to agree to the independence of any African country on any other basis than actual majority rule was to invite conflict and disaster. Britain had done this with South Africa in 1911; and Duncan Sandys had made a similar error over Zanzibar in 1963.

It seemed that the same mistake was about to be made with Rhodesia. Significantly, the 'Five Principles' enunciated for constitutional advance in Rhodesia by Sir Alec Douglas-Home in September 1964 and formally restated by Harold Wilson in February 1965 fell short of NIBMAR (no independence before majority rule). For the first of them stated:

> 'The principle and intention of unimpeded progress to majority rule, already enshrined in the 1961 Constitution, would have to be maintained and guaranteed.'

As we saw later, in successive proposals for a settlement, the principle of 'unimpeded progress to majority rule' could in British Government eyes be satisfied by a constitution that allowed Rhodesian whites a substantial majority* at the time of independence.

Ian Smith, who took power in April 1964 with the boast that he did not expect majority rule 'in my lifetime', had in nineteen months taken several steps that indicated he would indeed go to the limits in consolidating minority rule. He dismissed the Chief of Staff of the Rhodesian forces, Major-General Anderson, who was known to oppose a unilateral declaration of independence (UDI).

---

* 50 out of 67 seats in the *Tiger* proposals of December 1966, and 50 out of 66 seats in the Goodman proposals of 1971-72.

26

He resisted the scheme Bottomley produced in February 1965 for a 'blocking third' of African MPs who, assuming they all voted together, would just have the power to prevent retrogressive amendment of the constitution (the second of the British 'five principles'). And the general election that he called, much earlier than he need have done, in May 1965, he effectively turned into a referendum among white voters for independence although not specifically for UDI.

Finally, his reactions to the Heads of Government Meeting in June 1965 were ferocious. At that meeting, leader after leader from all continents called for a full constitutional conference, which all Rhodesian political leaders should be free to attend (Joshua Nkomo, Ndabaningi Sithole, Robert Mugabe and hundreds of others had been detained or imprisoned since June-July 1964, weeks after Smith took power).

Ian Smith's reaction was like a noisy banging of doors. In a cable to Wilson, he said:

"I must make it clear that to Rhodesia such a conference is absolutely unnecessary and out of the question, and that if such a conference were to be called, the Rhodesian Government would not attend, nor would any from our country.'

He went on to reject in October the idea of a Commonwealth mission, led by Sir Robert Menzies. Menzies would be welcome as an individual, he said, but a Commonwealth group certainly was not.

So it was in a mood of preparation for an imminent crisis that I made plans to visit Uganda, Kenya, Zambia, Malawi and Tanzania in early November.* I wanted to talk to the leaders of all these countries about the ways in which the newly launched Secretariat might be of help to young nations; but my more specific purpose was to persuade them that, if there were a UDI, they should keep cool. The problem, I urged, was not the illegality of a declaration of independence, but the long-standing racism. UDI would provide them with an opportunity to dramatise, on the world

---

* Harold Wilson made his final dash to Salisbury on 25 October, and hatched the idea of a Royal Commission, chaired by the Rhodesian Chief Justice, to undertake a revision of the 1961 Constitution so that it would fulfill Britain's five principles. Sir Saville Garner, who went with him, told me that Smith had been impressed by Wilson's warnings about the disastrous consequences of a UDI. I was not so hopeful; and in the last days of October revised my own schedule to leave London on 7 November, two weeks earlier than I had been planning.

and Commonwealth stages, the racial injustice and inequalities that had persisted for decades in Rhodesia. They should use the Commonwealth to help rally international action to deal with the Rhodesian situation rather than putting on an act, in their revulsion against British inaction, by withdrawing from the Commonwealth. Posturing, which was what a withdrawal from the Commonwealth would amount to, might make a leader feel better for a week or two; it might even make his people feel better, and hence make him more popular, for a few months if his people's minds worked slowly enough. But it was based on neo-colonialist thinking: the British were only one of a score of Commonwealth members, and they did not own or control the Commonwealth. And it would not improve the situation. My general message I summed up in a speech to the Zambia Association for National Affairs on 16 November:

> ' . . . Threats to leave the Commonwealth help no one; they diminish, not increase, the capacity of the withdrawing country to influence the situation. If the situation is to be corrected, if illegal rule is to be not merely ended but replaced by progress towards democratic majority rule, we as members of the Commonwealth must exert all our efforts through the Commonwealth channel and through all others to secure worldwide cooperation.'

I had asked, before leaving London, that in each country I might give press and TV conferences and talk to meetings of university students, in order to get my message across to a wide public; in effect, it was a way of bringing extra pressure upon the leaders. This was readily agreed; and I greatly enjoyed the sessions with students.

Of the five prime ministers and presidents, only one found much difficulty in agreeing with my thesis. But there was a catch, which was explained on my first stop – Uganda – by Milton Obote. He accepted that to take action against the Commonwealth over a UDI by Rhodesia was mere posturing, and even self-defeating. But, he warned, if any one among the African leaders withdrew from the Commonwealth, the pressures to follow this lead would break on all of them and the temptations to show solidarity in this way would be strong.

I was in an aircraft flying from Entebbe to Nairobi when Ian Smith broadcast his declaration of independence on 11 November. I found President Kenyatta expecting Britain to take firm action, now that UDI was declared. After all, it was treason. He had witnessed firm action in his own country; indeed, he had been imprisoned and detained by the British for nine years. Britain was a powerful country in his experience and, although African leaders had been told, by Douglas-Home in 1964 and by Wilson later, that Britain could not use force, he really did not credit Britain's impotence when the gauntlet was flung down by Smith. But he was prepared to give Britain time to crush this rebellion; he wasn't going to rush into any reprisal action against either Britain or the Commonwealth.

When I reached Zambia on 14 November, Kenneth Kaunda was naturally then a worried man. He realised how important it was for Zambia, landlocked and thrown into the front line of this crisis, to maintain contacts with many countries. He was not tempted to walk out of the Commonwealth, although he acknowledged that pressures could come from neighbours. (I myself thought they could also come from internal rivals.) I talked with him and Finance Minister Arthur Wina and Foreign Minister Simon Kapwepwe about how other Commonwealth countries could help Zambia in this emergency. Two weeks earlier in London Kapwepwe had told me he thought Zambia could 'keep afloat for six months' and he trusted that, before those months elapsed, economic sanctions would have brought down the rebel regime. Now, with UDI a reality, it did not seem so clearcut. Although the UN Security Council passed a resolution on 20 November recommending economic sanctions against Rhodesia, Britain delayed imposing oil sanctions until 17 December. Meanwhile, the stocks of oil supplies in Zambia were falling to a precarious level, dropping to only eleven days' supply by 11 December, while Rhodesia's stockpile during November doubled to three months' supply. Zambia was already a hostage of Rhodesia, and its lifeline of a railway through Rhodesia to Beira in Mozambique was being partially strangled.

Kaunda was also worried that the Rhodesians might cut off coal supplies from Wankie and electricity from the Kariba hydroelectric dam: but the dwindling of oil supplies was his most immediate anxiety. We talked about the tough economic prospects for his country, and about what various Commonwealth countries could do. At my suggestion, he sent a telegram to Pearson asking if Canada could help with an airlift of oildrums; and this airlift began with Hercules C-130 transport planes during December, supplementing the British effort with their older Argosies and Britannias.

Kaunda and Wina also asked that the meeting at Marlborough House of Senior Trade Officials scheduled for ten days later should have two additional items put on their agenda: sanctions against

Rhodesia and economic aid to Zambia. I agreed to arrange it. I also promised to send Nirmal Sen Gupta, director of my Economic Division, to Lusaka for a few weeks to help plan economic adjustments, and undertook to find a senior expert on a longer-term posting to help plan refugee resettlement. This turned out to be the Secretariat's first step in technical assistance.

During our four days in Zambia, our three-man team – Yaw Adu and Gerald Hensley were with me – visited Victoria Falls and performed a symbolic act. Gazing at the Zambezi river and at Rhodesia beyond, I suddenly remembered the first time I had met Jomo Kenyatta. It was in the ground floor washroom at Marlborough House during the 1964 conference, and we found ourselves standing side by side at the huge porcelain urinals that bore the manufacturer's tradename 'The Zambezi'. The conference was about to discuss Rhodesia, and I remarked on the symbolism to Kenyatta. Now, facing the real Zambezi, I remembered the incident and told the others. On an impulse we climbed down the steep bank to the river's edge and all three let fly into the torrent. Standing there, a Ghanaian, a New Zealander and a Canadian, we somehow felt that this was a pledge that we were not going to allow racial domination in Rhodesia to continue, and that the Zambezi was not going to remain a barrier to change.

On through Malawi, where Dr Banda told me he had no intention of leaving the Commonwealth, whatever anyone else said or did to Tanzania. I knew this would be the most crucial part of the trip. President Nyerere had several times talked publicly about Tanzania leaving the Commonwealth but during October had qualified this threat by adding 'if Britain acquiesced in a UDI'. By 20 November, when I reached Dar es Salaam, Britain had taken some relatively minor measures, stopping capital exports to Rhodesia, imposing exchange restrictions and banning imports of Rhodesian tobacco and sugar. It had not moved on the vital matter of oil supplies. British lack of action was looking suspiciously like acquiescence, in Nyerere's eyes.

I disagreed not at all with Nyerere's analysis of British inaction, but with his assertion that in certain circumstances he might have to break relations with Britain and leave the Commonwealth. I put my arguments to him in a robust way. There was a clear difference between his idea that he might have to break relations with Britain, and leaving the Commonwealth. To treat the Commonwealth as British property was perhaps understandable for a new country, I said, 'but we in Canada believe we invented it and think it is at least as much ours as British – and we would take a withdrawal as a personal affront!' As well, I had accepted the job of Secretary-General on election by him and the other leaders, and did not expect to be 'let down and stabbed in the back at the first crisis'.

We had a warm discussion. He said he was called Mwalimu, teacher, and he had been teaching his people that they must stand up for moral principles rather than make calculations of expediency. If he now failed to take a stand on principle and instead accepted something that was in his immediate interest, he would be letting down his people. No, you wouldn't be, I replied: your job is to take a long term view of what is in your people's interests – and preserve links and strengthen influence with other countries. Your duty is to try and shape the future. He would not make me any promises but, in the way he has of defusing a tense moment with a self-deprecatory remark, he added: 'Arnold, I sometimes think I would make a better preacher than president.'

I left Tanzania, believing that I might have made a dent in his thinking but not entirely reassured on his intentions. Back in London I gave a public warning on 26 November that one African withdrawal could lead to four or five others and have an effect on Asian countries, and that the Rhodesian crisis could lead to the disintegration of the Commonwealth if it were inadequately handled. 'Most African leaders are sceptical about the effectiveness in a reasonable time of the present level of sanctions. A complete trade embargo, coupled with measures to protect Zambia, would look more persuasive and sincere in their eyes.'

Early in December the danger to the Commonwealth increased. On 3 December the Foreign Ministers of African states, holding an OAU Council Meeting in Addis Ababa, passed a resolution calling on its members to break relations and 'links' with Britain if Britain did not crush the Rhodesian rebellion by 15 December. Although the resolution did not call explicitly for withdrawal from the Commonwealth, some African states began to interpret 'links' by coupling the two measures. I sent a long telegram on 8 December to the Commonwealth African heads of government, then numbering nine, urging them against such action. I tried many arguments:

' . . . Although it would demonstrate African seriousness, breaking Commonwealth associations could in itself do nothing to improve the Rhodesian situation. It would in fact worsen it by relieving some of the pressure on public opinion in Britain and other parts of the Common-wealth. To snap the links would abandon the field to those who might be only too happy to forget or ignore the demands of Africa.

'. . . I know you will understand my reasons for sending this message. The Commonwealth faces a major crisis. There have been suggestions for withdrawals during the next ten days. But in my judgement withdrawals could neither help the majority in Rhodesia nor widen Africa's freedom of decision. Once broken, Commonwealth ties would not easily be restored. I accepted the appointment which you offered me as Secretary-General in the belief that Commonwealth associations, if rightly used, can assist mankind in bridge-building between diverse regions of the world. If I am wrong, we are all losers and will continue to be losers long after this Rhodesian crisis is resolved.'

The two Commonwealth African governments that broke relations with Britain after the OAU's December 15 deadline were Ghana and Tanzania. Neither of them withdrew from the Commonwealth. In a speech in the Tanzania National Assembly, President Nyerere drew the distinction that I had hoped he would. The organisation was, he said 'no longer the British Commonwealth – it is a Commonwealth of free nations'.

In Ghana President Nkrumah went to the very edge of withdrawing from the Commonwealth. Yaw Adu had flown to Accra in early December to make the distinction clear to him, and found much less sense of crisis there than in Dar es Salaam, but was not able to see the President before the December 15 deadline. The following day Nkrumah said in parliament:

'Ghana's membership in the British [sic] Commonwealth has made it difficult for the country to pursue satisfactorily its African objectives. In the interests of African unity and the formation of an African Government which are Ghana's main objectives, Ghana must consider withdrawing from the Commonwealth, and will call on other States of the OAU to break links with former colonial powers which stand in the way of African unity – Britain, France, Portugal, Belgium and Spain.'

To carry out his plans he sent to London two senior officials, Michael Dei-Anang, who headed Ghana's African Affairs Secretariat as well as being a leading poet, and E. Adomakoh who was Governor of the State Bank. They were carrying two letters from Nkrumah – one to Harold Wilson, one to me – respectively making formal the breaking of relations with Britain and withdrawal from the Commonwealth. The Ghanaian High Commissioner, Kwesi Armah, was strongly opposed to this action, and managed to persuade the emissaries to keep these letters in their pockets while he engaged in a long-distance telephone argument with Nkrumah over several days. In the end he won at least half the argument – the Common-wealth part. Finally, when the two officials came to see me, we had a polite meeting, during which they never brought up the matter of withdrawal, and made no reference to any letter. We all knew, however, how close we had come to the brink.

It seems clear that Nkrumah was really of two minds. He felt that he could not afford to ignore an OAU resolution, even though it had been made without reference to heads of government, and he was also influenced by his friendship with Guinean president Sekou Touré and the unimpressive Guinean secretary-general of the OAU, Diallo Telli – and Guineans tended to see the Commonwealth in the same sinister neocolonialist light as that in which they viewed de Gaulle's French Community which they had refused to join in 1960. At the same time, Nkrumah was enthusiastic to turn the Common-wealth into a vehicle that could support African aspirations, and he had approved Adu's appointment in consequence. So he let himself be deterred from a walkout by his persuasive High Commissioner, although he boycotted the Lagos HGM the following month.

Soon afterwards, he was deposed in a military coup. Ghana's new leader, General Ankrah, quickly asked me to release Adu from his Commonwealth job to return to Ghanaian service and help reorganise its governmental structure. I could not afford to do so – as I told his emissary, 'It is written: Thou shalt not covet they neighbour's deputy.' But, as a compromise, Yaw went to Accra on loan for a few periods of two to three weeks each during 1966 and became in effect a pioneer in the top-level technical assistance that the Commonwealth was later able to offer to many countries.

Chapter 3

BREAKING NEW GROUND
The Ideas, Place and People

It was important to take time away from the political crises in the later months of 1965 to reflect on the changing nature of the Commonwealth and the needs which the new Secretariat should try to serve. It was important to accept, when possible, the invitations for public speeches and broadcast interviews, because there was not simply a great amount of ignorance, which was understandable since so much was new: new members and a new organisation. There was also, overlying the ignorance, a heavy sprinkling of national preoccupations, which was producing a general mood of neo-isolationism; and in this mood the usefulness of international organisations generally (and certainly of a fledgling like the Commonwealth Secretariat) was being doubted.

The doubts seemed heaviest in Britain. Among the older generation there, who had known the days when she was a (probably *the*) major world power, the Commonwealth had offered during most of the twenty postwar years an apparent salve to nostalgia for Empire. In more hardheaded terms, it also served to amplify Britain's voice, enhance its influence and increase its resources in the world. For this the British had to pay relatively little in military policing and trade preferences. But when during the later 1950s the British realised that the Commonwealth had ceased to be anglocentric, and Britain's lead was no longer automatically followed, there was a tendency among some British politicians and editors to cry 'sour grapes' and denigrate the Commonwealth because in selfish calculations they thought it an instrument that for them had lost its value.

As for young people in Britain at that time, many of them were rejecting the concept of world politics in terms of power – and rightly rejecting it. But that did not mean that they were attracted to the Commonwealth, as they perceived it. While they could become excited about the aspirations of developing countries, and about the links to those countries being forged by organisations like

Voluntary Service Overseas, yet the only image available to most of them of the Commonwealth as an association was the paternalistic one of a power relationship they inherited from the older generation. Understandably they were allergic to it.

In Australia during the final years of Menzies' long reign (he resigned the leadership in February 1966), the attitudes of the older generation in Britain found a resonant echo. The following fifteen years have seen a remarkably constructive reversal of those attitudes, and this is one of the most heartening stories of the Commonwealth, as will be described later*. But in the mid-Sixties Australia remained antipathetic to most of the new Commonwealth.

For their part, the public in many of the newer member countries tended to think of the Commonwealth in neocolonialist terms as a relic of Empire.

I set out in innumerable speeches and press conferences to dispel the notion that the Commonwealth was a ghost of Empire, pointing out that several countries Britain had once ruled – Egypt, for example, the Sudan, Iraq and Burma – had chosen not to join. It was not even a creation of Britain, but rather the creation of a string of leaders of successful liberation movements, starting with Canada's Sir John A. Macdonald and running on through Nehru and Nkrumah and Kenyatta. I summed up this thought in my first formal report to the heads of government in August 1966:

'When statesmen who have led their nations to independence have decided to seek membership in the Commonwealth, they have not appeared to be motivated by sentimentality about the past, but by a constructive vision of the future and by realistic assessment about their country's national interest. For many of them the past included memories of racial discrimination, political struggle and jail. The decision was taken because these leaders saw practical value for their countries and for humanity, in retaining and building on the positive aspects of an association that linked races and continents, and in surmounting past inequities, rather than in using unpleasant memories and resentments for nation building based on the perpetuation of suspicions and divisions, as lesser politicians have so often done.'

The practical value was seen in widely varying forms. Lee Kuan Yew once told me that part of its value to him was as a 'cover' for

---

* See Chapter 13.

maintaining the kind of links he wanted with countries – Britain, Australia and Canada – which otherwise might be called imperialist. The prime minister of Papua New Guinea, Michael Somare, saw the Commonwealth connection as useful for providing technical assistance from non-white countries, since he wanted to show his countrymen that sophisticated jobs could be handled by people other than Australians and kindred whites.

Most liberation leaders who applied for Commonwealth membership also grasped its larger value. On the eve of Tanganyika's independence in 1961, Julius Nyerere had described the Commonwealth in these terms:

'More than any other group of nations in the world today, the Commonwealth binds together in friendship and in likemindedness an astonishing variety of nations great and small, without distinction between them and without discrimination amongst them.

Stronger than ties and treaties, less selfish than alliances, less restrictive than any other association, the Commonwealth seems to my colleagues and myself to offer the best hope in the world today of lasting peace and friendship among the peoples of the world.'*

Kaunda once told me privately that he enormously valued the OAU because it symbolised, and helped member states to move towards, the unity of Africa. But, he added, the Commonwealth was even more important because it was an instrument which, if properly used, could help everyone move towards the unity of mankind.

Those who have regretted the elaborate structure of the United Nations, the rigidities of its voting systems, sometimes gaze wistfully at the freedom the Commonwealth enjoys. I found this wistfulness particularly strong among Americans, whose own revolution in 1776 was the logical beginning of the Commonwealth since it first taught Britain to be receptive to the demands of colonial peoples. In conversations in 1965-66 with Secretary of State Dean Rusk and Wayne Fredericks, the Assistant Secretary of State for African Affairs, I saw the untold value they put on the Commonwealth facility for regular and informal gatherings of leaders from all continents. And in 1975 Elliot Richardson, then newly arrived as US ambassador in London, called on me to voice his concerns about the souring of North-South relationships in the aftermath of

---

* Speaking on a Government Motion on Independence and Membership of the Commonwealth, Tanganyika National Assembly, 5 June 1961.

UNCTAD IV and to suggest that the Commonwealth Heads of Government who were soon to meet in Jamaica could play a significant role in lessening these dangers.

I had sat in as Canadian delegate in the late 1940s and early 1950s on many meetings of the UN General Assembly, its Security Council and its Economic and Social Assembly, and on many NATO meetings. There is no doubt at all in my mind that there has been more changing of attitudes, more implanting of fresh ideas, among political leaders who meet for a week or ten days in the relaxed circumstances of a Commonwealth meeting seeking consensus, than ever happened in the fixed lines of the United Nations or NATO. Sometimes it seemed, however, in the late 1960s and early 1970s that these facts were more widely perceived and valued in Washington than in London.

It was cheering to find, nevertheless, that several of the brighter Commonwealth leaders looked steadily beyond their own borders to provide themselves with the sense and the substance of effective community that humanity needs. Just as Arnold Toynbee suggested that the real units of history had not been nations but successive civilisations, so in modern terms they saw that the real unit for an effective international policy was not a nation-state but an association of countries. Not surprisingly, the leaders of little countries and their citizens realise more easily than those from big countries that they need to make the utmost use of international instruments: the United Nations, regional organisations like the OAU, the Organisation of American States, the EEC and the Association of South East Asian Nations – and the Commonwealth.

In my report to Heads of Government in August 1966 I developed this argument about a grouping of countries, of diverse backgrounds and opinions but with some common traditions, playing a significant role in moving mankind towards a cooperative world community.

'This diversity is a measure of the value of the Commonwealth, actual and potential, as an international association. Its significance lies not in achieving unanimity within a homogeneous group of the likeminded, but in the opportunities it affords to maintain and develop the habit of consultation and constructive co-operation among important representatives of so many regions, races and divisions of mankind. Consultation in the modern Commonwealth involves grappling with the major problems of world politics – those involved in relations between the races, between regions and civilisations, between the rich nations and the poor nations; the problem of world economic imbalance, of development, and of the search for a secure basis for peace . . .

'International understanding and co-operation are seldom easy to achieve, but there are a number of common factors among Commonwealth members which can help significantly in the search to attain them. Though only a small minority of Commonwealth citizens have English as their native tongue, nevertheless members of Governments, officials, businessmen, pressmen and educators can use English easily as a common working language. There are a number of similarities in Commonwealth countries' political, administrative, organisational and educational traditions, in fields as varied as the rule of law, military staff procedure, the concept of a non-partisan civil service, and the ideal of press freedom.

'Above all, there are habits of frank, informal and private consultation. These habits and traditions existed in the earlier, smaller Commonwealth, but they are of vastly greater significance and potential value for world politics as a whole in the modern multi-racial Commonwealth.'

But there remained the scepticism in important quarters in Britain. To them the Commonwealth seemed now a nuisance: once an asset, it seemed now a liability in many areas. It restricted Britain's freedom of choice. It inhibited British entry into the European Community and it made forbidding noises about a settlement in Rhodesia. What Britain could get out of the modern Commonwealth, I suggested, was what it offered to its other members,

'A better chance not only that she should have her policies understood by key countries in other continents but, even more important, a better chance to understand the real views, the real aspirations, the real worries and fears and problems of the leaders and governments and people in these other continents.'

These problems of attitudes were not limited to the British. During each of the next several years, I travelled some 150,000 miles, attending a conference here, a crisis there, independence parties for various new members, Commonwealth Parliamentary Association meetings or Commonwealth Games. I often combined these trips with stop-overs en route to and from special events in order to consult with heads of government, or persuade them to support some programme. Almost invariably I took the opportunity to address students and to give a press conference. I often felt that I was a sort of itinerant preacher.

Against this background of different perceptions of the nature of the Commonwealth, we had to get the Secretariat established.

In Marlborough House, loaned by the Queen, we had for our offices and conference rooms one of the most beautiful, prestigious and well located buildings in London. As we expanded, we rented some less ornate, additional office space nearby, beginning with a building in Carlton House Terrace that had once been Mr Gladstone's residence. A good official residence was clearly going to be essential, for quiet persuasion is often most effective during or after a good meal. Eve found the perfect solution in a new eight-floor tower block of flats in Carlton Gardens, directly across the street from the official residence of the British Foreign Secretary, and separated only by two formidable walls (happily with gates) from the spacious gardens of Marlborough House itself. The building had two flats per floor and by joining both of those of the fifth floor we had an adequate apartment for reasonably intimate entertaining. When we wanted to seat more than fourteen at one table or have a reception for more than about eighty people, we used Marlborough House itself. And I could walk back home from the office in three minutes through restful trees.

I used the metaphors of gardening to explain the nature of the Commonwealth when I gave the convocation address at the University of Michigan in April 1966.

'If one tends to think of political activity and institutions in terms of social engineering or architectural blueprints, then it is easy to conclude that the Commonwealth has no real existence . . . But there is a much more profound approach to politics and history, which can be conveyed by the metaphors of gardening.

'The gardener's approach has more humility, seeking to guide rather than control. It also recognises that, when we are dealing with life and growth, the intangible is even more important than the tangible. In politics as in other aspects of relations between men, the key factor is the human spirit. The laws of economic or geographic determinism can sometimes help us discern the conditions in which the human spirit has to operate, but it is the psychological factors that really shape the future. What matters most, in shaping history, are such intangibles as attitudes, values, intuitions, motivation, faith. It is in this field that the Commonwealth operates.'

Important decisions were involved in how to build the structure of the new functioning body, the Secretariat. How large should it be? What functions should it carry out? How much initiative was it to be allowed to take?

The Agreed Memorandum, the 1965 document that contained the terms of reference for the Secretariat, was ambiguous on all these points. But ambiguity can be an advantage, rather than a limitation. For example, on the question of the size of the Secretariat, the Agreed Memorandum says that 'it should operate initially on a modest footing; and its staff and functions should be left to expand pragmatically in the light of experience, subject always to the approval of Governments.'

As to functions, this would depend on the problems which Commonwealth governments, collectively or in groups, found over time were best tackled cooperatively on their behalf. Ideas and proposals emerged from meetings of ministers and officials, and from the Secretariat itself.

In interpreting 'initiative' the possibilities were limitless, and subject only to the varying realities of what was politically feasible. The provision in the Agreed Memorandum that the Secretary-General would have direct access to Heads of Government gave him the right to say anything he thought fit, to heads of government or at any other level. The right of freedom of public speaking was self-evident.

St Paul once wrote that 'The service of God is perfect freedom'. On a more mundane plane, I found being responsible to twenty or thirty heads of government collectively, but to no single one individually, a reasonable approximation to such freedom. However, it was best – indeed, when extra funds were needed, it was essential – that the initiatives and new activities be developed gradually, by precedent and steps.

I have already hinted that relations with some British officials were less than easy during the early days of the Secretariat. I should immediately add that relations with British ministers of both parties, from Alec Home and Harold Wilson downward, were almost without exception good. And I received great encouragement and much practical advice from several retired British ministers and diplomats such as Malcolm MacDonald, Lord Redcliffe-Maud and Sir James Robertson, and from many others – editors, journalists, professors and businessmen. But it is time to go into this matter more broadly, to show that, while antagonism to the Secretariat was not a universal attitude in Whitehall, it was powerful enough to cause a number of confrontations.

There were no problems in the early years with the Foreign Office, many of whose senior members I had known in Moscow, Cairo and elsewhere. Equally, the Colonial Office under Sir Hilary Poynton was as helpful and friendly as could be: it was working itself out of a job with decolonisation and seemed happy to be doing so. Its staff was not worried that the Secretariat began preparing and circulating papers on dependent territories: ones on Guyana, Botswana, Lesotho and Barbados were produced during the first year.

The Commonwealth Relations Office (CRO), on the other hand, felt itself threatened by the Secretariat – and the larger and more active the Secretariat, the greater the perceived threat. Not only was the CRO's handling of the Rhodesian situation under continuous challenge from Commonwealth member states, of whom the Secretariat was now the servant; the CRO's very existence as a separate department was being put further in question by our creation. For this issue of its separate existence had been simmering ever since India's independence. Skirmishing with the Colonial Office (CO) ended with a merger of the CRO and CO in 1966, and the unified diplomatic service recommended by the Plowden Inquiry was eventually formed by amalgamation into the Foreign and Commonwealth Office (FCO) in October 1968. But in the meantime CRO officials were anxious about their future; and relations between the CRO and the Secretariat suffered in consequence. While Sir Saville Garner, as Head of the Diplomatic Service as well as Permanent Under Secretary of State at the CRO, had none of these anxieties and was always personally cooperative, his attitude was not shared by some of his deputies nor did it permeate much into the middle ranks.

Their tactics were to try to keep the Secretariat as small, and its status as low, as possible. If it remained small, it would, they thought, be dependent on CRO help to service ministerial and officials' meetings. Equally, if the chairmanship of various committees remained in British hands, the CRO's influence would be maintained and its continuing importance would have to be acknowledged. From the Secretariat's viewpoint, it was essential to demonstrate that a major change had taken place: the Commonwealth in 1965 was not 'an Englishman's Club', if it ever had been. Some clashes were therefore not surprising.

They came sharply at the start. While I was sailing across the Atlantic in August 1965, the CRO made detailed arrangements, including dates, for a Commonwealth trade officials' meeting more than three months ahead, a matter that should obviously have been for the Secretary-General. Then, during my first days back in

41

London, I was shown a draft 'letter of appointment', prepared by officials who proposed that it be signed by Harold Wilson and sent to me. I was asked what day that week should be inserted as the date when I was formally taking up my appointment. This was altogether too much! Naming a date that week rather than at the end of June, when I had been elected, would have lost the Secretariat considerable funds from Britain, one-eighth of its first year's assessment, since the CRO intended to pro-rate their first fiscal year's promised contribution, an approach that would no doubt have been followed by other countries' treasury boards. To have accepted a letter of appointment from a British prime minister would, moreover, have meant walking into a trap: if he could appoint me, one of his successors could also conceivably fire me.

So I told the CRO bluntly: 'I took up my job actively from July 1. I was elected by all the Prime Ministers and it was recorded in their communiqué. That is the document recording my assumption of the office. That's all there is to it. I don't accept letters of appointment from the British or any other single prime minister. The President of the United States does not send a letter informing the UN Secretary-General that he has been elected.' Naturally Harold Wilson himself knew nothing of this. It was an impertinent but not (I suspected) naive try-on by some bureaucrats.

But the territorial skirmishing continued. In CRO press statements I was referred to as 'Secretary-General of the Commonwealth Secretariat'. A more concrete way of trying to diminish my office was to ask me and my Secretariat staff, then numbering about twenty, to move out of the main original buildings of Marlborough House after three months (I was in a splendid office which had been Queen Mary's bedroom) into the East Wing, which had been the servants' quarters. And a letter came from the CRO saying that, while the Agreed Memorandum stated that the Secretary-General should have direct access to all heads of government, each government had to determine by what channel that access should be exercised – a fine piece of Jesuitical metaphysics! – and that any appointment I wished to seek with the British Prime Minister must be through the CRO. Then, at the Commonwealth Finance Ministers Meeting in Jamaica in September 1965, the first ministerial meeting I attended as Secretary-General, I learnt in advance from the Jamaican organising officials that CRO officials had advised them to place me at a small table in the middle of the larger horseshoe table at which ministers would sit. This is the way that steno-typists are seated at UN council meetings; of course I insisted on sitting at the main table beside the chairman; the Jamaican officials consulted their Prime Minister, who naturally agreed.

None of these annoyances were hard to work out, when necessary at ministerial level, but if we had conceded these points they could have been serious, for the Secretariat and the Commonwealth links it served would have been perceptibly reduced in stature and importance.

On the issue of chairmanship of committees, it was important to have it established that, say at an officials' meeting in Marlborough House, the British would not automatically provide the chairman on the ground that he represented the 'host government' – any more than an American automatically chairs meetings at the United Nations. When nominations were invited in March 1966 for members for the Review Committee that was to study what relationship the Secretariat should have to existing Commonwealth agencies, the CRO wrote nominating Lord Sherfield as chairman. I had to take the position that the committee would elect its own chairman. I was delighted (and quietly instrumental in arranging) that Sherfield was in the event elected chairman by his fellow members, and he made an excellent one; but it was vital that Commonwealth equality be seen to be honoured.

There were some subtler moves I thought the British made about the Secretariat which we simply accepted with a shrug. After years in Moscow, I was not surprised to detect small signs that led me to suspect that the telephones in both my office and my flat were bugged. When I mentioned this to Mike Pearson in May 1966, he laughingly offered to send over from Canada a team of technicians to 'sweep' my rooms. We both knew that, if that was done, the bugs could soon be replaced. So for particularly confidential conversations with Secretariat staff or visitors, I used to suggest a walk in the gardens of Marlborough House.

A few words need to be said about the way the Commonwealth proceeds by consensus, and also about the impartial role of a Secretary-General. A Secretary-General, it is clear, must be impartial to the extent that he is responsible to the collectivity of member states and must not favour the interests of one group against another. But this need not mean he is neutral, nor that he steps carefully down the middle between the various views. Impartiality meant, in my interpretation, that we in the Secretariat made our own analysis of a situation and chose what seemed correct action in the common interest – and pursued it. On some issues this involved trying to change the minds of member governments and other people, and entailed some tough battles. But to have automatically taken a middle line, for example among various governments' starting views on the issue of EEC relations with developing countries – or to have been 'neutral' unless and until a consensus emerged without Secretariat leadership – would have been not merely useless, but disastrous.

Similarly, consensus does not mean unanimity, risking inaction or dangerous stalemate through a single veto; nor can it often involve the somewhat leisurely procedure described in the African phrase of 'sitting round a mango tree and talking until we all agree'. Consensus involves the support of a significant majority sufficient to make the action under consideration practicable. For example, the setting up in 1971 of the Commonwealth Fund for Technical Cooperation needed the support not only of a good majority but also of enough rich contributors to make it workable – but it was launched over Australian opposition. Again, the initial hesitation of many governments about Bangladesh's application for Commonwealth membership was turned by consultation and some persuasion into a positive consensus, and the few who remained reluctant acquiesced in it.

In short, the elected Secretary-General of a dynamic international community must embody for the association what Rousseau called 'the general will', and should act accordingly. It is also his responsibility to try, when necessary, to develop a general will, by discussion with heads of government and ministers and, when appropriate, with journalists and in public speeches.

Internally also, the Secretariat needed to be an organic growth. It could not, of course, spread in all directions like bougainvillea; but it had to respond to the stimuli and the demands of new situations, whether Rhodesia or the growing crisis in youth employment that led in 1973 to the launching of the Commonwealth Youth Program. And, precisely because we were a small staff dealing with matters in all parts of the world, we needed to use to the full the talents and geographical knowledge, as well as the subject specialisation, that each person brought.

Again, without undermining any director, I tried to make sure that ideas bubbling up in any division were not dismissed through a single negative decision. One means was the use of special assistants

44

of high calibre in my office, who played the role of outriders and picked up word of ideas and problems at every level. To those who were accustomed to a large, compartmentalised and almost feudally hierarchic, civil service (whether in Britain or in India), there was something subversive about this approach, and I had occasional disagreements on methods* with one or two senior colleagues who came from older and more conventional bureaucracies. But, having been a special assistant myself to Mike Pearson and appreciating the creative flexibility of the Canadian External Affairs Department in the first post-war decade, I persevered in this approach.

The Agreed Memorandum had stated that the Secretariat should start with a single Deputy Secretary-General (DSG) responsible for economic matters, adding that a second might be added later in light of general progress. My view was that circumstances in southern Africa and elsewhere could not wait for the years of quiet progress envisaged in the Memorandum, before a second DSG was appointed to deal with political matters. I was also concerned to establish that the Secretary-General as well as Heads of Government could make nominations for these posts, which (besides my own) were the only Secretariat posts to be filled by election by governments. Yaw Adu was my nominee for the political post, and Tilak Gooneratne who became the first DSG in charge of economic affairs was the nominee of the Sri Lanka Prime Minister, and a very sensitive and experienced Asian.

The Commonwealth was fortunate in the staff recruited to the Secretariat in those early years. They provided qualities different from those expected in traditional civil servants. I think of Nirmal Sen Gupta, like a Laughing Buddha round and smooth, but a man of excellent judgement as director of the economics division, who went on to be Chief Secretary of the West Bengal Government during the influx of millions of refugees from East Bengal, and later Secretary (permanent head) of India's Finance Ministry. I think also of Gordon Goundrey, a former professor of economics who had helped Alberta negotiate with the oil companies and Zambia recover from its membership in the Central African Federation before he joined the Secretariat. He is now an Assistant Secretary-General

---

* Years afterwards, I found my views on organisation broadly similar to those of Robert Townsend who, having given the Avis car-hire company a new breeze, sailed on to write *Up the Organisation: How to stop the Corporation from Stifling People and Strangling Profits* (Fawcett Crest Books, New York 1970). In the book's most important section, on People, he maintains that 'modern organisations are only getting people to use about 20 percent – the lower fifth – of their capacities.'

of the United Nations. And I think of Emeka Anyaoku, a chief's son from eastern Nigeria, whose diplomatic skills were most useful, notably among nationalist leaders in southern Africa and with all the African, Caribbean and Pacific members in the negotiations before the Lomé Convention.* All of them were soon working and advising at the level of ministers and often heads of government, who welcomed advice and initiatives as soon as they found that Secretariat staff had their interests genuinely at heart.

Others brought different qualities to the early mixture at the Secretariat. Patsy Robertson, warm and cheerful and practiced in jollying along the media in London ever since her days as press attaché for the West Indies Federation; yet, when it was necessary, a delightful deflater who could puncture stupidity or self-importance on the part of any pressman, Minister or colleague. Gerald Hensley, a quiet and modest but brilliant New Zealander with a creative mind that could soar; invaluable as a special assistant, for he intuitively recognised the moments when a Secretariat intervention could be timely with governments (say, during the Nigerian civil war) at the point when a problem was just visible but a fixed policy had not yet been moulded.

We were fortunate, too, in the British who came to the Secretariat, either from Whitehall or from outside government service. Two examples make the point. Tom Aston, seconded from the CRO as first head of the International Affairs division, came with useful experience of Africa and immediately assumed a Commonwealth stance with utter integrity. And Noël Salter, whom I recruited from the British Council of Churches, brought from his earlier experience as Deputy Secretary-General of the Council of Europe invaluable contacts with European bureaucrats; a Christian dedicated to both an international and a European vision.

They and others were a most unusual mixture, and the human chemistry between such different people might not have worked well. But they all had the quality that a small international machine needs above all to make it effective: they all enjoyed its diversity and took delight in the adventure on which the Secretariat was launched.

But how to keep good people? The Agreed Memorandum specified contracts of between two and five years, and home governments were often anxious to reclaim someone whose abilities were so noticeable. We managed to extend the contracts of at least some;

---

* In 1978 Anyaoku was elected Deputy Secretary-General of the Commonwealth.

and the others who went home have provided an enduring network of influential friends for the Secretariat.

The size and scope of the Secretariat depended on the conclusions of the Review Committee on Intra-Commonwealth Organisations set up at the request of Prime Ministers in June 1965. It had a daunting task, because there were then more than 250 organisations based in Britain and concerned with various aspects of Commonwealth relations. But the list was whittled down to ten intergovernmental organisations concerned with economic and educational matters, which the committee studied in detail to see if there was needless duplication either between them or with UN Specialised Agencies; which bodies might usefully be absorbed into the Secretariat; and how cooperation between the Secretariat and those that were not absorbed could be best achieved.

The Review Committee worked hard under the chairmanship of Lord Sherfield (who, as Sir Roger Makins, had been not only deputy head of the Foreign Office and British Ambassador in Washington but also head of the Treasury). It held twenty-eight meetings during the summer of 1966, and recommended that the Secretariat absorb the Commonwealth Economic Committee (CEC), with its staff of seventy-nine, mostly economists and statisticians, and the ten-person Commonwealth Education Liaison Unit (CELU). It found the arrangements surrounding the Commonwealth Scientific Committee (CSC) full of anomalies, but thought the CSC secretariat could in due course be integrated into the Secretariat.

The Sherfield committee concluded that nearly all the others (i.e. those concerned with forestry, telecommunications, air transport, aeronautical research, and the fourteen organisations that form the Commonwealth Agricultural Bureaux) had functions too specialised to be usefully absorbed into the Secretariat. In a category of its own was the Commonwealth Institute, which the committee said was doing an efficient job of educating and informing public opinion, mainly in Britain and at that government's expense, and should not be disturbed. The Secretary-General of the Commonwealth was made a member of its Board of Governors.

These were all sensible conclusions, and they gave the Secretariat important fields of work. Both the CEC and the CELU had executive functions and their absorption turned the Secretariat into more of an executive body itself. The staff of the CEC, which dated from 1925 and had once run the Empire Marketing Board, had in recent years been mainly engaged in compiling commodity reports, annual reports on Commonwealth trade and a series of financing development

47

programs. I was keen to deploy its (mostly British) economists on a broader front and more dynamically, for example in the work of export market development, which the Trade Ministers who met in June 1966 had recommended that the Secretariat undertake. Education was clearly a major area for Commonwealth cooperation, and I welcomed the opportunity to expand this work by taking over the CELU. Hugh Springer, the CELU head, a Barbadian, became a very able Assistant Secretary-General when we did so.*

Three other functional developments to which I attached great importance – the establishment of a Legal Division, a Medical Section and an Information Division – were only approved a few years later.**

Whether the Secretariat should act as a funding agency to promote and strengthen links between professional organisations around the Commonwealth had been a lively issue at the meeting of officials in January 1965. In the previous June, Alec Home had floated the idea of a Commonwealth Foundation, with initial resources of at least £250,000 a year for this purpose. Most of the developing country officials wanted such a Foundation to be a part of the Secretariat; the officials representing Britain, which had offered to pay half this fund, wanted it separate. I proposed a separate Foundation, in return for winning from the British support for some of the main terms of reference to the Secretariat. The Foundation's decisions, it was agreed, would be taken by a Board of Trustees with the Commonwealth Secretary-General as a member of that Board. So the Foundation was set up simultaneously with the Secretariat, and occupied part of the west wing of Marlborough House. John Chadwick directed its affairs with great devotion for the next fifteen years, launching new professional associations with regularity and funding professional centres in many countries.

A major concern for me throughout my years as Secretary-General was to set in train and then to extend multilateral programmes of technical assistance. All development assistance in the Commonwealth had been through bilateral, country-to-country channels, involving only four donors – Britain, Canada, Australia and New Zealand. The technical expertise and training places available in developing countries – there were many in Asian countries in particular – were quite unused. Prime Ministers in 1964 and 1965 had given verbal

---

* Later, as Sir Hugh Springer, he became Secretary-General of the Association of Commonwealth Universities.

** See Chapter 6.

backing to a scheme, first mooted by Sir Alec, for some joint Commonwealth development projects; but they made no financial arrangements.

After talking to leaders about the kind of development projects they would welcome, I put before the Heads of Government Meeting in September 1966 some detailed proposals with a modest target of £1 million a year. But any hopes for an immediate decision foundered in the wake of the stormy session on Rhodesia. The heads of government did, however, agree in their communiqué that these proposals should be examined at a meeting which I was to convene of senior officials concerned with aid administration, and this meeting took place in Nairobi in 1967 and authorised a start of technical assistance programmes using money from some rich countries to finance experts and training places drawn also from developing countries themselves.

Technical and functional cooperation is a part of such significance in the story of Commonwealth development that its start requires telling in a full chapter later.*

I followed up the Heads of Government Meeting with a five-week trip to Asia in November-December 1966, visiting India, Sri Lanka, Malaysia and Singapore.

It went down well in India when I said at press conferences that 'the Commonwealth as it exists today is the creation of Jawaharlal Nehru', and in Sri Lanka when I said that no single country or city was the centre of the Commonwealth. In all four countries there was animated discussion not only with heads of government but also with ministers of education, finance, trade and other functional portfolios about how Commonwealth collaboration could be improved for practical development. The themes of later UNCTAD meetings, and the thrust behind demands for a New International Economic Order, became clear to me at that early stage. It made me more determined than ever that the Secretariat's staff of economists, now strongly reinforced by the absorption of the CEC, should try to help shape policies on commodities rather than passively analyse them, and should tackle as a priority the problems of export market development for Asian and other developing countries.

A trip such as this was an excellent opportunity to get to know Commonwealth leaders in a relaxed setting. I remember in particular

---

* Chapter 6.

two dinner parties with Tunku Abdul Rahman in Kuala Lumpur. A man who mixed charm, dignity and often profound wisdom with a lively sense of humour, he asked me at the first, formal dinner whether I played poker. When I said I did, he invited me back for an informal dinner the following night, as well as for a game of golf in the morning. That second evening, we barbecued steaks and dealt the cards, and the Tunku told how during the HGM in London two months earlier he had gone to play poker at the Playboy Club. 'But it's not a good place for poker,' he added. 'Too distracting.'

I had found stiffer companions among some British and Australian MPs during the twelfth Commonwealth Parliamentary Conference in Ottawa that September. They challenged my right to give the wide-ranging address I did and suggested I should have confined myself to an administrative account of what the Secretariat had been doing. Australia's Air Minister, Peter Howson, went further and said the Secretariat should only prepare data papers and collate the views of experts. 'Their role is not to put forward policy, or even to express opinions on policy. I feel certain that, as the years go by, the Secretariat will realise the limitations of its role and not endeavour to exceed it'.*

But several Canadian editorial writers championed the Secretariat, in particular one on the *Toronto Star* who wrote:

> ' . . . .If the critics' view is accepted, and the Secretary-Generalship is reduced to a post office, ... some second-string functionary from the British Commonwealth Relations Office will suffice for the job.'

In subsequent years I continued to use my invitations to the annual Commonwealth Parliamentary Association meetings (which took place in different countries each year) as opportunies to propound analyses and recommendations to groups of legislators – as I also used press conferences, memoranda to governments and other channels. The appropriateness of this was never again challenged by elected legislators, either ministers or backbenchers.

---

* For my speech and the discussion, see appendix to *Proceedings of Twelfth Commonwealth Parliamentary Conference*, Senate of Canada, 28 September to 4 October 1966.

Chapter 4

RHODESIA 1965-72
Holding The Line

The fourteen years of Rhodesia's rebellion, from Ian Smith's declaration of independence in November 1965 to the Lancaster House agreement that was signed in December 1979, divide neatly into two halves. This chapter will tell the Commonwealth story during the first seven years, when Britain made repeated attempts to reach a settlement with the Smith regime that would give independence on terms that most Commonwealth countries considered would be a sell-out. The efforts of those countries' leaders, at four Heads of Government Meetings held during that period and through the Rhodesian Sanctions Committee, were essentially devoted to holding the line and preventing such a sell-out. The period ends with the most nearly successful of those settlement attempts, which collapsed in May 1972 when the Pearce Commission reported the emphatic rejection by the African population of the Anglo-Rhodesian proposals. The final seven years were of a different character, and will be covered in a later chapter;* for in them surely, if slowly, the guerilla armies became organised for liberation and Ian Smith was politically on the run, while using all his devious skills to prolong his survival.

Holding the line against a sell-out was as difficult as pulling on a greasy rope in a tug-of-war. The subject of Rhodesia always remained a slippery subject for Commonwealth and other governments to handle – and this suited British prime ministers. For each of them in his turn – Alec Home, Harold Wilson, Edward Heath – argued that, on the one hand, it was a domestic affair for Britain as the administering authority; but on the other hand that Britain had no direct control, since Southern Rhodesia had been a self-governing colony since 1923. Britain was relied upon by Commonwealth governments for most of their information on sanctions, just as they

---

* Chapter 10.

pressed Britain to take constitutional steps that would lead to majority rule. Although they were sceptical about how sharply economic sanctions were biting, they did not dream of mistrusting Britain to the extent of believing that British-controlled companies, one of them (British Petroleum) government owned, were the main sanctions-busters – at least, not until revelations began to surface in 1977 with the investigations by Martin Bailey and Bernard Rivers, and the inside information from Mozambique of Jorge Jardim.*

Harold Wilson, prime minister for most of the period covered in this chapter, had other preoccupations. Rhodesia, he often complained, was a millstone around his neck. He had no sympathy for the racist regime but his primary concern from 1964 to 1969, he makes clear at the outset of his book**, was to solve the problem of Britain's deficit in balance of payments. Instead of announcing a devaluation of the £ in his first weeks in office (and blaming the need to do so on the Tories), he yielded to Washington's wishes and maintained at too high a level the value of sterling, as the world's other reserve currency. He was forced onto the economic defensive, instead of being able to push exports from a competitive position.

So it was that any political event that hurt Britain's export trade or jeopardised its profitable investments abroad was a deplorable nuisance, with which he tried to deal as speedily as possible. Rhodesia was regularly top of that list of nuisances; but he dealt with it only spasmodically and shallowly. His Rhodesia strategy, which was based on economic sanctions, fell apart because he did not apply sanctions thoroughly at the start and never set up a system of demanding reports on their effectiveness that would have made his Ministers and officials energetic and aggressive in pursuing any whisper of a breach of sanctions.

Shamefully, the opposite happened. While two British companies, British Petroleum and Shell, continued to supply for twelve years after UDI – either directly or through devious 'swap' arrangements – more than half the oil needs of Rhodesia, he and his colleagues either remained ignorant or acquiesced; as did members of the Heath government after 1970.

Why did they not ask a few pressing questions of the oil companies? A major reason is that Wilson was appallingly badly served by his senior officials, whose connivance in the sanctions-busting by the oil companies has been exposed in the Bingham Report and in the

---

* *Sanctions Double-Cross: Oil to Rhodesia*, by Jorge Jardim, Intervençao, 1978.
** *The Labour Government 1964-70* by Harold Wilson, Pelican Books, 1974. Page 17.

remarkable account of this cover-up by Martin Bailey.* Their failure to enforce the law of the land is difficult to explain except in terms of reluctance to bring about changes in Rhodesia. Their connivance in sanctions-busting was as treasonable as Ian Smith's own act of rebellion.

The behaviour by his officials compounded, rather than corrected, three related failings in Wilson's own approach. He was excessively anxious to avoid confronting South Africa over sanctions, for fear of economic consequences to Britain. He was by nature a tactician rather than a strategist, and never planned for a long or systematic campaign. And he was therefore susceptible to illusory predictions of imminent success, the most memorable being his prophecy in January 1966 that the rebellion would be ended through the oil embargo in 'weeks not months'. When these predictions failed to come true, he did not as a tactician have the stomach to scrap his basic premise, and so the delusions were perpetuated.

Despite these deceptions, the Commonwealth achieved something substantial. Through the monitoring mechanism of the Sanctions Committee, and through the commitments extracted from British leaders by heads of government, the Commonwealth made it virtually impossible for Britain to conclude a settlement with the white minority regime and so saved the country from further years of racial strife. The Commonwealth did this more effectively than the United Nations could, because of its closer-knit and informal links, and because of its more sustained concern. Indeed, it led or prompted all the sanctions initiatives at the United Nations, and it stiffened the stand at the UN of countries such as Canada and New Zealand, which served on the Security Council during that period; and this in turn added to the bilateral pressures on Britain.

Unlike Wilson and Heath, the other Commonwealth governments kept a strategic objective in view: majority rule. Despite disagreements, despite occasional posturing when African governments were more concerned to make their own uncompromising case than to pull Britain onto middle ground, the Commonwealth stayed together and worked together to win from Britain a commitment to NIBMAR – no independence before majority rule.

Above all, the Rhodesia issue became a race between Britain concluding a settlement with Ian Smith and Britain recognising the

---

* *Report on the supply of petroleum and petroleum products to Rhodesia* by T. H. Bingham Q.C. and S. M. Gray. HMSO 1978; and *Oilgate, the Sanctions Scandal* by Martin Bailey. Coronet Books, 1979.

growing economic strength of Nigeria. Even before this strength was demonstrated, as it was on the eve of the Lusaka HGM in 1979 by Nigeria's deliberately ignoring British tenders and their nationalising BP, the implications should have been plain: Britain had at least as much to lose economically by upsetting Nigeria as by offending South Africa. As the British gradually realized that the financial see-saw was tipping towards independent Africa, the danger of a sell-out receded. But this point was years away in January 1966, when Nigeria first became a major actor in the Rhodesia drama.

Sir Abubakar Tafawa Balewa was a man of great moral courage and serenity. As prime minister of Nigeria from before independence in October 1960, he had to contend with powerful premiers in the four regions into which the country was then organised. He was best able to use his gifts of intelligence and calm perspective in foreign affairs, offering Africa and the Commonwealth a steadying hand. His last international action, in convening and hosting the HGM in Lagos 1966, was his most important.

Abubakar had been as shocked as I had at the resolution of OAU foreign ministers to break 'links' with Britain. (He told me later of the dressing down he gave his minister for being stampeded with the others.) And on 12 December he announced his invitations to a special Commonwealth HGM on the Rhodesian issue in Lagos the following month, and asked me to coordinate responses. The idea was attractive, because a meeting might produce a concerted programme of action, to end the Rhodesian rebellion and bring majority rule. Another important goal was to set up an aid programme for Zambia, so that it did not have to continue to rely on routes through Rhodesia for 95 percent of its exports and imports.

Nevertheless, the meeting almost failed to take place. Nkrumah and Nyerere (who both broke relations with Britain) refused the invitation; and so, from the other end of the political spectrum, did Menzies. Harold Wilson himself, who had been offended by a walk-out of African delegates when he spoke at the UN General Assembly on 16 December, began to tell other leaders that he could not attend a Commonwealth meeting 'merely to be put in the dock'. He was finally persuaded to go to Lagos after Mike Pearson followed up a meeting they had in Ottawa on 19 December with a telephone conversation on New Year's Eve. I had summarised in a message to Mike on 18 December my fears about the effects of a British refusal: increasing African mistrust of Britain, withdrawals from the Commonwealth, possibly some coups by extremist leaders. What African leaders wanted from Britain, I suggested, was an unequivocal commitment on objectives and means, but not an unrealistic timetable. Pearson made these points to Wilson.

Pearson, as he records in his memoirs*, sent me a cautionary message on 3 January expressing concern that the Commonwealth Secretariat 'should not appear to be taking sides rather than representing whatever consensus there may be'. It was drafted, I believe, by his officials after CRO officials had passed the word to Ottawa that they were disturbed by my active efforts in promoting the Lagos conference. I could not agree with the message's idea of consensus: in my view a consensus had to be built around credible commitments.

In organising an HGM outside Britain there were some unusual pitfalls we had to skirt with the Nigerians. We had agreed, in the allocation of responsibilities, that they should look after accommodation, hospitality and security, and the Secretariat be responsible for everything else. But when the Nigerian general in charge of security stood firm, on the eve of the conference, in refusing access for two hundred foreign journalists to the Federal Palace Hotel, where the delegates and Secretariat staff were to sleep and meet, he and I went to Abubakar. The Prime Minister accepted my argument that, if the press had no contact with any of the leaders, they would inevitably get the impression of disastrous disagreements; and he ordered that the hotel's international casino be cleared of roulette tables and transformed into a briefing room, where the press could meet delegates and myself twice a day.

During the meeting's two long days of talks, Wilson offered various assurances to his Commonwealth colleagues from eighteen governments, who included ten other heads of government. He would not, he said, negotiate with Smith, who would have to accept peace terms conveyed through the Governor, Sir Humphrey Gibbs. After the rebellion was ended, there would be a period of direct rule from Britain, leading to a constitutional conference; this conference, representing all sections of the Rhodesian people, would recommend a constitution leading to majority rule on a basis acceptable to the people of Rhodesia as a whole.

He kept his strongest assurances for the expected effects of economic sanctions: within a few weeks 75 percent of Rhodesia's imports would be cut off, while the oil embargo after only three weeks was

---

* *Mike*, Volume 3, page 284. University of Toronto 1975.

already having a crippling effect. As for the use of force, Wilson said that Rhodesia had some 23,000 fully equipped troops (he was including police reservists) and asked what those who advocated the use of force expected him to do. Pull 25,000 British troops out of Malaysia, spend two months transporting them to Zambia (letting the oil airlift to Zambia lapse meanwhile, so as to free the necessary aircraft) and then push them into Rhodesia on pontoons across the Zambezi? He ridiculed the idea witheringly.

But others made telling points. Milton Obote said he thought sanctions would be insufficient to bring down the rebel regime; furthermore time was on Smith's side, for the longer he lasted the more support he would gather inside and outside Rhodesia. Lee Kuan Yew said that he would accept that the British were in earnest, but why wasn't there more evidence of contingency planning on their part before UDI? Donald Sangster, the acting prime minister of Jamaica, thought that what this meeting should do was agree on what should happen if sanctions failed to work within a reasonable time.

It was into this atmosphere of continuing scepticism about sanctions that Wilson dropped his assurance, soon to become notorious, that 'on the expert advice available to me the cumulative effects of the economic and financial sanctions might well bring the rebellion to an end within a matter of weeks rather than months'. Afterwards no British official was eager to take responsibility for this 'expert advice'. It may be that Wilson culled his phrase from statements made by two other speakers at Lagos in a slightly different context. On the first day, William Nield, a senior official dealing with sanctions in Britain's Department of Economic Affairs, told a working party meeting that if the oil embargo was maintained, the Rhodesian reserve could last 'for weeks rather than months'. The next morning Pearson turned the same phrase around: if within weeks not months, he said, it could be seen that sanctions were not working, Canada believed it would be necessary to take measures under Chapter VII on the UN Charter.

That afternoon Wilson used the phrase himself, and followed this assurance by confiding in a private session attended only by the Heads of Government and myself that he had received word that senior members of the Rhodesian armed forces were preparing a coup against Smith and would invite the British in. They responded to his plea for time and restraint, to let these things happen. So the British policy of sanctions was approved for an experimental period.

But this approval was hedged with a time-limit and a control mechanism. On the eve of the conference Pearson and I had talked about the desirability of a committee to keep the progress of sanctions under review, and to study Zambia's needs for assistance. Pearson's formal proposal for this on the second day was welcomed on all sides. The Sanctions Committee, it was agreed, should consist of representatives of all Commonwealth countries, meeting regularly with the Secretary-General in London. It was to have more than a monitoring role, for the Lagos communiqué stated that 'the Sanctions Committee will recommend the reconvening of the Prime Ministers' Meeting when they judge that this is necessary'.

They also set up another committee to coordinate a Special Commonwealth Programme of Assistance in training Rhodesian Africans for the public service of a future independent Zimbabwe. Just before Christmas the ZANU representative in London, K.I.D. Mutasa, had come with the request that a crash programme be launched for African students at both university and Form IV (or, in British terms, 'O') level in countries anywhere in the Commonwealth. ZANU itself, he said, had set up a trust to collect funds and select students for scholarships, but much more was required. I prepared a memorandum for the prime ministers, pointing out that only about nine hundred Africans were then reaching 'O' level and only sixty completing 'A' level in Rhodesia, and recommending a special assistance programme. This was agreed, and proved useful.*

My memorandum itself had a separate, beneficial effect in establishing, at the first HGM that the Secretariat was organising, that the Secretary-General could put his own recommendations on the table and speak on them, rather than follow the previous line by which the British Cabinet Secretary sat mute at the main meeting and simply chaired the meetings of officials.

The Lagos meeting, then, began the process by which the Commonwealth had a direct, month-by-month involvement with the Rhodesian question. Although we lacked direct authority and had to work always by persuading Britain to act, our collective voice was established as the most powerful influence on Britain in favour of securing majority rule.

Yet I left Lagos with mixed feelings. The Commonwealth's serious view of the situation had been brought home to Britain, and controls had been agreed upon that ought to make sanctions more

---

* See Chapter 6.

effective. On the other hand, my own view for a long time had been that Britain should use force against the regime, as the quickest and cheapest way of ending the rebellion. In July 1965 I had urged Wilson to forestall UDI by moving paratroops into Zambia; and soon after UDI I urged him to send paratroops into Rhodesia as a rallying force around the Governor, arguing that this show of force would not be resisted, especially if the Queen broadcast an appeal. Canada could also, I thought, be persuaded to take part.* Wilson replied that 'Parliament would never stand for it. I have a majority of only three.' But even when he increased his majority to ninety-seven in the elections of March 1966, he did not change his views.

It was clear that only the sketchiest contingency planning had taken place in Whitehall before UDI. The Canadian Government had questioned how much was being done (and got no response) as early as the months leading up to the 1964 HGM, at a time when the British had troops engaged in 'policing' operations in Guyana and Aden; they were certainly not out of practice in planning such operations. In October 1965 Wilson asked Earl Mountbatten to be ready to fly to Salisbury as governor, and Mountbatten began gathering a 'bodyguard' of crack troops. If this scheme, which was only fully revealed in August 1979**, had been carried through without delay, the rebellion could well have been prevented without bloodshed.

Instead, the British government vacillated. Wilson publicly assured Smith in advance of UDI that force would not be used by Britain, thus disastrously encouraging the Rhodesian leader to take the fatal step. He had read, I learned later, a report prepared by his Defence Ministry that suggested that the British Government could not rely on the loyalty of its own troops if they were told to move into Rhodesia and confront their 'kith and kin'. This I found incredible! He had also been told by Sir Glyn Jones, an able man who was then Governor-General of Malawi, that in his judgement Rhodesian forces would resist British troops; years afterwards Sir Glyn told me that he had been mistaken and had learned as much when in Salisbury as vice-chairman of the Pearce Commission.

Since Britain would not use force, economic sanctions were the

---

* I sounded out Pearson on this issue, and he agreed that I put my view to Wilson. He did not raise the issue in the Canadian Cabinet, however, taking the typical Pearsonion line that 'I will risk falling off that bridge when I come to it'.
** Interview with Ludovic Kennedy on BBC television, and reprinted in the *Listener*, 29 August 1979. Wilson has a more limited reference to the episode in *The Labour Government 1964-70*, page 200.

only weapon. But these were applied like a course of innoculations. Consider only the timing of oil sanctions. Britain did not announce an oil embargo until five weeks after UDI, by which time Rhodesia had stockpiled three months' supplies and had reduced those of Zambia to eleven days, and it was not until May 1968, after further prodding by our Sanctions Committee, that Britain proposed in the UN Security Council comprehensive mandatory sanctions, a total ban on trade with Rhodesia. Rhodesia was fed a little poison at a time, like Mithridates in the first century BC. The Pontic ruler ordered these non-lethal doses to build up his immunity, and survived to control much of Asia Minor for fifty-seven years. In Ian Smith's case the course may have been less deliberate.

In the meantime, Zambia needed help urgently. Its oil supplies were completely cut by Rhodesia on 18 December, the day after Britain's sanctions order. RAF Britannias began ferrying in supplies from Nairobi, eighty-five barrels a load, and Pearson dispatched four much larger Hercules aircraft to operate an oil airlift from Kinshasa into Zambia. In early January, Zambia was down to a mere three days' reserves. But by April-May the main British-Canadian US airlift was ended, when road delivery through Tanzania along the 'Hell Run' road took over for two years; by August 1968 the Dar-Ndola oil pipeline, built by the Italian state oil company ENI after Wilson had said the scheme was beyond British means, was opened – and Zambia had no further problems of oil transport.

Back in London, Secretariat efforts were concentrated on making as effective an instrument as possible of the Sanctions Committee. A primary question to settle was that of chairmanship. Arthur Bottomley attended the first meeting on 25 January 1966 after insisting that he act as chairman. The British were anxious to retain the chair, even on occasions when their Minister was not present. As Joe Garner, the Permanent Under Secretary, explained to me, they feared the effects of a partial (i.e. unfriendly) chairman if sanctions were to prove to be unsuccessful. Others were equally vehement that Britain should not be in a position to control the meetings.

Just before the next meeting on 23 February a compromise was struck. A junior British minister took the chair at the outset and proposed Lionel Chevrier, the Canadian High Commissioner, as permanent chairman. Chevrier chaired the committee during its busiest period – it held thirteen meetings between January and the September HGM – and handed the job in November to Andrew Rose, High Commissioner of Trinidad.

From the earliest meetings members of the Sanctions Committee were disturbed about the continuing flow of oil to Rhodesia. From late January it came mostly by roadtanker over Beit Bridge from South Africa, rising to a peak of 3000 barrels a day in May. By March another 4000 barrels a day – amounting to half of Rhodesia's normal requirements before rationing – were rolling up the railway line from Lourenço Marques in Mozambique. And on 5 April the tanker *Joanna V* arrived off Beira with a cargo of 110,000 barrels of crude oil from Iran. The Sanctions Committee met on April 6, and members urged that action be taken through the United Nations to apply mandatory sanctions limited to oil.

In partial response to this appeal the British Government, after a Cabinet committee meeting the next day, decided to sponsor a resolution under Chapter VII of the UN Charter, giving Britain power to arrest on the high seas ships carrying oil to the port of Beira. This Beira blockade was continued until mid-1975, when Mozambique became independent. It cost Britain some £100 million, as it involved at one time or another seventy-six British warships. It prevented crude oil from reaching Rhodesia through central Mozambique, but did nothing to stop the flow of refined products from six hundred miles further south.

In May 1966 I tried to hit that target. At the end of April I was told by Malcolm MacDonald, then acting as Wilson's roving envoy in Africa, that some 150,000 gallons a day was moving into Rhodesia along the railway from South Africa through Mozambique by way of a junction thirty miles west of Lourenço Marques (now Maputo); this was three times the volume moving directly from South Africa by road over Beit Bridge. The British were reluctant to return to the Security Council, for fear its African members would reintroduce broad amendments involving action against South Africa, which Britain could not accept. In these circumstances I hoped the four Commonwealth members then on the Council (New Zealand, Uganda, Nigeria as well as Britain as a permanent member) could instead co-sponsor a resolution that tackled three-quarters of this traffic, avoiding mention of South Africa and calling on the Portuguese government 'not to receive any oil in Mozambique destined for Rhodesia, and to stop the passage of any such oil either by rail or by road.'

I put this plan to the Sanctions Committee meeting on 6 May, after an encouraging talk with Judith Hart, who had just been appointed British Minister of State for Commonwealth Relations. Chevrier asked his fellow High Commissioners to seek instructions from their governments, and a follow-up meeting was set.

On 10 May I had a stormy meeting with Bottomley, Britain's Commonwealth Secretary, who said he had become less happy about the whole idea of having a Commonwealth Secretariat and implied that I was putting ideas into the heads of some African representatives. (Of course I was, just as I tried to put sensible ideas into British heads. I considered that my job involved trying to shape events in sane directions.) But he eventually said he would attend the next Sanctions Committee meeting with Mrs Hart.

The Commonwealth initiative through the Sanctions Committee was, however, forestalled by a separate move of thirty members of the African group at the United Nations. They requested a Security Council meeting to consider a draft resolution that included a specific call to Portugal and South Africa to take any necessary action to stop the supply of oil and petroleum products to Rhodesia. It was defeated when Britain and other Western members abstained and denied it the necessary nine votes.

At Lagos it had been agreed that heads of government would meet again in July if the rebellion had not been ended by then. By mid-May Wilson asked that the meeting be postponed to September, believing that the sanctions policy would be showing real results by then and blaming what the British called 'South Africa's intervention' for putting back their timetable.

Wilson also hoped that the meeting could be held in Ottawa, to avoid his having to be chairman. At the end of May I talked to Mike Pearson about this. He gave me lunch alone at his Sussex Drive residence and, eating very quickly as always, said he would host a meeting if most others wanted it in Ottawa. But he was reluctant; his advisers were warning of a deep split over Rhodesia. He himself had doubts about Wilson's intentions, and would only risk being host if he received an assurance from the British prime minister that the Lagos commitments on direct British rule and an all-party conference were the starting point of any discussions.

In the end the meeting was fixed for London from 6 to 15 September. But an ominous word came from Zambia, in the person of Foreign Minister Simon Kapwepwe. He attended two Sanctions Committee meetings on 13 and 14 July, and gave his view that sanctions had failed and that he had deep misgivings about the British-Rhodesian 'talks about talks' that had begun in May despite Wilson's pledge at Lagos that he would not negotiate with Ian Smith. Kapwepwe told me in private that Zambia was considering leaving the Commonwealth. So I wrote a letter to President Kaunda, in which I argued that, despite his differences with the British

Government, he should not abandon the Commonwealth, which remained one of the best instruments for influencing other governments. I added:

' . . . There are also certain immediate tactical considerations. A Zambian withdrawal from the Commonwealth would inevitably seem like a slap across the face to many genuine friends of Zambia, in many governments across the world . . . Moreover (it) would give considerable encouragement to the illegal Rhodesian Front regime and to any elements inside any Commonwealth country who may advocate a sell-out of the principles to which Governments committed themselves at Lagos . . . The great need now is to hold Commonwealth Governments to the commitments they have made to one another, and to move forward from there.'

This letter had some impact in Lusaka. The Zambian Government decided against withdrawing from the Commonwealth, but made a gesture in holding back its team from the Commonwealth Games in Jamaica and not attending the Finance Ministers Meeting in Montreal. Regrettably Kuanda decided not to come himself to the HGM, but sent instead Kapwepwe and his Finance Minister, Arthur Wina. Kapwepwe could be at times a smoulderingly angry man. His distrust of the British dated from many years earlier, when he had fought with British forces against the Italians in Ethiopia, only to see Italians invited as immigrants into the Rhodesias to take African land. Now he was in no mood for compromise, and had his own reason for seeking trouble. He had ambitions (finally thwarted when he was detained in 1972) to supplant Kaunda as Zambia's President, and these would be advanced if Kaunda's pro-Commonwealth policies were shown to have failed. Kapwepwe almost succeeded in splitting the Commonwealth that September.

In a meeting with Wilson in his Downing Street office a few days before the HGM, I said there were two essentials to avoid a breakdown of the meeting. First, a categorical commitment against a sell-out – and the best form of such commitment was a pledge that there would be no independence before majority rule, NIBMAR. Secondly, an agreement on mandatory sanctions, at least against oil moving through Mozambique. It would be wise if he were to make these commitments at the start of the meeting, before arguments began. Wilson replied that Britain had never had a policy of granting independence only after majority rule: I said that the only two exceptions – South Africa and Zanzibar – had been disasters. He did make both these commitments under pressure before the end of that meeting, to take effect in December. He would have saved a lot of argument, and won credit, if he had made them voluntarily at the start.

I had also recalled, in my Report to heads of government*, the undertakings Wilson made at Lagos on constitutional change and his statement to the Commons on 25 January about the powers a Governor would wield in the transition period of direct British rule before independence. I did this to lessen the likelihood of any backsliding in the British position.

The talks on the Rhodesian issue at that September 1966 HGM, occupying four full days of plenary sessions and, in addition, five restricted sessions the following week, could in themselves provide enough material for a dramatic book. The characters were colourful, the issues large and the arguments powerful. There were many moments of suspense. It was undeniably a severe testing time for the Commonwealth. But this account cannot stray beyond a concentration on the three central issues and a few other comments from the Secretariat's viewpoint. All were agreed that the rebellion and racial discrimination had to be brought to an end in Rhodesia; the arguments, as before, were over means and tactics. So the first two points at issue concerned the *use of force* and the tightening of *sanctions*. The third was more fundamental: for it concerned a clear statement of objectives for the period after legal government had been restored, to assure *majority rule*.

Many leaders renewed their demands, made at Lagos, that Britain use force now that it was clear, at least to them, that sanctions would not be effective by themselves. To some familiar voices on this theme was added Forbes Burnham of Guyana. He argued that British use of force in Rhodesia would not mean war but 'a police action or punitive expedition in the tradition of Britain's high civilising role as a Colonial power'.

Lee Kuan Yew, in the surgical way he cuts through flabby thinking to hard realities, pointed out that if the major powers were not preoccupied with Vietnam, they might have interested themselves more in Rhodesia, to the advantage of its Africans. As it was, he continued, although he did not doubt the British Government's good faith, he could not expect it to send in troops. So he went on to suggest something that I had also urged on various occasions: the

* Report of the Commonwealth Secretary-General, 26 August 1966, pages 6-7.

pinpoint bombing of the railway lines from Mozambique and Botswana and the road bridges from South Africa, just inside the Rhodesian border. It would not involve any killing, he said, but it would be a sharp sanction on the Rhodesian economy. Several others supported his suggestion, but Wilson showed no sign of accepting his logic.

In consequence, discussion then centred on the tightening of sanctions. Wilson hastily admitted having been over-optimistic at Lagos about the effects of the oil embargo 'in weeks rather than months', and switched attention to the business of cutting Rhodesia's exports – chrome, pig iron, asbestos and especially the following year's harvest of tobacco – and to the need to help Zambia with aircraft and road vehicles, so that it could cut its imports from the south. Kapwepwe was infuriated, seeing this as diversionary tactics to avoid facing the fact that Rhodesia was surviving because of South African and Portuguese support.

The main discussion on sanctions focussed on whether it was good tactics to go to the Security Council for general mandatory sanctions, banning all trade with Rhodesia, or to be selective and pick strategic items. Milton Obote, who once again stood out as leader among the Africans, took the unexpected line that, if comprehensive sanctions would harm Britain's economy, which was then weakened by a seamen's strike and teetering on the edge of devaluation and a wage freeze, they should not be pressed. He therefore supported selective sanctions along the lines suggested earlier by Pearson.

The question of tightening sanctions was tied to the issue of majority rule by the thread that ran between London and Salisbury in the 'talks about talks'. There were deep suspicions about those preliminary talks with Rhodesian officials, and about the British secretiveness surrounding them. Kapwepwe quoted the suggestion that they were to pave the way to a legally independent Rhodesia still under white minority rule, and added: 'This would be to pave the way to another South Africa: one might as well pave the way to hell, so far as the African majority is concerned.'

Sir Albert Margai, the Sierra Leone prime minister, speaking from well-prepared material, argued that there was a close link between Wilson's six principles for a settlement and his refusal to support the NIBMAR principle. Strong pressure built up on Wilson to define his objectives for Rhodesia in less ambiguous terms, either by elaborating the words of his six principles or replacing them entirely. Kapwepwe won wide support for the second course when he proposed a two-clause declaration in what he called layman's language:

> '(a) A period of direct rule by Her Majesty's Government will precede the granting of independence to Rhodesia.
> (b) Rhodesia will not be granted independence unless and until it is governed by a Government elected by the majority of the people on the basis of one man, one vote.'

But it became plain that Wilson would not concede NIBMAR by accepting such clearcut phrases – at least, not yet. During the weekend and in the restricted sessions he began to speak of 'giving Smith one last chance' with a settlement proposal, in order to placate British public opinion, even though he implied it would be a formality as his terms would be too tough for Smith to accept.

Instead, on that Monday Harold Wilson produced a nine-point proposal for a constitutional settlement 'in conformity with the six principles', which 'might involve an entirely new constitution or simply entail amendments to the 1961 Constitution through the addition of external guarantees.' What was new about his proposal was the pledge that, if in these circumstances the regime was not willing to give way to a broadbased government under the Governor, he would withdraw all settlement proposals made before UDI, particularly those that envisaged independence in advance of majority rule. He would also agree, during the next UN General Assembly session (i.e. before the end of December), to mandatory sanctions against selected Rhodesian exports, and perhaps some further limited action later on oil control.

The second restricted session that followed his proposal was a disastrous occasion. The heads of government ill-advisedly decided, at the end of an afternoon session, to reconvene late on Monday evening, after a scheduled reception, to which I had invited editors, politicians, diplomats and others to meet them. Tongues were loosened, animosities unrestrained. The unpleasantness culminated in a complaint from Wilson: 'Britain is being treated as if we are a bloody colony.' There were angry protests and Wilson added: 'All right. I withdraw the word "bloody".'

The session broke up in confusion. It was a dark hour, although Kapwepwe and I stood smiling together in the front porch of Marlborough House for the benefit of television cameras – I kept talking to him until his car arrived under the portico and he drove off, for I feared a media question to him would provoke an explosive outburst. He was restrained then, out of courtesy to me, but soon afterwards at London airport he told journalists he was leaving the conference and called Wilson 'a racialist'. The next morning Wilson lost his temper in turn, complaining of character assassination. However, Kapwepwe had not withdrawn the Zambian delegation, which remained under Arthur Wina.

The meeting was finally rescued by two things. The first was the realisation that they all needed each other's help in this crisis, that for any of them to be lost to the Commonwealth through withdrawal would mean a diminution of each one's influence. The second was the solid amount of hard work that was done by those drafting a communiqué, to make the final bridges between leaders who think they have shifted to the limit from their original positions and then are shown that a few steps further will take them on to common ground.

There is a special skill of timing as well as phrasing that distinguishes such bridgebuilders. My successor Sonny Ramphal has it, and so had Mike Pearson. It was Pearson who, when others had exhausted themselves with a week of talking through this issue, was given the task of taking drafts for the communiqué from the British and the caucus group and marrying these texts. He worked through most of one night, and the next day was asked to do further drafting. It was almost too much: Pearson said he was not willing to continue the marriage of various drafts, for 'the next round would amount to incest'. But he ended by chairing an eight-member committee to amend his own work.

Tensions evaporated when Senator Hector Wynter of Jamaica suggested that the majority wished to record in the communiqué their firm views on the three central issues (use of force, NIBMAR and sanctions) and Wilson raised no objection. This led to agreement that Britain should similarly state its own views. The Rhodesian part of the communiqué was ready within three hours, and the HGM ended in a far friendlier mood. A bargain was struck. The Commonwealth had agreed to give Britain three months to reach a settlement with Smith that would need to be proved acceptable to the people of Rhodesia as a whole; if that did not happen, Britain would accept NIBMAR and mandatory sanctions through the UN.

Two general aspects of the HGM caused concern. Although like-minded prime ministers tend to gather in varying groups to solve particular problems at HGMs, this was the first time that a caucus was institutionalised. Wilson in particular took strong objection to the African-Asian-Caribbean leaders caucusing, partly because it held up plenary meetings, partly because he thought it produced fixed positions. But he was mistaken in thinking the 1966 caucus worked to harden the stand against Britain. On the contrary, its real purpose was to moderate or contain the views of Kapwepwe and Margai, and in particular to prevent Kapwepwe causing a crisis by staging a walk-out, which could have put many delegations on the spot. In general, however, caucusing, especially on racial lines, is a mechanism that limits manoeuvre and the scope for spontaneous ideas. This is why not only Pearson but the Tunku disliked it. Asked by journalists why he was not taking part in the Afro-Asian caucus, the Tunku quipped: 'We are Malaysians. We are non-Caucusians.' I am glad that the practice of strict caucusing was never taken up at subsequent HGMs.

The second aspect was the HGM's overwhelming preoccupation with a single issue, Rhodesia, and the determination of African leaders to keep focussing on it to the exclusion of other issues. At one stage I had to say to Obote that, while leaders from other parts of the world had taken a great deal of sympathetic interest in the Rhodesian problem and were trying to find solutions, there were other problems in the world. The prime ministers of India, Pakistan and Ceylon had decided the meeting was not worth their personal attendance (two Foreign Ministers and a Justice Minister led those delegations), and this was a sign that he would do his fellow Africans a disservice if he disregarded the interests of people elsewhere. He took the point – one which I took opportunities that arose to make also to other African leaders – and the time of later HGMs was more evenly spread between issues and continents.

We had to wait for Wilson to carry his 'talks' with the Rhodesians to the climax of a meeting with Ian Smith, which took place aboard HMS *Tiger* on 2 to 4 December 1966. It was a difficult time of suspense, holding our breath up to the hour when the Rhodesian Cabinet rejected the *Tiger* proposals. It is always unwise to get into a position where one's future depends on the enemy's making a mistake. The Rhodesian Cabinet rejected these proposals because they did not want to dissolve parliament and return legislative powers to a broad-based government appointed by the Governor before the testing of Rhodesian opinion. Foolishly, from their viewpoint, they threw away a chance to assure continuance of minority rule for a generation.

Mr Wilson thereupon carried out the pledges he had made to Commonwealth leaders in September. Britain proposed to the Security Council a mandatory ban on the purchase of Rhodesia's main exports (tobacco, asbestos, chrome, iron, copper, sugar and meat and hides). But it used the 'veiled veto', by being one of seven abstentions, to defeat an amendment requesting 'the United Kingdom to prevent by all means the transport to Southern Rhodesia of oil or oil products', explaining that it feared a confrontation with South Africa. It supported instead a weaker amendment imposing a ban on 'the supply of oil and oil products to Southern Rhodesia'. This ban was ignored by South Africa and Portugal – and ignored also, as the rest of us learned later, by Shell and British Petroleum.

Four days later, Wilson accepted the NIBMAR commitment. On 20 December he withdrew all offers of an independence constitution and said that no settlement of the Rhodesian problem was now possible unless it provided for majority rule before independence.

The Sanctions Committee did its best to tighten pressure on the regime. It held eleven meetings in the two-and-a-quarter years between the 1966 and 1969 HGMs, and its first meetings in this period were devoted to reviewing progress in the implementation of mandatory sanctions on Rhodesian exports.

Committee members quickly came to the conclusion that new ways were needed to increase the effectiveness of the sanctions policy. In September 1967 it set up a working party with representatives of seven governments (Britain, Canada, India, Jamaica, Kenya, Pakistan and Zambia), meeting with me or my deputy, to recommend whether it would be desirable and feasible to propose a total mandatory ban on all Rhodesian imports and exports, or to concentrate on tightening existing sanctions: and specifically what might be done about oil sanctions. After four meetings the working party reported back in December 1967. The most striking paper it submitted contained a scheme for strangling the supply of oil through Mozambique by a three-stage squeeze, of which the final stage involved extending the Beira naval blockade to patrol the southerly port of Lourenço Marques. But Britain was not interested in providing a much larger patrol of some fifteen frigates, saying supplies could anyway go in directly from South Africa!

In March 1968 an international furore followed the hanging of five Africans in Rhodesia and in this heightened atmosphere the committee reached general agreement to recommend comprehensive sanctions to the Security Council. In May the Council adopted Resolution 253, covering trade, shipping, travel on Rhodesian passports, airline travel and emigration (but not posts and telecommunications traffic). The UN also set up its own supervisory committee, matching the Commonwealth Sanctions Committee.

It looked like impressive action, even if belated. I had been unhappy with the lack of interest in Rhodesia shown at UN headquarters from the first visit I had paid there after UDI, in March 1966. Secretary-General U Thant was understandably preoccupied with the Vietnam war, but I had argued he should spare time for another problem that would grow if neglected. Even after May 1968 I was disappointed. I suggested that he recruit a team of sanctions investigators, including chemists who could by analysis detect tobacco and chrome originating in Rhodesia; and that UN members be authorised and encouraged to have suspect cargoes examined, and freighters carrying Rhodesian contraband seized. But he did not act; and in 1972 I had to tell his successor Kurt Waldheim that his only weapon between moral extortion and military force was economic sanctions and, if he allowed sanctions to become a laughing stock, he would be damaging not only the Zimbabwean cause but the credibility and authority of the international community.

Nor was there any strong support to be found in Washington. I had seen Dean Rusk as early as March 1966 in an effort to win backing for an effective sanctions policy. But preoccupations with Vietnam crowded out any real concern for southern Africa by the Secretary of State or the White House or Congress until the Angolan civil war drew in Cubans, South Africans and the CIA in 1976. There was, in fact, as Dean Rusk and later his successor William Rogers emphasized to me, a feeling of resentment among Senators about the attitude of most Commonwealth countries towards the Vietnam war and the lack of any help from Britain. So Rhodesian sanctions were given low priority – and indeed widely ignored.

By the last months of 1968 Commonwealth leaders had settled into a mood of accepting that sanctions tactics had shifted from 'quick kill' to 'long haul'. They (and I) rested our assurance on Wilson's commitment to NIBMAR.

The shock came in October 1968, when for the second time Wilson flew to Gibraltar for a meeting with Smith aboard a British warship. The settlement offered him on HMS *Fearless* should have been more attractive to the regime than *Tiger*, in that there was no longer any reference to a Governor taking control or to parliament being dissolved as part of the return to legality. Smith returned to Salisbury on 13 October, after five days at Gibraltar, without accepting or rejecting the proposals. Once again we were left waiting to see if (and hoping that) he would be foolish enough to pass up a bargain, and wondering how otherwise we could prevent a British sell-out.

I called on the new British Foreign Secretary, Michael Stewart, on 28 October and warned him that a *Fearless*-type settlement would drive much African opinion towards Chinese and Soviet influence, and would tend to increase racial violence in southern Africa, rather than diminish it, as he suggested it might.

On the same day there was a sharp, but not over-emotional, meeting of the Sanctions Committee, at which George Thomson, then Minister without Portfolio, had to face the complaints that Britain was about to abandon the NIBMAR pledge. A key point was how the British would be going back to Commonwealth governments for a review of the NIBMAR commitment. If they dealt separately with governments through their missions in different capitals, they might win majority assent; but, if the review took place at a meeting, there was little risk of a majority agreeing to reverse it. My line was that the decision should go to the next HGM, due within three months, since the pledge was a multilateral agreement made at the September 1966 HGM. The Trinidadian chairman, Andrew Rose, put emphasis on this point and the draft communiqué prepared by the Secretariat had a paragraph to clinch it:

> 'The meeting took note of the British Government's position that there would have to be a substantial and guaranteed change of circumstances to justify its going back to its Commonwealth partners for a review of the question of NIBMAR, and expressed the firm view that such discussions should take place at a meeting of senior Commonwealth representatives.'

Unfortunately, the African representatives were so taken up with making sure their own views were firmly expressed elsewhere in the communiqué that they paid no attention to a British move to weaken the rest of it. When Thomson suggested deleting the crucial second clause of this paragraph, they raised no objection.

In the end, it was not a fatal mistake. Ian Smith himself made that, in rejecting further British overtures conveyed by Thomson during two visits to Salisbury in November, and setting down a further eight reasons for not accepting the *Fearless* settlement. Nevertheless, the British Government left the *Fearless* proposals 'on the table' for several more months in the hope that Ian Smith (or some more moderate successor) might pick them up after further thought.

The January 1969 HGM took place at the height of the Nigerian civil war and attempts to bring the two sides together for talks during the meeting shifted a good deal of attention away from the Rhodesian situation. Nevertheless, there were two full days' debate on the issue, and Julius Nyerere (who had resumed diplomatic relations with Britain) led a devastating attack on the *Fearless* proposals and on Wilson's contention that his NIBMAR policy remained unchanged. But the most significant discussion centred upon the precise form that a 'test of opinion' would take, for by then the British were talking about appointing a Royal Commission for that purpose.

Kaunda argued for 'a full and free referendum'. When Wilson took credit for defending the rights of 23,000 Gibraltarians who had overwhelmingly voted in a secret ballot in the presence of Commonwealth observers to reject any transfer to Spain, he was asked if the same referendum procedure could be used in Rhodesia. George Thomson intervened to say it was too difficult to organise the speedy registration of millions of voters, and the British put the argument that a test of opinion carried out by Royal Commission had paved the way for the accession of Sabah to Malaysia, a point somewhat blunted when the Malaysian delegate said the decision had really been based on the results of an election.

Despite these differences the atmosphere was far more cordial than in 1966. Nobody challenged George Thomson when he said Britain's overriding consideration had been to 'fulfil its trusteeship' to the African people, or Harold Wilson when he said his government was 'particularly alert' in making sanctions effective, with a separate department set up in the FCO to seek out evaders of sanctions among other governments and to warn them of their neglect. For none of us knew then – or for years thereafter – that the Right Honourable George Thompson at least had been told of the 'swap arrangement' between oil companies eleven months earlier.

The continued offer of the *Fearless* proposals did not slow down Ian Smith's move to a republican constitution, which would divide the electorate starkly on racial lines and (in Smith's own words) 'sound the deathknell of the notion of majority rule'. Just after a referendum held among white Rhodesians in June 1969 had approved a republican constitution, the Commonwealth Sanctions Committee met and set up a special working party with representatives from seven countries to review the operation of the UN mandatory sanctions. But evasions continued, and Britain was heading into the uncertainties of an election period, while Smith had carried his 1969 constitutional bill through parliament and also made land segregation more rigid than before with the Land Tenure act.

When the Conservative Government of Edward Heath took power in June 1970, it lost no time in declaring it would make a further effort to find a 'sensible and just solution' to the Rhodesian problem. I had an ominous hint of the shape of this 'sensible solution' when I called on Heath that September. He said his Conservatives had never said they accepted NIBMAR or mandatory sanctions, and he did not expect a Commonwealth meeting to discuss these matters of British policy, any more than he would question the Tanzanians about the Chinese presence in their country. I found his mood and attitude chilling. NIBMAR, after all, was a British Government commitment, and sanctions were an obligation under the UN Charter.

However, the Heath government's first preoccupation in southern Africa became the issue of arms sales to South Africa;* and it was not until late in 1971 that Alec Home, by then the Foreign and Commonwealth Secretary, busied himself about the question of Rhodesia. Heath was anxious to concentrate upon the entry of Britain into the European Community during 1972, and thought it important to clear Rhodesia out of the 'pending' file.

Lord Goodman had prepared the way with regular visits to Salisbury through 1971, and Home signed the Anglo-Rhodesian agreement for a proposed settlement at the end of a brief visit in November. Based as they were on the 1969 constitution, with only four significant modifications, these proposals scarcely fitted (as Home claimed they did) the Six Principles. Lord Goodman himself defended the agreement in a curious way. He said: 'The terms of settlement were not a sell-out. The African had been sold out long before'.**

When the Commonwealth Sanctions Committee met on 10 December, the focus was upon the Fifth Principle, the test of opinion, since this was the only remaining means of preventing a British surrender to the Smith regime. Several representatives recorded in the communiqué their regret that the test 'was not to be carried out through the normal democratic process of free elections or a referendum'. But the British representative, Sir Martin Le Quesne,

---

* See Chapter 10.

** *The Past is Another Country: Rhodesia 1890-1979* by Martin Meredith, André Deutsch, 1980, page 84.

argued that it was impossible to frame an appropriate referendum question on such a complex issue, and a commission was the practical way as most people were illiterate. More to the point, Lord Pearce had already been named commission chairman, together with two deputies. So the committee concentrated on calling for the release of political detainees to participate and be given access to radio; and on telling Lord Pearce to take enough time so that people who had for years been surrounded by censorship and propaganda could learn about and debate the issues properly.

The Secretariat, which then had the services of a young Zimbabwean research officer, Ariston Chambati, worked hard on analysing the conditions for the test of opinion. Fortunately also I was able to talk at length to a deputy chairman of the Pearce Commission, Sir Maurice Dorman, a former Governor of Sierra Leone and Governor-General of Malta, who stayed with us in my flat during a few days of preparation in London. We discussed many aspects of the commission's work, and particularly the procedures that could best draw out a full opinion.

Procedures were much in my mind when I called on Lord Pearce in the week before he flew to Salisbury. Lord Pearce, a retired High Court judge, could be relied on to show judicial detachment. But I was not sure he realised the extent to which Rhodesian Africans could be inhibited from speaking out after years of repression. I began by telling Pearce frankly that many Commonwealth governments thought his Commission was conceived as a whitewash, because it was chosen instead of a referendum. With some trepidation I said that the prestige of the judiciary was at stake, and that it was very important that his procedures be seen to be impartial. After reiterating the points made by the Sanctions Committee, I warned him not to rely on the Rhodesian Government to supply interpreters, and not to expect Africans in vulnerable positions to express candid views in front of people who might be government informers. In particular, I pointed out the danger that the 18,000 African teachers, whose contracts forbade them to take part in 'political activity', could be intimidated by authorities into silence during any public discussion on the proposals. I also suggested that his commissioners should tell the people that, if the proposals were accepted and became the basis for legal independence, there would be no chance of Rhodesia being admitted into membership of the Commonwealth or the United Nations; for several heads of government had made their views plain enough on this matter, and there had been an overwhelming vote in the UN.

To my relief, Lord Pearce took my words of caution well, and thanked me for them. I was also relieved that the Rhodesian Africans, after an initial period of discussing whether or not they would boycott the Pearce Commission, decided to form what had to be called a non-political body – the African National Council – to oppose the settlement terms.

During the two months the twenty-four Pearce Commissioners moved around Rhodesia, from 11 January to 11 March 1972, another large Commonwealth drama was being played out: the birth of Bangladesh and the withdrawal of Pakistan from the Commonwealth.* I returned from Islamabad early in February in time to meet Bishop Abel Muzorewa on his first visit to London since assuming leadership of the African National Council. The bishop told me how the Smith regime was strictly limiting the scope that African leaders had for taking part in the campaign: Joshua Nkomo, for example, had not been allowed to leave his detention camp and so had no access to radio and television. I suggested that the ANC make use of radio stations in Zambia and Botswana, and that the bishop himself should record some radio tapes for use in case he was arrested after his return to Salisbury.

Then the unexpected happened. Guy and Molly Clutton-Brock describe it well in their book, *Cold Comfort Confronted*:

'The Commission arrived. Their members went to meet Africans; asked their opinions and listened to their answers. In the eighty years since the colony had been occupied, this had never happened before; they had never been consulted nor their opinion sought. This dramatic event suddenly gave the people a feeling of dignity and worth; it was democracy in action for a moment. A sense of unity grew, a consciousness of being African and opposed to colonist domination. . . . A resounding 'No' began to echo across the land in urban and tribal areas; even Chiefs and headmen began to disobey their masters and affirm the feelings of their people.'**

The Pearce Commission had a clear report to make, and handed it to Alec Home on 4 May. He tabled it in the Commons on 23 May, and I saw him immediately afterwards in his office. He was obviously deeply disappointed at the outcome. He thought the

---

* See Chapter 7.

** *Cold Comfort Confronted,* by Guy and Molly Clutton-Brock, Mowbrays, 1972, page 190.

whole situation would now polarise, with the Rhodesian whites moving further into the South African pattern. He had little confidence in sanctions being effective, especially with the United States lifting its embargo on Rhodesian chrome. Did the Africans really know what they had thrown away?

I thought they did. Muzorewa and the Rev Canaan Banana had told me they were prepared for sanctions to continue and would risk imprisonment, if they could defeat the settlement; they had said one had to pay something for one's freedom. But the British Government had acted honestly over the Pearce Commission, and stood honourably by its report. I suggested to Sir Alec that he could capitalise on this demonstration of Britain's reliability to improve British relations with Nigeria and other African countries, and to increase the confidence of the non-European world as a whole. These were far more important to Britain than the position of the Rhodesian minority regime.

I have always liked Sir Alec and respected the sincerity of his motives. I wanted to comfort him in his disappointment. But I also wanted him to understand the depth of and reasons for my own relief at the Pearce Commission's findings – and that I considered them best not only for Africans but for Britain, the West and the world. It was crucially important to prevent a sell-out and to hold the line in Rhodesia until the necessary international and domestic pressures could be developed to bring about majority rule.

Chapter 5
WAR IN NIGERIA
The Tangled Path to Peace Talks

While it is everywhere accepted that the mighty empires of past centuries – whether Roman or Mughal or British – encompassed peoples of many nations and languages and cultures, it is often suggested that there is something abnormal in modern times about running (or trying to run) a democratic state of more than one culture and language. Canada and Switzerland may have been exceptional in this way some generations ago, in pioneering a plural democratic society. But among the countries that have become independent since 1945, plural societies are the rule rather than the exception. Examples abound in the Commonwealth: India, Sri Lanka, Malaysia in Asia; Papua New Guinea and Fiji in the Pacific; Mauritius and nearly all the African states; Guyana and Trinidad in the Caribbean.

To make democracy work in a multicultural, multinational or even in a large multiregional society requires more than having the support of a simple majority. The political leaders need to have at least the acquiescence, if not the enthusiastic support, of a working majority in each major grouping. Most Canadian politicians have known this in their bones, and the successful ones have acted accordingly in forming alliances and cabinets, and formulating national policies. On the world scene, as we move beyond nation-states to an interdependent global society, the statesmanship involved in making a plural society work becomes increasingly important. If a political leader has passed the test of building a nation in his own plural society, he is on his way to being statesman enough to contribute at world level. His success is an encouragement to others grappling with similar problems; and for international relations he will have learnt sensitivity and balance. The Commonwealth has had many such statesmen, who pass on some of their wisdom at heads of government meetings. Pierre Trudeau once aptly termed these meetings 'graduate seminars for heads of government'.

Some Commonwealth leaders have failed this test and their

plural society has broken up; the prime example is Pakistan, whose self-destruction in 1970-71 is recounted in Chapter 7. Another great Commonwealth country that was plunged into the ultimate crisis of a plural society – open warfare between its ethnic parts – is Nigeria; and it is intriguing to compare the characters of the two men principally responsible for taking the plunge, Zulfikar Ali Bhutto in Pakistan and Odumegwu Ojukwu in Nigeria. Both were charismatic and intelligent, but neither believed in compromise; for each the choice was 'all or nothing'.

The complexity of Nigeria's plural society needs stressing. The country has more than two hundred tribes and languages. Three major tribal groups certainly dominated the country's three original regions: the Yorubas in the West, the Ibos in the East and the Hausa-Fulani in the North. But the minority tribes taken together are equal in number to these three; the Efik, Ibibio and Ijaw made up about one-third of the population of the Eastern Region when Ojukwu led it into secession in 1967; and the 'Middle Belt' tribes were a distinctive part of the old Northern Region. These minorities formed the basis for General Gowon's action in dividing Nigeria first into twelve states and later into nineteen. And Nigeria gave an example to other plural societies when, in drafting the constitution under which Shebu Shagari was elected President in 1979, it laid down the requirement that the successful candidate did not only have to lead the polls nationally but he had also to win a quarter of the votes in at least two-thirds of the nineteen states.

Today the Nigerian civil war remains a puzzle to many people. Why did the war go on for so long, for two and one-half years, when Biafra had lost control of the oil installations as well as most major population centres within a year? Could the suffering and the hatred have been as intense as portrayed in the media, considering that the country recovered its equilibrium swiftly and without retribution soon after Colonel Ojukwu slipped into exile in January 1970? And weren't there any serious and sustained attempts to break the military deadlock with peace talks? If there were, why didn't they succeed? Who was to blame?

This chapter sets out to give an account of the several efforts by the Commonwealth Secretariat to bring the Nigerian and Biafran leaders together for peace talks, and in the process it may provide some answers to the other questions posed above.

There were other international organisations, of course, that might have played a major role as mediator or interlocutor: in particular, the United Nations and the Organisation of African Unity. But UN Secretary-General U Thant was deeply preoccupied during much of 1967 with the aftermath of the Six-Day War between Israel and Arab states, while in 1968 the Vietnam war was reaching a climax. Moreover, the UN traditionally finds it difficult to deal with domestic crises or problems, except for the issue of apartheid. The Organisation of African Unity set up in September 1967 a Consultative Committee of six Heads of State* led by the Emperor of Ethiopia who tried intermittently to end the war. But the OAU's basic principle, of unquestioning respect for national boundaries of member states, put the committee on a narrow course when trying to deal with the problem of a secessionist force.

In contrast, the Commonwealth Secretariat had a flexibility the others lacked. It could move far less formally than a committee of six African Heads of State bound by a charter and by their own self-interest, or a United Nations with similar rigidities and an unhappy memory of its operations in the Congo half-a-dozen years earlier. The OAU approach was to enlist prestigious leaders to bring pressure on the combatants. Our approach was the lighter one, of simply bringing the Nigerian and the Biafran leaders, or their deputies, together to reason with each other. This involved a series of secret meetings in my London office or apartment, scores of telephone calls, visits to Enugu and Lagos by Secretariat staff and talks in other African capitals in the course of (or under the cover of) other Commonwealth events. It led us on from merely trying to effect meetings between the adversaries to proposing substantial parts of a political settlement and working out plans for a Commonwealth peace-keeping force. And in the Kampala peace talks of May 1968, this approach came closer to success than any subsequent effort.

The reason for the failure of peace talks lies mainly in the character of Colonel Odumegwu Ojukwu. A man of sharp intelligence as well as high ambition, he joined the Nigerian army because he saw it as the ladder to political influence; his long-term assessment of Nigeria's future led him deliberately into seeking this path to a strategic position of power. As well, he was more than an Ibo nationalist; his horizons were broader than his tribe. But by stages they narrowed, and one significant stage came after he appealed to

---

* They were the leaders of Ghana, Liberia, Zaire, Cameroon and Niger, besides Ethiopia.

Ibos who had survived the first pogrom in the North in July 1966 not to flee their homes. Many of those who listened fell victims to the second wave of slaughtering in late September, and Ojukwu carried a load of guilt for their lives. During the years of war, the tough aspect of some Nigerian army commanders – notably Lieutenant Colonel Murtala Mohammed and Colonel Benjamin Adekunle (known as the 'Black Scorpion') – no doubt reinforced his reluctance to step out from behind his barricades.

Another reason for Ojukwu's bid for independence was the lure of lucrative revenues from the oil-fields that were beginning to be exploited by British and French companies. Two-thirds of the oil was being produced in 1966-67 in the Eastern region (which became Biafra) but even the one-third produced in the Mid-West was shipped out through the East, and the refinery near Port Harcourt was also under his control. The revenues quarrelled over during the first half of 1967 only amounted to £7 million, but Shell-BP had some £150 million invested in the East.

When he decided for secession, Ojukwu soon showed himself dominant and persuasive over his Biafran followers, but he was blindly unrealistic in the broader arena of world politics. He somehow believed he would win if he persevered until a magic number of countries recognised Biafra. Like many others, I came to the view that he was determined to play for all or nothing, although many of those around him were sincere seekers of a compromise settlement. Even in the later stages, therefore, although disillusioned with Ojukwu, we could not, while so many were suffering, abandon attempts for a settlement; and a further major effort was made at the time of the 1969 Heads of Government Meeting. For three years Nigerian affairs took up a considerable proportion of my time and that of Yaw Adu and my special assistants. The returns were often meagre, but it seemed to me a necessary investment in the future of one of the Commonwealth's most important members.

The first military coup was carried out on 15 January 1966, just as Commonwealth leaders were dispersing from the special Heads of Government meeting in Lagos called to deal with the Rhodesian UDI; Archbishop Makarios was, in fact, caught in the crisis as he had stayed behind to tour the Eastern Region. It shocked all those who, only a day or two earlier, had been conferring under the chairmanship of Sir Abubakar Tafawa Balewa. He was murdered only a few hours after I took my leave of him.

However, for many months Commonwealth leaders (like others) treated as an internal affair the overthrow of the Nigerian Government and subsequent events: the brief ascendancy in Lagos of Ibo intellectuals in the administration of Major-General Aguiyi Ironsi and their declaration of a unitary state; the fierce reactions of Hausa-Fulani people in attacking the Ibo artisans and businessmen in their cities, and of Northern officers and soldiers in mutinying and shooting their Ibo officers, including Ironsi, in July; and the restoration of control by the youthful army chief of staff, Lieutenant Colonel Yakubu Gowon, after the senior surviving officer Brigadier Ogundipe found it impossible to restrain the rebels. When Commonwealth Heads of Government met in London early in September 1966, they observed one minute's silence in tribute to Sir Abubakar. The Ghanaian delegate referred obliquely to 'areas of tension in Africa' where he hoped 'a spirit of understanding and compromise would prevail'. But Brigadier Ogundipe, by now Nigeria's High Commissioner in London and chief delegate, only acknowledged problems in South Africa and Portuguese Guinea. The implication was plain: his people would handle the Nigerian crisis on their own.

Gowon's achievements – bringing the rebel soldiers under control, turning back the headstrong pressure of some Northern officers to take their huge region out of the Nigerian federation altogether – were soon submerged by other troubles. The savage pogrom of late September, which took the lives of more than seven thousand Ibos in the North, the retaliations in the Eastern Region, wrecked hopes of a constitutional conference. One million Ibo refugees trekked back to the Eastern Region, from which Ojukwu as military governor started in his turn to expel non-Ibos. From August Ojukwu had refused to recognise Gowon as supreme commander and had declared that there was 'no genuine basis for true unity in the country'. Mutual suspicions for months prevented any meeting of the Supreme Military Council within Nigeria, but a ray of hope began to shine when they met on 4 and 5 January 1967 at Aburi in Ghana. Britain's roving ambassador in Africa, Malcolm MacDonald, and Ghana's General Ankrah helped arrange the meeting.

The Aburi agreement was a major success for Ojukwu, for it would have turned Nigeria into a loose confederation in which the regions were to run their internal affairs, apparently without any central control of the armed forces, and in which any member of the Supreme Military Council could hold a veto over national matters, including top appointments in the army, police and public service. A group of federal permanent secretaries were quick to point out the implications to Gowon, when he returned to Lagos. He tried to retrieve some of the ground ceded by declaring at a press conference that 'We definitely decided against regional armies', but went ahead to promulgate a decree on 17 March 1967 that carried decentralisation of powers a great distance. Ojukwu however, rejected the decree and issued an edict ostensibly on revenue collection that amounted to taking control of federal services such as railways, airports and electricity within his region. Eastern Nigeria was far on its way to secession.

Watching from London, I was concerned at the breakdown of relations after the temporary buoying of hopes at Aburi. I heard that Ojukwu had severed communications with Lagos, and thought of offering my 'good offices'. When Hugh Springer, then serving as Assistant Secretary-General, flew to Lagos in mid-January to make preliminary arrangements for the next Commonwealth Education Ministers Conference, he carried a letter from me to Gowon expressing my hope to visit Nigeria. He brought back word that I would be 'welcome any time'. Senior assistants of Ojukwu gave a similar reaction to overtures from Springer, but since General Ankrah was still active in mediation moves, I waited in the hope he would succeed.

In March Dr. Kenneth Dike, who had left his post as Vice-Chancellor of Ibadan University and was to become a senior Biafran emissary, came to see me for one of many talks. I emphasised what became a constant plea: avoid irrevocable decisions to split up, allow a lengthy cooling-off period and keep open the channels of communication. The same day Emeka Anyaoku, whom I had re-cruited to the Secretariat from the Nigerian Mission to the UN, left on an unofficial 'home leave' visit to Enugu and had a long conversation with Ojukwu. Ojukwu, alleging (with some justification) that the British had consistently favoured the North, told him that the East would not accept any mediation that involved British Government participation.

Yaw Adu also flew on a scouting mission to his native Ghana and on to Lagos. General Ankrah had been trying to resolve differences over the interpretation of the Aburi agreement, inviting Ojukwu back to a meeting in Accra in March and working with financial officials from all four Nigerian regions and some Ghanaian counterparts on fiscal reallocation to help the Eastern Region meet the cost of resettling refugees. They had not made much progress. Nevertheless, federal officials felt positive about General Ankrah continuing to offer the help of a 'good neighbour', and were not interested then in any outside assistance. Adu sensed that this attitude was based on a fear that outside assistance would internationalise the Nigerian issue and open the door for Ojukwu to press for more formal intervention by African heads of state. So I shelved an idea, which had been discussed with General Ankrah and the British, of a small and informal Commonwealth mission.

Ironically on 16 April, even before Adu returned to London, there was an attempted coup in Ghana. It failed, but the weakness it revealed in General Ankrah's base of domestic support diminished his standing as a conciliator in Nigeria. The idea of a second Aburi meeting had to be dropped. As a result, the Commonwealth Secretariat began to seem a more necessary instrument of mediation.

I intended to go to Lagos after attending in May the Planning Officials' meeting in Nairobi that launched the first stage of the Commonwealth's technical cooperation programme*. In Nairobi Jomo Kenyatta expressed his deep concern about Nigeria, which he thought could only hold together through a very loose federation. But before the officials' meeting ended, irrevocable steps were taken in Nigeria, which created a new situation. Ojukwu made a marathon address on 26 May to the Eastern Consultative Assembly, demanding a mandate for secession, which the chiefs and elders formally gave him on the following day. That evening Gowon declared a state of emergency throughout Nigeria and announced a new decree to abolish the four Regions and replace them with twelve states under military governors. And at dawn of 30 May Ojukwu declared Eastern Nigeria a sovereign state as the 'Republic of Biafra'. South-Eastern and Rivers States, which three days before had been created by Gowon's decree from populations of a non-Ibo majority among the fourteen million people of the Eastern Region, were carried into rebellion until federal forces occupied them a year later.

On the day of secession Ojukwu wrote me a six-page letter, which did not arrive until 16 June. The authorities in Lagos, he wrote, 'have decided politically and militarily to dismember this Region by force'. By the twelve-state decree Gowon had 'staged a one-man coup (and) subverted the fundamental law of the land'. But Ojukwu went on to say that Biafra left the door open for a total reorganisation into 'a commonwealth of sovereign states', an association that could comprise a common market, common citizenship and common services including ports, road and air transport. He ended by saying

---

* See Chapter 6.

that Biafra 'wishes to remain a member of the Commonwealth'.

When I heard in Nairobi about Biafra's declaration of secession, I decided to fly to consult with Obote, Nyerere and Kaunda while in eastern Africa. They all stressed the importance of Gowon not starting hostilities against the secessionists, nor trying to separate by force the two non-Ibo states created from the Eastern Region. Kaunda, in particular, urged me to go personally to Lagos to make these points strongly to Gowon. I agreed to go, but decided first to go to London to consult my political officers at the Secretariat.

In London I told Edwin Ogbu, Nigeria's Permanent Secretary for External Affairs, something of the views of the East African presidents; and added my own view that both Gowon and Ojukwu seemed to be proposing in some ways a similar structure that combined a centralised authority for common services with extensive autonomy for the states. I made clear that I believed Africa needed further union rather than balkanisation. Ogbu promised to get Gowon to wire me suggesting an early date when he could see me. But, instead of returning at once to Lagos, Ogbu was called away to Moscow, and two weeks were lost while waiting.

Then came disturbing news from British sources. Their High Commissioner in Lagos, Sir David Hunt, was sending advice that nobody should be urging Gowon to refrain from force, since it was inevitable that he would use it, and any counter-advice would be interpreted as concurrence in secession. A senior CRO official visiting Lagos to discuss oil revenue payments was told not to visit Enugu, because they had now taken a definite decision to launch 'police action' against the East. And Gowon, I learnt on Monday 3 July, had asked Britain to supply a large amount of small arms within three days. So I cabled him directly that afternoon, received a reply on Wednesday and flew off to Lagos with Gerald Hensley the next day.

When we drove into Dodan Barracks on Friday morning, 7 July, it was the first time I had met Yakubu Gowon. I found him a most disarming person. We came to know each other well, and he soon made no secret of the difficulties he had with several of the more hawkish members of his Military Council and officials. He resisted as long as he could the building up of federal forces, hoping the crisis could be resolved without a large conflict; and throughout the fighting he steadfastly argued that there should be no vindictiveness and no post-war occupation of the Ibo homeland. He was something

83

of an anomaly: a Christian from the Muslim north; a gentle soldier who knew how to use some of the ablest politicians in the country. He was, in fact, the best possible person Nigeria could have found to lead it through terrible times. He had humour, too. He once thanked me for having saved his life during the January 1966 coup: for he had just returned from staff college in Britain and had reserved a room at the Federal Palace Hotel but, finding on his arrival that the entire hotel had been taken over for the Commonwealth summit conference, he had stayed privately in Lagos, and so escaped the assassination groups who were hunting down senior officers.

On this day, though, he was deadly serious. After I had offered all the help the Secretariat could give to get talks resumed and prevent hostilities, he led me through an account of the past year to show that all peaceful measures had been of no avail. He could not now meet Ojukwu unless he withdrew his declaration of independence and accepted the authority of the federal military government. The decision to use force was a very painful one to have to make. Even now, he was keeping it to a minimum. Every federal soldier had been issued with a strict Operational Code of Conduct (and he gave me one of the card-sized booklets), which stressed that the army was not fighting a foreign enemy or a religious war, and only the minimum of force should be used; it had been read and explained to them by their commanders, and they had to carry it into battle.

I suggested that Ojukwu had almost certainly been disappointed in the consequences of his declaration of independence. The economic blockade on the oil installations was tightening, and no country had moved to recognise Biafra. Was it not worth exploring the possibilities for further talks? I was prepared to go at once to Enugu, to talk to Ojukwu. A visit by myself would not raise the question of status and sovereignty that could arise from intervention by some outside government or Head of State.

He replied that the problem was with the personalities of Ojukwu and a clique of his advisers. Ojukwu had made no secret of wanting to become Nigerian Commander-in-Chief. Having been denied this Ojukwu had decided that he would rule a sovereign Biafra. On April 27 Gowon had written Ojukwu suggesting a meeting without pre-conditions on either side, and Ojukwu had retorted that only a fool would agree to such a meeting.

I pressed Gowon further. Would it not be worth a visit by myself or Yaw Adu? What was there to lose? Why not delay the military action for a couple of days, to let me try? Gowon seemed to hesitate for a moment, until Brigadier Ogundipe, who had at the last minute flown out with us from London, intervened to say such a visit was 'not on'; it was too late, the troops could not be stopped in time. And Gowon agreed, saying Ojukwu had not yet been hurt enough to want a genuine meeting.

So our meeting ended after ninety intense minutes, with plans to talk again two days later. Although it was clear that the outbreak of hostilities was imminent, I did not know – until it was announced the following morning – that fighting had started on the northern front on 6 July, a few hours before my first meeting with Gowon. But the news put some of his comments in a clear light.

Gowon had asked me to call next day on Chief Obafemi Awolowo, a veteran Yoruba politician whom he had released from prison and brought into his government as Vice-Chairman of the Federal Executive Council. Speaking privately, Gowon said that he would like me to maintain contacts with the Biafran leadership and himself, to seek an agreed settlement within the framework of 'One Nigeria'. Any confidential messages to him on this subject, Gowon added, should not be sent through Nigerian diplomatic channels but through Chief Awolowo. I agreed to do so. Gowon then said that he wanted to give me a signed letter setting out his desire for my 'good offices'; his reason was that my contacts with the rebel leaders might become known, and this would expose me and therefore the Commonwealth to serious criticism. I said this was not necessary, but as he insisted I accepted the letter.

As Gerald Hensley and I drove up to Ibadan in a battered government Cadillac on the Saturday morning for a talk with Chief Awolowo, we ran into the signs of war: lengthy road blockages as police controlled cars heading for Lagos, and a checkpoint at which we were halted for more than an hour.

Awolowo, playing with three grandchildren, told us of his own conciliation mission to Ojukwu in May. He had returned greatly encouraged, thinking that a settlement was possible – only to be publicly repudiated within a day by Ojukwu. He felt deceived and he echoed Gowon's view that, unless Ojukwu was removed, talks on any sincere basis could not begin. 'I have written him off', he said. He said he would bear in mind the possibility of Commonwealth Secretariat assistance in various forms, but everything now depended on the progress of the military operations.

At our second meeting next day Gowon was not in uniform, but talked mainly about the Federal Army's tactics. Since the few roads had been mined or blocked by Eastern soldiers, and the heavy rains anyway made mobile warfare impossible, they had reverted to a traditional campaign of moving slowly through the bush in foot-columns. But he was fairly confident of an early result. 'Once Nsukka and Ogoja are taken,' he said, 'it's in the bag.' Again I offered him Secretariat help at any time, in reconciliation or postwar reconstruction. Gowon replied: 'It's relatively easy to undertake military operations; the most difficult problems come afterwards. We will require very great help in this phase.' It was a moving moment, watching this lissom young soldier in a white suit, sipping ginger ale and facing up to the job he had never sought, that of shouldering the fratricidal problems of his sixty million people

I found a bluffer mood at Christianborg Castle, overlooking the ocean outside Accra, the following evening when General Ankrah served champagne and explained to us how he would invade Biafra, if he were Gowon. He would attack at division level, send two brigades to converge on Enugu and also plan an attack through the Mid-West State. Gowon, he thought, had started his war with far too few troops. General Ankrah then, to the surprise of myself and Yaw Adu who was in Ghana giving technical assistance, moved on to the question of military assistance. Commonwealth membership, he believed, involved an obligation to help any member who asked for military aid, especially against secessionists. Although he would do nothing to put the idea into Gowon's head, if the Nigerian leader asked him for a squadron of Lightning fighters to provide the air-cover he lacked, Ghana would feel bound to supply it, together with pilots. He would also urge other non-white Commonwealth countries to give similar aid. This notion was far from my offer of diplomatic support in getting talks going and of aid in postwar reconstruction. There is certainly diversity in the Commonwealth.

For the next eleven months I was heavily engaged in efforts to arrange direct talks between the two sides at a ministerial level and with an agreed agenda. It involved advancing by slow steps from procedural points to conversations of substance, to find some firm common ground. Often there were setbacks. Mutual suspicions undermined the common ground. Some envoys seemed to me more sincerely peace-seekers and trustworthy than others. Especially on the Biafran side, there was a frequent rotation of emissaries, and it was difficult to know which of them at a particular time carried real influence with Ojukwu.

It would be tedious for the reader to be given details of the talks at every stage, for many points came to be repeated. So this account tries to illustrate more the general flow of negotiations rather than to identify every rock we encountered or sandbar we scraped upon.

Each side in the early stages was naturally anxious to gain immediate political advantage from a military success. Thus, when Biafra reached the highwater mark in mid-August 1967 by flooding across Mid-West State and came within one hundred and thirty-five miles of Lagos, Ojukwu sent Sir Louis Mbanefo, the former Federal Chief Justice who had taken up the Biafran cause, to London to lobby for a ceasefire and negotiations and he himself broadcast his willingness to enter peace talks on condition that Biafran sovereignty was recognised. After consulting widely, I sent a letter to Gowon on 22 August, and a similar letter to Ojukwu, urging negotiations without preconditions except for a temporary truce. Gowon replied that Ojukwu had refused a meeting without preconditions in April, and 'so much has happened since. Ojukwu is now in open rebellion . . . ' So he laid down two conditions that were to be repeated many times: that Ojukwu renounce secession and accept the twelve-state system. Ojukwu, for his part, wrote repeating his own pre-condition.

Biafran occupation of Mid-West State lasted only two months, and by early October its troops had streamed back across the River Niger. On the northern front the Biafran capital of Enugu had fallen on October 4, and in the South federal troops had taken Calabar by a sea-borne attack. At this point Mbanefo seemed to soften Ojukwu's line. He told Yaw Adu that sovereignty was not a pre-condition for negotiations so much as the objective they would seek to obtain. Conversations with other Biafran envoys suggested their side now genuinely wanted talks. This time I wrote Gowon suggesting a secret meeting in London with representatives of both sides, and Hugh Springer flew out to Lagos within a week with the announced purpose of discussing dates for the Commonwealth Education Ministers Conference but with the added job of seeking Gowon's reactions to my proposal.

Events moved well from that point. In Canada for a few days on other business, I received messages that representatives of both sides wanted to see me in New York. There on 8 October I first had a long talk with Okoi Arikpo, the bright historian-politician from an Eastern minority tribe whom Gowon had appointed External Affairs Commissioner, and Chief Simeon Adebo, then Nigeria's ambassador to the UN. Both suggested it would be necessary to give the Ibos effective guarantees that they would not be occupied and punished.

Arikpo suggested that I should propose, at an appropriate moment, an armed Commonwealth peacekeeping force adequate to provide such a guarantee. I made similar progress with the Biafran representative, Ozumba Mbadiwe, towards agreement on a secret meeting. Many international phone calls were needed to clinch it, but it was soon agreed that teams of three representatives each should arrive in London the next weekend.

The rest of this episode was an anti-climax, but it gave me a first sight of Ojukwu's pattern for wrecking talks. While keeping an international reputation for being ready to enter negotiations – a reputation for reasonableness he recognised as essential if he was to win sympathy and, best of all, recognition for Biafra – he was wary of entering any real discussions that might involve compromise. So he allowed them to be set up, and then played for a breakdown. On this occasion two of his team (his powerful cousin C. C. Mojekwu, and James Udo-Affia) were delayed by 'mechanical difficulty' and arrived ten days late, after the federal team had packed up and gone back to Lagos, but saying they would be prepared to return. In the meantime, he objected to London as the venue and to the level of federal representatives (Alison Ayida, Philip Asiodu and Ahmed Joda were all Permanent Secretaries). During the week of waiting, I managed to bring Kenneth Dike and a more junior Biafran together with the Nigerian trio in my flat for exploratory talks, but the Nigerians' patience was running out. After Mojekwu finally arrived, there was a reappraisal by the top men in Lagos. Was Mojekwu there to make sure nothing substantial was conceded? Or did his presence signify that Ojukwu was in earnest about talks? In a tough Cabinet meeting on 29 October (a Sunday) the hardliners wanted to pull out of the talks, but Gowon and Arikpo carried the day, and Arikpo promised that his team would be back in London by Wednesday. But by then Mojekwu had disappeared again to France.

As I recorded in my diary: 'All this skittishness on both sides is tiresome. It takes a lot of persistence and sense of proportion to try to midwife these negotiations . . . At least, this is easier than the job of the poor bloody soldiers on both sides . . . '

General Ankrah's style of midwifery was more muscular. He did not mince words in the parallel communications he carried on with both leaders. In a letter to Gowon on 22 August he regretted that 'leaders of Africa have been virtually forced to remain silent and impotent to intervene in this fratricidal struggle. The contention that it is a purely domestic issue may have some merit, but I am afraid it is un-African. The tragedy of Nigeria is the tragedy of the whole continent of Africa'. And in the midst of the October episode he was in London and told me he planned to advise Ojukwu that 'he should get out and hand over to a group prepared to negotiate in good faith for the best terms they could get. Ojukwu has played for high stakes and lost. He should get out and with his family's money live in Switzerland or somewhere for the rest of his life'.

It was under pressure from Ankrah that the African Heads of State appointed the OAU Consultative Committee. But when the Emperor eventually led three other Heads of State (including Ankrah) to Lagos in late November 1967, the committee held only a one-day meeting with Gowon and made no contact with any Biafrans. It issued a brief communiqué advising 'the secessionists' to renounce secession and accept Nigeria's twelve-state structure. After this unproductive effort the OAU did not take any further initiative for another eight months, and the responsibility for attempting mediation meanwhile fell more clearly on the Commonwealth Secretariat.

For the next three months I tried to get the secret meetings started again, writing to both leaders, meeting individual envoys and telephoning contacts in different capitals. At first the Biafrans objected to London as a meeting place, saying the British Government was too biased. Later, when I began having confidential consultations separately with each side, the Nigerian team of permanent secretaries sensibly focussed on the three questions that needed solving if Biafrans were willingly to rejoin Nigeria: physical security, job opportunities and control of resources. The Biafran envoys, Mojekwu and Dike, seemed genuinely to want a negotiated settlement. But they clearly did not have any formal authority to put forward compromise suggestions.

Then in January 1968 came what I thought was a real break-through, from an unexpected corner. Dr Michael Okpara, who had been premier of the Eastern Region before the first coup and was briefly imprisoned by Ojukwu but later became one of his top political advisers, arrived at Mojekwu's base in Paris and said he wanted to talk with me – but was not prepared to pass through British Immigration.* So five of us (for he brought Mojekwu and Dike along) met at London Airport outside immigration control in a tiny glass-partitioned office in a lobby where passing travellers could have overheard every word. I noticed no loiterers, though the

---

* His was an extreme anxiety. Other Biafran envoys were prepared to come to London, but not to meet in Marlborough House since they might be seen by journalists or other diplomats. So meetings almost invariably took place in my nearby flat in Carlton Gardens.

discussion was worth hearing. For Okpara was businesslike, wasted no time on propaganda and was quick to build on the peg that I had been hammering home with his colleagues: that they would have to accept an overall Nigerian personality with exclusive powers in international representation and a central authority over certain common services.

Okpara was understandably concerned that Biafra should control its own internal security and have exclusive powers in certain other fields: and he wanted a ceasefire to be supervised for a short period by some outside 'presence', preferably a Commonwealth force. We talked also about state boundaries, and whether plebiscites might be taken in disputed areas. The outcome was so encouraging that during the next week we drew up a set of proposals as the basis for a package to establish conditions for a ceasefire agreement. The Biafrans initialled it on February 2, after Okpara and Mojekwu had made a hasty trip back to win Ojukwu's support. It began with the momentous sentence: 'A ceasefire to be agreed on the following basis: (a) There will be a united country . . .' So by early February I felt that I had a worthwhile proposal to put to the Lagos authorities, and made plans to fly there.

But something more should first be said about ideas for a Commonwealth 'presence'. The idea was that armed Commonwealth troops move in after agreement on ceasefire conditions, and act as military observers in the disputed and occupied areas of the former Eastern Region to ensure both that Ibos were not attacked and that Biafran forces did not use a cease-fire to build up their military strength. But other, often diluted, versions were produced later.

As Arikpo had expressed a preference for Canadian troops, I asked Mike Pearson informally in late November 1967 about their availability. After the winding up of UNEF in the Sinai that year, Canadian troops were not overstretched and Pearson saw no problem in principle, although by February 1968 some key officials in External Affairs had grown very cautious, glimpsing parallels to some future drama about Quebec. The British, on the other hand, were enthusiastic to the point of insisting that they had to be part of any such Commonwealth contingent, possibly under a Canadian commander. I hoped for Ghanaian and Indian troops, as well. Ankrah agreed, and the Indian Government said it would give sympathetic consideration to such a request if approved by the Nigerian Government.

I also borrowed a British colonel, who moved into Marlborough House on February 6 and began making contingency plans for the deployment of a brigade group, totalling some 2850 men, of three battalions with scout cars, light aircraft and helicopters. In the end, they remained simply contingency plans, as far as Nigeria was concerned. But twelve years later, a similar Commonwealth military observer group – although kept down to half those numbers – played a crucial role in helping Zimbabweans move through all the ceasefire problems to surprisingly peaceful elections.

The package of proposals that I carried to Lagos on 9 February 1968 was not, however, well received. In two days we had ten hours of meetings; but the first three-and-a-half-hour session with the Supreme Military Council was the decisive meeting. At it there were fourteen federal representatives, but only one civilian commissioner, Arikpo. The military force commanders were firm, but even frostier were some of the senior civil servants. Gowon and Arikpo, the latter very noticeably nervous, were clearly under pressure not to make any concessions. When I had introduced the 'One Nigeria' outline agreed by Okpara, and had argued that the major concession made by his side – a readiness to accept a federal Nigeria and a twelve-state structure – needed to be matched by offers that could save the Biafrans' pride, and had then introduced the three conditions Okpara had stipulated, Arikpo hastened in to say this took his government back to where it was before the war, and everything his negotiating team had worked for in London had been brushed aside.

He maintained, and Gowon supported him in this view, that the proposals amounted to a confederation or loose association. They rejected Okpara's three conditions: the boundaries of the 'Biafran' state to be determined by plebiscites to decide whether it should include any of the parts of the Mid-West, South Eastern and Rivers states, and specifically Port Harcourt; and for it to control its own internal security and its own mineral and economic resources, while guaranteeing Lagos 'independent sources of revenue adequate for its functions'. Gowon argued that the federal government had to control internal security in an emergency, had to have enough control over resources to promote national development, and could not allow a precedent to be set on holding plebiscites on boundaries, which could be properly settled by a commission. In a private talk later he told me that the key issue was Port Harcourt. This major port was now in Rivers State and, although a majority of its population were Ibo, it served the vital transport interests of several states, including notably some parts of the Muslim North. If it were to be excised from Rivers State through a plebiscite, the Ibos could use it as a strategic threat in any future quarrel.

The matter of a Commonwealth 'presence' came up sharply in Lagos, for newspaper speculation on the subject had made the Nigerians particularly sensitive. At the meeting with the Supreme Military Council an army member demanded to know where this idea had originated. My eyes turned to Okoi Arikpo, for I expected him to explain that he and Chief Adebo had raised it with me in October. Instead, his silence coupled with his expression made me realise how delicate his relationship was with the hawks on the Council, and persuaded me not to reveal the source.

The same evening, the subject came up again when we met with a team of senior officials. One of the most hawkish officials maintained that there could never be an independent 'peace force' separating combatants. Biafrans (he said) would have to be disarmed, the federal troops would not withdraw from any part of the East-Central State they already occupied, regular Nigerian police would look after internal security, and any outside observers would only be invited on the basis that they stayed at strategic points occupied by federal troops and reported to the federal authorities. It seemed a formula for post-conquest administration, not for a negotiated settlement.

All this was negative. The positive new point that finally emerged was federal willingness to have direct talks with the Biafrans without any preconditions – an offer Gowon had not been prepared to make since hostilities began. The suggestion actually came during the council meeting from a military man, Brigadier Ejoor, and was elaborated by Arikpo and the team of senior officials. So in the end I left Lagos, not with agreement on the Okpara proposals I had brought, but with something that was at least promising.

Back in London, I had to persuade Kenneth Dike, Ojukwu's most understanding envoy, who did not want any more meetings with permanent secretaries, that some of them were extremely influential – more so than many military members of the Council, or some civilian Commissioners; and that what mattered was 'plenipotentiary authority'. And on February 17 I sent a message to Ojukwu asking him to send 'high-level representatives, with full authority to negotiate' and transmitting a skeleton agenda of five items. This was a list which Adu and I had negotiated in Lagos involving no pre-conditions. After sending it, I saw Mojekwu who passed on a message from Ojukwu hoping I would visit Biafra soon.

I answered Mojekwu cautiously, knowing the sensitivities in Lagos at the time. These were underlined by receiving a tough message from Gowon on February 22 calling for me to produce 'convincing evidence' that the rebel leaders were ready to accept a united Nigeria of twelve states before he sent delegates to the secret meetings I had suggested.

His message reached me at London airport, just before I boarded an aircraft back to Lagos to attend the Commonwealth Education Ministers Conference. Two days later, we were back in Dodan Barracks for what turned into a three-hour meeting with Gowon and two officials. It was a pleasanter occasion than the encounter with the Supreme Military Council, and it was rounded off with a lunch of chicken curry: but it was impossible to get any clear answer from Gowon on the basic question of whether the federal government was willing to make any concessions to the Ibos in order to buy a negotiated settlement. Gowon said he wanted to wait until I had an answer from Ojukwu to my message of February 17 – and he would not agree to my visiting 'Biafra' because he said Ojukwu would make the same propagandist use of it as he recently had of a visit of some envoys of the Pope.

The Education Conference allowed me to spend two weeks in Nigeria in less strained circumstances than a purely political shuttle-visit, and to meet a range of leaders. It was reassuring to find, on a visit to Kaduna, that Colonel Hassan Katsina, who wielded wide influence as chairman of the council of the six Northern governors, said he favoured ending the war as soon as possible by a negotiated settlement. He even suggested the solution to the Port Harcourt issue might be a joint administration by the Rivers and Ibo states. And I took the opportunity to meet every accessible civilian commissioner. By far the most productive encounters were the three conversations I had with Chief Enaharo.

Tony Enaharo had reason to be grateful to Gowon. Abubakar's government, in its quarrel with the Action Group party that Awolowo led in the Western Region and Enaharo headed in the Mid-West, had imprisoned both chiefs in 1963. One of Gowon's first moves in 1966 as supreme commander was to release them; and in June 1967 he brought them both into his government. As Commissioner for Information, Enaharo was no match for the Biafran propaganda machine. The Markpress organisation, run from Geneva by William Bernhardt, a public relations expert from California, was extraordinarily effective in influencing opinion in Europe and North America, mainly through concentrating on humanitarian appeal rather than political argument and skilfully publicising the problem of starvation among Biafran civilians in 1968. Although he later tried to compete with Markpress by writing open letters to British MPs, Enaharo had no great interest in the subject of information. But he was an able and ambitious politician; and, while he was completely loyal to Gowon, he realised that if he could be prominent in a successful peace settlement he would greatly enhance his chances of becoming the next civilian prime minister. So he was energetic, that March, in refining an agenda and tactics for the proposed direct talks and, in the process, promoting himself as Lagos' chief negotiator.

He was self-confident enough to advance a new proposition, and then go to Gowon to persuade him of its value. Together we worked out a package of four main points that seemed to balance the key demands of both sides. It set up the acceptance of 'One Nigeria', against the assurance of security of life and property; and it balanced the question of how police and administration would handle the immediate post-war vacuum against plans for later, wide-ranging constitutional talks among all the states. I was not too hopeful of Ojukwu's reaction, because this plan entailed holding over two points of importance to Biafrans – territorial boundaries and their economic future – to be settled at a conference of all the states. But it was a fresh approach and, before I left Lagos, Gowon told me he supported it.

A further two months passed before Chief Enaharo and Sir Louis Mbanefo came together in London for talks to prepare for substantial peace negotiations. The reason for the delay was because Ojukwu was not prepared to accept the basis we had worked out in Lagos. He first wanted talks without any advance agenda, and then suddenly suggested an immediate start in Dakar, Senegal, under joint Nigerian and Biafran chairmen, with each side using the good offices of an African head of state. These proposals were calculated to place Biafra on an equal footing internationally with Nigeria, and (as Ojukwu obviously anticipated) could not be accepted by Lagos. In turn, Lagos produced a seven-point agenda for peace talks that began with Biafran reintegration into a twelve-state Nigeria; it was not an unreasonable list, except that it could be interpreted as moving away from the earlier commitment to start talks without pre-conditions.

Finally Enaharo and Mbanefo arrived for preliminary talks on the venue and agenda of a main conference. They met in my residence for eleven days until 15 May, and it was soon clear that Sir Louis was under tight constraints. A man of honour who deeply desired peace, he was apparently under Ojukwu's instructions to be a wrecker: to play these negotiations for a breakdown, as long as it could be blamed publicly upon Lagos. So he raised a series of objections – to the venue, the agenda, the starting date, and the issue of a chairman – that tested Enaharo's tolerance and my ingenuity. As the former federal chief justice and a member of the World Court in The Hague, Sir Louis had a high international reputation, which was the reason Ojukwu used him for the peace talks. But he was not politically astute, and proved a poor negotiator because he employed the adversarial style of a courtroom lawyer rather than the business approach of a corporation solicitor in a smokefilled room. He gave the impression that he expected some *deus ex machina* to render judgement for the advocate who made the better case: whereas a pre-trial deal was somehow immoral 'collusion'.

However, there were strong pressures on both sides to begin peace talks. On Ojukwu the pressures were military, and on Gowon they were diplomatic. The federal army had finally captured Onitsha after six months' fighting across the Niger River, while from the south it was moving on Port Harcourt. On the other hand, Dr Nnamdi Azikiwe, father of Nigerian nationalism and the country's first President, had toured five African countries and three – Tanzania, Zambia and the Ivory Coast – announced over a period of weeks their diplomatic recognition of Biafra, starting with Tanzania on 13 April. As well, Ojukwu's appeal in a long letter to British MPs to call for a ceasefire and the reports of federal bombing of Biafran women and children by Soviet-made aircraft flown by Egyptian pilots were having an impact in western capitals. Lagos had to prove it was not waging a vengeful and indiscriminate war.

Ojukwu's suggestion of holding talks in Dakar posed some risks. President Senghor had not recognised Biafra, but he was close to de Gaulle and to the French Secretary-General for African affairs, Jacques Foccart, who was pursuing a devious but strongly pro-Biafra policy. Ojukwu was financing much of his war operation by selling oil rights to French companies, and relying on arms supplies from France. So the French connection made Dakar a dubious venue for peace talks.

By stages the path was cleared for the main talks. I asked both sides to write down a list of acceptable sites, and agreement was reached on Kampala in Uganda. Mbanefo finally accepted that the talks might begin without a chairman, after it was arranged that Dr Obote as host President should make an opening address and that some foreign observers might be present, for this gave the talks the international standing Ojukwu sought. We eventually produced a 'neutral agenda' by listing two broad categories 'conditions for ending the hostilities' and 'arrangements for a permanent settlement' and the Nigerian seven-point agenda was separately mentioned in a different communiqué (which may or may not have satisfied the hawks in Lagos). A final argument about the date of starting the Kampala talks – Mbanefo at one stage threatened to withdraw all agreement if his early date was not accepted – was settled by scheduling an informal, and then a formal, start.

By the time the full negotiating teams arrived in Kampala, the hopes of the two sides seemed cast in opposite directions.* Port Harcourt was captured by Colonel Adekunle's marine commandos on 18-19 May, but on the other hand Zambia announced its recognition of Biafra on 20 May. In his opening address President Obote called for compromise and flexibility, and suggested that 'political solutions are fundamental to these talks and should be given more emphasis than the military aspect'. I am convinced that Enaharo, with Gowon's backing, was confident enough to take initiatives at Kampala to secure a peace settlement and would have had a good prospect of selling it to the powers in Lagos. It would have ended the war eighteen months earlier, saved countless lives and probably preserved more in resources for the Ibo people. But this was not how Kampala was to turn out, for Ojukwu's destructiveness cast a long shadow.

In the Uganda Parliament Buildings in Kampala the Nigeria and Biafran delegations, five on each side, met for nine formal sessions lasting some twenty-one hours over a period of eight days from 23 May. Only one prominent northerner, Aminu Kano, had been included in the Nigerian federal delegation, which had representatives from all three states of the former Eastern Region. There was a clear attempt to make discussions more intimate and 'southern', and to remove the risk of religious friction. Together with the Commonwealth Secretariat team, it was arranged that both sides should stay in the Apolo Hotel. The scene was set for old friendships to blossom and reasonableness to flourish.

* See John de St Jorre, *The Nigerian Civil War*, Hodder and Stoughton, 1972, page 200.

96

Yet there was no real coming together at the formal part of the talks. The Biafrans asked to stay instead at the Grand Hotel. And the two opening statements were predictably strong: Mbanefo made an emotional recital of the irreparable wrongs done to his people ('To force Biafrans back into the Federation would be like forcing the Jews that had fled to Israel back to Nazi Germany'), and Enaharo focussed upon 'the reorganisation of Nigeria into twelve states which has removed one of the root causes of discontent, mutual fear and instability'. Then the Biafran delegation led the talks back into the tangled bush of procedural matters which I hoped had been virtually settled in London; and for two days they argued whether there should be a chairman or any foreign observers. On the third morning, which was Saturday, it was agreed to ask President Obote to nominate a single observer and he chose at my advice his Foreign Minister, Sam Odaka, to serve in a personal capacity.

But the talks were already on a knife-edge. Enaharo received a cable from Lagos during Saturday ordering him to suspend the talks because of the disappearance of a confidential clerk, Johnson Banjo, who was last seen photocopying his speech on Thursday. (Banjo's body was found three weeks later, but no explanation for his murder ever came out.)

Enaharo showed me this cable and said. 'Give me twenty-four hours and I'll get this rescinded'. But in the meantime he could not respond to Mbanefo's proposal for an immediate ceasefire.

His stonewalling exasperated Mbanefo. By Sunday evening he wrote me a formal letter, saying he had concluded that Enaharo and his delegation were not serious about negotiations, and that the Biafran delegation would therefore leave the next day. To journalists he said: 'Our patience has run out. If they are waiting for a military solution, let's pack up and go home. We are ready to continue fighting. Death does not matter to us now.' It was a strong exit line, and spectators of the Nigerian drama would easily be able to identify the heroes and the villains.

Mbanefo was, in fact, under extreme pressure to leave. To delay this I asked Obote to summon him, with Enaharo and myself, to a meeting on Monday, and Mbanefo, reluctant to offend Obote, agreed to stay on at least until Enaharo replied on the subject of a ceasefire. Mbanefo sent Mojekwu and Kogbara away in his place. Meanwhile private talks were begun between the two delegation leaders, with Odaka as the observer-cum-conciliator, Yaw Adu and myself; and the five of us made progress, especially when Professor

Eni Njoku (the former Vice-Chancellor of Lagos University) deputised for the indisposed Mbanefo. Njoku was more flexible, more courageous and under less personal pressure from Ojukwu than his chief Mbanefo.

Three versions of a ceasefire and peace formula were produced in Kampala. The first was contained in Mbanefo's opening statement and could only be interpreted as a bargaining position as it was the extreme Biafran position: in the order of priorities it put a ceasefire first and in the most favourable terms (immediate ceasefire, immediate removal of economic blockade, removal of troops behind pre-war boundaries) and then a political settlement based on Biafran sovereignty before any thought could be entertained of economic cooperation or a plebiscite in non-Ibo areas of the old Eastern Region.

Enaharo's countering move, offered five days later, was more subtle in that it addressed the problem of Biafran fears for their security if they were asked to lay down their arms without visible guarantees of safety. So he produced a twelve-point programme that 'would allow a number of things to happen at one and the same time', in particular the renunciation of secession and a general ceasefire and freezing of troop positions supervised by an observer force. It also offered an orderly timetable for the disarming of Biafran troops and the handover of administration, and guarantees that Ibos would play a prominent role in policing and running their own state and in all branches of the federal service. But Mbanefo answered by trying to undo the package and extract the four items he liked, amounting to an unconditional ceasefire. When Enaharo resisted this, he said the Nigerian proposals were little more than surrender terms.

A third set of proposals, put forward as a compromise, was worked out by Yaw Adu and myself in separate meetings which we and Sam Odaka held with Njoku, Mbanefo and Enaharo in the final days in Kampala. It involved an immediate ceasefire and establishment of a Commonwealth observer force that could police any no-man's-land; relief arrangements including a partial lifting of the blockade; and a constitutional conference (without mention of the twelve-state structure). All these arrangements were to be attached to a basic acceptance by both sides of 'a new Nigerian union'. Njoku said he thought Mbanefo would agree to it (and indeed, three months later, a group of Biafran leaders wanted to press a similar formula); and Enaharo did accept it *ad referendum*, while saying it went far beyond his terms of reference. So I proposed that, if both delegations would accept our formula, we should agree to adjourn for a week, to allow Enaharo to fly back to Lagos to win over the Federal Executive Council; while Mbanefo, whether returning to his home base or not, should try to persuade the Biafran leadership to accept it. We would then reconvene, and sign an agreement.

But this plan did not succeed. Pressures on Mbanefo increased sharply from Biafra. He learnt that he had been burnt in effigy, and his family threatened, because of rumours spread by Ojukwu's men that he was selling out. Unhappily, too, the first anniversary of Biafran secession fell that week and Ojukwu made a midnight radio broadcast, in which he strongly attacked the federal leaders.

I nevertheless thought that, if Sir Louis Mbanefo agreed to the adjournment and publicly proposed the compromise, the pressure on Ojukwu could be irresistible. But Mbanefo felt he could not do this. On Friday 31 May, he addressed what turned out to be a last meeting of the resumed formal sessions of the peace talks. He accused Lagos of preferring extermination to a negotiated settlement and said his side was not prepared to talk 'with bayonets in our backs'. He made his final remarks from a text that Dr Azikiwe later told me had been worked out well in advance at Ojukwu's headquarters, and Enaharo was quick at the time to point out that these carefully prepared remarks dispelled any doubts that Mbanefo had been under instructions to break up the talks at that meeting. Then Mbanefo flew off to London to put the Biafran case to those of the international press that had not journeyed to Kampala. Enaharo stayed on for a few days 'in the hope that something might happen'. But by the following Tuesday we all dispersed, disappointed.

There were scores of international press representatives in Kampala, and I was strongly tempted to expose Ojukwu's posturing to them as a man only pretending a willingness to negotiate. But Mbanefo asked me, just before his departure, to do everything to keep the atmosphere reasonable. If this could be done, he was confident (he said) that he could persuade the Biafran leadership to let him come back to London to resume talks within a month. Eni Njoku reinforced this hope, and though sceptical of Ojukwu I felt (perhaps wrongly) that I should not jeopardise the hopes that I knew they were sincere in expressing to me. So I did not 'come clean' with the press; I wanted to give the optimism of Mbanefo and Njoku a chance.

In fact, neither Mbanefo or Njoku were allowed by Ojukwu to return to London.

For the next months of 1968 the main initiative in promoting peace talks passed to the Organisation of African Unity. Its consultative committee met in Niamey in July and discussed further a demilitarised zone and an international observer force; and throughout August delegations to the OAU summit in Addis Ababa (which heard a two-and-a-half hour tour de force by Ojukwu) met but made no real progress.

In late September a group of senior Biafran emissaries (including Azikiwe, Mojekwu, Okpara, Dike and Njoku) met in Paris. Hopes that had been raised by France in mid-summer of outright support and recognition of an independent Biafra were by then deflated; and in the light of this they decided to fly home and recommend that he accept the concept of 'One Nigeria' and negotiate a ceasefire and transfer of administration. The Commonwealth, they hoped, could help with the resettlement of refugees and with observers during the transition. These Biafran doves did fly home but were brushed aside, and Ojukwu vowed to fight on.

This marked Azikiwe's final disillusionment with Ojukwu. He called on me in October, and told me that he had been able to persuade Nyerere to recognise Biafra in April mainly because he was carrying an assurance from Ojukwu that such recognition would be used only to increase his bargaining power at the Kampala peace talks, and therefore make an agreement more likely, since Ojukwu would at the talks accept as the basis for a settlement the principle of a united federal Nigeria. Ojukwu did not fulfill this promise, and 'Zik' told me he felt that he had been used to mislead Nyerere by Ojukwu's false pretences. Much later, in January 1972, I had a visit from Dr Okpara, who had come to England to take medical refresher courses. He confirmed Zik's analysis of Ojukwu's character, and said that he was essentially an 'all or nothing' man who would instinctively shift away from any compromise settlement.

I had some hesitations about speaking publicly on Nigeria when asked during a visit to Ottawa to give evidence before the External Affairs Committee of the Canadian House of Commons in October 1968. But when I had lunch with Pierre Trudeau, who had recently become Prime Minister, he said it would be helpful to him if I gave my views; and it seemed important to face the growing talk, skilfully promoted by Markpress information material, that the Nigerian Government was pursuing a policy that bordered on genocide. So I spoke to the Committee.* I was pressed on the issue by one MP,

---

* Report of the Standing Committee for External Affairs and National Defence, House of Commons, Ottawa; 8 October 1968.

Robert Thompson, who had connections with a relief agency, and said that I thought that, though there had been atrocities on both sides, charges of genocide were 'entirely unfounded'. One of the key points for Biafran negotiators in a settlement was physical security, but breakdowns had come because of a rigid stand on sovereignty. 'There have been many occasions in the past eighteen months,' I added, 'when compromise deals guaranteeing physical security and economic viability could have been attained at the cost of concession on this point of separate sovereignty for Biafra'.

There was understandable press criticism that the Commonwealth Heads of Government, at their meeting in January 1969, did not discuss the Nigerian war on the formal agenda and made no mention of it in their communiqué. The fact was that Lagos remained adamant that their 'domestic situation' should not figure formally on the agenda. But they were receptive to proposals I had put forward in the month before the HGM that the occasion of the Meeting be used informally to advance a peace settlement.

I sent a message to Ojukwu urging him to come to London or nearby and saying I would do all I could to arrange a meeting with the chief Nigerian delegate, who was Awolowo; alternatively, I asked him to send a team to meet with Nigerian plenipotentiaries and myself at my flat. I got agreement from Gowon that Awolowo would meet with Ojukwu and Nyerere said that, if wanted, he would sit in on any such meeting; as did Obote. They both pressed Ojukwu to take advantage of this plan and Ojukwu did send a team to London (Pius Okigbo, Dike, Nwokedi among them) some days before the HGM was due to begin on 7 January. I had preparatory meetings with them – and then suddenly they received instructions from Ojukwu to leave London and not to meet Awolowo under any circumstances. Once again Ojukwu was proving he did not genuinely want a settlement and was pinning his remaining hopes on more diplomatic recognitions.

Even after the team had disappeared, leaving only Kogbara their London representative, the federal leaders remained willing to talk. as I recorded in my diary for the first day of the Commonwealth Heads of Government conference: 'At the Palace on Tuesday night I had a chat after dinner with Chief Awolowo. He said he would welcome an informal meeting in my flat with a senior Biafran minister. The previous day Nyerere and Kaunda had both told me they thought such talks would be desirable and I should try to arrange it.' But when, on Wednesday, I arranged for Kogbara to come to lunch, he did not turn up and that afternoon his office and

101

home gave conflicting stories of his being sick or sent somewhere urgently.

Chief Awolowo also made clear his willingness to discuss the war with all Heads of Government if I arranged an informal session without officials. So Harold Wilson as chairman adjourned a regular session of the conference in Marlborough House, and we moved over to Lancaster House for 'coffee and sherry'. There was an intense discussion about the war with Chief Awolowo; and I gave an account of the preparations made for Nigerian-Biafran talks during the HGM and of Ojukwu's change of mind and removal of his team.

A professor of international law at Harvard University, Roger Fisher, who for many years has specialised in problems of international conflict and much later became an adviser on Middle East affairs to President Carter, suggested to me a different approach after he had developed contacts with both sides for about a year. He drafted a letter, which he hoped Ojukwu would sign, that would authorise me to make arrangements on Biafra's behalf with Lagos for a military truce while a conditional settlement was worked out. The letter was shown to the Biafran envoys Ignatius Kogbara and Pius Okigbo, who after discussion with Ojukwu made some changes to the wording: and Enaharo on the federal side was told of the initiative.

Early in 1969 Professor Fisher telephoned to say that Okigbo was keen that I should fly to Biafra to get Ojukwu's acceptance of the proposal and signature on the letter; Roger Fisher offered to accompany me. I needed the federal government's agreement for such a visit and sent a message to Arikpo raising the question. When I met with Enaharo in London in mid-March, however, he said he thought there was little possibility of the Supreme Military Council giving its approval to a truce. He offered to raise with Arikpo again the question of my flying into Biafra; but he thought the timing was unfavourable, as Harold Wilson was about to visit Lagos, and the OAU was becoming active. The field was crowded. So we had to let Fisher's proposal lapse.

Throughout the rest of 1969 there was no shortage of would-be peacemakers: the OAU consultative committee met in April, the OAU summit in September, when Gowon attended and Ojukwu stayed away. Senghor tried to mediate in May and Dr Busia, newly elected prime minister in Ghana, in November. There were also reports that Zambia and Gabon made attempts. Finally in December, the Emperor of Ethiopia called the two sides to Addis.

It was a year of widening concern through many countries for the plight of civilians inside Biafra. I did my utmost to keep in touch not only with governments but also through well-informed observers working with relief agencies. Some were so committed to one side that their comments lost all objectivity; and I was shocked to learn that some Church relief organisations were paying Ojukwu large landing fees in US or Swiss currency (which would obviously be used to buy arms) for the privilege of flying in medical and food supplies. But men like Adam Curle, taking leave from Harvard to work with the Quakers, and Hugh Elliott who had been a senior official in Eastern Nigeria before and after independence, gave me valuable help on many occasions.

One of the more fascinating characters whom I met in this connection was Colonel Mike Hoare. He had led mercenaries in the Congo, but told me that, though Ojukwu had tried to hire him, he would never serve Biafran secession which he thought morally wrong. Instead, he went to Lagos to see Gowon in December 1967 and, the following April, wrote him from South Africa suggesting the quickest way to end the war would be for Gowon to halt his troops and declare a demilitarized zone in which a neutral peace-keeping unit could be deployed. This would remove the Ibos' declared fear of genocide and open the way to peace talks. He offered to raise and train a unit, and gave General Mobutu as his reference.

When he saw me again in December 1969 he was more concerned about a way to get relief supplies to the starving people of Biafra other than through Uli airstrip, where arms-carrying aircraft also landed. Hoare's plan was to insert a 'third force' of about four hundred African troops (he suggested Ghanaians and Congolese) into a neutral zone adjoining Biafran-held territory, to organise the distribution of airdropped relief supplies. With the Colonel's concurrence I wrote to Gowon suggesting a modified version of this scheme.

But time was running out for Biafra, although Gowon was one of the few to know how close the end was. Within a month the war was over. Strengthened with Soviet 122 mm artillery, the Nigerian divisions advanced and sliced the remnants of 'Biafra' in pieces. Ojukwu took flight, leaving Sir Louis Mbanefo and Major-General Philip Effiong to negotiate a surrender. Gowon, as I always believed he would, stood steadfastly for reconciliation. There would be no second-class citizens, he said. Instead of a victory parade, he ordered a national day of prayer.

I was witness to one such scene of reconciliation, between Ignatius Kogbara who had been Biafran representative in London and S. U. Yolah, the acting High Commissioner for Nigeria. I introduced them to each other at Kogbara's request, nine days after the surrender. At first they stood rather awkwardly in my office in Marlborough House, and we talked about a fairly neutral subject, the reestablishment of a stable currency. Then Kogbara said he had wound up his office but offered to help the High Commission contact the five thousand or more Ibos who were somewhere in Britain. Yolah was glad to hear this, and said he was starting to arrange passages back to Lagos. Kogbara said he had already distributed widely among exiles the two hundred and fifty copies of a conciliatory letter Yolah had sent over to his office. Yolah asked him his personal plans, and Kogbara said with a smile he had finished with diplomacy and wanted to return to being a businessman in Port Harcourt; a Rivers man rather than an Ibo, he was worried about violent recriminations among the minority tribes and wondered if the federal government could provide some protection. They discussed this a little, and then Yolah asked him to come any time to Nigeria House and he would ensure that no embarrassment was caused to him. Kogbara said simply: 'Thank you. I understand.'

There were hundreds of similar scenes. I think the Commonwealth helped them to happen. It was the first organisation to bring the two warring sides together for peace talks, and helped Gowon to create an atmosphere of non-vindictiveness. Emissaries who had taken part in talks, even though they failed, gained a perspective that made reconciliation easier: when Azikiwe returned to the federal fold in August 1969, when Mbanefo flew to Lagos to deliver the final surrender, they were surer of themselves for having kept in some sort of pace and touch with the other side. Working through many rounds of negotiations was a painstaking exercise that often seemed unrewarding, but it had in the end some far-reaching effects.

Reconciliation in Nigeria after their civil war was much quicker, and deeper, than reconciliation in the United States after theirs. Gowon was a devoted and admiring student of Abraham Lincoln – and he survived in power long enough to implement his generous vision. In Chapter 9 I mention my visit to Addis Ababa in 1973 to represent the Commonwealth at the tenth anniversary summit meeting of the OAU: General Gowon startled his security guards and others by making a point of having the aircraft in which he flew to Addis Ababa piloted by an Ibo who had served with the Biafran air force a few years earlier. The gesture was symbolic and constructive.

Chapter 6
DEVELOPING MUSCLES
Sharing Skills and Common Sense

Happily, only a small part of the time at Heads of Government Meetings, ministerial meetings, professional and technical conferences and seminars has been spent consulting about political crises. Much more time has been spent in discussing new ideas and old problems of development; often this leads to a recognition that these are common problems, and out of this realisation comes a plan for a programme of cooperation. The political crises that did endanger the association simply reinforced my determination to try to strengthen functional cooperation, both for its own sake as it was facing the real problems of human development and also because this was the way to maintain the Commonwealth as an instrument useful in the modern world.

The special understandings that came from sharing an amount of history, from growing up with similar institutions and from being familiar with a common working language, were the basis for planning cooperation in many fields. Not to make use of this potential would be like starving – or, at the very least, not exercising – a human body. It was crucially important for the Commonwealth to develop muscles and build some sinews.

This was a truth so self-evident that it seems strange that, although technical assistance programmes were authorised in 1967 and started in 1968, it took more than five years to make the funding fully multilateral and to launch the Commonwealth Fund for Technical Cooperation in 1971.

Yet within another eight years this cooperative effort had grown to the point where it was supporting some 330 experts on long-term assignments, and helping 2,200 students on courses and training programmes hosted by thirty-five Commonwealth governments – all on the cost-effective basis of a £9 million Fund to which forty-one countries had made voluntary contributions. The Prime Minister of Barbados, Tom Adams, did not overstate facts at the Lusaka Heads of Government Meeting in 1979 when he said, 'The CFTC is one of the major unifying influences of the Commonwealth'.

Why then did it take so long to start? The best civil servants are, of course, creative innovators; but there are many others who feel they have done their duty by God and history – or, if they have not the wit to care about that, who feel they have earned their keep or even done a good day's work – if they have found sophisticated reasons for saying 'no' to any new idea. I call them 'the Abominable No-Men'. They are particularly numerous in the larger bureaucracies. In this case they found a range of reasons for advising their political leaders to be cautious: 'Let us not rush things . . . be careful it does not duplicate other efforts . . . we prefer to run our own bilateral programme . . . we are not sure there are the extra resources . . . we are not sure the needs exist . . . the administrative costs can grow out of control . . . '

The CFTC and the other divisions of the Commonwealth Secretariat that are now active in functional cooperation – in such areas as rural development, food production, science and technology, health care, youth leadership, legal affairs and public administration – had to survive these chilly winds of bureaucratic caution as they took root. Although it attracted few newspaper articles compared with the political crises, it is the part of the Secretariat's work of which we can perhaps be most proud. For it has built a latticework of positive relationships between many countries.

There had to be a strategy to build a programme by stages and even by stealth, and by seizing any opportunity to set a precedent in technical assistance. Many opportunities occurred, for the needs were as numerous as the visits any Secretariat person might pay or letters he might send to a developing country. The period of preparation and experimentation could have been briefer; but it helped to refine plans, so that the CFTC continued the way it eventually started, as a lean and professional unit.

The meetings – of Health Ministers, Education Ministers, Law Ministers – helped broaden the views and stimulate ideas among a great number of participants. A common theme was the recognition that traditional methods were inadequate to deal with the pressing problems of development. School curricula which had been taken from Britain as the basis for schools in colonial capitals where the children of the elite were prepared for secondary schools and universities, needed drastic revision for new village schools in countries where most children in the present generation will not receive more than four years' schooling. Inappropriate village schooling in many countries was leading to dissatisfaction and the drift of unemployed school-leavers to shantytowns in the cities. So we ran regional and Commonwealth-wide conferences and workshops, and we commissioned studies, on curriculum development, on the adoption of 'new maths' in developing countries, on education in rural areas, on teacher training and textbook writing. We organised regional meetings of school inspectors and of teachers of handicapped children.

The Health Ministers and their officials were concerned with the imbalance of health care between cities and rural areas, and this led not only to our supporting an expansion of the East African flying doctor service but to a study of how the 'barefoot doctor' service of China might be adapted in Commonwealth countries. Ministers would discuss ways to make life in villages more interesting, ways to introduce village industries. And out of such discussions, and out of the caucusing of Commonwealth ministers at UN conferences – for example, Agriculture Ministers with my deputy Hunter Wade, at the World Food Congress – came fresh plans and, in the Secretariat's structure, a new division concerned with food production and rural development. It has been exciting to watch the inventive imagination of some participants stir the others, the experience and common sense of some guide the rest. It was the Commonwealth at work, often on a shoestring.

The first layer of functional cooperation, the cement that would hold the association together, was already in place in 1965. Finance Ministers had been meeting annually since the 1950s, although their concentration was upon the general world situation and the sterling area's balance of payments. Education Ministers had also met on two occasions and, at Ottawa in 1964, they had set up the Commonwealth Education Liaison Unit (CELU). When the staff of CELU and of the Commonwealth Economic Committee, who serviced the Finance Ministers, were brought into the ambit of the Secretariat in 1966,* it was possible to add two functional divisions – Trade and Commodities, and Education.

Putting in place the next layer of cooperation was a lengthier process. Commonwealth Trade Ministers, who had a lively meeting at Marlborough House in June 1966, chaired by Douglas Jay, offered the Secretariat a stimulating challenge by listing four areas we should explore; the feasibility of establishing a Commonwealth

---

* See Chapter 3.

Market Development Fund, and of reviving the Commonwealth Shipping Committee which had been suspended in 1955; the organising of a meeting of tourism experts; and the convening of a meeting of senior planning officials who could particularly discuss trade promotion.

I was determined to put formal and specific proposals for a Commonwealth Joint Aid Programme to the Heads of Government Meeting called for September 1966. The instructions to us from the Trade Ministers, and the recommendation of the Law Ministers meeting in April 1966 that we set up a Legal Division, seemed to presage a favourable climate. So, early in August, I made five suggestions in a circular sent to all governments:

1. To take advantage of the help that the older developing countries could give, in training places and experts available to travel, and to finance from a central source some of the foreign exchange costs incurred, particularly passages for experts going to other developing countries. This scheme we called 'Third Party Technical Assistance'.
2. To plan for joint consultation and cooperation in regional assistance programmes in Africa, the Caribbean and Mediterranean to the same modest extent that the Colombo Plan did in Asia.
3. To set up a small team of specialists inside the Secretariat to advise governments in such areas as university education, public administration and statistical services.
4. To carry the idea of joint development projects (approved in principle by Heads of Government in 1964) to the stage of organising and financing feasibility studies.
5. To set up a Commonwealth Planners' Service.

This last was the brainchild of my economic Deputy, Tilak Gooneratne, who believed many governments would welcome advice on the formulation and implementation of national development plans. I suggested that a fund of £1 million a year (which was about 0.5 percent of the total aid budgets of Commonwealth donor countries) would cover these services.

But we soon ran into the cautious negativeness of bureaucrats. One senior British official told me that two aid agencies could not possibly be allowed to exist in the same country. I could only reply that it was fortunate that no one ever told the Americans this, for otherwise the World Bank and the United Nations Development Programme would never have been born.

This same CRO official prepared a critique of our proposals, which was sent to the Secretariat in August 1966 over the signature

109

of Sir Andrew Cohen (a former colonial governor who was then head of Britain's Overseas Development Ministry – a good man who should have known better than to lend himself to such nonsense). After an imperial flourish* authorising me to forward the (already circulated) proposals to Commonwealth Prime Ministers, its bleak comment on 'third party technical assistance' was that the British Government had never yet financed experts from another country 'and we would see real difficulty in doing so in present circumstances'. The item on regional schemes brought a ponderous warning against duplication.

The proposals for a Joint Aid Programme were discussed towards the end of that exhausting Heads of Government Meeting, and ran into some heavy weather. They were strongly commended by the Sri Lanka Minister of Justice, Senator A. F. Wijemanne, who had first-hand experience of the Colombo Plan. But the two other main speakers were not so enthusiastic. Arthur Bottomley, who had become Britain's Minister of Overseas Development, approved of the principles behind my proposals but said Britain was in no financial state to pledge any funds. Swaran Singh, India's Foreign Minister, was in favour of a fund to pay the passages of developing country experts, but said that any further institutionalising would detract from the pragmatic approach he admired in the Commonwealth, and suggested that I should identify needs on a case-by-case basis.

The Secretariat's proposals survived the 1966 HGM by dint of getting authority to organise and refer them to a special meeting of senior officials on 'cooperation in planning, Commonwealth assistance and trade promotion'. This meeting took place in Nairobi in May-June 1967. In an attempt to weaken the opposition of British officials to the proposals ahead of that meeting I had gone to see Harold Wilson and he strengthened the British delegation by adding two outstanding economic experts from outside the CRO and the Overseas Development Ministry: Dr Thomas (now Lord) Balogh, economic adviser to the Cabinet, and Sir Donald McDougall, director-general of the Department of Economic Affairs. At Nairobi McDougall was asked to chair a committee on Regional Cooperation. Gamini Corea, later to become the Secretary-General of UNCTAD, took charge of a committee on Com-

---

* 'I am authorised by the Commonwealth Office to say that . . . they would see no objection to its circulation to Commonwealth Prime Ministers, if Mr Arnold Smith is satisfied that such circulation would be in accordance with the Agreed Memorandum of the Commonwealth Secretariat.'

monwealth Cooperation in Technical Assistance; and Philip Ndegwa, Kenya's top official in economic planning, was the overall chairman. The gathering included many of the Commonwealth's best planners, and prospects seemed excellent for a worthwhile step forward.

There were useful warming-up sessions on planning techniques and regional cooperation. The crux of the meeting came with the discussion on technical assistance. I stressed the various advantages a multilateral program could offer: how it could pool the expertise of a team from several countries, recruit experts for countries with limited foreign contacts, and draw them from developing countries that had highly trained people but could not afford to finance assistance programmes of their own. I also pointed out that an expert from another developing country would often be the most appropriate person to send, because of a background of working with limited resources.

These arguments, though supported by the speakers from developing countries, did not prevail. The Canadians expressed doubt whether more resources – either of experts or of financing – could be found inside the Commonwealth, and thought the recruitment of experts from a distance raised many problems. The British and New Zealanders warned against duplicating other agencies' efforts, and the Australians said flatly that they distinctly preferred bilateral arrangements and anyway thought that any recruitment of multinational teams would bring a confusion of techniques.

The chairman, Philip Ndegwa, made a superb speech castigating the rich for stingy negativity, and in the end we won qualified agreement for a modest programme. Instead of hiring experts through a central fund, the Secretariat was to be allowed to recruit them on lines of credit provided by Britain, Canada and New Zealand who would approve individual assignments. They were to concentrate 'on meeting the planning, rather than the operational, needs of governments.' We also won approval for a headquarters group of about six staff (development economists, statisticians, public administration experts) who could respond quickly to requests to visit countries, identify problems and recruit specialists who could deal with them. A useful loophole phrase conceded that this headquarters group might on occasions undertake short-term operational work themselves, for this enabled us to experiment with a resource development team (later called the Technical Assistance Group or TAG). The headquarters group was similarly to be funded by a line-of-credit from Britain, Canada and New Zealand; and the assignments they undertook were happily left to the Secretariat's discretion.

Even more important, now that some sort of technical assistance programme was established, the nature of ministerial meetings changed and became more action-oriented. Requests for assistance to the Secretariat could come from any group – whether law, health, finance, trade or education ministers – rather than exclusively from some central point in each government. Meetings which had previously been mainly consultative now took on new dynamism. As well, we were able to work with non-governmental organisations like the Association of Commonwealth Universities. We could not directly finance some like E. F. Schumacher's Intermediate Technology Group, but I told him we could respond to requests for his help if they came from Commonwealth developing countries; and this we did.

The plans for trade promotion were sharply trimmed, however. Early in 1967 the Indian Government had circulated through the Secretariat a proposal for a Commonwealth Market Development Fund of between £10 to £15 million, to support many activities including product development and design for export. A Secretariat paper for the Nairobi meeting suggested a more modest start with an initial commitment of £3 million. In a standard delaying ploy the officials from rich countries asked for a detailed study; so an expert group with members from Britain, Canada, India and Pakistan was attached to the Secretariat for eighteen months. Two of the institutions they recommended in their final report – a small Commonwealth Export-Import Bank and a commercial-type corporation to undertake export sales and investment operations through joint ventures with agencies in developing countries – were rejected after a brief debate among Heads of Government at Singapore in 1971. The other recommendation was a fund to support activities such as market research, participation in trade fairs and exchanges of trade delegations. This became the essence of a new Export Market Development division, which has helped developing countries organise many successful buyer-seller meets – a form of two-country trade fair – both within and beyond the Commonwealth: for example, a buyer-seller meet for Jamaican goods in Toronto, Indian goods in Cologne and Kenyan goods in New York.

The Nairobi meeting recommended that the technical assistance programme cover national and sectoral planning, project preparation, statistics, finance and public administration, all areas in which there were similarities of experience and practice in most countries. So for the headquarters team that was established by April 1968 I appointed Alfred Pusar, a Lithuanian-Canadian transport economist; Ikhtiar-ul-mulk, the former Director-General of Statistics in Pakistan; John Kaboha, a senior administrative officer from Uganda with experience in UNICEF: and Ed Dommen, a British-Swiss economist who, like the others, had experience in planning and project appraisal. They worked under Gordon Goundrey, who had been a senior adviser on economic planning in Zambia and who had come to us on the recommendation of Kaunda.

Members of this team were soon busy filling many requests. Ikhtiar-ul-mulk, for example, helped the Gambians put together the economic papers for their budget exercise; he advised Malta on the training needs for its statistical service; he worked with the Associated States in the Caribbean to plan a population and housing census; he advised the East African Community on a more rapid processing of trade statistics; and he helped the three southern African countries – Botswana, Lesotho and Swaziland – organise their trade figures according to the Brussels system. As well, he was responsible for making a success of the periodic meetings of the top Commonwealth statisticians. It may seem hardly the most glamorous work; but it was fundamental to development planning for small countries who could not get this kind of expert advice on an intensive, short-visit basis from other agencies.

Alfred Pusar helped draw up plans for repairing and maintaining the Tanzanian road system; with two other Commonwealth advisers he produced a basic document on how to measure the costs and benefits of public works in Singapore; he visited Sierra Leone with Goundrey to advise about difficulties in the cement and other industries; he drew up a regional planning scheme in northern Nigeria; and he went to Malta to advise on the conversion of its shipyards into a shipbuilding and repair centre for vessels of many nations, after the closure of the British naval base.

Among many other jobs, Ed Dommen helped Fiji with their national accounts and input-output tables; and John Kaboha helped set up a public administration documents section for a centre in Morocco that organises training courses throughout Africa. But, rather than give a pepper-pot impression of the work done for several countries, it is better to describe the impact that the Commonwealth programme could have on a single country in a short period. Take, for example, Botswana.

Botswana became independent in September 1966, at a time of crippling drought and famine for the 600,000 people who mainly lived from cattleherding. It was vulnerable geopolitically, being surrounded by Rhodesia, South Africa and South African-controlled Namibia. The railway running through Botswana was managed by Rhodesia Railways. Many of its young men went as bachelor migrants to work deep underground in the South African gold mines – you could see the graduates of these contracts wearing a yellow miner's helmet as they walked through the bush with their cattle. They were the only 'graduates', for the country did not have a single complete secondary school, let alone a university. Their currency was the South African rand, and with Swaziland and Lesotho it was part of a customs union in which, on a formula worked out half a century ago, South Africa apportioned tiny shares of the customs revenue to its three small partners. For five years after independence the Botswana Government had to accept grants-in-aid from Britain to cover its recurrent budget expenditure.

The Secretariat's headquarters team helped Botswana find planners for the education and agriculture sectors, and for the tourist industry; it recruited a Ghanaian to do a salaries review for the public service; and it launched a major study of rail operations. But in terms of securing for Botswana a larger and steadier flow of revenue on which it could plan its national development, the Commonwealth group scored a disproportionate impact with two other missions. First, a headquarters team led by Goundrey made a detailed study of other common currency arrangements (Belgium and Luxembourg, for example), then banking experts seconded to us by Britain and Canada advised the three countries on the costs and benefits of introducing a currency separate from the rand; on the basis of this work the 'pula' (the Tswana word for 'rain' also used as a blessing in that dry land) was inaugurated in Botswana. Secondly, over a period of eighteen months Gordon Goundrey headed a team of advisers who helped the Botswana Government gain maximum advantage in the mineral negotiations over large diamond and copper-nickel discoveries.

The tax and royalty arrangements that were worked out during 1968-69 with the De Beers Corporation over the two diamond 'pipes' discovered at Orapa and Letlhakane and with American Metal Climax (Amax) over the copper-nickel deposits at Selibe-Pikwe, were complex. Goundrey made five trips to Botswana, and others to Washington and New York. A first-class accountant was borrowed from Britain's Overseas Development Ministry and a top metallurgist from Canada's Department of Energy, Mines and Resources. The results were rewarding to Botswana. From nothing at the time of independence, by 1976 the total value of mineral production was US $101 million, and government was taking a fair share of the revenue. Wisely the government specified that the terms and conditions under which production should take place would be limited – and subject to renegotiations if conditions turned out to be significantly different from those envisaged at the time the agreement was signed. And indeed the revenues turned out to be significantly higher, and the costs significantly lower, than those used for the original negotiations. When a new discovery of diamonds was made at Jwaneng, far to the south under Kalahari sand, and turned out to be the third biggest in the world, similar conditions were specified.

The Secretariat followed up this work with help in negotiating with the World Bank on funding the infra-structure of these mining developments, advice on staffing needs in the public service to meet the demands arising from them, and advice on setting up an Industrial Development Corporation. As well, a New Zealand tax administrator joined Ed Dommen in reviewing the country's financial structure and tax system, to advise on how to promote economic development with reasonable incentives for foreign investment, with an improved system of tax collection and with a fairer distribution of income. And, behind all of this, the Goundrey team helped start annual meetings of the planners of Botswana, Lesotho and Swaziland, to discuss common problems; New Zealand gave us finance for the first two meetings, after which they were supported by a central fund when the CFTC was launched.

A further and unusual occasion of Secretariat help to Botswana came when the South African foreign minister sent a sharp note to Seretse Khama's government asserting that Botswana and Zambia did not possess any common border, on the grounds that Rhodesia and the Caprivi Strip (the eastern 'finger' of Namibia) met instead at that point. This was a matter of importance for Seretse, as he was negotiating with the United States for aid in building an all-weather road to Botswana's northernmost point, Kazungula, from where a ferry had for many years crossed to Zambia. It was also then an area of some tension, for South African and Rhodesian troops were often visible in their respective corners.

The case was a tricky legal issue, because this may be the only national quadripoint in the world, the only place where four countries meet; and the historical arrangements in colonial times had

115

been left vague. As well, the confluence of the Chobe and Zambezi rivers (which formed the borders) had produced some shifting of landmarks. The Secretariat's lawyers worked hard on dredging up precedents and building up a case for Seretse, while I gave political advice to the effect that he would be wise not to force the issue to a conclusion but simply to state his differing view for the record. I argued that if the case ever came to the International Court, he would have the United Nations speaking for Namibia and Britain appearing for Rhodesia; and time was generally on his side, for an unfriendly Rhodesia would before long become a better neighbour as Zimbabwe.

The Botswana example should give the flavour of the whole assistance programme, and show that it was doing a job no other agency could tackle. A national technical assistance agency like ODM could not have drawn on the range of expertise from several countries, while the UN could not have responded as quickly and flexibly to a dozen requests. As well, both the UN and donor governments have consistently avoided giving technical assistance in negotiations with transnational corporations. One senior British aid official told me it was 'immoral and politically untenable' to do so; I asked him whether he had never heard of the practice of using taxpayers' money to provide legal aid to citizens being prosecuted by the country's attorney-general. Anyway, after the work done in Botswana and many other places, we could return to Commonwealth governments with an impressive early record, to ask approval for an expanded programme.

I had hopes of starting a multilateral fund at the time of the 1969 Heads of Government Meeting in London. Although it had been possible to put together some teams at short notice by drawing heavily on the headquarters group, we were not able to field many such teams although the demand was heavy from the outset. In a visit to Ottawa in 1968 I obtained a broadminded offer from Maurice Strong, a man combining idealism and great entrepreneurial skills who had taken over as President of the Canadian International Development Agency (CIDA). Noting how effectively the Commonwealth programme was providing technical assistance to the smaller countries, Strong offered to provide $10 million from the CIDA budget to get a multilateral Commonwealth fund started, without any conditions of matching amounts from other countries. The Secretary of the Cabinet was on our side. The only condition was the approval of Pierre Trudeau, who had become Prime Minister in April 1968, and during that same visit I met him, and he promised sympathetic consideration to the idea.

Three weeks before the 1969 HGM, I had word that a senior External Affairs official was advising against this move, on the grounds that such a sum could not be offered to the Commonwealth programme without similar support being given to a proposed francophone agency, which he feared France would use to promote separatism in Quebec. I myself argued that Ottawa should indeed support the francophone agency, outdo Quebec in its backing for *L'Agence* and thereby neutralise any mischief France could conceivably plan. I also saw no reason why the Commonwealth should suffer because of the fear that francophone cooperation might be used to subvert Canadian unity.*

Trudeau came to the London HGM, the first he had attended, with a prepared speech in which he would strongly support the Commonwealth programme and make an unconditional $10 million offer to get a central fund started. Although support of this nature for our programme had been formally approved, his Cabinet Secretary was not sure on that January morning whether Trudeau was going to deliver. As we entered the conference room, I asked him if he had anything for us and he shook his head.**At the last moment, apparently, he decided not to make the speech. The Commonwealth has never come so close again to such a generous offer, and the CFTC has had to build itself up much more gradually than was necessary.

There was, at any rate, a favourable response from senior officials who met at the Finance Ministers meeting in Barbados in September 1969 to carry out a review programme. The Secretariat paper that was prepared for this review proposed a trebling (four to twelve) of the headquarters group to allow the formation of a resources team (experts in law, accounting and resource economics) after the Botswana experience and to add educational and manpower planners. This was agreed.

Our paper also proposed a £1 million central fund to provide 'third-country financing': it was estimated that this could cover

---

* See Chapter 9, for a fuller account of relations between the Commonwealth Secretariat and *L'agence de coopération culturelle et technique.*

** I was told later that much of the evening before he had been on the phone about the problem of getting an invitation for Canada as well as for Quebec to the francophone conference. (See Chapter 9.)

the costs of 'topping up' the salaries of one hundred operational experts who would fill established posts, and the total salaries of another forty experts or advisers badly needed but not budgeted for by developing countries; and, as well, the cost of training three hundred students from developing Commonwealth countries in other such countries.

The Barbados meeting accepted these ideas in general but delegates from the developed Commonwealth countries asked for much more detail before any new commitments could be made.

So another year was spent in working out with governments agreement on the terms of reference of the Board of Representatives that would supervise the fund and the size of the Committee of Management; in seeking offers of contributions; and in compiling details of the places and facilities at national institutions where third-country training courses could be provided. A draft Memorandum of Understanding setting out the framework for the Secretariat's operation of the fund was circulated to all Commonwealth governments, and this was approved by senior officials at the Finance Ministers Meeting in Nicosia in September 1970.

Australia, which had shown no enthusiasm for the program at any stage, only attended the Nicosia planning meeting as an observer. But enough delegates announced pledges from their governments to allow us to hope we could meet the pre-set conditions for making the Fund operational: a majority of Commonwealth member governments agreeing to take part, and contributions amounting to at least £250,000 pledged. Canada had given it a good start by offering at Barbados to contribute forty percent of the total fund or a maximum of C$350,000. Britain offered thirty percent or a maximum of £110,000 a year. Countries like Cyprus and Jamaica as well as New Zealand made cash pledges, and several more countries such as India and Zambia made generous offers of places at universities and institutions. It was a hard-headed three-day meeting, hammering out the administrative details, but there was the satisfaction of finally getting a viable scheme accepted.

Plans for establishing the CFTC were blessed by Heads of Government at a cheerful session on the last day of the Singapore HGM in January 1971, when the dust was settling that had clouded the earlier days on the issue of proposed British arms sales to South Africa. At my request President Seretse Khama of Botswana opened the discussion, and his moderation and the practical examples he could give on Commonwealth cooperation set a positive mood. He spoke of his country's having received since 1967 'invaluable assistance ranging from mining, taxation and monetary policy to tourism and communications'; he also pointed out that through it Botswana had been sent expert advisers from Ghana, Zambia and Kenya, and found this expansion of technical assistance through third-country financing an excellent innovation. Pierre Trudeau for Canada and Alec Home for Britain reiterated their country's pledges of forty and thirty percent of a total with a ceiling that could start the Fund off with resources of £335,000 a year; and both of them offered to raise the ceiling in later years.

By September 1971, no fewer than twenty-nine countries had pledged money to the Fund, and by 1972 Australia had finally been converted to its usefulness and, once converted, acted with typical openhanded generosity.

So at last, the brakes were off. Since Canada offered the largest contribution, I accepted their suggestion that I appoint a senior Canadian diplomat, George Kidd, who was then serving as senior vice-president of CIDA (Canadian International Development Agency) to be an Assistant Secretary-General of the Commonwealth and first Managing Director of the CFTC. Under his guidance for the first three years, and then that of Tony Tasker who had headed Britain's Overseas Development Institute, the fund doubled for each of the next five years and, though still small, earned a reputation for excellence. It had also much the lowest overhead costs of any aid agency.

The Board of Representatives, consisting of one representative from each government participating in the Fund with an elected Chairman, settled down to meeting twice a year to review progress and the inevitable new problems. Between these meetings, policy guidance has been provided by an eleven-member Committee of Management, chaired by the Secretary-General, which includes the major donors and is representative of the several regions of the Commonwealth. The CFTC is an integral part of the Secretariat; for the Secretary-General is, under the Memorandum of Understanding, 'responsible for conducting the operations of the Fund in accordance with the decisions of the Board of Representatives and the Committee of Management'.

The CFTC's own borders of technical assistance soon began to broaden beyond the original confines of support in planning. But the importance of the CFTC spread even further, because it provided a central point to which could be attached all the various efforts at cooperation in different fields. Having a multilateral fund that could legitimately support functional cooperation in health care and book development and legal training courses and rural technology allowed some fledgeling divisions of the Secretariat to spread their wings and look more confidently at the wide skies.

Full accounts have been given in Secretariat publications of the activities carried on in the dozen divisions of the Secretariat that now promote and help coordinate practical cooperation among Commonwealth countries.* The best that can be attempted in this space are a few illustrations of the sort of activities that have been undertaken because they needed doing and because no other organization was in a position to carry them out. This was more than filling gaps; it was often pioneering.

Take as first example the Legal Division. Law Ministers, who met at Marlborough House in April 1966, had endorsed the recommendation of a committee of officials for a clearing-house of information on legislation and other legal matters. But cautionary words soon began to flow from some governments, including Canada, which suggested that lawyers were well enough organised already and the addition of a Legal Section could start an expansionist trend in the Secretariat. To counter this nonsense I argued that such a section should be seen as a form of technical assistance to the smaller countries, which it did become (although it also proved very useful to all members, rich or poor). Nevertheless it was not until 1969 that the division could be launched under Tom Kellock, a British barrister who had worked in Africa and Asia and had been among the first to call for the Secretariat to play an active role in Commonwealth legal affairs.

At first, its primary function was to provide information about legislation in Commonwealth countries to other countries that were thinking of enacting laws on similar subjects, whether it was public health or noise abatement, citizenship or the office of ombudsman. By 1974 the division was able to move under Kutlu Fuad, a Turkish-Cypriot judge who had sat in the Uganda Court of Appeals for nine years, to the stage of launching an ambitious publication, the *Commonwealth Law Bulletin*. This was a large advance on simply

---

* *Commonwealth Skills for Commonwealth Needs*, 1979, gives the fullest account of CFTC operations, while the *Reports of the Secretary-General* of which, up to 1981, there have been eight, detail the activities of individual divisions, as well as other Commonwealth developments.

replying to inquiries about other countries' legislation. It has involved the stimulative role of gathering and scanning a large amount of law documents and then writing abstracts of new legislation and of court judgements that could be of interest and use in other countries, and also of proposals for law reform. Periodic meetings of the heads of Law Reform Commissions of member countries have been a logical development.

Another logical advance was to inaugurate a series of training courses for parliamentary draftsmen. After organizing such courses for five years and having provided basic training for some 140 young legislative draftsmen, the job was far from done. For Fuad had still to write in 1979: 'There is a desperate shortage of legislative draftsmen throughout the Commonwealth at large, particularly in the developing countries, which depend heavily on legislation to promote developmental programmes.' Another initiative was to run refresher courses for judges.

In a similarly pragmatic fashion the office of Medical Adviser evolved. When Commonwealth Health Ministers met for their second conference, in Kampala in 1968, they realised that, for lack of staff, few of the recommendations from their first conference three years earlier in Edinburgh had been followed up. So they suggested a doctor should be appointed to the Secretariat as Medical Adviser, particularly to provide continuity between these triennial ten or twelve day meetings; they also agreed to meet every year for one day before the World Health Assembly, with regional meetings preceding that. Dr Vedast Kyaruzi of Tanzania, and later Professor Sir Kenneth Stuart of Barbados, have in turn tackled the awesome job of trying to help raise health standards in member countries in three broad ways: through support at ministerial meetings, commissioned studies and regional secretariats.

They used the triennial meetings of Health Ministers to spotlight a theme – the allocation of scarce resources for the improvement of health services, for example, in Colombo in 1974 – and so give delegates an opportunity to learn how similar many of their problems are and to share some possible solutions. In between these meetings they carried out studies, often through consultants, on matters of common concern: two that were commissioned after the Colombo conference dealt with ways to avoid waste resulting from expensive medical equipment lying idle for want of maintenance and repair skills, and with ways to cut heavy expenditure on the procurement of medicinal drugs by bulk purchase and quality control. Interestingly, each of these studies pointed to solutions through regional cooperation. This confirmed the good sense shown years earlier when regional health secretariats had been set up in Barbados, Lagos and Arusha (Tanzania) and a major emphasis of the Secretariat's health programme (with accompanying CFTC funds) was placed on regional cooperation. Regional projects have included the harmonising of health legislation in the Caribbean and the preparation of an environmental health strategy for those islands, while the African secretariats have concentrated more on mounting training programmes and avoiding duplication of costly facilities in each country's university.

The idea of regional cooperation has also helped to transform the work of the Commonwealth Science Council (CSC). In the early years after the Commonwealth Official Scientific Conference in 1946, cooperation consisted mainly in collaboration and exchange of research results between the scientifically more advanced countries. When the CSC began meeting every two years after 1960, this was still the general pattern; but by 1971 the CSC had a membership of representatives from twenty-two governments, and was becoming far more concerned with advice to developing countries on how to plan their research and development.

The energy crisis of 1973 turned minds further away from 'high technology'. The Science Division within the Secretariat, which is answerable to the CSC and the Secretary-General, made a virtue of its limited resources (even in 1978-79 it had only seven professional staff and a budget of less than £400,000) and began organising regional committees that would pursue action programs in sectors of high priority in that region. In effect, the CSC and the Science Division became a priming group. It held meetings in various regions where the scientists worked out their own collaborative programme: those in the Caribbean chose research in biogas and solar experiments, those in Asia and the South Pacific chose rural technology, while fourteen other Commonwealth countries in Africa and the Mediterranean began collaborating on standardisation and quality control of their manufactured goods to improve their export trade. The CSC then has a further role in disseminating the findings of these regional groups and in encouraging their application. The work has a multiplier effect, and it also avoids duplication of efforts by isolated scientists.

The Education Division has filled many worthwhile gaps, in encouraging greater self-reliance. One example is in the book development program that was launched after the Singapore HGM, to follow up on work on curriculum development. The attempt to increase the immediate flow of books by a Commonwealth low-priced book scheme did not make much distance; but the Division addressed the longer-term needs by encouraging book production and the setting up of national book development councils in the smaller countries. Regional seminars to study the various problems led on to actual training courses: a six-week course in Guyana, for example, drew thirty participants from eleven Caribbean countries and during their course they produced some fourteen booklets, ranging in subjects from West Indian literature to backyard farming. Equally practical has been the encouragement of local production units which make low-cost science equipment for schools, and regional workshops have spread the experience: people in Papua New Guinea now know, for example, how the Zambian JETS (Junior Engineers, Technicians and Scientists) coordinate school science clubs and make equipment for them; and how in Africa bananas and lime juice, among other natural products, are used in making chemicals.

The problems of out of school youth were quite as pressing. At the 1969 HGM Harold Wilson had argued that there should be more Commonwealth cooperation in many areas of youth activities. At the NGO level in Britain, a brilliant English historian, David Dilks, brought a number of organisations active in the youth field together in a National Youth Affairs Council and, as its chairman, put creative suggestions for new Commonwealth initiatives both to the British Government and to the Secretariat. The Education Division organised two regional seminars on the subject of youth and development during 1969-70. Then for the 1971 HGM in Singapore the British Government submitted a second paper, concentrating on the problems of unemployment of young men and women, and Edward Heath wrote me a supportive letter expressing his personal concern; and the Secretariat proposed the launching of a Commonwealth Youth Programme. To produce a multiplier effect, it was to focus on the exchange of youth leadership training and an information exchange about youth in development.

The person behind many innovations in the Education Division and the moves towards a Youth Programme was Dr James Maraj, of Trinidad. Jim Maraj was one of the most creative people to work for the Secretariat, full of ideas and blessed with green fingers – for many of his ideas took root and grew. More skilful as entrepreneur than administrator, he had a talent for getting to know ministers and senior officials in many countries, and not only persuading them of the value of some scheme but also leading them on to writing papers or making speeches about it at the next conference, so that it appeared as their idea. Often he would write notes that added meat to their speeches. It was in this manner that he promoted the Commonwealth Youth Programme, first as Director of the Education Division, and later, when ministers responsible for youth matters met in Lusaka in January 1973, as Assistant Secretary-General. The ministers at Lusaka approved proposals for a programme that would focus on encouraging youth's involvement in national development through a system of awards and travel grants, on training for youth leaders, and on exchange of information on national programmes and plain good ideas.

The planning of the Commonwealth Youth Programme increasingly concentrated on the setting up in 1974 and 1975 of three regional centres – in Lusaka (Zambia), Chandigarh (India) and Georgetown (Guyana) – where leadership training courses were to be run on a 'sandwich' basis, with classroom studies broken by some months of fieldwork. By 1980 more than four hundred youth field workers and administrators had gained a Commonwealth Diploma in Youth Development, and a great deal of important experience besides.

A programme that I had wanted to launch from the outset of the Secretariat was one of Information. Such a large job needed to be done in bringing home to all sorts of people the benefits and the potential in the association that was the new Commonwealth, that every available ally was important. Many were extremely effective: the Queen herself, heads of government on visits abroad and senior Secretariat staff from many countries, all helped in speeches to emphasize the lively collaboration between countries; so in their own spheres did the Commonwealth Institute and the Royal Commonwealth Society. But there was still a gaping hole at the centre, in the Secretariat, where for some years we even had to pay our press officer from part of the administration division budget because there was no budget voted for her post.

The reason for this was a long-held objection to a Commonwealth information programme from British and Indian officials, who argued that material coming from an Information Division might be tendentious on sensitive issues. Only blinkered officials in large bureaucracies could have proffered such a crass argument. In the late 1960s UNESCO's public affairs department had a $1 million budget.

By 1968 the need was becoming obvious to many people. The British Government had ceased to support their magazine *Common-*

wealth Today, although it had achieved a circulation of 200,000. An independent ally, Derek Ingram's Gemini News Service, was beginning to make its way with feature articles in scores of newspapers. For the 1969 HGM I produced a memorandum that tried to show, with examples such as the Colombo Plan Bureau, that an information programme need not be costly. Sonny Ramphal, for the Government of Guyana, pressed a well-argued proposal for such a programme. There were still objections from powerful officials, which were only overcome after a survey mission of twenty-one countries by Donald Kerr, an Australian who had held senior posts in the British Government's own information service, produced strong proof of the demand for such a service, which Heads of Government then acknowledged at their Singapore meeting in January 1971.

The Kerr survey stressed the importance of working through existing channels – newspapers and government information departments, primarily – rather than creating new ones. And by recruiting directors like Tony Eggleton of Australia and Nick Harman, a British journalist and television reporter, the Secretariat has always secured a fair hearing from journalists.

But it also became inevitable that the Secretariat should try to reach various publics in Commonwealth countries more directly than by relying on a 'piggy-backing' process. So still on a tiny budget, the Information Division has since 1977 increased its own publications and developed a direct mailing list: the bimonthly *Commonwealth Currents* magazine, the Commonwealth Day posters aimed at school use, the radio tapes that are mailed from London to a network of more than sixty-five radio stations around the Commonwealth and a film about the CFTC appropriately called *Making Ends Meet*. These all help to put across the liveliness of the Commonwealth connection and are a great improvement on what was available a decade earlier.

All these functional divisions of the Secretariat just described – whether they deal with law, health, science, education, youth affairs or information – can turn to its CFTC arm if their activities require an expert to give advice in some developing country or if some training programme or workshop is involved. But the major parts of the funds available to two other divisions, called General Technical Assistance (GTA) and Education and Training (E & T), go directly to answer requests from individual governments. The list of projects is almost endless, for today more than 2200 students and trainees attend CFTC-supported courses in a year and more than three hundred experts are abroad on long-term assignments. So only a few points can be made here. One is that they draw on expertise and institutions that never fitted into the older aid programmes. By 1975 some fifty percent of experts on long-term assignments were themselves from developing countries. For example, a Singaporean had been appointed Director-General of the Fiji Ports Authority, while a Trinidadian was advising the South Pacific Islanders on the establishment of a regional shipping line. The recruitment of such experts and advisers was, on average, speedier and less expensive than that by other international or national agencies.

On the E & T side in that year, twenty-five Tanzanian technicians were training in India for the job of promoting small-scale industries in rural areas, while a team of Zambians was studying weather forecasting in Kenya. Since the training was carried out in countries with conditions familiar and relevant to the students, it had an advantage over courses offered in northern countries. The programme claims an extremely high success rate – the figure in 1979 was ninety-six percent – and there is no brain drain, for all the trainees return home. The cost-effectiveness is a tribute to the careful planning of the division's director, Peter Snelson, a British educational expert who had had years of service in what was then Northern Rhodesia (now Zambia).

Two training programmes deserve special mention. These are the Commonwealth Programme for Zimbabweans, which predates the CFTC since it was authorised by Heads of Government at my request in January 1966, and the Commonwealth Programme for Namibians that was similarly agreed in 1975. The Namibian programme is still small, for by 1980 less then four hundred students had been helped by Commonwealth governments. But the Zimbabwean programme was both extensive and extremely helpful to the new government that took power in April 1980. For by that date more than six thousand Zimbabweans had been offered study places, scholarships and employment experience in more than twenty-five Commonwealth countries. Four-fifths of these awards were provided either by the host governments themselves or by drawing on UN and other international funds; the Commonwealth Secretariat acted as the clearing-house for applications, places and awards. It administered the other fifth more directly, drawing on the multilateral Commonwealth Zimbabwe Scholarship Fund that had attracted £2 million in contributions over seven years; this Fund not only paid for four hundred and fifty students to undertake courses in twenty-two developing countries of the Commonwealth but also covered the cost of three hundred students who took correspondence courses from inside Rhodesia for their 'A levels' or a first degree.

In terms of producing for a developing country government a high return from an intensive effort, the resources team in the Technical Assistance Group (TAG) at headquarters has done outstanding work not matched by any other multilateral agency. Let me end this chapter with an account of the tough but successful renegotiation by Papua New Guinea of tax arrangements for the largest copper and gold mine in the region.

Papua New Guinea did not reach the stage of internal self-government until December 1973. In the meantime Australia, the administering government, had concluded an agreement with Bougainville Copper Pty Ltd, a subsidiary of Rio Tinto Zinc, which allowed the company a three-year tax holiday until 1976. It turned out that production in the first year was three times what had been estimated at the start of negotiations, and the price of copper had risen. Consequently, the company in 1973 earned $A158 million (£103 million), of which royalties of only $A35M went to the government. When it was clear that profits in 1974 would be even higher (they were $A118M in the first six months) the new government of Michael Somare was anxious to re-negotiate the agreement.

Previously Michael Faber, a resource economist who had worked with the Zambian Government to liquidate the British South Africa Company's claim to mineral royalties from its Copperbelt, had written in 1972 a report for the World Bank and UNDP recommending that the agreement be revised. He argued that fundamental changes in the projected size of the mine and in conditions prevailing in the copper and gold markets had clearly rendered the terms of the original concession inappropriate even before production from the mine had started. Nothing happened for a year until a colleague from Zambia, Anthony Martin, went to PNG and made the connection for the Somare government. The situation then was politically explosive, because Bougainville Island is closer to the Solomon Islands than to most of PNG and a secessionist group was active, and because the Somare government was an unsteady coalition.

The Secretariat was called in early in 1974 to help prepare a negotiating strategy and to advise during the negotiations on an alternative taxation and financing arrangement. Gordon Goundrey had returned to Marlborough House from an interlude with Memorial University in Canada (where incidentally he helped the Newfoundland premier negotiate resource deals with Ottawa). He was joined by three other members of our staff: Mike Faber, Roland Brown (a British lawyer who had been Attorney General in Tanzania recruited by Julius Nyerere at the time of independence) and Soomer Lallah, a Mauritian lawyer. The arguments were long, and lasted for four sessions, from April to September. That month a Canadian who was Director of Planning to Somare, David Beattie, wrote to the Secretariat: 'Hundreds of millions of dollars hang in the balance. These are momentous talks. . . So much of PNG's future is wrapped up in these talks.' By then the TAG team had produced an original proposal for an additional profits tax, or resource levy, of seventy percent once a fifteen percent return (taxed at ordinary rates) on an adjustable capital base had been exceeded. When the company still resisted, Somare announced in the National Assembly that there would be 'one final round and, if it fails, the government will feel obliged to introduce legislation in October'. This was not a bluff. Legislation had been prepared, and a lawyer had advised on its international implications.

The final round was as tough as any. Goundrey had sat with the PNG negotiating committee led by Beattie and Mekere Morauta, and excelled according to a colleague, at 'verbal trench warfare', contesting every issue across the table. In the very final session the company's top men faced a Committee of Ministers headed by Somare, but the PNG side yielded on only a few technical points.

At last it was agreed, and calculations gave the PNG Government $A72 million of the $A118 million profits earned in the first half of 1974. Yet the company's shares rose that same week, which showed that shareholders had expected worse results, and were relieved that the new taxes were related to profits and did not involve an increase of royalties. Over the next seven or eight years PNG stood to gain extra revenue of at least $A300 million (£200 million) from the re-negotiation. It was worth the effort.

In the Secretariat we sometimes called this technical assistance in negotiating with multinational corporations 'Operation Robin Hood', although it was really also in the long-run interests of the international corporations that developing countries be enabled to negotiate a fair deal – otherwise the corporation would lose its investment through nationalisation.

The TAG team has helped the smaller countries of the Commonwealth negotiate many resources agreements, although the Bougainville case is probably the most dramatic. During work for Swaziland in diamond negotiations in 1979, it acquired a computer terminal in London that gives these smaller governments the ability to match multinational corporations in the sort of complex financial analysis that is often involved in mining agreements. And TAG has also moved offshore, to help the island and coastal states negotiate agreements over the resources, both fish and mineral, in their 200-mile exclusive economic zones. The importance of these zones to some states can be illustrated by the Solomon Islands, which now has sovereignty over fifty-three times as much sea-area as it has over land.

Few of the original sceptics still doubt the usefulness of the Secretariat's activities in functional cooperation and development assistance. From the Secretariat's viewpoint, although it made a laborious start, it has been the most consistently satisfying part of the job.

Chapter 7

THE BIRTH OF BANGLADESH
Bhutto takes Pakistan out

India has offered at its apex in New Delhi a memorable example of what the Commonwealth has been built on: the forgiveness of sins. In the years after independence, a visitor fortunate enough to be invited to a State banquet in what used to be called Viceroy's House and is now Rashtrapati Bhavan may notice around the walls of the former Durbar Hall, where such gala dinners are served, a continuous line of portraits. There is no break in this line between the portraits of British viceroys which end with that of Mountbatten, and those of the Presidents of the Republic which start with that of Dr Rajendra Prasad. While other countries have pulled down statues of imperial lords, India has made this symbolic act of generosity, signifying that each contributed something of good to the modern country – and what was bad is buried.

Jawaharlal Nehru was not only one of the founders of the post-war world but one of its better interpreters. He was able to spread the influence of India internationally by establishing the principles of non-alignment, and by inspiring a younger generation of leaders in many other lands. He was also able to educate people in western countries in the respectability, indeed the wisdom, of non-alignment for so many Third World countries. And by his request for continued membership as a republic, and in other ways, he helped lead the Commonwealth into a new era.

Indian officials held two reservations about the Commonwealth Secretariat in its early days. One was the suspicion that the Commonwealth might try mediating over Kashmir. The other was the pettier attitude, particularly prevalent in the Foreign Ministry, of discouraging the growth of several Secretariat functions in order to keep as low as possible India's levied contribution (amounting to just over ten percent) to the Secretariat's general budget. In terms of India's own budget, the amounts involved were miniscule.

Those reservations aside, there was in Delhi widespread goodwill and often enthusiasm for the Commonwealth in the later 1960s. The great personality of Nehru was gone, and Bahadur Shastri too; and Indira Gandhi, with other preoccupations, was sometimes unimaginative about the Commonwealth. But Morarji Desai as Finance Minister and the heads of the Trade and other economic ministries often offered an Indian lead, particularly in schemes for export promotion. There was good cooperation also from law and education ministries: and India contributed senior staff to the Secretariat, and offered hundreds of training places and scores of experts.

But there was deep bitterness in the subcontinent. Although Pakistan and India had forgiven the sins of the colonial power, they had not healed the wounds left between them in Kashmir after Partition. Twenty years later, in 1967, I visited Ayub Khan and posed a parallel to him from Canadian history. Canada could, I suggested, have spent decades feeling aggrieved about the land-grab by which the United States possessed itself of the tip of the 'Alaskan panhandle' when Teddy Roosevelt sent troops north in 1902, or about the much earlier boundary dispute between New Brunswick and Maine. We could have spent our energy in trying to right these ancient wrongs. Instead, we had grumbled for a time at the unfavourable decision of an international tribunal, and then settled down to cementing good neighbourly relations and to developing the vast resources and spaces we had left. The Pakistan president seemed fascinated by this New World pragmatism, but maintained that, while that might seem a logical way to end the Kashmir dispute, it was not practical politics among Punjabis. Peoples' psychology differed.

So it was with deep concern that I watched the catastrophic events of 1970-72 on the sub-continent begin to unroll.

Of all the crises faced by Commonwealth countries since 1965, the breaking up of Pakistan and the caesarian birth of Bangladesh was the most bloody and devastating. The full toll of lives crushed and people tortured will never be known. The destruction wreaked in East Pakistan during the liberation struggle brought further delays in the development of that country, which had never in the years since 1947 received the share of central government investment and effort to which it was entitled on any criterion – whether size of population, or need, or the amount of foreign exchange that its exports earned for the whole of Pakistan.* And, sad to say, the upsurge of Bengali nationalism that in the elections of December 1970 made Sheikh Mujibur Rahman and his Awami League the indisputable choice of the people was not adequately harnessed in the first few years, a head of steam unused. The energies of the Bangladeshi nation, a very creative people, are only now being effectively marshalled to develop what can become a prosperous country.

The break-up of Pakistan was very much a Commonwealth concern, for it soon drew in its big neighbour India, first as haven for a flow of many millions of refugees and then as safe retreat and source of re-equipment for guerilla forces under hot pursuit by Pakistan troops, and finally as interventionist force in a sharp two-week war. But despite sustained efforts by certain Commonwealth leaders and by the Secretariat, the Commonwealth was not able to influence President Yahya Khan to follow a path that would bring civilian rule peacefully to both wings of his country, nor to avert war between Pakistani and Indian forces. It was a melancholy experience to see the constitutional quarrel between Yahya Khan, Zulfikar Ali Bhutto and Mujib end by their laying the country waste. And it was sharpened by the concluding episode in January 1972, when Bhutto, who had finally achieved the presidency of a broken country, abruptly announced Pakistan's withdrawal from the Commonwealth only two hours before I was due to meet him. The redeeming part of this tale comes right at the end when the Secretariat was able by some unconventional diplomacy to win general approval for Bangladesh's membership of the Commonwealth. Among other things, this opened the way to its government securing large amounts of international aid for reconstruction.

By January 1969 Ayub Khan was in deep political trouble. In that month eight opposition parties formed the Democratic Action Committee in Dacca, and called for an end to Ayub's four-tier system of 'Basic Democracy'. They also called for regional autonomy for East

---

* During 1958-68 East Pakistan's jute, tea and hides and skins provided fifty-nine percent of all Pakistan's exports; yet East Pakistan was allowed only thirty percent of the country's foreign exchange earnings. In 1968 the population of the West wing was 61 million, of East Pakistan 71 million. West Pakistan took two-thirds of the foreign aid provided by the US and over ninety percent of the aid provided by other countries. For details of other disparities, such as in the civil service and military leadership, see *The Asia Magazine*, 27 February 1972, p. 5.

Pakistan along the lines of the Six Points set out by Sheikh Mujibur Rahman as early as February 1966. These stipulated that the federal government would be responsible only for defence and foreign affairs, while the provinces controlled taxation, their own foreign exchange and trade – and also their own militia. In West Pakistan, too, there was agitation, led among others by Bhutto who formed the Peoples Party in 1967 and had been arrested in November 1968. Ayub offered concessions; he promised regional autonomy in general terms and direct elections – the first such elections in eleven years – and in February 1969 he freed Bhutto from prison. But it was all too late. A peasants' revolt began sweeping away his 'Basic Democrats' and installing Peoples Councils. In turn, his army chief General Yahya Khan took over in March 1969.

Discussion of Pakistan's problems was frankly tackled when I visited Karachi, Islamabad, Dacca and Chittagong in September 1970. Yahya Khan admitted that economic progress was not only lopsided in its benefits to West Pakistan (even the new wheat and rice strains of the 'Green Revolution' did better there), but it had not produced any real spread of wealth among the people. Despite the views of most of his fellow generals, he was determined to base the December elections for a constituent assembly on a fair census and an honest count of the ballots. This meant that East Pakistan, with about ten million more people, would have a majority of seats. He thought Mujib's Awami League would win about seventy percent of the seats in the East wing, and would thus have to form a coalition with some Western parties, which should produce a balanced and moderate government.

He also added that he too was part of the constitution-making process, and I left with the impression that he intended to offer the politicians further 'guidance' if they did not suppress their wrangling over parties and personalities. Indeed, his Legal Framework Order of March 1970 gave the National Assembly only 120 days to frame a constitution and the President power to validate it or conversely to refuse to do so – and to dismiss the Assembly. Nevertheless, despite this glint of iron, he gave the impression of being a well-meaning and sincere if not brilliant man.

Within three months, however, his calculations began to fall apart. East Pakistan suffered in November a cyclone in which more than 200,000 were reported killed. Yahya did nothing to improve his standing among Bengalis when so little help in the disaster came from the central government in contrast to the aid from overseas.

But the greatest blow to his plans were the election results.

Although twenty-three parties had contested the elections, Mujib's Awami League won all but two seats in East Pakistan and thus an overall majority in United Pakistan. Equally shattering, Bhutto's Pakistan Peoples Party won eighty-one seats and thus a majority in West Pakistan. Instead of being able to manipulate a multiparty coalition, Yahya Khan was faced with two strong parties, one representing Bengali nationalism and the other West Pakistan Islamic socialism. And they were poles apart.

Some commentators blame Yahya Khan for almost all the horrors that followed and indeed assert that he never intended to transfer power to an elected assembly.* I do not myself believe there was such total conspiracy. It seems clear that by February 1971 Yahya was party with Bhutto to deceiving Mujib into the belief that they were seriously negotiating when he was in fact gaining time to reinforce the troops he had in East Pakistan. But by then he had yielded to the hawks among his military junta and he had also surrendered to the wiles of Bhutto.

Clever and charming, Bhutto was buoyed up by his electoral sweep of the West wing; he did not wish to be either opposition leader or junior partner in a coalition government. The die was cast when in mid-February Bhutto said he would not attend the National Assembly in Dacca on March 3 and 'would break the legs' of any member who went there from the West; and when Yahya, without consulting Mujib, postponed the session two days before it was to meet. The other events of March – the civil disobedience campaign of all Bengalis from the judges down, the abortive negotiations between Yahya and Bhutto and Mujib, the acceptance by West Pakistani troops of insults and provocation from students until they could hit back devastatingly, shelling the university on March 27, and the arrest of Mujib – all followed in the mad logic of escalation.

Commonwealth countries, and the world generally, were slow to react. Partly this was a normal reluctance to interfere in a country's internal affairs. Partly it was due to a lack of detailed information, for foreign journalists were expelled from East Pakistan on March 25.

In late March I sent a message to President Yahya saying that, if he was prepared to listen, I would do everything possible to organise Commonwealth assistance in a genuine search for a political

---

* See Anthony Mascarenhas, *The Rape of Bangladesh* (Vikas Publications, Delhi, 1971).

134

solution. There was no response, but several envoys came with messages from different sides. On 26 April I heard a full Bengali account from Judge Abu Sayed Choudhury, whom Yahya had appointed to the 'hot seat' of Vice Chancellor of Dacca University in 1970. He urged a suspension of Western aid to persuade the Pakistan Government to release Sheikh Mujib and resume negotiations. On 1 May Arshad Husain, a close friend who had been my colleague as Ambassador in Moscow and later Foreign Minister, came as Yahya's special envoy to talk with Kosygin, Pompidou and Heath. He was incidentally a brother-in-law of my Deputy Secretary-General, Azim Husain, a former associate head of India's Foreign Ministry, whom I had asked Indira Gandhi to nominate for the Secretariat post. On his trip Arshad also had a meal with Azim and me, and claimed that security operations were successfully completed, and that most of the Awami League MPs would be prepared to sit at least in an East Pakistan provincial assembly. I questioned whether he really thought they would cooperate after the traumatic events of recent weeks, and he replied, 'I think so. Otherwise, it is all over with poor Pakistan.'

The following is from my diary: 'I said that I thought they might need Mujib, if they wanted Bengali cooperation. I hoped they were treating him well. Arshad assured me that Mujib was in good health and being well treated. . . . I wonder, however, whether the generals around Yahya are really prepared to be sufficiently flexible . . . It is possible in circumstances to rule for a long time by force, but usually only with a good ideological and mystical cover. The Pakistan regime has gone a long way to destroying its fig-leaf. It will be quite a feat if they can get it replaced in time to preserve unity.'

I was also in touch with Indian leaders. Jayaprakash Narayan argued that Pakistan unity was no longer possible and that India should recognise the independence of a Bangladesh government as legal cover for responding to a request from it for military intervention. Swaran Singh, the Foreign Minister, seemed more flexible and moderate. He said no solution should be ruled out, when I suggested that India's influence with the Awami League leaders might be in favour of a federal compromise. I was trying to lay the basis for a 'good offices' operation, which would certainly need Indian cooperation.

At the end of May the Canadian High Commissioners in Delhi and Islamabad, Jim George and John Small, combined in a long, authoritative cable to Ottawa. The two diplomats said the refugees' welfare must be Canada's first concern. But there were broader concerns: the threat of administrative breakdown in East Pakistan and also in India's West Bengal; China's support of Pakistan with a $200 million credit, and the fear that China might advance through Sikkim if war started between India and Pakistan. While urging speedy humanitarian aid, George and Small also argued that Canada and other middle powers were in no way obliged to pursue 'a rigid parallelism' in policies towards the governments of India and Pakistan, and suggested the meeting of the Pakistan consortium of aid donors in June was a time to exert pressure on Pakistan for restraint. This indeed happened. The eleven donor nations, influenced by a withering report of the reign of terror in East Pakistan from a World Bank-IMF team, decided to suspend aid, which in 1969-70 had amounted to $316 million.

Then on June 26 I received an urgent message from the Ceylon prime minister, Mrs Bandaranaike, asking me to consult immediately with all Commonwealth Governments on measures or machinery to reduce tension between India and Pakistan. She had, she said, 'grave apprehension' that the situation was likely to escalate from a local to an international problem. This message was stimulated in part by talks which Azim Husain and I had with Tilak Gooneratne, then the Ceylon High Commissioner in London.

Her message came on a Saturday night, when I had snatched a weekend to attend with my daughter Alex the Aldeburgh Festival, to listen to Benjamin Britten's music and marvel at Euripedes' *Phaedra* and *Medea*. I hurried back to London to draft a reply. It was not, of course, the first time that I tried to intervene in the crisis. There had been the message to Yahya Khan in March, repeated through Arshad Husain in May. On June 16 I had wired to President Yahya directly, reflecting Commonwealth concern about the refugees and saying I was ready to visit Pakistan at any time; and a message in similar vein had gone to Mrs Gandhi. But Mrs Bandaranaike's message was the first formal request from a Head of Government for a Commonwealth initiative in mediation, which I thought desirable in this case.

After talking with Gooneratne, I sent a reply to Mrs Bandaranaike suggesting that she invite four or five Commonwealth Heads of Government, or preferably Foreign Ministers, and myself to meet in Colombo under her chairmanship 'to consider the situation and action that might be taken to ameliorate it'. On the following day, June 29, a response came from Mrs Bandaranaike: she too preferred a committee of Foreign Ministers – and she agreed to chair it. She asked that the governments of India and Pakistan should be consulted about which countries should be represented on the committee. She added that she had already written to Yahya Khan and Mrs Gandhi expressing her concern and offering her assistance in any mediatory role.

My hope and plan was that a Commonwealth team – comprising, say, the Foreign Ministers of Australia, Canada, Ghana and Malaysia, plus myself – could meet under Mrs Bandaranaike, and first send messages as a group from Colombo to Yahya and Mrs Gandhi, and then visit Islamabad and Delhi, and probably Dacca and Calcutta (where the other Awami League leaders were operating in exile). Yahya Khan would find it difficult to ignore a high level team, including two significant aid givers, particularly as it would be going beyond discussion of Pakistan's domestic affairs and would be visiting Delhi. At the same time I hoped Mrs Gandhi would welcome the team, since it would be dealing separately with the Pakistanis and also responding to the call she had several times made to the 'international community' to shoulder responsibilities in the East Bengal situation that had burdened her country by June with expenditure of $1.5 million a day for the welfare of the refugees. Neither side, I felt, could rebuff the team without glaring public inconsistency.

So on 30 June I spoke to the Australian and Canadian heads of Mission in London to find out whether their Foreign Ministers would participate if invited, and to the British Foreign Secretary, Sir Alec Douglas-Home. He thought it might be limited to a regional committee (including Australia as part of the Asian region); his doubts that India and Pakistan would accept any committee at all seemed to melt as we talked.

I was planning to fly to Colombo the following day to discuss the scheme directly with Mrs Bandaranaike. But her Permanent Secretary phoned me and pleaded that I should not come unless I had the prior agreement of Mrs Gandhi and Yahya Khan on the committee and its membership. He seemed terrified, and the reason was not far to seek. The Indian High Commissioner in London, Apa Pant, had heard word, without detail, from his Ceylon counterpart that 'an important Ceylon and Secretariat initiative' was afoot; this alarmed and upset Mrs Gandhi who had not been told of any specific initiative in the letter that she had received from Mrs Bandaranaike. Quietly Mrs Bandaranaike was told, I believe, from Indian sources to mind her own business if she did not want her precarious domestic situation involving Singhalese relations with the Tamils in the northern part of the island to worsen. India, while not wishing to reject openly a Commonwealth initiative after appealing for international help, was taking strong informal steps to discourage any such development.

Reluctantly cancelling my flight, I sent messages to both leaders on July 1, giving them details of what had passed between Mrs Bandaranaike and myself and seeking their agreement. A hint of the Indian reaction came that day from Apa Pant, when I gave him my telegram to send to Mrs Gandhi by Indian cipher; to Delhi, he thought, the Commonwealth initiative appeared to equate the situations in India and Pakistan, and this was a false equation since Pakistan's actions alone had created the vast exodus of refugees from which India now suffered. I explained that the committee would want to talk to the Awami League leaders in exile in Calcutta. We were not at all equating the Indian and Pakistan governments, but would welcome the Indian Government's views and advice. But no official replies came to me from either capital and Colombo again on July 19 discouraged me by telephone from flying out for a quiet talk with Mrs Bandaranaike unless the two big neighbours approved in advance.*

What of other mediation efforts? The United Nations Security Council had not been at all eager to tackle the issue, although at the request of U Thant the Secretary-General of the Islamic nations, Tunku Abdul Rahman (the former Malaysian Prime Minister) flew to Islamabad in June to urge a political settlement – but to no avail.

Another conceivable mediator had been Henry Kissinger, then at the height of his influence in the Nixon administration. The United States had disbursed some $10 billion to India in development assistance and food aid since the 1950s, but any influence in Delhi was greatly diminished by Washington's already evident 'tilt in favour of Pakistan'. Yahya Khan and his Ambassador in Washington, Aga Hilaly, had been useful intermediaries for Kissinger as he developed the belatedly sensible policy of an opening to China; and no doubt this weighed with him and Nixon. But Kissinger never used what influence he had to restrain Yahya Khan during the middle months of 1971. He was busy on missions to Peking and to secret meetings with North Vietnamese envoys. He made the

---

* A reply was eventually sent by President Yahya Khan to Mrs Bandaranaike on 10 August suggesting that the best way to reduce tension was to 'dissuade India from interfering in the internal affairs of Pakistan and creating a situation of crisis and confrontation'. No reply from Mrs Gandhi is recorded.

classic diplomatic error of arriving on the scene too late to prepare his ground as a mediator and, after a last-minute effort to bring Yahya Khan together with Awami League exiles, picked the wrong side. He forgot Napoleon's dictum that 'in war the moral is to the material as three to one', and supported a man who was clearly in the wrong in trying to suppress with great cruelty the results of a democratic election. The tilt towards Pakistan became even more pronounced in December when the United States blamed India for 'the broader hostilities' and sent the nuclear-powered aircraft carrier *Enterprise* and seven other warships into the Bay of Bengal. It was the ultimate gesture of futility in an increasingly unwise course of policy.

But meanwhile the situation had worsened by the week. In July Yahya Khan was declaring that a secret military trial of Sheikh Mujib would soon begin, and the charges would carry the death penalty.* And, in the wake of the suspension of British and Canadian aid, a Pakistan spokesman said his country was seriously considering leaving the Commonwealth – and Pakistanis began talking about giving retaliatory support to Catholics in Northern Ireland and to separatists in Quebec.** A committee of Pakistani officials, set up to study the costs of breaking Commonwealth relations, reported to Yahya Khan overwhelmingly in favour of staying in, although his own economic adviser, M. M. Ahmed, argued for withdrawal. What added more uncertainty to the whole situation were reports that Yahya Khan had taken to drinking heavily. War between India and Pakistan was being widely predicted for November, after the monsoon rains had ended; and Bhutto himself was announcing that he would either be in charge of Pakistan by November, or else back in prison.

Open warfare in fact broke out on December 3, when the Pakistan air force flew from West Pakistan to bomb military airfields in Western India. It was not only an inept operation but a desperate move of aggression, possibly aimed at precipitating United Nations intervention, because their forces in East Pakistan were under such pressure from the Mukti Bahini guerrillas who were armed and supported from India. In October Yahya Khan had accepted an offer of 'good offices' from U Thant but Mrs Gandhi had turned it down on the grounds that this was not an Indo-Pakistan dispute. Now to

---

* *Financial Times,* London, 4 July 1971, interview with Neville Maxwell.

** *Daily Telegraph,* London, 16 July 1971.

their delight, those top Indians who had long wanted to carve up West Pakistan saw the opportunity. Fortunately Mrs Gandhi took other advice and the Indian Cabinet decided to limit the war. Personally I do not believe that the movements of US warships in the Indian Ocean, or long-range pressure from Washington via Moscow, deserve credit for influencing the Indian restraint, as Kissinger has claimed. On the contrary, these moves merely served further to sour Indian-US relations.

I had admiration for the generous and compassionate way in which Indian officials were dealing with the enormous problem of millions of refugees, and for the remarkable maturity of the ordinary people of India. For most of the refugees were Hindus or 'Biharis' – Urdu-speaking Indians – but there was virtually no communalist or anti-Muslim reaction; there was simply help. But this admiration was mixed with regret at the cynical way in which Indian politicians had been pleased to watch (if not contribute to) the deterioration of the East Pakistan situation for many months, and had on specious grounds blocked all international efforts at mediation. I myself had made a final effort on November 29, telling the Pakistan High Commissioner that I would fly to Islamabad at once if Yahya would receive me. Yahya sent no reply. But, in any case, it was really too late for any mediation.

The war was over within two weeks. Mrs Gandhi declared a ceasefire on December 16, the day after Dacca fell, and Bhutto flew back from a UN Security Council debate to be promoted from Foreign Minister to President on December 20. He had been back in government for less than three weeks, and could start with a clean slate. I cabled him congratulations on taking the presidency 'at this testing hour', and wondered (to his High Commissioner) if he would be smart enough to release Mujib forthwith and prepare the people of West Pakistan for recognition of Bangladesh as an independent state. He did the first; but his fight to prevent the diplomatic recognition of Bangladesh was foolish and did his country lasting harm.

I should digress briefly on the general issue of diplomatic recognition. A trap, into which countries too often fall, is to believe that by not recognising a regime of which they disapprove they will cause it somehow to lose influence, if not entirely to vanish. It is in particular an American heresy, which they learned in the years before World War I when their diplomatic activity was mostly

limited to Latin America. There were frequent coups among banana republics, and Washington's recognition or the lack of it did
often mean survival or not to the new regime. But the Americans
seemed to think this a law of political nature that would work on a
wider stage. Not so. It took the United States seventeen years to
recognise the Soviet Union, for example. This helped Stalin stimulate xenophobia among his people, and built an iron curtain around
them; it did the West no good.*

Later, the United States took another twenty-five years after
1950 to recognise the Peoples Republic of China. There are several
other examples to show that a stand of non-recognition almost
invariably constrains the subject more than the object. Rhodesia is
the single exception, and that because we envisaged and encouraged a take-over by an alternative and majority regime. So I was
concerned that Pakistan should soon recognise Bangladesh and that
the West and the Commonwealth should also do so, believing that
only Moscow would gain from delay.

When Bhutto had a preliminary talk with Sheikh Mujibur late in
December, before releasing him, he made it known that he would
be angry if other nations took what he called 'premature measures'
over East Pakistan. He was threatening to break relations with any
country that recognised the new regime in the east, in effect propounding his own 'Hallstein doctrine'. That doctrine had done no
good for its originator, West Germany; and Willy Brandt had done
his people and the world a service with his 'opening to the East'. I
began before the New Year to suggest in messages to those Commonwealth governments that were aid donors that they should
quietly warn Bhutto against an Asian 'Hallstein' approach. He
might well resent that advice, but it was better to try earlier than
later, before anyone took up a public position.

Unfortunately Alec Home was concerned to avoid provoking
Bhutto, and Mitchell Sharp stated in a pre-recorded television
interview** that Canada could not recognise Bangladesh so long as
there were 100,000 Indian troops on its territory, because there was
not a government in effective control. This was not the argument
used in 1944, I reminded him, when the government of General de
Gaulle was recognised long before it controlled France and while

---

* My own general view of recognition is that, if Satan had a kingdom on this
earth, I would appoint one of my best young men or women as Ambassador
there – to keep a good eye on him.

** Interview with CTV, Toronto, 2 January 1972.

the country was full of foreign troops. But Britain and Canada may well have hesitated in face of the extraordinary pro-Pakistan line being taken in Washington.

In the midst of these hesitations Sheikh Mujibur Rahman arrived, with one hour's notice to British authorities, at Heathrow airport early on Saturday, January 8. He came straight from nine months' imprisonment to a suite at Claridge's Hotel, and was staying only a single day in order to see senior Bengalis before flying to Dacca. I arranged through Judge Choudhury to call on him that evening, in between interviews he had with Edward Heath and Harold Wilson.

He talked cheerfully about himself, saying he was fit after nine months' rest. I began the substantive discussion by observing that, in relations between peoples as between individuals, the forgiveness of sins could prove a remarkably constructive act. He grinned and said that he personally would not disagree; but it was politically impossible to keep any constitutional links with West Pakistan, after what its army had done to Bengali women and children. His own home village had been razed and all its young men hunted down as troops tried to find his son. He was eager to return home and start the task of reconstruction. He very much wanted Bangladesh to be a member of the Commonwealth. The earliest possible links with Commonwealth countries would be helpful. I said that, if separation from West Pakistan were to prove inevitable, I would do my best to get a consensus on Commonwealth membership.

It was after this that I suggested to several governments that they simultaneously tell Bhutto they were considering a request from Mujib for recognition. Bhutto publicly announced and began applying his version of the Hallstein doctrine by breaking relations with Bulgaria, Mongolia, Nepal and Poland, when they recognised Bangladesh; although he tried to persuade the Polish Ambassador to stay on as trade commissioner, and he meekly accepted Soviet recognition of Bangladesh without a whisper of any reprisal.

William McMahon, who was halfway through his brief time as Australia's Prime Minister, liked my idea and gave himself two weeks to gather a group of countries that would take simultaneous action; he saw some advantage, in an election year, in Australia being a pace-setter in Asian events. But Douglas-Home counselled against any joint Commonwealth move. Don't face Bhutto with the Commonwealth issue, he told me; let the West Europeans move first. In any case, British recognition would come within two months, he said. Ottawa was talking of a longer delay, of three to six months.

Central to this diplomatic tiptoeing was the attitude of President Bhutto. What did that clever, brave, proud, guileful and inconsistent man really hope to happen? Did he still truly believe in the territorial integrity of West and East Pakistan, when he asked governments to avoid precipitate action and give the leaders in Dacca time to respond to ideas about a continuing link? Was he hoping to bargain for the return of his 90,000 troops and civil servants from Indian hands with his 'card of legitimacy', his acquiescence in the international recognition of Bangladesh? Was he sincere in asking governments to wait while he prepared his own people to accept inevitable changes, including the sovereignty of Bangladesh?

As January passed, his actions made many doubt such intentions. Instead of preparing the ground with his own people, he went travelling in the Islamic world, as far as Libya, reportedly urging his hosts to discourage their Western and Third World friends from recognition of Bangladesh. And, much though his hopes focussed on an early return of Pakistan prisoners of war and civil servants, he separated this issue from that of recognition. For he did not withdraw his acceptance of Heath's offer to mediate a return of prisoners when Britain (telescoping its original timetable) passed a diplomatic word on January 18 that it intended to announce recognition 'in a week or so'. But on a television interview* Bhutto threatened to leave the Commonwealth if Britain recognised Bangladesh before he had further talks with Mujib and before Indian troops were withdrawn.

This statement reinforced my concern to meet and talk with Bhutto as soon as possible. From early January I had been trying in messages sent through the High Commissioner, Lieutenant General Muhammad Yusuf, to get a date for a visit to Bhutto in Islamabad, saying I could possibly help to work out a new deal with the East Bengalis that would be in Pakistan's interest; but these messages, which I had asked be forwarded to Bhutto as he shuttled around the Middle East, seemed to produce no result. I sent another message the day he returned to Pakistan, and received a cable saying he hoped I would come as soon as I could. It was brought to my flat at about midnight on Friday, January 28. I knew Bhutto

---

* Reported in the London *Daily Telegraph*, 21 January 1972.

was leaving on the following Monday for a visit to China, and thought it best to have my say first. So I left on the first available flight on Saturday with Emeka Anyaoku, director of my International Affairs division, and David McDowell. We reached Rawalpindi just after lunch on Sunday.

But already, unknown to our party, the die was cast. That morning the British High Commissioner, J. L. Pumphrey, had delivered a note from Alec Home in response to an invitation to stop off in Rawalpindi on his way to Delhi the following Saturday. Home's note first said that he would stop off and then said that Britain was going to recognise Bangladesh, and planned to announce it on February 4, just before Home set out for India. The British Foreign Office had given me no advance warning of this, but had said Pumphrey would keep me informed of developments. However he did not send anyone to the airport or make contact that afternoon. Although he knew when I was arriving, and knew from an earlier posting in Zambia how the Commonwealth can too easily be entwined in reactions against a British move, he did not wait a few hours to tell me about the note and give me an opportunity to try and talk sense about the Commonwealth to Bhutto before he delivered it. It was a costly lapse.

For, when we arrived at the airport, the Protocol officer told me that President Bhutto was meeting with his Cabinet to discuss what reaction they should make to the British decision. And at 5 pm, while a military attaché from the president's palace was on the telephone inviting me to meet Bhutto at 7 pm for a private talk before having a working dinner with him together with his four provincial governors and half his Cabinet, Anyaoku heard over Radio Pakistan a news bulletin announcing Pakistan's decision to withdraw from the Commonwealth. An hour later Bhutto held a press conference, which Anyaoku attended for the Secretariat, and made clear that the decision was in retaliation for the British move.

Bhutto and I met as arranged, at 7 pm in his small study at the Rawalpindi residence and he asked at once: 'Why couldn't they have waited a few days?' I answered, equally bluntly, 'Why couldn't you have waited a few hours – until we'd talked?'

I was annoyed that he had been so stupid in taking such an Anglocentric view of the Commonwealth, and told him so. In his book *The Myth of Independence* he had written, 'The Commonwealth has passed the point of mutual benefit. It has become a vestigial institution'; but he had also written, 'In international dealings there is no such thing as an irrevocable constant.'* He was capable of making use of any instrument or organisation. But his action that day – for he had bulldozed the decision through his Cabinet – was based on the notion that Britain owned the Commonwealth, a humiliating and also a silly idea. At the same time, I realised that by his earlier public threat he had painted himself into a corner. He felt that he had been treated with contempt by Britain and that he had to react. With 200,000 Pakistani immigrants in Britain, he was not going to risk retaliating against her directly. The Commonwealth was the substitute target. It was stupid and sad; but the Commonwealth had only lost a trick, and Pakistan had lost a war – and a country. The important task now, I considered, was to heal relations between the Punjabis and the Bengalis and Indians.

I urged Bhutto to recognise the new regime in Bangladesh without delay, and thereby to build on the great goodwill which he had gained, at the very start of his assumption of the presidency, by releasing Mujib. It was now in his 'honeymoon period' that he had maximum flexibility and could use it to engender new attitudes and relations between the three great units of South Asia; Pakistan, Bangladesh and India. They could develop either way.

I also set out to warn him against *revanchisme*, saying that forty million lives had been lost as a result of the Germans' traumatic reaction to loss by seeking retribution and scapegoats after the first World War. How much more constructive the moods and policies in Western Europe after World War II – reconciliation and the search for economic, political and defence cooperation, through common initiatives such as the EEC and NATO.

We had a pleasant conversation, sitting in his study for a good hour and sipping whisky. I told him of my talk in London with Mujib and of my intention to fly on from Rawalpindi to Dacca, if he would agree in principle (and if he wished, in complete confidence) to release Bengali civil servants and recognise Bangladesh independence. Pakistan could have the greater advantage in a package including an exchange of prisoners-of-war and also significant amounts of international and Commonwealth aid. He suggested I could still arrange a meeting between him and Mujib on exchanges of civilian officials and prisoners-of-war, and we mentioned Ceylon as a possible meeting place. We discussed where events in the subcontinent would move from this point. I suggested

---

* *The Myth of Independence*, by Zulfikar Ali Bhutto, Oxford University Press, 1969, pages 24 and 185.

there could be a new arrangement, involving close working relations and trade with an independent Bangladesh. Mujib would not want to be too exclusively dependent on India. He would, I thought, welcome the extra elbow room that relations with Islamabad could provide. Bhutto expressed interest and receptivity to all these possibilities. I suggested there might even be sense in an eventual federation or confederation of all the parts of the subcontinent – Pakistan, India, Bangladesh – and asked whether Bhutto would rule this out as impossible. He said he would by no means rule it out as an eventual solution. But he asked me not to quote him on this point to his Ministers or others. It was a frank and stimulating talk.

Nevertheless, he maintained that he could not offer, however conditionally, to recognise the independence of East Bengal. He would need months. I said this delay could prove costly. Coupled with his announced withdrawal from the Commonwealth, it changed the leverage I had thought could prove useful.

During the working supper of curry and tandoori chicken, he was the charming host, eager for debate. For the benefit of his Cabinet he repeated his question, 'Why couldn't Britain have waited a few days?' And I repeated my counterquestion. When he added the question why had Australia and New Zealand also decided to recognise Bangladesh (they announced it the following day), I replied they could speak for themselves but they probably had three reasons: a basic assessment that Bangladesh was an independent entity, a concern that it might fall into extremist hands if the Mujib regime were not recognised, and a dislike of being threatened. Bhutto said he had not threatened anyone, and I said that the Hallstein doctrine was a form of blackmail, as had been his threat to leave the Commonwealth.

Why couldn't they have waited before dealing with Mujib? he asked again. I said that, when a couple were getting a divorce, it was outrageous if the husband pressed mutual friends to put the heat on the estranged wife, and cut her off from friendly contact. They would want, as Commonwealth countries did in this situation, to retain the friendship of both parties, while regretting their quarrel. On and on the discussion went about recognition and non-recognition. I realised that one element in his calculations had been that, by breaking with the Commonwealth, he might consolidate relations with Islamic countries and China. But by the end of the evening he and his Cabinet seemed somewhat shaken and showing genuine regret at their precipitate action.

Bhutto urged me to stay on as his guest for a few more days, to have further talks after he returned from Peking. But under the circumstances, unless he could authorise me to promise Mujib recognition as part of a deal I would try to work out, I felt that our party should return to London the next evening. He asked his cousin Mumtaz Bhutto, the Governor of Sind, to look after us in Karachi while we were there. Bhutto hoped that though Pakistan was leaving the Commonwealth, we would keep in close touch. Nobody could have been more charming.

At a press conference back at the hotel, I issued a statement expressing regret at the Pakistan Government's decision, while saying that 'the Commonwealth goodwill to all concerned remains'. I added the hope that there would now be 'a period of realism, generosity and determination to develop the practical cooperation and mutual confidence so much needed.' And I ended with a phrase suggested by my brother Wilfred, who happened to be staying with me in London the evening before I had flown to Rawalpindi, and who is an Islamic scholar:* 'Bitterness and fear must be replaced by what the Holy Koran calls *Talif ul Qulub* – reconciliation and a binding together of hearts.'

This went down well in the press; and the following week the Pakistan newspaper *Dawn*, pointing out that thirty countries had by then recognised Bangladesh, suggested that soon their 'East Pakistani brethren would be justified in thinking that in the whole world we are the only ones who are against them'.

Nawa-i-Waqat put it more curtly: 'President Bhutto is supposed to be an expert in foreign policy, but he should not make Pakistan's foreign policy a laughing stock.'

He was doing something more sinister and far-reaching than that. I would have put my arguments about reconciliation even more strongly to Bhutto and his colleagues if I had known then what had been the major purpose of the new President's visit earlier that month to Libya. Years later (through a BBC television team's investigation in 1979-80) it was revealed that Bhutto was primarily seeking Libyan money to finance the purchase of a nuclear weapons industry and that in January he had summoned a group of fifty Pakistani scientists to a desert rendezvous to tell them, 'we are going to have a bomb!'**

Back in London, one problem that Pakistan's withdrawal caused

---

* He was then Director of the Centre for the Study of World Religions, at Harvard University.

** *Toronto Globe and Mail*, 19 June 1980.

was on a very different scale from some of the issues discussed above, but important. This involved at once personnel, principle and politics. Naturally we had some Pakistanis on the small Secretariat staff, and two in particular were treasures. I have already mentioned Ikhtiar-ul-mulk, a statistician of world class. The other was Sufi, a superb organiser as conference officer, for he was quietly and cannily persuasive in getting governments to adapt plans, even buildings, to meet the needs of an intimate international conference for which they were to play host. There were others, as well. The question which Bhutto's abrupt withdrawal of Pakistan's membership seemed to pose was whether they had any other course but to resign or be dismissed. I told them that, while we could employ only Commonwealth citizens, under both Pakistani and British law dual citizenship was permissible. If any of them applied for dual British citizenship, we would facilitate continuation of employment. I was delighted that Sufi and Ikhtiar-ul-mulk and some others took this course.

A month later, when in Delhi, in response to a press question I described Pakistan's decision to leave the Commonwealth as 'hasty, unwise and foolish', but added that any application for re-entry would be sympathetically considered. This earned a rebuke from the Pakistan Foreign Office spokesman: 'The statement is highly impertinent. . . . The decision to quit the Commonwealth is final and Mr Smith should stop being a busybody.'

He wasn't quite right. A move to apply for re-entry was started by the Pakistan Cabinet in 1973, but was abandoned when news of it was prematurely leaked from Islamabad. Later General Zia began taking soundings in 1978, and one motive that took him to the Zimbabwe independence celebrations in April 1980 was the opportunity to meet Commonwealth leaders. He also talked to me frankly there of his desire to see Commonwealth membership restored. But Mrs Gandhi made clear to other Commonwealth guests her opposition to Pakistan's re-entry 'at this time'.

A few weeks after leaving Pakistan, I visited Mujib in Bangladesh, as a first step in seeking a consensus on its membership of the Commonwealth. I arranged to visit Malaysia, Singapore, India and Ceylon on the same trip.

Dacca, two months after its capture from Pakistan forces, was still a shattered city. The university, shelled by tanks a year earlier, had many buildings smashed. Houses had machine-gun holes in their walls. The streets were comparatively uncrowded, because the millions of refugees were still moving back across the border. Basic services were erratic. I had flown there with David McDowell and George Kidd to discuss the recognition issue, an exchange of prisoners and civilians, and aid for rehabilitation. Judge Choudhury, who had become Bangladesh's first president, gave a dinner for us and the lights went out as I was replying to his speech of welcome. This had been happening also in Britain because of an electricians' strike, and I was able to say, 'It's just like London.'

But there were many worrisome aspects we could glimpse in February 1972. Bangladesh was already an arena for manoeuvre by the big powers. The Chinese were busy among the Naxalites, the Bengali extremists who had also a strong base in West Bengal that alarmed the Indian government. The Russians had established themselves on the Bay of Bengal through offering to run salvage operations in the harbours of Chittagong and Khulna. The American Seventh Fleet was cruising alertly in the Indian Ocean. And, as our party moved on through Singapore, Malaysia and Ceylon in the last week of February, the depth of the fears of a new regional imbalance were evident: India had suddenly become the dominant country in South Asia.

All these signs of trouble and fear pointed to the need to help establish Bangladesh as a strong and independent country. A great deal depended upon the character of Bangladesh's leader, and I was concerned that in some ways Mujib was (as after a talk with him I commented to David McDowell) 'airborne' and impractical. He had charm and charisma. He spoke and acted like a prophet. But he was not an administrator; nor did he make the effort to build a machine to follow through on his verbal decisions and pronouncements.

We talked in Dacca about an exchange of civilian officials with West Pakistan, for each had some 8000 of the other's. Bhutto was ready for an immediate exchange. Could these be transferred by ship or by sealed trains through India? Mujib kept saying that he was only prepared to talk to Bhutto about such an exchange after he had recognised Bangladesh. I suggested they could talk, with or without recognition. 'Don't feel you only exist if he recognises you.' He repeated, 'But I exist, I exist.' He was deeply affronted at this lack of recognition. This was silly: if he did not 'recognise' Bhutto's regime, this would put him on a footing of equality, I urged. After all, Bangladesh was the larger of United Pakistan's two successor states, and his election was democratic and overwhelming.

We talked, also, about a new constitution for his country – for

149

Bangladesh had asked the Secretariat to provide a constitutional adviser. Mujib said he would bring in a Westminster type of constitution and full democracy. When I suggested it was important that the Bangladesh leader have strong reserve executive powers at his command, he demurred. 'My strength is the people's support. If I say do this, they do it. When I asked them to surrender their arms, they surrendered them. No force was needed; no new laws. If the people stop following me, I will go. I have fought all my life for democracy.' They were fine words, but they did not suit the tough circumstances he faced.

Commonwealth aid for relief and reconstruction began flowing in March. The worst crisis was in housing: 24 million people, or one-third of the population, were without permanent shelter. I had sent two circular messages to governments focussing on Bangladesh's need for food grains, housing materials and transport craft for rivers and waterways. There was a particularly large and speedy response from Canada, which committed $45 million in aid for the first year and shipped 140,000 tons of wheat ahead of the monsoons in May. Canada however was (for budgetary reasons) ridiculously slow to establish a resident mission in Bangladesh – though the technical assistance Mujib most needed was independent political advice, which a good resident High Commissioner might have developed the position to give.

But it was important to win approval for Bangladesh's application for membership of the Commonwealth, which had been formally circulated by the Secretariat to the heads of the other thirty-one governments. Replies were slow to come in, as I expected. So I had to discuss and indeed sometimes argue the issue with several heads of government individually. As in the case of Singapore in 1965, when Pakistan was reluctant to give its approval, I took the line that the decision should be by general consensus in which certain countries could simply acquiesce. But it took until mid-April for that consensus to be clear. Bhutto during his travels in January had appealed for Moslem solidarity to considerable effect and was able, through his Islamic socialist approach, to sweep aside the fact that Bangladesh contained more Moslems than his own country. As well, there were countries that decided to make a slow and careful assessment, wondering about the implications of India's greatly increased influence in the region or (as Nigeria – and Canada – did) about the precedent of recognising a breakaway state.

Most Asian members of the Commonwealth required real persuasion, for they were fearful of Indian hegemony in South Asia.

I took the line that Mujib would be more independent of India if his regime were widely recognised, and certainly if its desire for Commonwealth membership were accepted. This argument won them round. Tun Razak, Prime Minister of Malaysia, and Lee Kuan Yew of Singapore announced their approval during my visit to them in late February. Other countries in the region – Ceylon and Mauritius – carefully separated the issue of approval of Commonwealth membership, which they granted, from their own formal recognition of Bangladesh. This made me pleased that I had not taken the British advice to wait on the Commonwealth issue until most countries had recognised Bangladesh bilaterally. In mid-March there was need to prod the Commonwealth African governments for their views, and Emeka Anyaoku travelled to Nigeria. By the end of March Gowon sent me word that Nigeria 'would not object' to the admission of Bangladesh, if this represented the wish of a majority of governments. Ghana used the same phrasing a few days later, and Sierra Leone and Tanzania also accepted during the same week.

Eventually only Malta and Amin's Uganda had not replied, two countries with links to Gadaffi's Libya which Bhutto had visited in January. A deadline loomed on April 18, when some heads of mission were due to present credentials in Dacca and it would be publicly evident by the title – Ambassador or High Commissioner – by which the Commonwealth diplomats were received at that ceremony whether Bangladesh's application was being approved. If not, the new regime would lose face. So I telephoned Dom Mintoff in Malta the previous evening and we had an extraordinary half-hour talk, while he produced a list of suspicions: that Mujib's was a puppet government, that Britain and India had pushed me into acting on their behalf, that he had no proof Mujib actually wanted Commonwealth membership, and that the procedure was highly unusual. Little by little he came round; it was clear he was under strain because of his battle with the British over the future of their bases on Malta, and he felt (wrongly) that the Commonwealth had been no help in this dispute. In the end he said he would support Bangladesh membership as long as he received assurance that they wanted it.

The next morning I phoned Amin and reached his Foreign Minister, Paul Etiang. Amin was chairing a Cabinet meeting, so I simply told Paul that I was announcing Bangladesh's membership that afternoon since all other governments had agreed to the announcement. I would be interpreting Uganda's silence as acquiescence. Etiang, worried about his leader's reaction, said he would interrupt the Cabinet meeting and telephone back. I said I must make the announcement anyway – there already was a consensus. In the event, no call came back.

So Bangladesh was received into the Commonwealth.

Bangladesh membership in the United Nations took much longer. Not only Pakistan, but China with its Security Council veto, was opposed. Waldheim, with whom I discussed the matter that October, told me that when he had been in China a few weeks earlier Chou En-Lai had begun their conversation by talking about Bangladesh, saying it could not possibly last and did not deserve to survive. It was the product of a Soviet plot to encircle China.*

Much more slowly than need have happened, the wounds of that war were dressed. Bhutto refused to allow the negotiations with Mrs Gandhi in June 1972 that produced the Simla Accord to encompass a package settlement, tackling all issues including Kashmir and Bangladesh. Early in the negotiations he told an Indian negotiator, 'No, no, not a bouquet of roses. One rose at a time.'** Elegant, but unwise, in his usual style. As a result, he did not move to recognise Bangladesh until just before the Islamic Summit meeting in Lahore in February 1974. By then Mujib's hold upon his people's support was slipping, and he finally lacked the power to prevent the army coup during which he was assassinated in August 1975.

But the winning of agreement on Commonwealth membership in April 1972 swiftly opened a route for Bangladesh to request and receive large amounts of multilateral aid. By the rules of the World Bank, it cannot make loans to a country that is not a member of the United Nations or of one of the UN specialised agencies. The first opportunity to secure such a membership came in May when the World Health Organisation held its annual meeting. Health Ministers from Commonwealth countries have traditionally held meetings of their own a day or two before the World Health Assembly opens. I flew to Geneva for this meeting to press the case for Bangladesh, and the Commonwealth ministers agreed to sponsor Bangladesh's admission to the agency, and join me in canvassing support among other countries. WHO, on whose Director-General I paid what was much more than a courtesy call, made generous commitments itself to Bangladesh; an immediate $432,000 in 1972

---

* Diary, 2 October 1972.

** *Bhutto – a Political Biography*, by Salmaan Taseer. Ithaca Press, 1979.

rising to $3 million in 1979. But, more important, the way was open to UN Development Programme and World Bank support. Bangladesh's call for basic help was beginning to be heard.

For an authoritative new view on US involvement, as outlined on pages 138-9, see *'The Tilt Policy revisited: Nixon-Kissinger geopolitics and South Asia'* by Christoper Van Hollen (who was deputy assistant Secretary of State for Near East and South Asian Affairs 1969-72, and United States Ambassador to Sri Lanka 1972-76), in *Asian Survey*, Volume 20, No 4, April 1980.

Chapter 8

FROM CYPRUS TO TUVALU
Membership, Small States and Regional Cooperation

The issue of Commonwealth membership for Bangladesh, a country of 75 million people in 1972, came at one end of the scale. Towards the other end were several countries, often of very small population. Should there be any rules setting the bounds for membership, or should all comers be welcome? Are some countries too small? Should some be excluded for historical reasons? What criteria could there be?

The question whether to impose a minimum population requirement for membership was tackled in 1960. There were then only ten Commonwealth members, with Ghana the single representative of black Africa. But it was foreseen that Cyprus and Malta, with populations of a half-million or less, would soon be independent, and other applications might come from Caribbean islands. So Cabinet Secretaries from member countries were called to a meeting at the British Prime Minister's country home of Chequers, to talk numbers; Bob Bryce went for Canada. They discussed the possible disadvantages of loss of intimacy, uneven representation, different levels of concern. They also acknowledged that the coming of more members would bring the larger countries the advantage of meeting a greater cross-section of opinion, while for the new countries the association would offer a window on the wider world and links with some useful friends. It was the classic argument that must sometime occur in every club. In the Commonwealth there was also the ideal of non-racialism, which the following year would be powerful enough to drive South Africa out the door. The Cabinet Secretaries concluded that the Commonwealth should do nothing to exclude countries for reason of size.

Cyprus joined in 1961, and long afterwards Archbishop Makarios told me one of the reasons why he had been happy to take this step. His people's connections were obviously strongest with two non-

Commonwealth countries, Greece and Turkey; but he wanted a third option rather than have to choose between them, which in effect would mean *enosis* or union with Greece. Commonwealth membership helped him to opt for independence, without explicitly rejecting *enosis* and so alienating the powerful Eoka extremists.

Other countries with a population of less than one million achieved independence from Britain and became full members of the Commonwealth during my first months as Secretary-General: The Gambia in 1965, and then in 1966 Botswana and Lesotho in Africa, and Guyana and Barbados in the Caribbean.

Unlike France, which has maintained *départements d'outre-mer* and arranged that the people of Guadeloupe and Martinique and elsewhere send *deputés* to Paris and receive the same social welfare as Parisians (while in return France now has large claims to offshore minerals in the Pacific and Caribbean), Britain has hastened to shed its smaller dependencies. Malta under Borg Olivier wanted to become an integral part of Britain, and offered many attractions – a Mediterranean base, sunshine for tourists without foreign currency, among others – but the idea was brushed aside, like an embarrassing temptation. (This even though there was by then the success of the Americans' grant of statehood to Hawaii as an example.) The smaller Caribbean islands were sent away by stages, first to an unheated halfway-house called Associated Statehood, with the stricture that they could not return but only move on to full independence, separately or in a federation. Everyone had to stand on his own feet.

When Britain negotiated the concept of Associate Statehood for five Caribbean islands in 1967 (Antigua, Dominica, Grenada, St Kitts-Nevis-Anguilla and St Lucia – St Vincent followed in 1969) this posed a new question of representation at Commonwealth conferences. For they became internally self-governing, leaving Britain responsible for their external affairs and defence.

I wanted to see these Associated States exercise as much autonomy, and engage in as much international consultation, as their premiers desired. So in discussions with Joe Garner at the Commonwealth Office in London during 1967 I took the line that they should be invited to all Commonwealth conferences in fields where they were self-governing – to the annual Finance Ministers Meeting, in particular, but also to trade, medical, educational and legal conferences. And it was so agreed, although the British argued that airlines policy was part of external affairs; this annoyed Eric Williams, who hoped to establish BWIA as the Caribbean regional airline and considered that Britain was using its remaining powers in the Associated States to promote BOAC interests. When Commonwealth countries formed an expert group in 1968 to discuss reduced airfares in the interests of tourism development, it was Britain that spoke for the Associated States.

The concept of Associate Statehood was invented, not by Britain, but by New Zealand in the Cook Islands Constitution Act of 1964. The group of fifteen Cook Islands can by unilateral vote of its legislative assembly become fully independent, but it has chosen to leave external affairs and defence of its 19,000 islanders in the hands of the New Zealand Prime Minister, who acts after consulting the Premier. At the time British civil servants thought New Zealand was setting a dangerous precedent for many of their own colonies but, a few years later, Britain adopted the system in the Caribbean, while stipulating that these states had either to federate or else hold a referendum or further election before moving to full independence.

New Zealand also maintained a liberal stance over the vexed question of Nauru in 1968. A remote coral island on the Equator, closer to the Gilbert Islands (now Kiribati) than to the Solomons but a good distance from either, Nauru had profited from being a restingplace for sea-birds over the centuries. The phosphate deposits – some 60 million tons – gave the 6000 islanders a per capita income as high as that of the United States. But how was Nauru to defend itself if it exchanged its status as a UN Trust Territory (under the joint guardianship of Australia as chairman, Britain and New Zealand) for total independence? It was a rich prize for some modern pirate. The island's chieftain, Hammer DeRoburt, was worried at its vulnerability and approached the Secretariat through my New Zealand special assistant, David McDowell.

He needed independence, he told us, so that he could sell phosphate to the Japanese and others at a proper market price. He had had trouble with the corporation – called the British Phosphate Commissioners, and principally responsible to Australia's Minister of External Territories – which was exploiting the deposits, not only about a price but also over his desire to get them to replace land after strip-mining, rather than offer his people another island in place of their scarred rock. So he wanted to have close links with the Commonwealth, to help the island through such crises, but he recognised that some special form of association would be necessary because of Nauru's tiny size. He foresaw difficulties with the Australians and British, who might claim the right to canvass Commonwealth members on his behalf while themselves being cool, as he feared, to the idea of broad association.

I suggested that, immediately after the independence ceremony in January 1968, he should send me a message applying for membership so that I could do the canvassing without dispute. This he did, on a holding basis, and over the next few months he and the Secretariat designed a new category of Special Member, which meant that its government would not be invited to prime ministerial meetings but could attend any technical and functional meetings and in any case receive all the papers from such conferences. In case of a political crisis involving a threat to Nauru's independence, I told him that he could communicate through the Secretariat with all the Commonwealth Heads of Government and propose emergency consultations. In 1978 Tuvalu (the former Ellice Islands) with a slightly bigger population of 8000 also chose to become a Special Member, while its neighbour Kiribati, with a population of 55,000, requested full membership in 1979.*

Any visit to Nauru is likely to be memorable. I went there some years after independence when Air Nauru had been launched and it was no longer necessary to stay two weeks between flights. Many things were on a grand scale: the especially wide aircraft seats for the big Polynesian frames; the affluence of Nauruan youth with their outboard motors in Anibare Bay and Honda bikes on the perimeter road, while men brought from other islands worked the great flexible shovels that scraped the phosphate from the coral pillars. The President acknowledged as a major problem the easy life enjoyed by his young people, who could attend Australian universities free and not worry to pass exams. He himself was more puritanically inclined. One evening, after giving me a delicious informal dinner, he sat down at an organ and led his Cabinet in singing Methodist missionary hymns. I thought of another of my clients of that time, Ted Heath, an outstanding musician, and I wondered if he had ever tried to orchestrate his Cabinet in this way.

I had some discussion in the late 1960s about several other additions to the Commonwealth, which did not in the end take place. In 1967 I was invited to Nepal as a guest of the Foreign Minister – we had been Ambassadors together in Moscow – and talked to King Birendra and his Prime Minister; they saw advan-

---

* Michael Faber, who as TAG director paid many visits for the Secretariat to these islands that rise no more than a few metres out of the South Pacific, was once asked after a trip there 'How is Tuvalu?' and replied laconically, 'Keeping a low profile.'

tages in membership, but worried about Chinese reactions. There was also an approach from the conservative leader of the South Arabian Federation (Aden and the tribal hinterland) during the period of partial self-government and nationalist struggle which led into civil war. I was asked to visit Aden, as a preliminary to their applying for membership. I had often reflected that it was a pity the Commonwealth had no Arab member – say, the Sudan – but I knew how controversial among the non-aligned members an application from this regime in Aden would be. For its viability was, I thought, doubtful and its real motive seemed to be to gain a defence commitment from Britain which the British Government did not want to give. So I ducked the invitation and told the federalist leader that applications were not normally made before a firm date was fixed for independence. By the time that happened in 1967, his regime had been swept from power. His successors did not apply.

But the most intriguing exploration came with Irish leaders in 1968. Ireland withdrew from the Commonwealth in 1948 because it had decided to become a Republic, and because it did not occur to the Irish Goverment to ask (as Nehru did in 1949) whether the two institutions were compatible. Twenty years later, some top Irish officials were favouring a return to the Commonwealth, I was told. One reason was that they thought it would make it easier for Britain to be conciliatory over Northern Ireland; others, like the former Foreign Minister Sean MacBride, believed it would help Ireland to be more outward looking. Their ambassador in London asked me informally what the best approach should be, for they did not know how either their politicians or the British would react. I said I would make soundings, if they requested me to do so. Whether it was coincidence or officially inspired, I was soon afterwards (in December 1968) invited to be chairman in a debate at Trinity College, Dublin. During the visit I talked with the Taioseach (Prime Minister), Jack Lynch. His view was that an application to rejoin would be too controversial then in the current state of Irish-British relations, but that the time might well come when Commonwealth membership could help the evolution of either a united Ireland or a separate country of Ulster, and reconciliation between Protestants and Catholics there. I told Mike Pearson about this visit, and he was delighted at the thought of an Irish return.

Some senior CRO officials propounded a legalistic criterion, that only British colonies – and that meant excluding protectorates – could apply for Commonwealth membership. This was intellectual and political rubbish. As I argued in my Third Report to Heads of

Government in November 1970, the Commonwealth's significance lay in its heterogeneity balanced by certain common elements – political and legal traditions, some similarities in higher education and techniques of public administration, the ability to use English as a working language – that combined to make discussion among a cross-section of humanity less difficult. Several countries that had never been British colonies would be excellent candidates, in particular Namibia and Papua New Guinea. We will discuss Namibia later, in Chapter 10, and pass on here to Papua New Guinea.

Actually, Papua was a British protectorate for twenty-one years, after the colonial carve-up was confirmed at the Congress of Berlin in 1885. But from 1906 it was administered as an external territory by Australia, which after World War I was also given the mandate to run the League of Nations (and later UN) trust territory of New Guinea, a former German colony. Over the post-war years of Australian administration, the policy had hardly wavered from that of extreme gradualism. The first secondary school was not started until 1957, and the consequent lack of skilled and experienced New Guineans was cited to justify a slow political development.

When I visited Australia in February 1967 and expressed a desire to visit the territories, I was disappointed but not altogether surprised at Canberra's objection. Obviously the Australians worried that a visit by 'Mr Commonwealth' would stimulate ideas of early independence, and they had no plan for that.

John Gorton began the positive shift towards independence with a speech in July 1969; Andrew Peacock was a progressive force as Minister of External Territories from 1971; and, when Gough Whitlam led the Labour Party back to power in December 1972 after an interval of twenty-three years, he told me he was 'deeply ashamed to be the last imperialist power'. He was proposing a high-speed move to independence, with self-government in December 1973 and a target-date for full independence in late 1974. I said I would like to visit PNG, because I had heard that some Australian officials of the old school were advising the PNG politicians that the Commonwealth was not worth joining and I wanted to encourage them to think of applying. Whitlam agreed, and I visited the country for a week in April 1973 togther with CFTC managing director George Kidd and two bright colleagues from Australia and New Zealand, Tony Eggleton and David Caffin. The new Administrator, Les Johnson, was full of progressive ideas and had indeed

159

come to Marlborough House in 1970 when still Assistant Administrator to ask if PNG could have technical assistance from us even though Australia was not then contributing to the CFTC. Naturally I agreed; but, as he told me later, Canberra forbade him to submit any requests at that time.

Papua New Guinea is one of the most fascinating countries in the Commonwealth, as well as being remarkably beautiful. There are other lands which offer a long perspective – in Egypt, for instance, one can gaze back over 2000 years as one explores the agricultural techniques of the villagers – but nowhere is it so long as in PNG. Here perhaps 20,000 years of social living are on view, because some of its people are still back in the Stone Age, existing without the wheel and without agriculture, gathering roots, spearing fish and hunting birds with bows and arrows. As an art collector I was excited by the variety of styles and by the powerful 'presence' in the masks produced by craftsmen who did not separate work, art and religion. While we in 'civilised' countries struggle to regain some wholeness in our lives, these tribal peoples naturally see life whole for they have never divided it into parts.

Enchanting, too, were some of the expressions in Pidgin, which passes for a *lingua franca* among the two-and-a-half million people because most of the country's seven hundred or more languages are mutually unintelligible. I found I was being described as *bik pella Commonwealth blongumeall* (the last four syllables meaning 'our'); and the term for independence – somewhat dismissive of the old-style Australians (whose nationality by ellipsis becomes 'Strine') – was *bik pella Strine piss off*.

There was some foreboding about independence, especially among the majority highland groups who feared it would put them at the mercy of the coastal peoples who had the advantage of receiving earlier missionary schooling. One evening at Goroka a dinner was arranged for our party with two Highland MPs and the local mayor. The MPs were noticeably reluctant to sit with us at all and, although language difficulties prevented me from directly finding out why, I guessed it was that my title of Commonwealth Secretary-General implied 'independence' to them. The mayor, who was more sophisticated as well as better lubricated, consulted them and then delivered me a warning:

'Secretary-General, we are religious people and I want you to know that white men who try to push us into premature independence will burn everlastingly in hell-fire.'

Michael Somare, who as leader of the Pangu Party had headed

the coalition government since 1968 and become Chief Minister in 1972, had his own worries about independence. He feared that the generous resettlement terms Canberra was offering its PNG administrators who opted to come back home would prompt a large exodus of Australians. He knew little about the Commonwealth, but during our talks he swiftly saw several valuable aspects. One was the educational value for his people of seeing CFTC experts – perhaps senior teachers at a training college – who were non-white, and thus realising that education and skills could be developed by people of any nationality and colour. He asked if the Secretariat could provide him, for the Supreme Court, with a non-white judge, expert in common law but trained in taking tribal customs into account; this proved easy. He also hoped to be able to rely on the Secretariat for large-scale technical assistance if there was a considerable exodus of Australians.

I was keen, therefore, to mount a special CFTC programme for Papua New Guinea, even before independence (which was in the event delayed until September 1975). And for 1974-75 the Secretariat had more than thirty-five projects of technical assistance and training there, and put one-sixth of CFTC's total expenditure that year of £3.5 million to this special programme. It involved not only advisers of many nationalities – among others, a Jamaican expert on national accounts and an Indian helping to set up the university's school of animal husbandry – but also a new category of 'operational experts' doing key jobs for one or two years, such as training nurses at rural health centres, and the fourteen New Zealand secondary school teachers who led teams of newly graduated New Guinean teachers. And, as I had hoped, the programme paid a different sort of dividend as well, for both Australia and New Zealand in 1974-75 increased by four times their contributions to the Fund's general resources. So the relatively large PNG programme did not cut into our aid to other developing countries, but helped it grow.

To coordinate this programme I appointed a special representative in Port Moresby, John Kaboha from Uganda. In efforts to encourage both decentralisation from London and regional cooperation, resident representatives were recruited for other regions. The Commonwealth's medical programme was decentralised with a West Africa Health Secretariat set up in Lagos, and a similar Health Bureau followed for East and Central Africa in Arusha. In the Caribbean a health director was appointed to the already existing regional secretariat, CARICOM; and the Vice-Chancellor of the University of Guyana, Dr Dennis Irvine (who happened to be Jamaican), acted as my part-time resident representative to encourage other projects of regional cooperation.

It is sometimes assumed that the Commonwealth and regional organisations are rivals for the loyalty of various countries. In nearly every part of the post-war world some attempt has been made to set up an organisation for regional cooperation and development: the EEC, the Organisation of American States (OAS), the Organisation of African Unity (OAU) and in 1967 the Association of South East Asian Nations (ASEAN). There were Commonwealth countries who had joined, or were qualified to join, each of these regional bodies. Was this a good move, or would it weaken the Commonwealth?

I have always taken the line that there is every advantage to be gained from Commonwealth countries being active in regional associations. I supported Britain's application to join the EEC, at a time of strong opposition from Australia, New Zealand, many African countries and many British Labour Party politicians, because I believed Britain could make Europe more outward looking. The same motive was behind urging Caribbean leaders to join the OAS so that attitudes in that organisation might be broadened a little. In turn this strengthens the Commonwealth for these interlocking memberships increase the Commonwealth's potential to help harmonise the policies and attitudes in different regions, and so help the world move eventually to a global community.

From the earliest days of the Secretariat, I preached that 'Like patriotism, regionalism is not enough.' Maps might suggest that the world's peoples are gathered on land masses and separated by water; but history has shown that the sea is a high road for many people rather than a barrier, and from the ancient Mediterranean civilisations to the modern Commonwealth the links have been made by cheap sea (and now air) communications. There has been logic in helping the smaller Commonwealth states – particularly in the Caribbean and the South Pacific – to build a foundation of cooperation within their own regions. But we tried always to take advantage of the fact that the Commonwealth spans all regions. For example, it was clearly understood that the three regional training centres set up under the Commonwealth Youth Programme would take in trainees as well as instructors from other regions, including the industrialised parts of the Commonwealth. We wanted the advantages and economies of regional cooperation and decentralisation without the potentially costly regional isolationism that could be involved.

Visiting the West Indies was always like going home. An ancestor, who was captain of a merchant ship operating out of Virginia in the 1770s, decided that the American Revolution was not for him. Instead of going north to Canada, as many did under the name of United Empire Loyalists, he put his family on a ship and sailed south to Grenada, where they settled. My own father was born and brought up on Grenada, and used to swear that Grand Anse Bay had the most beautiful beach in all the world. He was not far wrong. (My mother's ancestors, on the other hand, had fought with the American revolutionaries. Both my parents immigrated to Canada, but my North Americanism is balanced and of over two centuries' standing.)

But rivalry in the West Indies has never stopped at simply boasting about a beach. Britain, in its years of undisputed control, never tried to integrate the islands into a single political administration, as it had done with hundreds of millions of people of many language groups in South Asia. The West Indies Federation of ten islands was a brave but belated attempt to cover rivalries, but the thin surface crumbled when Jamaica withdrew in 1961. I remember the dismay I felt during my first visits as Secretary-General after 1965, finding little islands competing ridiculously among themselves for foreign capital and tourist developments, vying to cut off their own noses with tax holidays and other concessions to spite each other's faces.

On a visit to Trinidad in 1966, I talked to Eric Williams about the time when, after Jamaica withdrew, he had refused to try to pull the remaining nine islands together under his leadership into a new association, commenting with throw-away wit, 'ten minus one equals zero'. I said that I admired his aphorism but was not convinced of his judgement on that issue. He did not disagree about the need for more union but said that, if a single state were created, many people from the poorer islands would want to migrate to Trinidad and his people feared they would be swamped. (The West Indies, while wanting easy access for their migrants to Canada and Britain and the United States, have maintained strict controls among themselves.)

But throughout those years Eric Williams was fully aware of the dangers of inadequate cooperation. During a visit to London early in 1969, he said it was probable that such cooperation as still existed

163

after the break-up of the federation was going to come unstuck. He added that it was a pity I could do nothing about the situation. When I replied that maybe I could do something and offered to visit the Caribbean states in May 1969, starting with Guyana, he encouraged me to do so.

On my island-hopping tour of seven of the West Indian states I found that there were several boobytraps immediately ahead, all possibly connected.

The central issue was whether Jamaica would join the proposed Caribbean Development Bank (CDB). When CARIFTA, the Caribbean Free Trade Area, had been established a year before, Jamaica had joined it – and enjoyed a favourable trade balance from the outset with the other ten members, as so often the most advanced member of a free trade area (e.g. in East Africa or West Europe) has done. But it was apparently hanging back from commitment to the CDB for several reasons. It was still not sure whether it would be admitted to a larger grouping, the Organisation of American States, and thereby become able to join the Inter-American Development Bank; it thought the CDB would have only enough resources to help the smaller states; and it was offended that other states had tentatively decided the CDB headquarters should be in Barbados, rather than Jamaica.

This hesitation irked the Associated States, which were receiving little immediate benefit from CARIFTA, and some of their leaders were murmuring that, if Jamaica did not join the CDB, it would be expelled from CARIFTA. (Though this was technically not possible, the smaller states could themselves resign and create a new free trade association, without Jamaica.) As well, there was concern that Jamaica's Finance Minister Edward Seaga was talking about a separate university for his island, which would have meant the breaking up of the University of the West Indies after twenty years of successful growth. Another issue was Trinidad's desire to make its BWIA a regional airline, which carried broad implications for the development of tourism. Jamaica and Barbados wanted their own airlines.

The 'Anguilla affair', which had started in May 1967 when its 6000 people had ejected the St Kitts police and set up its own administration, also lingered on. This was another case of strains in a plural society, for the people of St Kitts-Nevis are mostly descended from plantation workers, and those in Anguilla from pirates and fishermen; their psychology was understandably different. Bradshaw, the St Kitts premier, had not bothered to get adequate Anguillan participation in policy-making. A conciliation mission from the four independent Commonwealth Caribbean governments and a ministerial conference of all interested parties, had both failed to resolve the problem. In March 1969 a British commissioner, supported by paratroops, had landed on a sandy beach and taken charge. It was fun for Fleet Street; but several Caribbean leaders took the affair of 'the mouse that roared' more seriously. If Anguilla could break away from St Kitts-Nevis (geographically it is separated by some 100 kms of water and some French and Dutch islands), then perhaps some day Tobago would split from Trinidad, Cariacou from Grenada and Barbuda from Antigua, or so they told me.

John Compton, the premier of St Lucia – a particularly beautiful island boasting 'the world's only drive-in volcano' – was then working hard on a plan to federate the Associated States. He considered Anguilla was a symptom of a wider malaise, a Caribbean tendency towards disintegration. And beyond that came the question of regional security, with perceived threats ranging from the mafia seeking a sovereign haven from taxes to the USSR wanting submarine bases. Schemes for regional police training and joint military contingents had collapsed with the West Indies Federation and, though Trinidad and Jamaica combined to criticise the British troops landing on Anguilla, there had been no alternative force. What would happen in any future affairs?

No-one was likely to settle all these issues at once, but their inter-relatedness led me to suggest that they should not be tackled piecemeal. Perhaps it would be better to place the future of Anguilla in the larger context of a commission on the future of the six Associated States? Perhaps the issues of CARIFTA, the CDB, the university and the regional airlines would be sorted out more easily if discussed together at a Caribbean Heads of Government meeting? There was some support for a summit meeting of this kind, but various factors prevented it. Among them were the desire of the Associated States premiers to talk first among themselves, and the suspicion in Hugh Shearer's government in Jamaica that any comprehensive talk of regional cooperation could be a prelude to proposals for political integration, which they saw as making Jamaica the milch-cow. Nevertheless, my suggestion did, I believe, help the leaders think in terms of positive trade-offs rather than withdrawals.

In visits in May and again in October 1969, I did my utmost to persuade the Jamaicans and others that they should not think of any regional organisations as mutually exclusive; that it was wise to have overlapping membership of CARIFTA and the OAS, of Commonwealth bodies and those bodies of whom only a minority were Commonwealth states; and that Jamaica would gain from joining both the CDB and the Inter-American Development Bank. The Jamaican position was complicated by the anticipated early retirement of Hugh Shearer. The leading contenders for the succession, Finance Minister Edward Seaga and Trade Minister Lightbourne, had taken up opposed positions on these issues. I worked on all of them, and was glad that Hugh Shearer, after some indecision, came down on the positive side for joining both groups.

In the end, the urgent issues were resolved, the longer term issues were set aside. Jamaica agreed to siting the Bank's headquarters in Barbados, the CDB was successfully launched in October, and CARIFTA survived with all members. The university also remained intact. The Anguilla problem was dealt with in a narrow context; a Commission for which the Commonwealth Secretariat provided the senior staff recommended a middle line – a certain amount of autonomy while remaining linked with St Kitts-Nevis – but the British eventually made it a separate, direct dependency.

Meanwhile, larger scale initiatives have faltered. Attempts to federate four Associated States, or to form a unitary state of five of them with Guyana, or to associate Grenada with Trinidad, all failed. Eric Williams emphasized to me that Trinidad alone could not take on the burden of supporting the smaller islands and absorbing their unemployed youth; but if Britain, Canada and the United States would combine in a special aid programme to help develop the smaller islands, a broad federation or association with Trinidad could, he promised me, be feasible.

So, to give some momentum to this idea of a union among the Windward and Leeward islands, linked with Trinidad and conceivably with Guyana, I tried to persuade Britain, Canada and the United States to see the advantages of a special aid programme. In talks in Washington I argued (in the aftermath of the landing of the Marines in the Dominican Republic) that they could not afford the odium of more military intervention against local regimes, and I suggested, both there and in other capitals, that it would make strategic and political sense to put considerable funds into Caribbean development.

In Ottawa I was given the impression that Canada would contribute to a special Caribbean programme, provided Washington also did so. In the State Department there was some agreement with my analysis, but it was made clear that Congress would not support significant amounts of aid to former British colonies when

Britain and Canada were critical rather than supportive of US military ventures in Indo-China. Indeed, the United States was already retreating into aid cuts and into Nixon's surcharge of ten percent on imports from all sources. So the opportunity was lost of fostering West Indian integration with large-scale outside support, even though a break-up of the existing cooperation was averted.

Almost as a last resort (and because they got no special privileges, in terms of free entry of goods and people, from the connection with Britain), four Associated States took their separate paths to independence and Commonwealth membership in 1974-79. Sonny Ramphal was moved to make a challenging speech, 'On being a West Indian', to a university audience in Trinidad in January 1978* in which he contrasted the giant states there will be in the year 2000 (India with some 1060 million people, Brazil with 215 million) against a still fragmented West Indies: 6¹/₂ million people in the region and a parliamentarian for every 11,000 people, a government minister for every 34,000 and an oil refinery for every 500,000 – and six international airlines. 'Are we really to prepare for the twenty-first century by retreating each into his tiny enclave? . . . Do we believe that, abandoning cooperation among ourselves, we can yet hope to secure the world's cooperation for our separate salvation?'

The Bahamas, as a necklace of seven hundred islands strung off the coasts of Florida and Cuba, has had to seek its own separate salvation. It has done so with all the self-confidence that is encapsulated in the tourism motto, 'It's Better in the Bahamas'. Its Prime Minister, Lyndon Pindling, set a precedent by hosting the Commonwealth Finance Ministers Meeting in 1971, two years before independence. The chartered aircraft that took the ministers on from Nassau to Washington, where they were to attend the World Bank's annual meeting, put down at Freeport for a few hours so that the Bahamians could show the visitors how industries and tourists had flocked to an island that was undeveloped in the mid-1950s.

We were all loaded onto a red doubledecker London bus for an island tour, and the spokesman for the Grand Bahama Promotion Board stood at the front to explain that Freeport had not existed in 1954 but now this new city of canals, built on what had been

* Shridath Ramphal, *One World to Share: Selected Speeches*, Hutchinson Benham, 1979, p 325.

167

uninhabited rock, was set to be 'the Venice of the twenty-first century, without danger of sinking into the sea'. He told us that $2 billion 'has been invested in development here' and more was being negotiated. I was sitting between India's Morarji Desai and Amir Jamal of Tanzania, and heard them gasp. They were shocked at the North American use of the word 'development', which to them meant helping the poor increase their productivity and gradually eliminate poverty, not bringing in new people and opening up empty spaces. Amir Jamal murmured wistfully, 'What could I not do in Tanzania with $2 billion!'

But even the Bahamas had its problems. Pindling's government wanted to maintain after independence the island's attraction as a tax haven. So it turned to the Secretariat for advice on how to increase its revenues without imposing income tax or taxes on capital gains, gifts or inheritances. We were able to send a CFTC expert, and word of this must eventually have reached the Isle of Man. This island, set in the Irish Sea and an ancient haven of missionaries, is not part of the United Kingdom. Instead, it is a Crown possession administered by the British Home Office, but with a considerable degree of self government. Exactly how much is sometimes disputed. An appeal to the Commonwealth Secretariat about offshore radio transmitting stations or ships was, I discovered later, blocked in the Home Office. But its House of Tynwald, the oldest of parliaments, was responsible for the island's tax structure and, during a pleasant springtime visit there with Eve in 1974 as guests of the Speaker, I was asked for technical assistance to turn the Isle of Man into a tax haven alongside Jersey in the Channel Islands. Since it could hardly be considered a developing country, the CFTC could not officially meet such a request; but I believe a tax expert on the Secretariat staff spent some holiday time on the island giving advice.

Commonwealth cooperation in developing tourism as an important earner of foreign exchange that should receive priority in national development plans was explored at a meeting in Malta in 1967 of representatives of twenty-two governments. It launched a working party, which produced schemes of promotional stand-by airfares to increase travel opportunities for young people between member countries; but it proved difficult to move in advance of IATA. Seminars were also held on how small islands could maximise the benefits of tourism while minimising the sociological costs – of family disruption, seasonal unemployment, racial tensions and crime. Attempts were made to help the South Pacific, for example, to learn the lessons of the Caribbean. I remember watching the superbly natural hula dancing, when the Queen opened an international airport in the Cook Islands, and wondering how long before the ill-effects of a tourist drive would be plain.

The special problems of small states have been a major concern of the Commonwealth Secretariat, both in my time and later under Ramphal. Ed Dommen, who had been among the original foursome in the Secretariat's technical assistance team, drew on a decade's experience to write the wide-ranging paper on these special problems for the Finance Ministers Meeting in 1977.

That meeting was held in Barbados and the host prime minister, Tom Adams, gave it proper prominence, so that the subject became an important issue at the first Asia-Pacific Heads of Government Regional Meeting in Sydney in 1978, and later an item discussed for a half-day session by the full Heads of Government in Lusaka in 1979. They listened to eloquent speeches by the Prime Ministers of Fiji and Grenada and by President René of the Seychelles, and in their Lusaka communiqué agreed that 'special measures of support were required . . . to offset the disadvantages of small size, isolation and scarce resources'; they pointed in particular to the need for specialist assistance in helping them take advantage of the new potential, the mineral and fish resources within their 200-mile exclusive economic zones.

Is there a danger that these small states, in their growing numbers and with their special concerns, will crowd out the bigger countries at HGMs? This fear has been regularly expressed as the numbers rose to the point where in 1980 there were twenty-five of the forty-four Commonwealth members with populations of under two million people. But experience thus far has not borne out these fears; they have not turned the old intimate gatherings into an unwieldy crowd. When some delicate diplomacy has been required, as over Rhodesia during the Lusaka HGM, half-a-dozen leaders have retreated in a group by themselves. When world issues are discussed, most of the leaders of smaller states are pleased to listen rather than speak.

Happily there are exceptions. The Commonwealth gives scope for leaders of great talent, who happen to have been born in small countries, to play the part they deserve. To give only three examples, from different regions of the Third World: Lee Kuan Yew of Singapore, Seretse Khama of Botswana and Sonny Ramphal of Guyana have all been able to contribute in a Commonwealth setting so much more than they could have done, if they had relied only on

169

their standing as representatives of one tiny country on the world stage.

And regional cooperation, despite the political stalling in the Caribbean and elsewhere, has advanced in many parts. An outstanding example was the initiative of the Sydney CHGRM in February 1978 and the functional collaboration between twelve Asian and Pacific countries that sprang from it.* And ministerial meetings on a pan-Commonwealth basis have also helped launch practical programmes on a regional basis, while at the same time producing an exchange of ideas between regions. To tell something of the origins of the Commonwealth Youth Programme (CYP) will illustrate this point.

In January 1969 there was a lukewarm reception at the Heads of Government Meeting for a British Government paper suggesting that the Secretariat make a series of studies of youth questions and then organise a conference at ministerial level to plan increased cooperation. The Australian foreign minister thought UNESCO was doing all that was needed internationally; the Indian minister of state said that ideas about youth varied too much from country to country for any international action; and the Malawi high commissioner argued that his country had worked hard to inculcate its Young Pioneers with a renewed respect for chiefs and rural life, and he thought any generalised cooperation could undermine these values. Only Milton Obote spoke up strongly for some sort of Commonwealth youth programme, partly (he said) 'to bring up the young to understand the horizons and magnitude of the Commonwealth'.

But the Secretariat's Education Division had already been studying the special problems of out-of-school youth in some countries which were giving priority to programmes designed to involve young people directly in development; and we were encouraged after the HGM to hold regional seminars on this subject in Kenya and Trinidad in 1969-70. To these meetings we invited, not government delegates, but individuals with expertise in youth organisation and training; and the reports of these seminars (*Youth and Development in Africa* and *Youth and Development in the Caribbean*)** were so well received that some of the earlier doubters were convinced by 1971 that cooperation in this field would be useful.

A specialist conference on Education in Rural Areas, held in

---

* See Chapter 13 for Australia's initiative.

** Available from the Information Division, Commonwealth Secretariat.

Ghana during the same period with delegates from twenty-three Commonwealth countries, dealt with the problem that even primary school education (which every government hoped to make universal after independence) tended to make students dissatisfied with traditional village life and encouraged a drift to the cities. So when the Fifth Commonwealth Education Conference met in Canberra in February 1971, the goverments had important evidence in front of them of the common nature of these problems and the usefulness of collaboration. They asked the Secretariat to organise a meeting of Commonwealth officials to prepare the way for a ministerial meeting on youth matters, and out of that second meeting (in Lusaka in January 1973) came plans for the Commonwealth Youth Programme. But before the ministers made their decision, a further regional seminar was held for member countries in Asia and the Pacific in 1971, and special seminars for Malta and Cyprus in 1972.

This process may seem laborious, but it ensured that the concerns of all countries were studied in detail and in comparison with other countries, and that the eventual programme was well founded on full consultation. Most of the countries that were initially cool to the CYP did in the process warm to the idea of cooperation; indeed, India offered facilities so that one of the three regional centres could be established at Chandigarh. And, through the pattern of alternating regional seminars with Commonwealth-wide conferences to arrive at a programme which is then regionally based, the CYP began with the benefit of ideas cross-fertilised from other regions.

The Mediterranean is one area that does not fall into any particular region for Commonwealth functional cooperation. Malta has made good use of CFTC experts, especially since its government embarked on a large expansion of its ship-repairing and shipbuilding industry. Cypriot youth leaders have gone for training to the regional centre in Lusaka. And Cyprus and Malta have both taken a distinctive lead in cultural activities in the Commonwealth. The 'Viva Malta!' group's initiative in an early arts festival was the original inspiration for the Edmonton Arts Festival that spectacularly matched the Commonwealth Games in 1978, and Cyprus in August 1980 imaginatively pioneered the first Commonwealth film festival, inaugurated in an ancient Roman open-air amphitheatre with a Zambian drummer and Chinese dancers from Hong Kong. Such is the Commonwealth, full of surprises!

The strategic location of Cyprus in the eastern Mediterranean has meant that at least five outside powers – Britain, the United States and the Soviet Union as well as Greece and Turkey – are concerned in any moves to settle the island's future. By 1964 Archbishop Makarios was dependent on a United Nations peacekeeping force, after fighting had broken out between Greeks and Turks, and a UN Mediator was at work on the first of several settlement plans. I visited Cyprus twice during 1970, and was particularly worried that the younger people in each community were growing up as strangers to each other in a population of only half a million; there was also the disparity between the prosperous Greek parts and the run-down state of many Turkish-Cypriot areas, where people were dependent on remittances from Turkey.

I talked to Makarios about the possibility of launching some joint ventures in manufacturing and light industry between Greek and Turkish Cypriots; and he agreed in principle, providing Denktash the Turkish Cypriot leader also approved. I put the proposition to Denktash, who hesitated for some time and finally turned it down, apparently on instructions from Turkey. Which was a pity, because it was as opportune a time as any for positive action, with EOKA leader George Grivas out of the country and with Greek and Turkish communities still sprinkled together in many parts of the island, a situation that vanished after the polarising events of 1974.

A Commonwealth effort was more successful in the case of Gibraltar, which is not a full member but a British colony since the eighteenth century. At the height of Spanish pressure to incorporate Gibraltar, the British Government decided to hold a referendum among its 27,000 people in September 1967 and invited me to arrange a team of four Commonwealth observers. I appointed to this team ambassadors from New Zealand and Kenya who had postings in Europe, a senior lawyer from Jamaica and a top Pakistani civil servant, asking each to act in a personal capacity, not on instructions from his government. They spent ten days on the limestone Rock and their unanimous report, stating that the secret ballot and the conduct of the referendum allowed free expression of choice, helped reinforce the dramatic ninety-nine percent vote in favour of remaining with Britain and separate from Spain. It was a modest effort, but proved to be a useful precedent for urging that a joint Commonwealth group of observers from several countries should cover the elections in Zimbabwe in February 1980 and in Uganda in December 1980.

Another British colony, naturally of interest to the Secretariat although it will never probably become a full Commonwealth member, is Hong Kong. It was not until March 1972 that the Peoples Republic of China took steps to reassure Britain that it would not make any hasty moves over Hong Kong, even though it has repudiated the treaties under which Britain acquired it during the nineteenth century. But it had for years attended meetings of the Commonwealth Finance Ministers, as well as a number of educational conferences. I visited Hong Kong in January 1974, on the way to the Commonwealth Games in New Zealand, to talk to the political leaders there about taking a fuller part in the activities of the CFTC. I found a good response, and since then the Commonwealth connections have grown. Hong Kong has not only hosted the Finance Ministers Meeting (in September 1976) and several seminars in multilateral trade negotiations during the Tokyo round, but it has begun to play a considerable role in the CFTC as contributor both of funds and experts.

The number of South Pacific members of the Commonwealth grew swiftly. During 1970 Western Samoa, Tonga and Fiji all joined the Commonwealth, in time to play a significant part in the trade negotiations that led to the Lomé Convention, which will be described in the next chapter. For any traveller on the world's air routes, the extra time it takes to reach these South Pacific islands has always been compensated for by the great hospitality and the exotic feasts the islanders offer visitors – the suckling pigs and the local 'caviar', *palolo*, that rises over certain coral reefs at a magic moment each year after the second equinox. It may be these attractions that have drawn the attention of many Secretariat staff and CFTC advisers to this region, but if so it is well disguised or mixed with a concern for the special problems of development in small isolated communities. As four more island states moved to independence and Commonwealth membership – the Solomon Islands and Tuvalu in 1978, Kiribati in 1979 and Vanuatu (formerly the New Hebrides) in 1980 – the concern properly increased.

The amount of regional cooperation in the South Pacific is already impressive. The University of the South Pacific, from its main campus in Fiji and under a Vice-Chancellor, James Maraj, who is provided as an 'operational expert' through the CFTC and was formerly my Assistant Secretary-General, is a focal point for many forms of cooperation between the islands, including distance learning through the Peacesat radio satellite links. Another focal point is the South Pacific Commission, whose main concern is to coordinate economic development. But the diversity of cooperation goes beyond a few organisations to fit all kinds of situations: the sending in 1980 of some Papua New Guinea troops to Vanuatu to help police the islands after a miniature but awkward rebellion was a well publicised example. Many CFTC advisers on assignment to one country find themselves carrying out tasks through the region, whether it is a plant protection expert, Dr Edwin Dharmaraju, seeking an antidote to the threat of the coconut stick insect or a lawyer-turned-insurance-expert, Dr Ranjan Amerasinghe, who has helped nearly all the islands draft their insurance legislation.

Prospects have recently brightened for many small states. Not only have some of these island and coastal states gained a potentially huge inheritance with the declaration of sovereignty over 200-mile exclusive economic zones (EEZ), but oil companies are prospecting in offshore areas or remote parts where it was previously not profitable to do so. The Technical Assistance Group (TAG) of the CFTC has been quick once again to help the smaller countries take advantage of these changes; first, with advice on fisheries management and then more intensively with help to governments dealing for the first time with valuable energy minerals, both oil and uranium. After successful work with the Tanzanian Government in drafting legislation on hardrock minerals and in negotiating over uranium with a West German company, TAG found itself with similar requests from all parts of the developing Commonwealth – from Bangladesh and Cyprus, Botswana and Barbados, Grenada and the Solomon Islands. TAG can itself be a channel for one small country helping another, for the New Zealand Treasury has seconded to this team a succession of mid-career experts in taxation questions who in gaining wider experience for themselves are worth their weight in gold to the countries they advise.

Twenty years on from the Chequers meeting to decide what to do about small states in the Commonwealth, the question is being cheerfully answered. They are able to do a good deal to help themselves and each other, with some imaginative support from the Secretariat.

174

Chapter 9
DEALING WITH EUROPE
Teaming up for the Lomé Convention

Two important challenges were posed to the Secretariat after 1969 in building bridges outwards for the Commonwealth. One was to make links with its francophone counterpart, l'Agence de coopération culturelle et technique (ACCT), which was set up in 1969-70. The other was to help the developing countries of the Commonwealth bargain for the best terms of association with the European Community after Britain's entry into the EEC.

Bridging was all the more difficult because of the different approaches of Britain and France to the disposal of their empires. The independent Commonwealth states, having been sent briskly on their road by the 'mother country', were suspicious of the ways in which France tried to keep her former colonies in the family circle with all sorts of ties – military pacts, reciprocal trade obligations, technical assistance programmes – that put French officials into key positions in African ministries. For their part, the French and some of their leading protégés like President Senghor of Senegal found difficulty in understanding the looser Commonwealth pattern. Coming from a country of both British and French parentage, I thought the work of trying to span this gulf particularly important.

I had spent a year, soon after the battle of Dien-Bien-Phu, as an International Truce Commissioner in Indo-China; and after Suez nearly three years as Canadian Ambassador to the United Arab Republic at the point when that parish included Syria. But my own first involvement with the French post-imperial system as a whole was in 1963, when after three years in Moscow I came back to External Affairs as Assistant Under-Secretary of State, supervising the Divisions handling Canada's relations with Africa and Europe, as well as the Middle and Far East. I was shocked to find that about ninety-six percent of Canada's aid programme went to Commonwealth countries, although nearly one-third of the country's tax-payers were French-speaking. There was then not a single Canadian diplomatic mission in any francophone country in Africa. I joined Marcel Cadieux, the Under Secretary of State, in urging that this imbalance be corrected at once.

Early in 1964 Mike Pearson was persuaded that it would be both courteous and politic to speak personally to de Gaulle on the subject of a Canadian aid programme in francophone Africa, to assure him that it was being planned not as a challenge to French influence but simply from a desire to support the assistance already in hand. An official visit to Paris was arranged, and that first meeting was a *tête-à-tête dans l'intimité*, which meant that de Gaulle and Pearson met with only one adviser-interpreter each, while Paul Martin as External Affairs Minister went with Cadieux to a separate meeting with the French Foreign Minister. So I accompanied Mike to this meeting in the Elysée Palace, where de Gaulle opened the conversation with words of poetic balance:

> 'Monsieur le premier ministre, je veux vous assurer que la France est pour un Canada fort et uni, parce que seul un Canada fort et uni saura faire face aux États-Unis.'

It sounded very reassuring at the time, especially when he added a promise of cooperation in West Africa. But, as we thought over his words later (especially his emphasis on the two-edged conjunction *parce que*), we saw the threat they carried: that, if Canada was not sufficiently anti-American, he would cease to see usefulness in its unity. It fitted in with his later support for Quebec separatism, and his support for Biafra, in that his instinct in world politics (learnt, perhaps, as a young captain fascinated with tank warfare) was to cause splintering in regions or countries – especially in the English-speaking world, whether in North America or Nigeria, or in Anglo-American relations – whose size he saw as an obstacle to the expansion of his own influence.

Canada's relationship with francophone countries in Africa and Asia began to change rapidly. Pierre Dupuy, the former Canadian Ambassador in Paris, toured many of them to prepare the ground for new missions, while in Ottawa plans were made for stepped-up recruitment. By 1967-68 the bilateral aid programme for francophone Africa had grown to $8 million (today it is more than $130 million) and Canada had become active on this different stage.

In my 1965 'election speech' to the Canadian Universities Society of Great Britain, I reflected on this and other changes produced by Quebec's 'quiet revolution' led by Jean Lesage, a man I had known and greatly admired when we both worked in Ottawa in 1963-65.

'The most exciting single development in Canada these days is the surging renaissance – cultural, educational, industrial, and political – of Quebec . . . In my own field of international politics, not many years ago, the pressures from Quebec on Ottawa were largely negative – to avoid this entanglement and spurn that commitment. Today these pressures are positive, and impatient . . . Why do we not join the Organisation of American States? Why have Canadian aid programmes been so largely concentrated on English-speaking countries? These are good questions. Speaking personally, I welcome these pressures!'

It was in this spirit that I faced the question of what links the Secretariat should make with l'Agence in 1969.

Although the concept of *la francophonie*, or closer relations between French-speaking peoples, was first written about by the geographer and anarchist Elisée Reclus in the 1880s, it was not until the late 1960s that any organisational plans began to be made; and the movement then started with African leaders rather than with France. But already a network of parliamentary and professional organisations had grown up, among them l'Association des universités partiellement ou entièrement de langue français (AUPELF), with a well-known Quebec journalist Jean-Marc Léger as its founder-secretary. As well, francophone ministers – of education, youth, justice and so on – had begun holding regular meetings after about 1967; they were normally serviced by French civil servants working with the host government.

In the drive towards setting up an organisation similar to the Commonwealth Secretariat, various tendencies were at work. Senghor, as a member of the Academie Française, was more interested in cultural aspects than in economic cooperation. The latter concern was represented by Hamani Diori, the Niger President who was also president of l'Organisation commune africaine et malagache (OCAM), the fourteen-member grouping of sub-Sahara states. President Habib Bourguiba of Tunisia was talking then of a 'French Commonwealth', and was particularly interested in development assistance and pragmatic cooperation.

In the months before the first Niamey conference took place in February 1969, there were mixed views in Ottawa about how Canada should deal with the prospect of l'Agence. The shout by President de Gaulle from the balcony of Montreal City Hall of *'Vive le Québec libre!'* in 1967 had reverberated across continents. Early in 1968 there had been clashes over the status of Quebec's representation at an education minister's meeting in Gabon which French officials organised and to which the Canadian federal government was not even invited. Certain officials in Ottawa were worried that de Gaulle was going to use *la francophonie* and l'Agence to goose Canada over Quebec and for that reason seemed inclined to play down, even try to sabotage, l'Agence. Although I was no longer a Canadian official, I made clear to Ottawa my strong belief that the right and prudent course was for the Canadian Government to do its utmost to support l'Agence enthusiastically and to become influential in it.

Hesitation between the two 'options' in Ottawa lasted past the January 1969 HGM and prevented an expected pledge of $10 million by Pierre Trudeau to launch the CFTC, because these officials did not want to give an equivalent amount to the ACCT. Within the next few weeks, however, Trudeau decided to go strongly for Canadian federal participation in l'Agence and to that end began to sweeten President Diori, host of the conference, with talk of a substantial Canadian aid programme in his country.

So the first Niamey conference went smoothly. As *Le Monde* noted, there was goodwill on all sides in the Niger capital when thirty delegations approved a resolution to create an agency for cultural and technical cooperation and when the Quebec delegation proposed Jean-Marc Léger as provisional secretary-general, with the task of bringing detailed proposals to a second Niamey conference in March 1970.

I sent Léger a telegram of congratulations, suggesting we should meet, and received a friendly reply. Although his Quebec separatist views were well known, I hoped that he would see his new job in terms of global integration, rather than as an opportunity for disintegration. I wrote at the time:

'I attach tremendous importance to encouraging the development of *la francophonie* in the direction of seeing the main goal as practical cooperation across the lines of race, wealth and poverty, and geography: I hope we can work in parallel and cooperate.'

This was not the attitude in Ottawa, however. In mid-April I was faced with a message from External Affairs Minister Mitchell Sharp, written in suspiciously impeccable French, suggesting that it would be dangerous to want to make too close a parallel between the well established, relatively stable Commonwealth and the ill defined *francophonie* that was still in a state of gestation. In particular, Sharp wrote, Canada 'with most African states' hoped to keep the proposed organisation apolitical. The African states wanted to use it mainly for diversifying their sources of aid; and Canada feared that a political organisation would offer too handsome an opportunity for French intervention in Canadian domestic problems. 'Quebec itself would perhaps find it difficult to resist the temptation of using *la francophonie* as a political instrument.' Mitchell Sharp ended by hoping that I would be 'very circumspect' in my dealings with Léger, and adding a veiled threat that any 'bidding up' (*surenchère*) between l'Agence and the Commonwealth Secretariat could create serious difficulties for Canada 'from which the Secretariat itself could suffer'.

Far from blackmail or reciprocal 'bidding up' for Canadian aid, I felt that Léger's new agency and mine offered great opportunities for Canada to reach out from its lonely corner. No other country had more to lose if the world became frozen into separate continental blocs; and bridges across to other continents were especially valuable to Canada. In the end, this view was echoed in Ottawa.

Meanwhile, Léger and I went ahead to forge links. We compared notes about organisations when he and an assistant visited London for three days in November 1969. He made an interesting distinction between the two associations in saying that, while the Commonwealth had first had a sense of community and then, through the establishment of the Secretariat, had acquired a formal identity, the opposite process was occurring in the case of l'Agence: it was being created as a legal entity and it would then try to create a greater sense of community between the French-speaking countries.

He was scrupulous in noting that, as the name of the Agency implies, it was not envisaged that *la francophonie* would be a forum for political exchange. Indeed, he spent little time with my political officers and showed much greater interest in my functional divisions and in the work with professional organisations sponsored by the Commonwealth Foundation. He asked why the Foundation was a separate structure from the Secretariat and, when the plans for ACCT were completed in 1970, one of the five integral institutions was a Consultative Council made up of non-governmental people who would make recommendations for ACCT activities outside the governmental field. In turn the Council working with its associated NGOs might organise conferences or publications on behalf of the

Agency. It is an original idea, which has some advantages over the looser Commonwealth pattern.

The second Niamey conference was overshadowed by the messy tussle between France and Canada over Quebec's status. The Canadian delegation included representatives from three other provincial governments besides Quebec, to show that French was spoken broadly across the country. This, together with the fact that Canada was prepared to pay one-third of the Agency's budget as well as to finance a large road-building project in the host country of Niger, swung support to its viewpoint; and it was agreed that only sovereign states could sign the convention setting up the ACCT, but Quebec could become a 'participating government' and sign the Charter annexed to the convention.

The French presidency could not for long have thought it possible to use Léger for its own purposes to split Canada. For during 1969 the Gaullists discovered that Léger was no puppet and had his own, completely honourable, ideas for the future of l'Agence as the servant of all its member states. Significantly, in the *avant-propos* of the ACCT's draft convention, Léger stated that the organisation should not be at the service of the French language, but rather should be in the interest of cooperating through the medium of the French language. Paris also disliked his expansive view of the future functions of l'Agence on the technical cooperation side, which corresponded with the Commonwealth Secretariat ambitions and with the mellowing Canadian attitude towards both. So at the second Niamey conference the French were eager to replace Léger with an African nominee as Secretary-General, and only reluctantly accepted him for a four-year term. But they managed to cut his proposed budget for 1970-71 by forty-five percent.

I had an excellent meeting with Léger in Paris in July 1970, snatching a day from the crisis over arms sales to South Africa and from the Commonwealth Games in Edinburgh. He had with him his two Deputy Secretaries-General, from France and Senegal. We talked about differences in our resources and functions: l'Agence was ahead of us with a multilateral fund for projects, but it was inhibited from much economic work and entirely from political affairs. Rather than competitive athletics like the Commonwealth Games, the ACCT hoped to stage a festival in which all countries could participate on some basis of equality – athletics certainly, but also poetry, theatre, ballet and handiwork, and a gathering place of young people. Indeed, the Commonwealth itself made lively efforts in this direction: first the 1965 Commonwealth Arts Festival in

London, and much later Festival 78, the arts and culture programme of the XI Commonwealth Games in Edmonton, Alberta.

We also talked about our similar programmes and concerns: in book production, teacher exchanges, tourism. Léger had organised an adventurous expedition of young people in Upper Volta, and asked about hiring a ship for educational cruises, as the Royal Commonwealth Society had done, or as the Comex organisation of Colonel Lionel Gregory had done with intercontinental buses and train, for hundreds of Commonwealth youth. He also had hopes of launching a satellite, from which French-language programmes could be beamed to the Caribbean and North Africa as well as West Africa, New Brunswick and Quebec. I commented how important it was to go beyond regional cooperation and the 'continental land-mass approach', and Léger replied:

> 'Our two Secretariats are fighting the same battle. We in *l'Agence* have entered the field more recently, but the battle is not being fought any less keenly.'*

French opposition in the early years made progress in joint programmes much slower and more tentative than Léger or I had hoped. I visited l'Agence headquarters in Paris again in September 1974 to meet Léger's successor, Professor Dankoulodo Dan Dicko, a former Minister of Education in Niger, and he paid a return three-day visit to Marlborough House in December. This second visit caused some fluttering of suspicions among French officials and, the very next day, Xavier Deniau called on me in his capacity as chairman of a French government committee on *francophonie*. He was concerned to learn what he could do about any plans Dan Dicko had made with us, and also about the Secretariat's activities in international (i.e. political) affairs; he asked how often member states withheld support from our activities. I pressed the argument that some practical cooperation between the Secretariats would

---

* My assistant and good friend, Noël Salter, who was taking notes of the meeting, added in his account: 'I sat back at this point and suddenly saw a vision of two old countries, England and France, who were resolved not to see their cultures disappear but, realising that in future these would have to be on a multilateral rather than a bilateral basis, were "seeking to maintain" cooperation through essentially Anglophone and Francophone agencies; and that for this work it was not Englishmen or Frenchmen who were leading the work, but two Canadians coming from a country which uniquely represented the bringing together of the English and the French traditions within a single country. I found this dialogue across the table between two Canadians symbolic.'

finally dispose of the charge that the Commonwealth and *la francophonie* were attempts to perpetuate the division of Africa. He said he agreed.

Dan Dicko himself said he wished Léger had been politically able to take initiative in more fields, and he was particularly thinking of remodelling their youth programme along the lines of the CYP in linking the training with national development. We also talked about cooperation in language training, and this went ahead. From 1976 the CFTC has provided one hundred scholarships a year for university lecturers and teachers from the Gambia, Ghana, Nigeria and Sierra Leone to attend six- to eight-week courses in French language training in Lomé, Togo. And in February 1979, after return visits between the two Secretariats, plans were made for closer cooperation in youth work and scientific activities, including post-harvest technology and alternative energy.

The relationship between l'Agence and the Commonwealth Secretariat has been sunny, whereas it might have been clouded with mutual suspicions. We should pass now to a story which began with deep suspicions but ended in useful cooperation: the transforming of developing countries' trade-and-aid association with the EEC from the Yaoundé Convention, which had several partly concealed but dangerous disadvantages, to the improved Lomé Convention.

From my first months as Secretary-General, I preached that British entry into the European Community should be good for the Commonwealth.

I had indeed consistently urged on my British colleagues the view that Britain should be part of a European Community, starting in the 1950s, when I was Counsellor in the Embassy in Brussels (and West Europeans hoped Britain would join the Coal and Steel Community) and then when I was Canadian Minister in the High Commission in London at the time when most West Europeans wanted Britain to join in the negotiations that led to the Treaty of Rome in 1957. Britain could of course have written her own ticket and avoided the problems later posed by the Common Agricultural Policy.

In June 1971, in both an article in *Crossbow*, the Bow Group's magazine, and an interview with Louis Heren of *The Times*,* I argued that Europe and the Commonwealth were not alternatives

---

* *The Times,* London, 25 June 1971, page 1.

for Britain, but could be complementary and mutually supporting. But there were plenty of despondent voices. On the same day, 25 June, *The Times* reported a gloomy speech by the Australian High Commissioner, Sir Alexander Downer, who forecast a rash of ill effects: a decline in mutual trade and investment, a withdrawal of reserves from Britain, job discrimination against Commonwealth citizens, a general loss of goodwill. If all this happens, he concluded, 'As inevitable as rain in the English summer, the whole Commonwealth association will weaken to the point of becoming an empty shell.'

In May 1972, after Britain (with Denmark and Ireland) had signed the Treaty of Accession, when it was waiting to enter the EEC in January 1973, I enlarged on my view in a speech to the Foreign Press Association:

'With British entry, Europe has the opportunity of 'tuning in' to this ready-made international network encompassing almost a quarter of the world. In its turn the Commonwealth has an unprecedented opportunity for closer relationships with Europe, and with the Francophone countries.

'As a Canadian, as a Commonwealth man and as a friend of Africa, I rejoice at the dramatic revival of the *entente cordiale*. I hope we shall now see the best of the liberal traditions of both Britain and France reinforcing one another, to develop generous and forward-looking relations between Europe and the other continents.'

But there was to be a good deal of illiberal manoeuvring in 1972-73 before the *entente* spread beyond the nine to draw in the forty-six associate members from Africa, the Caribbean and the Pacific (ACP) through the Lomé Convention in 1975.

Within four months of Edward Heath's crucial visit to Paris in May 1971 to win from President Georges Pompidou the approval for British entry that de Gaulle had denied Harold Macmillan in 1963, the Commonwealth Secretariat was plunged into technical and inevitably political work on the consequences. For the Commonwealth Finance Ministers at their meeting in Nassau in September 1971 invited the Secretariat 'to study and prepare papers on the issues which would arise for consideration by those Commonwealth countries to which the offer of association has been made'. I was particularly happy to take on this work because I believed that the advice the Secretariat could offer the twenty 'associables' would be a major example of the functional cooperation and technical assistance in which the Commonwealth was beginning to excel.

So it turned out. Hunter Wade, who had acquired a practical knowledge of the world economic scene as New Zealand's Ambassador to Japan before joining the Secretariat as Deputy Secretary-General, worked closely with me and D. K. Srinivasachar, director of our Economic Affairs Division, in marshalling the Secretariat's own expertise. The Secretariat supplied the 'associables' with papers on a range of commodities including beef, cocoa, coffee, sugar, jute and pineapples, and on several other issues including the implications of the Generalised System of Preferences (GSP). Aware that grave and legitimate controversy might be stirred on the issues among various parts of the Commonwealth, I made a particular point of arranging contracts as consultants with top economists from three different regions – Professor Alister McIntyre from the Caribbean, H.M.A. Onitiri from Nigeria and Dharam Ghai from East Africa – to contribute to these studies and to two meetings that we convened in London of officials from the twenty capitals of the 'associables' (and ten other interested countries) in April and July 1972, when we discussed these subjects in depth.

The Commonwealth countries that did not receive an 'offer of association' under Protocol 22 of the Treaty of Accession fall into two groups: the three developed countries – Canada, Australia and New Zealand – and the five Commonwealth countries in Asia.

Of the three developed countries, Canada had the smallest adjustment to make, because by then no more than eight percent of its exports went to Britain. For New Zealand it was a much bigger problem, as in 1971 Britain was buying ninety percent of its butter and its lamb exports and eighty percent of its cheese. Throughout the sixties its government worked quietly to diversify its markets and without exaggeration to plead its case for special treatment. Australia went through a period of opposing the whole idea of Britain joining the EEC, but by the time that Whitlam took power its government more calmly acknowledged that the country had been given enough time for adjustment.

The brush-off by the EEC of the five countries in Asia was more perturbing. Bangladesh needed all the help it could get to recover from the devastation of the war, while the other four – India, Sri Lanka, Malaysia and Singapore – seemed to be paying the penalty of having actually achieved a significant measure of development.

For the reason why they were excluded from the list of 'associables' in Protocol 22 was succinctly given to me by a French cabinet minister whom I met by chance at a private dinner while on a holiday at 'Aux Anjeaux', the farm in Aquitaine that my wife and I had bought in 1967 as a country hide-away. He said there was no question of their being allowed free entry into the EEC 'because they produce manufactured goods, and they would get American-style technology and management, and with cheap Asian labour they would flood the European market.' In other words, those countries that could take real advantage of the free entry into the EEC market that association involved were to be excluded from it.

We did a broad study of the implications of British entry for each of the five countries. It would mean the end for them of the British preferences to which they had for years been accustomed. We argued for generosity by the EEC in applying its GSP to Asian manufactures and (especially for Singapore as an entrepôt trading state) and for generosity over rules of origin. In my speech to the Foreign Press Association in May 1972 I recalled that the Asian countries were covered in the Treaty of Accession by a joint (but vague) declaration of interest on the development of trade relations and added: 'We trust that the enlarged Community will recognise that its responsibilities toward Asia are no less important than those toward Africa.' And certainly the EEC has developed its trade with the five countries (including Singapore and Malaysia) in ASEAN.

Sugar was a major and special issue in the EEC negotiations from the start of Britain's own bargaining about its entry. In May 1971 the British Government secured from the EEC something less than a 'bankable guarantee' on behalf of the Commonwealth sugar producers. The French text – that the enlarged Community *'aura à coeur de sauvegarder'* – was officially translated eventually as 'will have as its firm purpose to safeguard' the interests of Commonwealth developing countries whose economy depended heavily on sugar exports. Ten Commonwealth countries – seven in the Caribbean, plus Mauritius, Swaziland and Fiji – fell in this category, and they had hoped that Britain would have been able to secure a generous quota for them from the outset. As it turned out, the British tactics were probably wise, for Britain would not in 1971 have won these producers the quota of 1.4 million tons it finally gained in 1974-75.

It is time to set out on the board the main players in the 'Protocol 22 negotiations' in 1972-73.

First, there are the eighteen Yaoundé 'associates' in July 1969. They called themselves the Associated African and Malagasy States (AAMS) and they had a coordinating council in Brussels with the chairman's post rotating every six months and a Secretary-General from Mali, S. D. Sylla. His nationality is significant because, while fourteen of these countries also belonged to the OCAM and had particularly close ties with France, Mali and three others (Burundi, Mauritania and Somalia) did not. President Léopold Senghor of Senegal was the current president of OCAM, and Mali's relations with its coastal neighbour Senegal had been cool since the failure of a federation ten years before. As I discovered, Sylla and Senghor had differing views on the best form of association to succeed Yaoundé II.

Of the twenty Commonwealth 'associables' listed in Protocol 22, there were the four independent Caribbean States (Barbados, Guyana, Jamaica and Trinidad), three from the South Pacific (Fiji, Tonga and Western Samoa) and thirteen from Africa. The last group has to be subdivided further. Mauritius was in mid-1972 on the point of signing Yaoundé II.* Three East African states – Kenya, Uganda and Tanzania – had signed their own Arusha Convention with the EEC in 1969. Nigeria had signed its own Lagos Convention in July 1966, but, in the turmoil preceding the outbreak of the civil war, it was never ratified, and Nigeria's relations with France soured over French support of Biafra. Finally, the three southern African states – Botswana, Lesotho and Swaziland – had a particular problem through being part of a customs union with South Africa (since 1911). During 1972 we sent a Secretariat team to advise them on ways to reconcile these obligations with any possible EEC arrangements.

I was myself far from happy with the restrictions placed on the offer of association. For Protocol 22 listed only three options: a Yaoundé-type convention, a convention on the Arusha model, or a simple trade agreement dealing with specific products. The Arusha Convention was essentially a commercial treaty, and lacked the technical and financial assistance provided through the European Development Fund (EDF) to the Yaoundé group (which was worth $730 million during the Yaoundé I period of 1965-69 and a prom-

---

* Since it did sign during 1972 and began meeting with the Yaoundé associates, the number of the 'associables' is sometimes given as nineteen, and the associates' number increased to nineteen.

ised $930 million during Yaoundé II). The Arusha Convention also obliged them to offer 'reverse preferences' to EEC exports. The East African countries were having to grant a tariff preference of up to nine percent on some fifty-seven items, which made up about one-tenth of their imports from the EEC: these included wines and spirits, films, glass, typewriters, radio sets and clocks. The greatest benefit they received was a tariff-free quota for 56,000 tons a year of unroasted coffee. It was a poor agreement, negotiated as a defensive act to avoid being squeezed out of the European market for agricultural products by the Yaoundé group.

Yaoundé II was an improvement on Yaoundé I in several ways. Aid under it was more directed towards industrialisation (the manufactured exports of these eighteen African countries were very limited and posed no threat to European producers such as the French had perceived from Asia) and there was a new emphasis on trade promotion and marketing. But it still had its own considerable drawbacks. To judge from trade statistics, the commercial advantages to the Yaoundé group during its years of operation had been unimpressive. As a percentage of the total exports of all developing countries to the EEC, the AAMS' share had dropped from 22.7 percent in 1958 to 20 percent in 1968, while the share of the non-associated African states had risen from 15 percent to 22.5 percent. Free trade in temperate agricultural products was restricted by the Community's Common Agricultural Policy, and AAMS paid the penalty of association in the form of reverse preferences. These were not explicitly obligatory – Zaire and Togo never extended them – and varied between countries; but a survey in 1967 showed that the average margin of reverse preferences on goods made in the EEC was 14 percent in Ivory Coast and 21 percent in Senegal.

In April 1972, when the Secretariat began the twin series of meetings with officials from the capitals of the Commonwealth 'associables' and with their High Commission representatives in London (the so-called 'London committee'), I had two major concerns. The first was to impress upon the 'associables' the extra bargaining strength they would have if they worked together among themselves; I also hoped to win over the francophone AAMS or at least some of them. The second was to say that, if they combined, they could negotiate better terms than those being offered in any of the three options; in particular, they could get rid of any obligation to extend reverse preferences to the nine industrialised countries of the enlarged EEC.

A Canadian or an Australian, living in a country blessed with many minerals and raw materials, can easily forget the basic dependence of Western Europe upon various sources, in Africa and elsewhere, for their primary products and can minimise the pressures that have led them to tie these sources closely to them, in colonial days by outright administrative control and later by a preferential trading bloc. I had frequently to remind myself that the 'most favoured nation' principle of liberal trading arrangements came far less naturally to a French politician than to a Canadian. Nevertheless, I felt there were strong objections to the system of reverse preferences.

My objections to reverse preferences were both economic and political. So far they had not entailed a heavy direct cost to either the Yaoundé or Arusha group; but they involved diversion of trade from less expensive or more convenient sources, and they placed irksome constraints on both the domestic economic and external commercial policies of a developing country. Reverse preferences would also undermine the whole concept of non-alignment. Beyond this the principle was established in the GATT and, most recently, in the Generalised System of Preferences that trade and economic relations between developed and developing countries should not involve reciprocity on the part of the latter.

The political objections I explained in these words:

'An inward-looking group comprising the enlarged Community and the thirty-nine developing countries could be a formidable bloc. Exclusivist bloc-thinking is a form of isolationism and would create grave dangers . . .The party could get rough. A trade war – or an aid war – between powerful continents would not be in anybody's interest. Certainly not in the interests of developing countries. Not would such a scramble among the rich to carve out spheres of influence in the Third World, in a sort of latter-day Yalta, be in the real interests of the industrialised nations themselves. Surely they too have an interest in cooperation – commercial, strategic and political – that is more than regional.'*

It was important to move as fast as possible in this preliminary stage of forming a common front of associates and associables because otherwise some of the smaller Commonwealth countries might feel that, since they could not afford to lose their market in Britain, they had no viable alternative but to agree to a disadvantageous Yaoundé-type arrangement (The Gambia actually did so, for a time).

---

* Speech to Foreign Press Association, London, May 1972.

These moves seemed to have a brisk start. Simultaneously in April 1972 the officials from Commonwealth capitals agreed with my proposal that I try to arrange a meeting for them with their Yaoundé counterparts by September, and a ministerial meeting of the Yaoundé group asked Sylla to explore with me the idea of a joint meeting at ministerial level. Hunter Wade and Sylla met later that month in Santiago during UNCTAD-3, and tentatively fixed a compromise schedule, by which officials of both our groups of member countries would meet in Geneva in September for an informational meeting, to learn at first hand the experience of the AAMS. If all went well, ministers of both groups would meet before the end of the year to start building a common negotiating position vis-à-vis the enlarged EEC.

But it soon became clear there were many crosscurrents that would divert such straightforward progress. Nigeria and Senghor of Senegal were to become principal influences on the stream of events.

Nigeria did not know how it wanted to handle the problems, but it did know that it did not want to be hurried. As the giant of Africa, independent for a dozen years and feeling its strength after surviving the fever of its civil war, it was not going to agree without a good deal more study to the terms the smaller countries of the Yaoundé group had accepted when they were recently emerged from the colonial cocoon. There was a widespread and understandable feeling in Nigeria that it should reject any form of association, so great was its resentment of recent French actions in arming the Biafrans and undermining efforts to form a West African Common Market. Nigeria's Trade Minister, Wenike Briggs, strongly reflected these attitudes. I sympathised with these well-grounded feelings, but felt strongly that Nigeria ought to assume leadership and use its superior bargaining power in negotiating better terms for all the developing countries rather than nurse its doubts in the background.

President Senghor had different ideas about Nigeria. He came to London in early July and asked to see me. At a reception for African ambassadors at his embassy on July 3, he kept the party waiting for half an hour while putting his views very candidly to me in the next room. It was imperative, he said, that Nigeria should be excluded from any new Yaoundé arrangements; the existing principles (I believe he meant the Development Fund) could not accommodate so big a country. If it were included, the balance would be destroyed and the rest of them would be 'inundated'; Nigeria could make its own trade agreement, he said.

He also insisted that reverse preferences were 'of the essence' and 'the foundation stone of the association'. They were fundamental to African self-respect, in that African states were offering something to Europe in return for technical assistance, and fundamental to the maintenance of African influence on the West Europeans. He did not believe in universality; but rather in regional blocs. The United States had a special relationship with Latin America, and it was right that Africa should have a special relationship with Western Europe, which would keep out unwelcome influences from elsewhere. He spoke scornfully of those (mostly Germans and Dutch) in the EEC, whose eyes strayed beyond his cherished Eurafrican community: *'les mondialistes'*, he called them.

The views he eloquently expressed about Eurafrica were no doubt formed by his schooling in France and his membership of L'Academie Française. He impressed me as being like some black philosopher living 2000 years ago in Alexandria, convinced that Greek culture reflected the highest civilisation and proud of his Roman citizenship. We spoke enthusiastically about French-English bilingualism, and he quoted a Senegalese proverb that a man walks better on two legs than on one. He told me he had been translating T. S. Eliot and planned to translate Yeats. He wanted further talks with me, he said, but it would be 'embarrassing' for him to come again to London. So he urged me to come to see him in a private flat he maintained in Paris for a longer meeting in September, and I said I would.

A conversation that same week with Jean-François Deniau, EEC Commissioner for development aid, confirmed me in my view that France as well as Senghor feared Nigeria's general influence inside an association. France also feared that, if Nigeria participated, a large slice of the EDF pie might have to go to development in that country, leaving less aid than before for the French-speaking AAMS. He himself thought it unrealistic to expect France's partners to increase their contributions to the Fund enough to accommodate Nigeria. I told him, as I had told Senghor, that I did not think Nigeria was approaching the question of association chiefly in terms of the aid it might get out of Europe.

Within two weeks of Senghor's visit to London, Sylla and the plans he had been making with us for the joint meeting of senior officials in Brussels in September were pushed aside. A letter on July 12 from Ambassador Jean Poisson of Niger, chairman for that half-year of the AAMS Coordinating Committee, informed me that the 'associated' states had decided that the first contacts should be between AAMS ministers and their counterparts among the associables who had already chosen the Yaoundé option. At the same time Senghor sent an AAMS team, headed by his own Foreign Minister, to tour various Commonwealth African capitals to discuss plans for a meeting in Dakar in November, probably restricted to African heads of state. Finally, FCO officials (including the most senior pair, Sir Denis Greenhill and Sir Martin Le Quesne) told me that the British Government was committed to doing all it could to get the twenty ACP 'associables' to choose the Yaoundé option, reverse preferences and all; if Nigeria refused these terms, I was told that did not much matter – the important thing was to get the others. I wondered if the British Government was hoping for French approval for a greatly enlarged EEC regional development fund (which would help depressed areas of Britain) in return for supporting the general French line over association and producing circumstances that would keep Nigeria out.

It was an awkward time. To cover the AAMS retreat, which may have been inspired as much by Deniau, or indeed by Jacques Foccart, as by Senghor, some EEC officials were throwing suspicion on the motives of the Commonwealth Secretariat. It was said in Brussels that I was criticising reverse preferences under the influence of the Canadian and Indian Governments, and the point was made that the two members of my staff most involved with this work were from New Zealand and India – so naturally (or nationally) as 'outsiders' we were against the Protocol 22 options. At the same time, the Nigerians found the terms of Ambassador Poisson's letter quite unacceptable, and suggested talking to the European 'Nine' rather than to the Yaoundé group.

Nevertheless my second meeting with Senghor went ahead, fortunately after I had had a private talk with Sylla, who was optimistically preparing for the day when a majority of EEC associates would be anglophone by taking a few weeks' crash course in English Language at Cambridge. As we drove out together to London Airport, he told me that Senghor's views about excluding Nigeria, perpetuating reverse preferences and fostering Eurafrican unity were not shared by several of the AAMS. They had insisted the Yaoundé Convention be renegotiated every five years precisely because, he said, they were prepared to grant reverse preferences only so long as they needed development aid, and France demanded the reverse preferences as the *quid pro quo* for aid.

Senghor, at our second meeting on September 5 in Paris, was more flexible, at least on procedural points. I had made clear my view that to expect Commonwealth developing countries in Africa, the Caribbean and the South Pacific to choose in advance for or against a Yaoundé option (or any other of the three 'options' offered by the EEC), before discussing its content and implications, was preposterous. Senghor said the condition set out in Poisson's letter, that only those prepared in advance to accept a Yaoundé-type association should attend a joint meeting, could be ignored. All the twenty 'associables' were to be invited, without prior commitment. But his stand on substantial points had not changed: the meeting had to be at ministerial level, and reverse preferences were still 'of the essence'. On Nigeria he appeared more flexible than in July: he said he personally would welcome cooperation with that country, but he felt the most that Nigeria would agree to was a trade agreement. His greater flexibility on this point may have been occasioned by the fact that with me this time was the Director of my International Affairs Division, Emeka Anyaoku, a Nigerian.

He followed up the meeting with a letter to me on September 18 in his capacity as President of OCAM, setting out what he called a compromise: that all the twenty associables 'including Nigeria' would take part in the joint meeting, but those who wished 'to participate in Yaoundé III would accept reverse preferences'. He also wrote to the AAMS Heads of State on September 18 about our meeting and about stressing to me that reverse preferences 'were foundation stones of the Association. If we were to abandon them, we should by this act accept the position of the *mondialistes* who wish to transform the Association into a simple Free Trade Area'. The 'London Committee' of the ACP High Commissioners did not consider his letter much of a compromise, and few of them had reactions from governments about a joint meeting. We were no further ahead.

I did not find much new thought when I talked with Edward Heath on September 25. He pointed out that Commonwealth countries had granted reverse preferences for many years without suggesting they were neo-colonialist. (The Caribbean countries were extending an average 10 percent preference to Britain in 1967 but the African states offered nothing.) The choice was up to the developing countries, Heath said. If they did not want association, they could still have entry rights to the Community's GSP. I raised the problem of Commonwealth countries in the Pacific being asked to choose between losing their British market or undertaking to discriminate in favour of the EEC and against India, Australia or New Zealand, and of Jamaica and Barbados being asked to choose between losing their British market for rum and bananas or discriminating against Canada and the United States; but Heath did not seem greatly concerned about 'details'.

However, we heard in early October that a political row was brewing with the AAMS as a result of Senghor's message to its Heads of State on September 18. Several of them, particularly those who were not also in OCAM, were angry at the way they thought Senghor was trying to dictate a common line to them over reverse preferences. Zaire had actually threatened to leave the Association years ago over the issue and had been assured that reverse preferences were a matter within the competence of national governments, because the Yaoundé arrangements were bilateral pacts between the EEC and individual associates, creating eighteen free trade areas and not (as Senghor suggested) a single customs union. Zaire stood strongly on that position.

It was at this point that I thought it helpful to write a circular letter on October 12 about the political aspects to the Foreign Ministers of the nineteen 'associables'* (Mauritius had by then signed Yaoundé II). I started by setting out the extremes of possible results, to get the ministers to think more broadly than the three options offered. One outcome (the best for them) could be ready access to larger markets, stable commodity arrangements, generous new sources of aid – all without affecting their relations with other countries and without accepting political ties 'to any one power bloc'. The worst outcome could be discriminatory aid-and-trade arrangements between Western Europe and some (perhaps only the weaker) developing countries, leading to competing blocs of rich countries trying to carve out exclusive spheres of political and economic influence in the developing world.

The developing countries could by their own efforts determine where in the spectrum of possibilities between these two extremes the coming negotiations arrived at. But, with negotiations between the enlarged EEC and themselves due to begin in August 1973, it was important to form a common front among the Commonwealth associates and with as many of the French-speaking AAMS as possible, and to 'get together with them in good time'.

---

* This letter and several other documents referred to in this section are contained in *Relations with the Enlarged European Economic Community: Records of Meetings of High Commission Representatives April-Dec. 1972*, Commonwealth Secretariat (restricted).

I suggested that there was a greater danger of their underestimating their bargaining power than of overplaying their hand, and that, although the associables had only been offered three options, 'the substantive position is far from being cut and dried'. Why should the developing countries not put forward their own proposals?

To back up this argument, I developed a critique of the three options offered, and concentrated on the first of them, the Yaoundé-type association, because it alone included development assistance. And I tackled its two most controversial factors – aid and reverse preferences – in some detail. Summing up on the latter, I said:

'In my judgement, participation together in negotiations with the enlarged EEC of a significant number of Commonwealth countries which were resolved *not* to accord reverse preferences could not fail to induce an amendment of the Community's policies . . . Although officials (of the EEC and their governments) may initially take the line that discriminatory tariff concessions are essential, it would prove politically difficult to make this stick in a crunch.'

As for aid, I also argued that the associables would be able to obtain it from the EEC 'without strings', that the resources of the European Development Fund would almost certainly be doubled or trebled, and that parliaments and the public in West Germany and the Netherlands (to say nothing of Britain) would make sure that the 'more populous, and economically and politically not less interesting, Commonwealth developing countries' received their fair share alongside the Yaoundé associates.

As a courtesy, I gave the other Commonwealth countries copies of my circular letter to the ACP associables. As expected, the British as well as the French objected strongly to my letter, the British even sending a circular message of their own which commented adversely on my letter and said that it was 'only a personal opinion' (whatever that might mean!).

But my letter made an impression on the ACP countries which proved useful. The strategy it advocated was in fact the one eventually adopted, and it proved successful, although the tactical procedures were different from those I envisaged when I sent it. In the short run my letter helped the Commonwealth associables to stick together during the doldrum period in the closing months of 1972 when the technical studies had been done and the political meetings were being postponed, as plans for both a Commonwealth and a joint ministerial gathering were twice put back. When Dr Arikpo, Nigeria's Commissioner for External Affairs, saw me on December 1, he said he entirely agreed that the possibility of a wholly new relationship should be examined, but in the meantime urged me to write another circular letter addressing the advantages and disadvantages of options two and three – the Arusha model and the simple trade agreement – before a meeting was called of Commonwealth ministers early in 1973. But instead of that measured progress, events began to take a dramatic turn in the New Year.

There are often difficulties in scheduling meetings at suitable times for ministers from twenty or more countries, which do not clash with important Commonwealth occasions in other spheres. A witty correspondent of *West Africa*, who had been following the 'games of hide and seek' between the Commonwealth and AAMS Secretariats in 1972, called the proposed joint meeting of associates and associables in early 1973 'the hardest rendezvous to set up since Pyramus tried to meet Thisbe at Ninus' tomb'.*

But eventually we scheduled a meeting of Commonwealth ministers and officials from the twenty 'associables' in State House, Accra, on February 26 to follow immediately after the UN Economic Commission for Africa (ECA) had completed its biennial ministerial meeting. Africa's relations with the enlarged EEC was an item on the ECA agenda, so that the occasion could be turned into a joint Yaoundé-Commonwealth group meeting; and the omens seemed good, since there were signs that the Community itself was becoming more flexible on both reverse preferences and aid matters, and was even studying ways to help stabilise the export receipts of associates (a first step to the eventual Stabex scheme that was a major innovation of the Lomé I Convention).

When I stopped in Nairobi on my way back from the Youth Ministers meeting in Lusaka in late January, I found the Foreign and Finance Ministers, Dr Mungai and Mwai Kibaki, cool to the idea of the February 26 meeting. Philip Ndegwa, Permanent Secretary to the Treasury, who was also present appeared to be their chief strategist. The timing was still not appropriate, they told me. What was important was to establish a unified African position, and they were confident of doing that. They regarded Senghor's own lobbying as ineffective. They dismissed the problems of the

---

* *West Africa* 5 March 1973, p 298

Caribbean and Pacific countries as minor, compared with the priority of a common African front. A week later, nevertheless, we were notified by the Kenyan High Commissioner on February 12 that they would attend the February 26 meeting.

On the way to Accra, however, they stopped in Lagos for a meeting of Commonwealth African economic and trade ministers called at the request of the East Africans, who proposed setting up a secretariat at Arusha for the thirteen Commonwealth African countries to study and coordinate their approach to the EEC. Eight Commonwealth countries' ministers met in Lagos on February 16, approved this idea and decided to ask the ECA to remove this subject from its agenda. Some also decided to propose that our Commonwealth meeting in Accra be cancelled but this was by no means welcomed by others.

At a reception which Nigerian Trade Commissioner Wenike Briggs gave that Friday evening for the African ministers and also for the British Foreign Secretary Alec Home, the rumour was passed round that I myself had sent a telegram from London cancelling the meeting. Hunter Wade, who was already in Accra to prepare for the meeting, was astonished to be told by ministers from various countries that the source from which they got this extraordinary rumour was Martin Le Quesne, Home's Deputy Under-Secretary. There was of course no truth whatever in the rumour. When Wade later had the opportunity of talking to Le Quesne about it, he did not deny telling African Commonwealth Ministers that I had cancelled the meeting, but said lamely that he had heard it from the Commercial Counsellor at the British High Commission! Naturally, it gave momentum to the proposal for cancellation.

Over the weekend Commonwealth ministers moved to Accra, where on Monday they met their francophone counterparts. The francophone ministers were split among themselves after a ferocious argument in which President Senghor was criticised for attributing his own views about reverse preferences to them all in his September letter to me. In that divided state, they agreed to ask that the EEC item be taken off the ECA agenda, and Briggs did so on behalf of the rest. Wade was told by the Ghanaian Government, rather sheepishly and full of apologies, that these Commonwealth countries did not feel able to take part in our subsequent meeting, and that Ghana as host government was therefore compelled to cancel it altogether. I then had no choice but to inform Caribbean and Pacific countries accordingly.

It seemed at first that everything had suddenly fallen apart. The

Ghanaian hosts were upset. Robert Gardiner, the Ghanaian executive secretary of the ECA, felt his organisation was being by-passed. The Fiji prime minister, Ratu Mara, who had already left the Pacific for the meeting and met me in London on the day it should have begun, felt brushed aside and concluded there would now be no full meeting of Yaoundé associates and all Commonwealth associables before negotiations with the EEC opened in August. Sylla, who had worked hard to bridge gaps among his own AAMS and had made a good impression on Commonwealth representatives at an informal meeting I had arranged in December, was deeply depressed. A common front seemed further off than ever, and time was getting short.

The situation was pulled together by an unexpected person in an unlikely way. The first Secretary-General of the Organisation of African Unity, Diallo Telli, had been a difficult person with whom to cooperate. Coming from Guinea, he projected his strong views on French colonialism in all directions in an immature, almost silly, way. His urging of African Foreign Ministers to break links with Britain, and those in the Commonwealth to withdraw from it, if the Rhodesian rebellion was not suppressed by 15 December 1965, would – if his Commonwealth clients had left the association as he wished – have been utterly counterproductive: it would have facilitated a British 'sell-out' to Ian Smith. His influence in the OAU team, which under Kaunda came to London in October 1970 to protest to Heath about arms sales to South Africa, was particularly insensitive. After two four-year terms, he was impressively beaten (thirty votes to ten) by Nzo Ekangaki, who by the age of thirty-eight had acquired much practical experience as Cameroon's Minister of Public Health and Population, and Minister of Labour and Social Welfare – and international contacts as Deputy Foreign Minister. Ekangaki's powerful speech as OAU Secretary-General at the opening session of the ECA ministerial meeting at Accra in February 1973 proved to be the turning point in the long journey towards a better arrangement than Yaoundé for the EEC associates.

When we met in London the following week, he told me that he had regarded the Lagos meeting of eight Commonwealth African countries as 'splitting tactics' for it seemed to be setting up a rival to the OAU, and he had believed the Commonwealth Secretariat had organised the meeting! Emeka Anyaoku, who had been a schoolfriend of his, and I were able to convince him otherwise; and in doing this my letter of October 12 to ACP Foreign Ministers (of which we gave him a copy) was useful. He told me that he was astonished that the Secretary-General of the Commonwealth should hold and advocate such views. He added that he was inclined to agree with the strategy I was suggesting.

In the meantime his vigorous speech to the ECA meeting had altered the pieces on the board. The speech was a passionate call for African unity and African action, to organise themselves in their own interests as effectively as the EEC countries did for themselves. Many of his phrases struck non-African observers as xenophobic:

> 'We must not allow others . . . to use us as pawns or treat us as nitwits . . . We need to ward off the danger of allowing inter-African economic cooperation to become an instrument at the service of the interests of foreign industrialists and investors, instead of a means to the accelerated development of our Continent . . . The first architect of African development can only be the African himself.'

There were important figures present, like Botswana's Vice-President (now President) Quett Matsire, who were unhappy with these expressions; and the Ivory Coast and Senegal were worried that the other Yaoundé countries were moving towards a more independent stance. But Ekangaki was clearly reflecting, and amplifying, the general mood. He did more than that. By dwelling on 'the lamentable failure' of UNCTAD III and pointing out how at UN meetings Africans always had to withdraw to work out a common strategy privately, he skilfully if rather brutally asserted the primacy of the OAU over the ECA in African economic as well as political affairs (and incidentally of himself over the veteran Robert Gardiner).

In talking with the Fiji prime minister on February 26 I agreed that the African decision to refuse without notice to attend the meeting they had agreed upon with Ministers of the Caribbean and South Pacific countries was unwise as well as rude; but I added that the assertion of a solid African group could prove to be 'not necessarily a retrograde step. The differences of view that have to be reconciled go deeper in Africa than in other regions.'

The reconciliation moved at speed, especially after Nigeria's General Gowon (who ended by chairing the OAU Summit in May) took the initiative over from his Trade Commissioner. The French were afraid of the influence of Nigeria over the francophone states, but the countervailing influence of Senghor had waned since his controversial efforts in the previous year. A meeting of African trade ministers in Abidjan in May, under OAU auspices and in collaboration with ECA, worked out a strategy based on eight principles, of which the most important three were that reciprocity (i.e. reverse preferences) should not be required, that aid should not be dependent upon any special association, and that there should be a guarantee of 'stable, equitable and remunerative' commodity prices.

The eight principles were endorsed later in May 1973 at the OAU's tenth anniversary summit in Addis Ababa, to which I was invited as a guest of honour. There Okoi Arikpo, Nigeria's External Affairs Commissioner, told me that at the preliminary Foreign Ministers' meeting the Senegalese representative was still fighting strongly against the principle which specified that there should not be reverse preferences. The situation was far from settled. We discussed under whose auspices further consultations should take place. He agreed that there was value in the Caribbean and Pacific countries joining in talks with the Africans, but thought it by now unnecessary to have further formal Commonwealth consultations, which encouraged separate francophone consultations. Instead, he was in favour of using the auspices of the OAU.

I said he was probably right. I had been trying to draw together with a strong bargaining position as many Commonwealth and Yaoundé countries as possible, although I thought we might lose some of the latter. But his was a bolder and more imaginative approach; by using the OAU he could hope to draw all of them in, the Africans first and the others later. I was, however, still worried about the intentions of Nigeria itself, having fought for its inclusion, against the discouragement of France, Senegal and even Britain – and against the opposition of some influential Nigerians, too. Nigeria, I insisted, had a duty to lend its leverage to the weaker developing countries. Arikpo was still uncertain whether his government would opt for association at the finish, but he said: 'We will go along during the negotiations, to lend our bargaining weight to the others, even if we decide ourselves not to sign in the end.' That was a big step forward, and in the event they went all the way to Lomé.

Gowon as OAU chairman called a meeting of all thirty-eight Commonwealth ACP and Yaoundé states in early July to coordinate tactics for the first meeting with the EEC Council of Ministers later that month. An all-night session under Briggs put together a platform for the Brussels meeting (although Senegal and the Ivory Coast still clung to reverse preferences). At the EEC-ACP preliminary meeting Briggs spoke for all the African states, Ratu Mara for the Pacific and Sonny Ramphal for the Caribbean. They made a strong trio, Ramphal particularly impressing the Europeans and in his turn rejecting the notion of reciprocal trade preferences. The EEC Council agreed to start negotiations in earnest in October, and seemed to take to heart Ramphal's complaint that the EEC's first proposals were 'very disappointing' and his call for 'arrangements more relevant to the needs and mood of the 1970s and beyond.'* They realized there would be tough negotiators facing them and this proved to be the case in the eighteen months leading to the signing of Lomé I in February 1975.

There was an intriguing swing in the British view in the twelve months after May 1972. After Senghor's visit to London and, even more (I suspect), after a more Gaullist prime minister Pierre Messmer took office in Paris, the FCO began to press the Commonwealth associables to consider the Yaoundé (or first) option exclusively, and to accept reverse preferences. While other parts of the British Government looked at this question more broadly, considering both the North American viewpoint and that of developing countries, the FCO continued to appease de Gaulle long after he was dead. Only the week before the ECA meeting in Accra in February 1973, a senior FCO official flatly asserted to me that a united African approach would not only be impossible to achieve, but actually wrong, as EEC precedents dictated a certain set of tactics. The associables, he said, should 'sign-up' for negotiations in August on the basis that they were discussing the first option only. Only if the results were unsatisfactory would they then move on other options. Of course, this rigid approach was not followed, and by May 1973 the FCO was in line with the rest of the British Government in opposing reverse preferences and looking liberally upon the ACP position.

When the OAU so dramatically asserted itself in February 1973 and Nigeria's top leadership – Gowon and Arikpo – began to take a personal part in building a common front, the Commonwealth Secretariat's major task in these negotiations was done. We continued to help the South Pacific countries in their special position in trading relationships with Australia and New Zealand and in economic cooperation with other members of the South Pacific Forum; and Mike Faber was sent as a CFTC adviser to help them develop their negotiating position. But our earlier work, in drawing the twenty 'associables' together on the foundation of technical studies that cut across regions and in building the bridge to the Yaoundé

---

*Bridget Bloom, *Financial Times*, 27 July, 1973.

group in 1972, together with my circular letter on the political aspects and prospects, laid the basis for the ACP's common front in the later negotiations.

There was a productive side-show with the Foreign and Finance Ministers of Kenya during 1973. After playing their part in getting the Commonwealth associables' meeting in Accra cancelled, Mungai and Kibaki came to London in March as guests of the British Government. They met me the morning after having dinner with Edward Heath, and were obviously still chewing it over. For they told me that they thought Britain's membership of the EEC would inevitably diminish the relevance of the Commonwealth, and that Africans' confidence in its viability had been shaken by the quarrel with Britain at the Singapore HGM.

I pretended to lose my temper and said, angrily but pityingly: 'I can understand that a poor country, only recently independent from Britain, might think that British Government decisions and moods must determine the value and uses of an international association that belongs to all of us. You've been so accustomed to seeing Britain as the boss. But you should understand that I come from a much older country than yours, much richer than Britain, and one that had to decide in 1940 whether to accept Churchill's plea to make plans, should the need arise, to be host to a wartime British government-in-exile. Britain is not the centre of the world for us. When you grow up, you may have a more mature attitude about the Commonwealth and make your own proposals about what future activities you want it to undertake.'

This outburst shocked them into talking positively about Commonwealth cooperation and Philip Ndegwa, who in 1967 had played a central role in the Nairobi planning officials conference that led to setting up the Secretariat's technical assistance programme, said it would be useful if I worked out a five-year programme of cooperation. Further correspondence followed with Dr Mungai, which resulted in Vice-President Daniel Arap Moi, who headed Kenya's delegation at the Ottawa Summit in August 1973, proposing the establishment of a Commonwealth Development Bank. The proposal was combined with another from the Finance Ministers for a Commonwealth finance corporation, and the two were studied by an expert group of bankers and financial specialists from six countries. They recommended setting up a Commonwealth Investment Bank, with initial paid-up capital of £15-20 million, to mobilise finance from various sources for directly productive enterprises, and joint ventures. It was a well-researched proposal, and would have achieved a bridging between regions that is still needed in financial institutions below the quantitative level of the World Bank and IMF; for all that has grown since then is the activity of the regional development banks.

To my regret, the proposal was turned down in 1975 at the Jamaica HGM, when many countries were still shaken by the first oil price rises, and when imagination, as well as the generosity of the rich, had dwindled along with foreign exchange. But it is a scheme that awaits revival.

There was a further occasion on which a positive Commonwealth voice was helpful on this subject of British membership of the EEC. Opposition within the Labour Party forced Harold Wilson, after he returned to power in 1974, to promise a national referendum on the issue. I was approached by a former Conservative Minister in April 1975 to be a member of the 'Yes' committee. After thinking it over, I said it would be better for me as a Canadian not to accept since it was at this point an issue for British voters, but I would do my best to secure a supportive statement from Commonwealth leaders at the HGM the following month. This was achieved. The Jamaica HGM authorised a statement that Commonwealth countries welcomed British entry into the EEC, as creating a Europe that would be more compatible with good relations with the Commonwealth and other parts of the world. Wilson, who had hoped for such a statement unsolicited by himself, was delighted with this ammunition for the referendum. And, remembering the gloomy words of the Australian High Commissioner four years before, I was specially pleased that Gough Whitlam joined in the positive declaration.

A scheme which was revived in 1978-1980 was the proposal for a French Commonwealth. In 1978 it was Pierre Trudeau's initiative, and the Canadian External Affairs Department official who had been coordinating Commonwealth relations in Ottawa was shifted to working on this new but parallel scheme for francophone countries. Trudeau wanted such an association to discuss world political issues, and President Senghor was asked during the Franco-African summit of heads of government in 1978 to prepare more specific proposals. He produced the idea of an 'Organic Community', which would handle exchanges between member states in fields such as education, communications, science and economic issues and which would also include a conference of francophone leaders. He defined the Organic Community as 'a flexible structure for dialogue among heads of state and government founded on the assent of the partners debating, freely and in private, issues and proposals of interest to their countries within the framework of a network of organised solidarity'.

It sounded, in fact, remarkably like a Commonwealth Heads of Government Meeting. And in a press interview in 1980, some months before his retirement, he said he wanted the Community to have a Secretariat headed 'like that of the Commonwealth by a man of political stature'.

It was disappointing that an eruption of the old quarrel between France and Canada over the status of Quebec pushed back into 1981 further action on Senghor's proposal. A Committee of Experts who met in Dakar in September 1980 accepted a broad definition of cultural exchanges, and suggested the community should have three spheres of interest: cultural, economic and 'a contribution to peace among peoples'. The Canadian Government took this as confirmation that it would be dealing with major international issues, especially as the organisational meeting planned for Dakar in November to precede a summit was at the level of Foreign Ministers; it announced it would send two federal ministers, and invited officials from Quebec and New Brunswick to join its delegation. France, on the other hand, emphasised the cultural aspects and insisted that the Quebec Government should be there in its own right, as cultural affairs are a provincial responsibility in Canada. But Ottawa was not prepared to have a Quebec minister: it would have given at least a symbolic victory to Quebec separatists at the end of a year that had seen a heavy setback handed to them at a referendum of Quebec voters. The quarrel was not resolved, even though the Foreign Ministers meeting was postponed to December. Eventually it was cancelled, and the whole proposal put on ice.

I hope a thaw soon comes. L'Agence has found its feet as a technical cooperation agency, but it has clear limitations on its functions, compared with the Commonwealth Secretariat. In particular, the consultation between Heads of Government which the Commonwealth enjoys percolates through the whole association. For its francophone equivalent to have the same amount of ferment and stimulation – to be, in fact, an 'Organic Community' – it needs a regular conference of Heads of Government 'debating freely and in private'. Is this what France wants? If it is, attitudes in Paris as elsewhere will have changed considerably since the events described early in this chapter. It will have been a worthwhile journey.

Chapter 10
LIBERATION IN SOUTHERN AFRICA
From Arms Sales to Zimbabwe

In the 1970s the political struggles in southern Africa became increasingly inter-related. The South African government had begun pursuing a 'forward defence' strategy and strengthening friendly administrations to the north that could act as a buffer zone. South African troops were patrolling in the Zambezi valley alongside Ian Smith's forces. South African investment funds were being poured into two vast hydroelectric projects, the Cunene dam in southern Angola and the Cabora Bassa dam in central Mozambique, in order to stiffen the resolve of (and increase the profit for) the Portuguese government to remain in Africa, holding the two flanks of this southern bloc.

It was inevitable, therefore, that the Commonwealth Secretariat should be concerned about events in all these countries. An earlier chapter dealt purely with Rhodesia, and the lengthy effort to hold the line against a British sell-out after UDI in 1965. This chapter voyages more broadly across southern Africa in the 1970s. It carries the Rhodesian story through the years of armed struggle, to the crucial Heads of Government Meeting in Lusaka in 1979, and on to Zimbabwe's independence day which I was fortunate enough to witness in Salisbury. But it also tells how the Commonwealth took on a special responsibility for training Namibians for their own day of independence, not without argument from some officials. And it further describes how I was able to help start, and then help break an impasse in, the early negotiations between the Frelimo nationalist leaders and the new Portuguese government in 1974, which led to peaceful independence for Mozambique; this in turn, transformed the whole strategic prospect for Rhodesia.

Of course, all these threads lead to South Africa itself, and the relationship of Commonwealth countries with its government. So this chapter also covers one of the most difficult episodes faced in my years as Secretary-General, caused by the announced intention

204

of the British government of Edward Heath to resume arms sales to South Africa.

Many writers have said that the Commonwealth went to the brink of disintegration on the arms sales issue in the months leading up to the Singapore HGM in January 1971. The crisis was real. Happily, however, no country left the Commonwealth then and several positive programmes were an outcome of that meeting, including the launching of the CFTC. Perhaps the major lesson of the arms sales incident is the enormous value of candid consultation among Commonwealth leaders that can head off a crisis and save a member state from an appalling blunder. I have no doubt that, if Heath had gone ahead with large sales of arms to South Africa, he would have done even more damage to Britain's standing and influence in the world than Anthony Eden did through the invasion of Suez in 1956. He was saved from this because the Commonwealth had matured into a representative association whose leaders acted quickly, spoke frankly and finally produced a pair of agreements that saved everybody's political face. So the story is as much about the talks that went on quietly from July to December 1970 as about the climax at Singapore.

The South Africans skilfully baited a trap for the incoming Conservative government in mid-1970. There was a general indication in the party manifesto, 'A Better Tomorrow', that the Conservatives would lift the non-mandatory embargo on arms sales, which had been approved by the UN Security Council in 1963 and which the Wilson government had honoured; but it had not been in any sense an issue in the June 1970 campaign. The South African officials, however, knew that many Conservatives regretted that the French and Italians had taken over a lucrative market, and that Heath had been alarmed at the Labour government's plan to withdraw British forces from 'East of Suez'. For while still Opposition leader, he had made visits to the Gulf States and to Singapore and Malaysia in 1969-70, to discuss a continuing British role in the region.

So it was no courtesy visit that Hilgard Muller, the South African Foreign Minister, paid on his new British government counterpart, Alec Home, within a week of the Conservatives' election victory on June 18. He was able to refer to the Simonstown Agreements of 1955 when Britain had handed over the naval base near Cape Town and had agreed to supply anti-submarine frigates as part of South Africa's programme of naval expansion to guard the sea-route around southern Africa. The orders had all been filled by 1964, at a

205

cost of £18 million, but the agreement to cooperate in defence of the sea-route remained and had involved some joint naval exercises. Now Home, who in July 1969 had published an article in the *Daily Mail* on 'Why the Tories will sell arms to South Africa', gave Muller an assurance that he would live up to his word, and indicated this to the press, even before the matter was discussed in Cabinet.

The first crisis came quickly. On July 11 the British Prime Minister sent a twenty-paragraph letter directly to the Commonwealth heads of government referring to the Simonstown Agreements and saying that Britain could not 'continue to benefit from these valuable defence facilities without being prepared to consider requests for equipment directly related to the security of the sea routes which we believe to be implicit in these agreements'. He added that a statement of specific intentions would be made within ten days 'to keep in check the wilder speculation'. Although Heath stressed that the equipment would be for external defence and not internal security, he gave no hint of whether he was considering only some helicopters for which the frigates had been adapted, or a whole new range of equipment – more frigates, Buccaneer bombers and Nimrod patrol aircraft.

Nor was there any mention of consultation. Earlier that week, on July 6, Alec Home had also proclaimed British freedom to act alone, when he painted for the Commons an alarming picture of Soviet naval expansion: 370 modern submarines, significant activity in the Mediterranean which, as soon as the Suez Canal was reopened, would spread eastward from a base in Aden and probably Somalia. 'The British government alone must accept the responsibility for Britain's security,' he said. 'No one else can decide that for us. No one else can judge our needs.'

Sonny Ramphal, then Foreign Minister of Guyana, was passing through London and saw Home the next day. He put the view strongly that it would be extremely tactless for the British government to make a decision and simply inform Commonwealth countries. He urged delay until consultations could take place, and went on to press Sir Alec not to make any decision until after the HGM in January, when leaders would listen seriously to a genuine case about defence of the western world.

I first saw Heath's letter during a meeting on July 13 with Alec Home, who asked for my comments on it. When I gave them, he asked me to put them in writing, which I did in a letter four days later. I was glad to learn that my letter was circulated to other Ministers and various department heads. I argued, during an hour's discussion, that the security of the east and west coasts of Africa depended primarily on political attitudes within black African states, and the proposed British actions could mean they would find it more difficult not to lean towards either Moscow or Peking. Home's rejoinder was that the Russians might in any case increase their influence in Nigeria (which they had supplied with arms during the civil war) and, if the Chinese built a base as well as the railway line in Tanzania, then the Simonstown base and the agreement with South Africa would be absolutely essential for Britain, in order to maintain a presence in the Indian Ocean. He did, however, say he wanted to take fully into account the feelings of African leaders.

These were soon made plain to him. Kaunda sent messages to all Commonwealth heads of government expressing his grave concern and a note to Britain, indicating that he might take economic retaliation, possibly by cutting copper exports. But he made no threat to leave the Commonwealth on this issue. I was glad I had sent him a message on June 30, foreseeing the new strains and underlining the value of the Commonwealth as a 'a framework within which governments can maintain free exchanges of view . . . to help overcome the dangerous stresses that could fragment mankind on racial or regional lines'.

Ironically, the Commonwealth Games opened that week in Edinburgh, and many High Commissioners as well as British Ministers flew up for two less political days among the pipe bands and sprinters. But, the day after returning to London, I learnt that Julius Nyerere had sent a message to the British government, saying he would withdraw from the Commonwealth if Britain went ahead with its announcement of a definite decision to resume arms sales. It was by then Saturday afternoon, July 18, and the British statement was due to be made on Monday. The timing was tight.

It was not the most restful of weekends. In Tanzania the President was by then hundreds of miles upcountry, staying in a village, and the admirable British High Commissioner, Horace Phillips, hurried there to be a soothing influence as well as front-line communicator. At Chequers on Saturday, Heath and Home were conferring with top officials about what exactly they would say on Monday. And at my flat a group of my senior staff gathered, to plan how to dissuade Nyerere from withdrawal or (if he persisted) to prevent a chain reaction that could involve Zambia, Uganda, India and Ceylon.

Late that day we heard from Sir John Johnston, the Deputy Under Secretary, that the Chequers meeting had tentatively agreed to postpone any decision on arms sales and to tell Nyerere that none would be made until there had been an opportunity to talk the whole subject over with him and others. But this was subject to confirmation after a further meeting on Sunday at Number 10, and we feared that the demonstrators who had gathered near Downing Street might have put the backs up of Tory Ministers. So I asked the Tanzanian High Commission to open its cipher channel and sent a 'most immediate' message to Nyerere urging that 'no irretrievable action' be taken. I said it would be particularly unfortunate when the Commonwealth as a whole had not had an opportunity in a meeting to discuss the question. Three hours after this frank personal message had been sent, word came from Downing Street that the British would indeed postpone action. The next afternoon, Alec Home made a mild statement in the Commons, reiterating the British government's view on the Simonstown Agreements, expressing its willingness to consult with Commonwealth governments, and saying it proposed 'to complete these consultations and discussions before decisions are finally taken'.

The Canadian government played a useful part in winning this respite. Through Charles Ritchie, the High Commissioner in London, I had urged that Canada try to restrain British action; and on July 17 Pierre Trudeau sent Heath a letter expressing his own 'serious misgivings', saying that many Commonwealth governments were likely to interpret any arms sales as 'an implicit gesture of acquiescence in the policy of the South African government toward the African population' and asking Heath to 'weigh carefully' their views. He also sent the gist of his letter in a message to Nyerere. I am sure this helped hold both sides within the bounds of reasonable action.

It was only a respite, though. The next danger-point would come in October, when the British Parliament reassembled, for Home gave an assurance that he would announce a decision first in parliament. It did, however, give time to look more coolly at the issues at stake.

There was no doubt that the sea route round the Cape was considered vital to Britain. Heath himself at Singapore described the world's sea lanes as 'the arteries of life' for Britain, and said that about fifty percent of its oil supplies and a quarter of its trade passed through the route around the Cape.*

---

*Nicholas Scott, MP for Paddington South, in a courageous debating speech to the Bow Group during the Conservative Party Conference in October 1970, gave what may be more significant figures. He said that only about five percent of the total tonnage of dry cargo shipped in and out of Britain went around the Cape, 'so it is hardly a question of life and death'; the importance of the Cape route would further diminish as oil imports from Nigeria picked up again after the civil war.

There was no disputing the Soviet naval build-up. My own view, after three sojourns in the Soviet Union, was that its leaders were determined to make it a world air and naval power after the 1941-45 war in which its aircraft had been merely ground support and its navy a coastguard, and in which its calls to the western Allies for a 'second front' had been answered by lofty talk of the actions of 'Strategic Air Command', and so on. Their first priority after 1945 was to become a global air power and, more speedily than the West expected, they developed a nuclear weapon, pioneered satellites and built up an armoury of missiles. Then, just as thoroughly and inexorably, they set about becoming a world naval power in line with detailed strategic studies. They built up the Soviet navy to gain political influence, and to escape the containment by breaking out first into the Mediterranean and then broader seas. Their deployment in the Indian Ocean began in 1968; by 1970 the Soviet force included one cruiser, three destroyers, five submarines and several supporting vessels.

But it was strategic lunacy for Britain to try to counter the Soviet build-up by a move that risked alienating all those states bordering the Indian Ocean (of which thirteen were in the Commonwealth) who accepted Britain's basic interest in the region. Obote, during a visit to Dar in late July to consult with Nyerere and Kaunda on the issue, put it mildly to the British High Commissioner: 'You have engaged the wrong policemen.'

At least the younger Bow Group MPs saw the folly. One of them pointed out that India had the largest fleet in the region, twice the size of the South African Navy, and asked: 'What conceivable strategic advantage do we gain if the price of an arms deal were a hostile or uncooperative Indian Navy?' Again, from a technical and logistical viewpoint, the sea-lanes near South Africa were hardly the best place for Soviet vessels to start any hostilities. The much narrower shipping lane at the entrance to the Persian Gulf or at the approaches to Europe was more vulnerable to Soviet attack than the wide route around the Cape.

Another consideration was how other western countries viewed the situation. After all, only one in twelve ships rounding the Cape was a British vessel. I asked David Newsom, the US Assistant Secretary of State for African Affairs, if Washington could help, as a NATO ally, in talking the British leaders out of an act of stupidity. I was delighted when a strategic assessment by the Pentagon left British military staff in no doubt that Washington would be more circumspect about the Indian Ocean situation.

By about the end of August it was apparent that some senior

British ministers and officials were beginning to see the folly of arms sales. Peter Carrington, then Defence Minister, seemed never strongly in favour; his efforts in the region were centred on putting together a five-power group (Britain, Singapore, Malaysia, Australia and New Zealand) to cover the defence gap that would be left when British forces in Singapore were reduced. Alec Home, author of the commitment, was having second thoughts.

The main protagonist now was Heath himself, who from all accounts had been doubtful earlier. He supported the policy, not because he had any sympathy with South African racial attitudes (his record on race, from an early visit in the Belgian Congo to his clashes with Enoch Powell over non-white immigrants, was a liberal one); nor because he saw great commercial profit to Britain or even military advantage, for a few frigates and helicopters would scarcely tip the strategic balance. He supported it because he was simply an extremely stubborn man, who thought that retreating from even an unconfirmed policy was a sign of weakness and would damage his government's credibility in other spheres, particularly in the tough negotiations he saw ahead of him in industrial relations, and with EEC countries on membership. His instinct also was to resent unpalatable advice, from civil servants or other Commonwealth governments.

Reasoning by itself, therefore, would not change his mind; although some of the closely argued letters he received from Commonwealth leaders and pressure from moderates within his own party must have had an effect. Still less would he be swayed by emotional attacks upon 'the British', at OAU meetings or the Non-Aligned Conference which took place in Lusaka that September; for Heath understandably complained about the 'double standard' applied in criticising British intentions and ignoring French actions over many years. During his last weeks at the Secretariat before returning to Ghana, Yaw Adu wrote an eloquent letter on this theme to his prime minister, Dr Busia. No, what was needed was neither reason nor emotion but a face-saving device, or what was called in official correspondence 'a constructive alternative'. And it would take time, probably some months, to find and promote the device with the best chance of success.

When I had a first formal meeting with Heath as Prime Minister early in September, I was anxious to discover if he had any time fixed in his mind for announcing his conclusions on the arms issue. He was working through a list of Commonwealth heads of government, many of whom he would see at the United Nations in October or as they passed through London to the UN twenty-fifth

Anniversary gathering. He told me he had been considering whether to refer the matter for discussion at the January HGM or settle it beforehand; on the whole, he thought it was not a sound principle to 'save up rows for Commonwealth conferences'. Although he said the timing was still an open question, I left with the impression he wanted to act as soon as he had gone through the motions of consultation, by the end of October.

October, therefore, became an extremely busy month. Although in September I visited Pakistan which was heading into crucial elections, I cancelled plans to fly on to Australia and to Fiji for its independence ceremony, in order to talk about the arms issue with a number of Commonwealth leaders who would be visiting London. I also wrote Heath a reflective letter on October 5, in which I argued that South Africa might be pursuing political or diplomatic objectives, rather than strategic requirements. That is, I suggested, South Africa might be trying to break up the Commonwealth, thereby isolating Britain from black Africa and gaining British support and apparent moral sanction for its regime. African threats to withdraw from the Commonwealth were impetuous and unwise, but Heath should see them not so much as an attempt to put pressure on him as a desire to uphold a fundamental principle of the Commonwealth, racial equality. His undertaking not to make a final decision before consultations with Commonwealth colleagues was most welcome and I suggested that such consultations should be multilateral, especially as Commonwealth governments had agreed to meet in Singapore in January.

My main objective with all the African and Asian leaders I met in October was, as it had been in November 1965 over the Rhodesian UDI, to prevent withdrawals before multilateral talks were held; and I warned them as well that South Africa was setting a trap. The mood was sombre. Their interviews with Heath made them feel his mind was closed to other options. Nyerere told me that he sensed among his British hosts a strong mood of tiredness with the Commonwealth, a feeling of being besieged and needing to assert themselves. If it would help lift the British Government out of this mood, he was quite willing to say publicly that Tanzania did not want to push Britain around, that it recognised the sovereign right of Britain to make its own security decisions and did not accuse its government of racialism.* He had told Heath all of this. Other heads of government I saw in September and early October

---

*He did say it publicly, in a signed article that appeared in *The Observer* on 1 November 1970.

– including Yahya Khan, Prince Dlamini of Swaziland, Forbes Burnham, Presidents Makarios, Seretse Khama and Kaunda – all agreed on the need for multilateral talks.

My efforts irritated the British Government. On October 19 Sir John Johnston raised the matter of a circular letter I proposed to write to all Commonwealth heads suggesting multilateral talks. He claimed that this looked as though I was orchestrating pressure on the British, which went beyond my mandate under the Agreed Memorandum; I had done all that was proper to do, he said, by suggesting in my letter to Heath that he discuss the issue collectively. To me this was a preposterous argument. I was not a Cabinet Secretary, with Heath as my boss, but someone elected by the representatives of nearly one billion people, and my job was clearly to facilitate multilateral consultations on major international issues. In this case, it was doubly important to do so, in order to ensure all Commonwealth governments thought very carefully before taking steps that might break up the association. We argued about this for some time, and could not agree. I sent the circular.

During later October and early November a succession of African heads of government and foreign ministers came through London, to make their concern clear to Heath; they also talked to me. Among the foreign ministers, Sam Odaka left the impression that Uganda would take drastic action if Britain announced they were selling arms, and Okoi Arikpo said African states would at least stay away from the Singapore HGM if an announcement were made beforehand. The Ghanaian Prime Minister, Dr Busia, told me he had written other African Heads of Government suggesting that, if a sale were announced, they consult together about 'expelling' Britain from the Commonwealth. Prem Haksar, the Secretary of the Prime Minister's Office in Delhi, indicated that India would withdraw from the Commonwealth if some African countries began such a move.

Some visitors struck more positive notes. The Kenyan Foreign Minister, Dr Mungai Njoroge, talked about the possibility of a Defence Ministers' meeting before Singapore to discuss security in the Indian Ocean, or else of making the topic a specific item on the HGM agenda. Arikpo made clear it was not Nigeria's intention to extract from Britain a declaration that it would not proceed with arms sales. He also thought heads of government at Singapore should set up a committee to study alternative arrangements for Britain, using perhaps Mombasa or Mauritius. The seeds of a solution were being planted.

The prickliest time came, however, during the visit of President Kaunda at the head of an OAU team of foreign ministers. Heath had been reluctant to see them at all, and in a private talk before they met him on a Friday afternoon, I urged Kaunda not to make any public threats. But they had an unpleasant session with Heath, in which the most that Heath offered was a joint declaration by the South Africans and British that the arms supplied would never be used against Africans, but only for external defence; and Kaunda came to a press conference in an emotional mood. He began talking about 'sanctioning' Britain out of the Commonwealth; he also broadened the issue by bringing in NATO's links with Portugal and western trade with South Africa. It was a disastrous press conference, compounded later by tension at a dinner at Downing Street where Heath insisted people were trying to push him around and the evening ended with Kaunda's abrupt departure. I sat next to Kaunda at a Grosvenor House lunch the next day, and we chewed over these unfortunate episodes; I think he accepted a number of lessons, and Lord Chalfont quoted to him the advice of an old Chinese strategist, 'Build your enemy a golden bridge on which he may retreat.'

This advice may well have spurred Kaunda into drafting, with some help from John Hatch, a Declaration of Commonwealth Principles to be presented at the Singapore HGM. He hoped this would give him and other African leaders a freer hand to seek a solution without upsetting the anti-western factions in their own countries. I liked the draft and encouraged the idea. So did Ivan Head, Trudeau's foreign affairs adviser who visited Kaunda and Nyerere in December and brought a copy back to Canada. Trudeau suggested three changes and also showed it to Heath during a five-hour meeting the two had in Ottawa on December 16. I was given a formal draft to circulate to all governments at the end of the month.

Late in November I visited Ottawa, where the crisis over the Front de Libération du Québec terrorism continued, for the British Trade Commissioner in Montreal James Cross was still being held by kidnappers. A soldier with a submachine-gun escorted me on my rounds. Despite his domestic preoccupations Trudeau was, I found, alert to the problems facing the Commonwealth and keen to help with solutions.

It was important to find a face-saver for the British Government, to allow it quietly to drop the policy of arms sales and provide an alternative way to protect the sea routes. East African leaders had suggested one alternative – a British take-over of the Simonstown facilities – but I knew the South Africans would not accept it. The counter-suggestion, that Commonwealth defence ministers should meet to discuss a defence system for the Indian Ocean, gained more support than might have been expected from countries that adhered to a policy of non-alignment. A representative for Indira Gandhi assured me India would support it as long as the purpose of the system was explicitly stated to be to safeguard trade routes rather than to counter the Soviet presence in the Indian Ocean. But I finally decided to press instead for the establishment at the Singapore HGM of a study group to examine the security of maritime trade routes in the Indian Ocean and South Atlantic. There was a separate proposal from Ceylon to declare the Indian Ocean a 'zone of peace'; the study group plan originated from ideas put forward by Kenya's Dr Mungai and Nigeria's Arikpo, combining with Hugh Shearer of Jamaica. The British Liberal leader Jeremy Thorpe also put the idea of an Indian Ocean study group to Pierre Trudeau in a private letter.

But we still had to arrive at Singapore intact. There were continuing fears that Britain might make an early announcement that it was going ahead with sales, which could prompt Tanzania to withdraw from the Commonwealth and trigger other retaliatory moves. I had also heard from a Mauritian Minister, who had visited Lagos for Nigeria's tenth anniversary of independence and had dined alone with General Gowon (they had been brother officers years before), that Gowon told him Nigeria would not hesitate to withdraw even if Tanzania were dissuaded because of its poverty.

Most disturbing of all was the report I heard in November from a former Indian ambassador that Mrs Gandhi, who was looking for a distracting issue on which to run for reelection, might plunge ahead and announce India's withdrawal before any British action. This would certainly produce a chain reaction among African states. I remember how, in reaction to British intervention at Suez in 1956, the President of India had called for his country's withdrawal from the Commonwealth and the Prime Minister, Jawaharlal Nehru, had argued against the gesture and carried the day. I noted in my diary:

'From my first talk with Alec Home shortly after the elections, I have emphasized the danger of an irrational over-reaction by India. We are faced with the danger of India jumping the gun as she did last spring when she was the first government officially to say that she would boycott the Commonwealth Games unless the MCC cancelled the invitation to the South African cricket team to play in England.

214

'The danger of the present situation is that . . . serious foreign policy decisions may be taken for . . . short-term reasons of domestic image-making and posturing. Nehru, thou shouldst be living at this hour!'

The danger passed, happily. Good advice from several countries, including the United States and Canada where Heath visited in December, helped cool the atmosphere on his side. And Mrs Gandhi held back from the brink. On the way to the Singapore HGM I attend the Commonwealth Law Ministers Conference in Delhi, and talked with her. By then the situation in India was calmer and she spoke positively about events in the Commonwealth. Although she stayed away from the HGM, her Foreign Minister Swaran Singh came and played a conciliatory part in the main debate.

I was still concerned, in the debate ahead in Singapore, that leaders would simply lecture each other, and not consult and listen. A few general arguments on the advantages of consultation I set out in my Third report, and it did not escape the notice of some newspapers, particularly *The Guardian*, that I was trying to convince Heath of the value of listening to advice from others without feeling it was gross interference in his own country's affairs. One passage was particularly pointed:

'It would be erroneous to interpret such multilateral consultations as in any sense an invasion of the sovereignty of member countries. It is accepted that sovereign governments each take decisions within their sovereignty on the basis of their assessment of their respective national interest. That is their responsibility to their people. The function of consultation is to reconcile this fact with the fact that nations live together on a small planet, which they must learn to share.

'. . . The disasters of history suggest that governments at times have made costly blunders due to tragic misjudgements which have usually arisen from a lack of sensitivity to the realities of the outside world in which foreign policy has to operate. Consultations, if approached in the spirit of sincerity, sensitivity and open-mindedness, can decrease the danger of miscalculations.'

The Singapore Heads of Government Meeting, which opened in a special conference hall on Thursday, January 14, was still the most uneasy summit that I remember. For both Heath and Australia's John Gorton were insensitive men and prepared to be irrational, and neither of them seemed to mind the prospect of the conference being a total failure.

There had been two previous Commonwealth Summit Meetings

held outside London: in Ottawa on trade in 1932, and in Lagos for the special conference on Rhodesia in January 1966. I thought the 1971 HGM should take place in Asia so that delegations might feel a balance to the perspectives of Africa and might reflect that more than three-quarters of the people of the Commonwealth were indeed Asian. It would be good to hold the HGM in a developing country which had achieved some spectacular development and Lee's intellectual stature and political acumen would make him a superb choice as chairman. So, as early as the first months of 1970, I asked him to invite us; and he did so.

In two respects the Singapore HGM was a smooth success. Lee Kuan Yew *was* excellent as chairman, and he managed the time-table so that there were more than five days' constructive discussions on topics that went far beyond African concerns. Yet the meeting will be remembered for the tensions over the arms sales issue, the uncertainties up to the final day about the Declaration of Principles, and for some sour remarks which, despite the achievements of the summit, left bad feelings that were not wiped away until the Ottawa HGM in 1973.

Understandably, many African leaders came to Singapore wanting to tackle the arms sales issue first and foremost, because it was the most important. For precisely that reason, I thought it most unwise to discuss it until the heads of government and I had had several days, including a weekend, for private consultations on the most controversial item. So I took the precaution of circulating to delegations a WHO document which gave frightening medical details of how changing time-zones could affect good judgement. The point was accepted, and the agenda was organised so that the subject did not come up until the fifth day.

It was important to keep work on the Declaration of Principles in parallel with discussion on arms sales. In the first few days that happened. Kaunda introduced his draft declaration disarmingly as 'neither a charter nor a code of conduct, but guidelines for the solution of Commonwealth and international problems' and it was then referred to a committee of officials, for clarification and amendments, to be discussed again by delegates under a late item, 'The Commonwealth in the Seventies'. This procedure for handling Kaunda's draft declaration was a British suggestion, to which African officials had agreed. In the event it meant that the Declaration was never discussed in full plenary session, and the changes made to the original Zambian version were worked out by officials or, in the final stages, by a handful of prime ministers.

216

The question of British arms sales was treated delicately in the general political debate that filled the first three days. Most African delegates barely mentioned it. Heath staked out his position by talking of the menace of Soviet naval power and saying Britain had more reason than the rest of Western Europe to be on guard against it in the Indian Ocean. All was running to plan, for the weekend was to be the time to work out compromises.

Then the plan went wrong, in two respects. Heath took himself out of range by going for a Sunday's sail on the yacht of a British military adviser and his daughter. And on Monday afternoon the Jamaican Prime Minister, Hugh Shearer, accelerated the timetable. He had missed a short discussion in which it had been agreed that delegation heads and I would meet privately the next morning to clear up some points in the Declaration draft, and, speaking hours later, he pressed for the meeting to be a secret session instead on the arms sales issue. In the flurry of altering these plans, the heads also agreed to meet without any advisers or note-takers. This forestalled a plan which Harry Lee and I evolved. We had been counting on winning agreement, when the time came, for each head to have one adviser; in particular, we wanted Alec Home to be sitting by Heath as a moderating influence. But now we were launched, without all the preparatory consultations completed, into a secret session of just the thirty-one heads and myself.

In the event, though, the twelve hours of secret session that followed through all of Tuesday and on Wednesday morning went more smoothly than one could have expected. Nobody made threats. African leaders carefully balanced their remarks: they left no doubt about their strong feelings, but at the same time acknowledged that Britain had a right to take its own decisions. Obote seemed typical of African rationality in these sessions when he made the point: 'We want to be non-aligned; but British military cooperation with South Africa would create strong public pressures on us to tilt towards the Eastern bloc.' Heath showed himself to be conciliatory at times, but for the most part he appeared not to be listening. Shearer, spokesman on this issue for the Caribbean leaders, was especially busy with suggestions for compromise. He offered to add to the conference record that no one was asking Heath to abandon the Simonstown Agreements. When this did not produce any corresponding offer from Heath, he said in gentle exasperation, 'Look, we're all under pressure from our people as politicians. Let's not pretend we're a bunch of virgins.'

Gradually a consensus grew around the scheme for a group of

217

countries to study the security problems of maritime trade routes. There was discussion about detailed terms of reference for the group – should it also study the legal aspects of the Simonstown Agreements, and the apartheid system, and so on? The wiser heads saw the study group in broader terms, as a means to give them all time to work their way out of the confrontation. But would Heath give them time? He had asserted Britain's right to sell arms, and they had recognised this right. 'Don't take us back to square one by saying it again in plenary,' he was begged by Kaunda. Heath was still offering nothing, beyond an assurance from the South African government that it would not use any British equipment for purposes other than maritime defence. The support for a study group began to dissolve among Africans (although Arikpo of Nigeria stood firm). We engineered a coffee-break, so that Alec Home could be brought into a nearby room to talk to Heath. Afterwards Heath volunteered that his government had not yet made up its mind about arms sales. This was taken as a sign that he would alter course, in his own time. So the secret session ended, with quarter-promises.

On Wednesday afternoon Lee read out to the plenary conference the agreement to set up the eight-nation study group,* and Heath stated three reservations on the basis of which Britain would join the group – in effect, asserting publicly Britain's right to sell arms. We then endured eight hours of speeches, boring rather than acrimonious, as delegation heads read prepared statements for the public record. During the secret session Dr Banda had kept silent, explaining only that what he had to say he wished to be on the record, so that historians could study it in the twenty-first century. Lee replied that he could guarantee him time to speak on the record, but he could not guarantee that future historians would take note. In the plenary session that night Dr Kamuzu Banda, sitting near the end of the sixty-foot table with a hollow centre filled with tropical pot plants, rolled out his oratory for more than an hour. It was a dismal scene, lacking all intimacy. Twice I whispered to the chairman that he should cut Banda short. Lee hesitated. The second time I suggested it, he recalled that he had given the Malawi leader extra security guards because he was thought to be a special target for Communist elimination squads and added: 'I won't cut him off, but I'm tempted to take away his guards!'

---

*It was to consist of representatives of Australia, Britain, Canada, India, Jamaica, Kenya, Malaysia, and Nigeria, plus the Secretariat.

218

Around midnight the session was enlivened by Trudeau giving a broad brush-sweep of what might happen in southern Africa over the years ahead, and asking many questions; what was the total picture? where did members want it all to end? It was a penetrating speech that established the Canadian Prime Minister among Commonwealth leaders; more immediately, it loosened up a taut session. The delegates headed for their hotels at 4 a.m. without retreating on the study group scheme.

But the Declaration of Principles had still to be tied up. It had been improved during the week, in particular with a stronger and more coherent paragraph on achieving a more equitable world society by fairer terms of trade as well as aid transfers. But the Australian prime minister, John Gorton, a plodding politician who had supported Heath solidly in the arms issue, was full of doubts about the draft just before lunch on the conference's final day. It was important to end the conference with an agreed Declaration, both because it was a valuable if imperfect statement dealing with world peace, citizens' rights, racial prejudice and Third World poverty, and also because without it African leaders would appear to have yielded to Heath on the arms issue and achieved little in return. Again, Trudeau proved a helpful fixer. He persuaded Gorton to drop some halfbaked ideas and to agree, as Heath also did, to the paragraph on combatting racial discrimination, when amended with a five-word insertion which then stated that no member should give assistance which 'in its own judgement directly' contributed to racism. It was not difficult to win African acceptance of this addition as the price of gaining the whole Declaration.

I had warned, at a press conference just before the HGM began, against countries outside the Commonwealth trying to 'drive a wedge' between Britain and the African nations. Most journalists took this as a reference to the Soviet Union, especially after the 19,200-ton cruiser Alexandr Suvorov steamed westward through the Straits of Malacca in full sight of all delegates on the meeting's second day, giving weight to Heath's argument about the threat in the Indian Ocean. After the HGM, resting before going on to Australia for the Commonwealth Education Ministers Meeting, Eve and I stayed at Lee's villa at Changi and went to a Chinese New Year's party, where Eve was seated beside the Soviet Ambassador. He questioned her vigorously throughout the meal about the British motives for wanting to sell arms to South Africa. He saw the political advantages to his own country, and thought there must be offsetting advantages to the British, for surely they were subtle, even Macchiavellian, in their diplomacy. He could not conceive that sometimes they could be plain stupid.

Another 'outsider' I had been referring to was South Africa, which in March and April 1971 tried to knock the wedge further in by informal requests to Britain to supply armaments on a large scale – six modern frigates and, it was also rumoured, a complete guided missile system. However, Heath's law officers had in February advised him that the Simonstown Agreements placed Britain under the legal obligation to supply only helicopters for three anti-submarine frigates, and some naval spares; and, one month after the Singapore HGM ended, he announced that Britain would sell seven Wasp helicopters valued at about £2 million. He ignored any other requests. Only six helicopters were delivered before Wilson returned to power in 1974 and scrapped the Simonstown Agreement.

It was a petulant gesture of defiance by Heath to sell the helicopters, and it led to the withdrawals of Nigeria, India and Malaysia from the study group on maritime routes. The whole idea of a study group was quietly dropped in July, but it had served its purpose in helping to push aside the arms sales question. Carrying through its work was not essential. The British Government had learnt a lesson, however unacknowledged, and drawn back from the outsiders' trap – across a golden bridge.

My involvement in the Mozambique peace negotiations began within a fortnight of the overthrow of the Caetano government in Portugal on 25 April 1974. I was interested for several reasons. One was Mozambique's strategic position along the flank of Rhodesia. Another was because the new leader, General Antonio de Spinola, had talked about a 'Commonwealth type of system' for Portugal's African territories, inaccurately equating that with a federation of autonomous states. A third reason was that the signatories to the Lusaka Declaration of 1973, whose principal authors were Nyerere and Kaunda, had undertaken to urge the liberation movements 'to desist from their armed struggle and to cooperate in the mechanics of a peaceful transfer of power from Portugal to the peoples of the African territories', if Portugal should change its policy and accept the principle of self-determination. This now seemed possible: so, in a news conference in Ottawa on May 10, I said of General Spinola's statement: 'If he wants assistance in setting up a Commonwealth, we will be only too glad to help him.' And, on my return to London, I wrote offering help.

His Foreign Minister, Dr Mario Soares, came to London on May 24 to open negotiations with the PAIGC nationalists of Guiné who had been fighting Portugal for thirteen years. I went to see him that evening at his hotel, to offer him Commonwealth assistance if he was serious in wanting a negotiated settlement with Mozambique involving independence. I told him of the Lusaka Declaration, and stressed that the help of Tanzania and Zambia, on whose territory the Frelimo forces were based, could be valuable. Soares saw the point and was immediately keen to use Commonwealth channels to start negotiations with Frelimo leaders. So I telephoned Nyerere's office in Dar es Salaam, and his Principal Secretary, Dickson Nkembo, flew north that night with a foreign ministry official. They met Soares and Colonel João de Almeida Bruno, an important figure in the April coup, in my flat the next evening. Soares spoke French but not English; so Soomer Lallah, a Mauritian lawyer on the Secretariat staff, acted as interpreter.

Nkembo was authorized by Frelimo leaders to tell Soares that if Portugal made a public acceptance of the principles of self-determination and complete independence and explained how independence was to be achieved, Frelimo forces would stop fighting. Soares argued that his government was sincere about self-determination, but could not say so publicly yet because of fear of how the white minority in Mozambique and the South Africans would react and what might happen in the coming elections in Portugal. He said he would give an assurance privately to an OAU meeting, but in the meantime Frelimo should trust the good faith of a government that had released political prisoners, disbanded the secret police and put in office socialists like himself who had been in exile and detention. Nkembo reported back to Dar over the weekend and on the Monday met Soares again in my flat to say that a meeting with Frelimo leaders was being arranged in Lusaka within the week.

The Lusaka talks in early June did not go well. A basic obstacle was General Spinola's line of thinking about self-determination. It did not alter from what he had said in his famous book *Portugal and the Future*, whose publication in February had triggered the revolution. Soares argued in May that Spinola had written guardedly under conditions of military censorship, but in June Spinola was still hedging on any pledge of complete independence. He was offering no timetable for self-government, and talking only about holding a referendum about what type of constitution the people wanted.

There was a good deal of activity in late June: Portuguese negoti-

221

ations with the PAIGC in Algiers, a tour by Spinola of both Angola and Mozambique. But the Portuguese-Frelimo talks in Lusaka had been suspended, and I wanted to find out if I could help to get them started again. So in early July I flew to Dar es Salaam, where as cover I had been invited to attend the Saba Saba (7/7) celebrations, for that year was the twentieth anniversary of the founding of the TANU party. I had arranged to see, while there, the Frelimo President, Samora Machel. Before leaving London, I told Jim Callaghan, by then Foreign Secretary, of my plan and got his agreement that I could use British channels to communicate urgently with Lisbon. Callaghan felt from his own conversations with Soares that the Portuguese leaders were still 'blinking in the sunlight' after the darkness of a half-century of dictatorship. He hoped to get Spinola to abandon his idea of a referendum, but he hoped also that the Frelimo leaders could be brought to understand the problems in Lisbon.

After a morning of Saba Saba ceremonies on July 7, I met the Frelimo leadership in private. Machel had with him Marcellino dos Santos and Joaquim Chissano, his chief colleagues. They were in an angry and suspicious mood: not suspicious of myself because Nyerere had vouched for me, but of Soares. They thought he had been merely playing at negotiations in June in order that Portugal would appear progressive to western countries, to get aid and to establish respectability at the United Nations; but that he was really stringing them along without any real intention of conceding independence.

I thought they were misassessing the situation badly, and told them so. Spinola was trying to tie Soares' hands, I suggested. Soares did not have adequate breadth of negotiating instructions to talk about independence, but he was sincere. I argued that it was worth their trying to see if something could not be made of this situation: for example, why not offer some concessions to the Portuguese as a way to allay their fears – perhaps a transition period of up to a year, and elections before independence? This provoked the retort from one of Machel's colleagues that the idea of reaching independence by negotiations and with a transition period might be a Commonwealth tradition, but it was no part of the Portuguese or Mozambican tradition and he saw no reason why it would work for them. I said it had worked in Tanzania, Zambia and many other countries on their continent. It had become an African tradition. They had nothing to lose by trying, and a good deal to gain: why not try? At this point Machel nodded and remarked, 'There's something to be said for this.'

He then delivered what amounted to a positive ultimatum for me to convey to Soares. When they had broken off the Lusaka talks in June, Soares had suggested that contacts should be renewed in the first half of July. Machel said he would wait until July 20 to see if the Portuguese government did make contact: if it did not, he would take its silence to mean that Portugal was 'refusing independence' and, he implied, he would order his troops to intensify the war. But, he added, if Soares did reconvene the meeting on the basis of negotiating independence, he could envisage various guarantees for the 250,000 Portuguese minority, assurances about investment, trading relations and cultural contacts, and a transition period.

It was a good outcome to this two and one-half hour meeting with the Frelimo leaders, which had begun in a combative, dingdong way. Both Emeka Anyaoku and I were heartened by it, and detailed conversations with Nyerere and Kaunda confirmed this view. Kaunda was confident that, given the establishment in Mozambique of a provisional (possibly coalition) government under Frelimo leadership, many safeguards could be negotiated as well as elections before independence. But (Kaunda added) it would be a tragedy if, through a lack of mutual understanding, the possibility of an agreed solution was discarded. I sent messages to Soares, by cipher telegram from Dar, Lusaka and Accra through Callaghan's office, reporting all this and adding my own assessment that the only way to end Portugal's wars in Africa was to concede unequivocally the principle of independence and to start serious negotiations to this end.

Events were moving fast in Portugal itself. The argument on exactly this issue between Spinola and Soares burst into the open. Spinola dismissed Soares, and immediately afterwards was himself removed from the presidency. By July 17, Soares had been reappointed Foreign Minister in a more likeminded government. Back in London on July 19, I sent him a letter that added the views of the Kenyan and Ghanaian leaders and urged him to move swiftly in negotiations. The Portuguese Chargé d'Affaires, who transmitted the letter, was worried about Frelimo's July 20 deadline and said that Frelimo forces had already begun to threaten the town of Murrumbala. I said I thought a major offensive would be delayed, in view of the ministerial changes in Portugal.

This part of the Mozambique story has a happy conclusion. The talks were resumed and, despite a brief effort in September by some white extremists in Lourenço Marques (now Maputo) to seize the radio station and stage a UDI, the country moved to independence in June 1975 after a transition period under a provisional government. Something of the Commonwealth tradition spilled over into Mozambique.

I raised another issue during my talk with Samora Machel and his colleagues, which proved no less important during the next few years: whether Frelimo, once it led the government of Mozambique, would enforce a complete blockade on Rhodesia, in accordance with UN sanctions, and give maximum help to bring majority rule to that country. Machel said that Mozambique was largely dependent on Rhodesia for food imports, and on transit payments from that country for foreign exchange. He would need a year after independence to get his administrative control effectively established. He would also need technical assistance, and significant capital assistance, to replace earnings from Rhodesian transit payments. Subject to this, he would do all he could to help. I promised to try to arrange technical assistance from Commonwealth experts; for capital assistance I hoped to arrange an initiative by Commonwealth members at the United Nations, in order to tap American and other sources as well as Commonwealth members. Help was indeed forthcoming from both Commonwealth and United Nations sources, and the director of the Secretariat's TAG team, Gordon Goundrey, eventually moved to the United Nations as an Assistant Secretary-General and continued to make the matter of assistance to Mozambique one of his special concerns.

On the same trip in July 1974, the first steps were taken towards a Commonwealth programme for Namibians. The original request came from Sean MacBride, the former Irish Foreign Minister whom I first came to know in 1966 when he was running the International Commission of Jurists in Geneva. By 1974 he was United Nations Commissioner for Namibia and when we met in Lusaka he talked confidently about the transfer of power by South Africa being completed within two years. It was, with hindsight, much too optimistic: South Africa had resisted since 1946, by every possible means, the assertion of any United Nations authority over the territory, and had taken scant notice when in October 1966 the UN General Assembly overwhelmingly voted to terminate South Africa's mandate and declare South West Africa (soon renamed Namibia) 'henceforth under the direct responsibility of the United Nations'. But it was in the nature of this remarkable man, his enthusiasm undimmed at seventy, to expect the good to happen and to plan to make it better. He thought the coup in Portugal, which would inevitably lead to independence in Angola, would in turn open the way for Namibia. He was anxious to set up a Namibian Institute in Lusaka, to train public servants for the future independent government; and he asked me for Commonwealth assistance in doing so.

I was equally keen to help, but had to say that we would first need to have the approval of Zambia as the host country and then of Commonwealth countries collectively, in order to extend CFTC assistance to the territory. I had authority to give CFTC aid to any Commonwealth developing country or dependency; I was prepared to argue that Namibians qualified because they had been Commonwealth citizens until they were deprived of this link by the racist actions of their administering power, South Africa, which led in 1961 to South Africa's withdrawal from the Commonwealth. Also I would argue that Namibia should be helped as a potential Commonwealth member in the near future. Sean MacBride liked these arguments. He said that he too hoped Namibia would join the Commonwealth, and that it would choose English as its official language. At that point two other languages – Afrikaans and German, surviving with the many farming families that remained from the days of its being the Kaiser's colony – had equal standing.

I soon found that others were not so eager about the Namibian connection. Three times my request was turned down: by the CFTC Committee of Management, by a meeting of Senior Officials (i.e. the heads of civil services of member countries) and in January 1975 by a Review Committee made up of seven cabinet secretaries. The main grounds given for opposing the scheme was that Namibia was not a Commonwealth country or dependency and that I was inviting undesirable controversy. The opposition was led by British officials; the British Government had been one of only three to abstain when the UN General Assembly terminated South Africa's mandate, so they were doubly cautious about stepping out of line with that country.

The lesson was plain: not to put new political proposals in front of government officials, however senior, but to take them directly to politicians. I circulated a memorandum to Heads of Government ahead (but not too far ahead) of the HGM that was held in Jamaica in May 1975, and it was not difficult at that meeting to win a consensus from the Heads of Government. A few months earlier Emeka Anyaoku had talked in Lusaka with Sam Nujoma, president of the South West African Peoples Organisation, and with my encouragement Nujoma himself submitted a memorandum to the HGM asking for Commonwealth assistance. Unlike his civil servants Callaghan, who had met SWAPO leaders during a trip to Lusaka in January, was particularly positive at the Jamaica conference.

Sam Nujoma called on me in London to express his delight at the Jamaica HGM decision. It so happened that my wife and I were holding a farewell garden party at Marlborough House the next day, and I invited him to come. The Queen was coming; and some FCO officials, who had learnt the guest list through security sources, told me they hoped I would avoid any photographs being taken when I presented the SWAPO president to the Queen. Obviously they spoke neither for Callaghan nor the Queen.

Implementation of the decision about Namibia took time, but the programme was not unimportant. The allocation was £87,500 in 1976-77 for the support of some seventy-six Namibian students and trainees in five Commonwealth developing countries. It was increased the following year to £200,000, which provided eighty more scholarships. At the same time a number of Commonwealth governments – including Australia, Canada, Nigeria and Britain – gave bilateral scholarship support for some seventy other Namibians. Through the UN Institute for Namibia and other UN programmes, to which Commonwealth countries also contributed, another three hundred Namibian students were being trained.

This was a start, and it was heartening to realize the broadening effect upon future Namibian leaders and professionals of taking, say, agricultural courses in Jamaica or carpentry training in Barbados as well as academic courses nearer home in seven African countries. And the Secretariat organised other technical assistance. At SWAPO's request, it recruited a consultant to do a factual survey of mineral developments in Namibia and analyse the legal position of foreign companies that had started mining operations after the UN ended South Africa's mandate. The report *The Mineral Industry of Namibia – Perspectives for Independence* was handed to Nujoma in 1978. As well, the Secretariat supported a workshop in 1978 to establish priorities for a Nationhood Programme for Namibia, for which UN agencies proposed various projects.

But a scholarship and training programme for fewer than five hundred students is clearly not going to meet the acute manpower needs of a disadvantaged country of about 1.5 million people, or the hunger for knowledge and advancement of the 35,000 Namibians who have fled into exile in Zambia and Angola. I hope that a much larger effort will be mounted by all those countries, particularly those in the Commonwealth, that in 1966 through the United Nations took a unique step in making Namibia their direct responsibility to bring to self government and independence. One scheme planned during 1980 was to set up in Lusaka a Namibia Extension Unit to tackle the basic educational needs of these refugees, by preparing correspondence course texts and audio-visual aids and training supervisors for a project in functional literacy to benefit at least 6000 refugees. If the Commonwealth is to live up to its principles of collaborating to help the most disadvantaged people in a practical way, Namibians have a strong claim to assistance.

The public approval by Heads of Government at the Jamaica HGM in May 1975 of programmes to help Namibians caused a minor press commotion, and two friendly South African reporters in London asked me why Namibia was considered eligible when it had not been a British colony. I replied that it had been a protectorate of a Commonwealth member, South Africa, which had left the Commonwealth because of race discrimination but Namibians were not to blame for that. If it later wanted to join the Commonwealth, when it had gained independence, I was sure that Namibia would be very welcome. They asked if South Africa itself would ever be considered eligible, and I answered: 'Of course, if South Africa should decide to come in out of the cold, and abandon the race discrimination policies that have made it an outcast from the international community. I feel confident that Commonwealth governments would welcome a nondiscriminatory South Africa under majority rule into Commonwealth membership.'
They seemed pleasantly surprised at the idea.

I turn now to the final years in the Southern Rhodesian story before it was transformed into independent Zimbabwe.
A political pause followed the Pearce Commission on Rhodesian Opinion in 1972, described in Chapter 4, and Commonwealth countries became more concerned to plan for the future Zimbabwe. The important task was to train administrators and technical people for the years ahead. The Special Commonwealth Programme for Zimbabweans had provided scholarships for three hundred and fifty Zimbabweans by 1972. The programme needed expansion on a large scale. This started in May 1972, when the Canadian Government signed an agreement to provide up to $75,000 a year to let the Secretariat pay for the education and training of Zimbabweans

in Commonwealth developing countries. Thus began the multilateral Commonwealth Zimbabwe Scholarship Fund (CZSF). In the eight years from May 1972 over four thousand more students were assisted through the programme, four-fifths of them through bilateral offers of places from Commonwealth governments (for which the Secretariat played a coordinating role) and about 750 of them through the CZSF.

The special programme will be wound down when by 1983-84 the students abroad will have completed their courses. It is a programme of which all the Commonwealth countries that participated, from Fiji to Sierra Leone, can feel proud. The Secretariat followed up with a questionnaire to graduates of these courses, and was able to make available to the Mugabe government data on more than nine hundred trained Zimbabweans. Probably no other African country has gone to independence with such a large cadre of people who have had solid training and worldwide experience and Zimbabwe, as an independent member of the Commonwealth, will continue to benefit from CFTC training and education assistance, and from the Commonwealth Scholarship and Fellowship scheme.

The Rhodesian issue was less explosive at the Ottawa HGM in August 1973 than at any summit in recent years. Nevertheless, just before the HGM there was a flurry of activity in Rhodesia. Ian Smith reluctantly started talks with the African National Council, led by Bishop Muzorewa. To show he still wielded an iron fist, he detained some top ANC officials at the same time and, in the middle of the HGM, his police arrested 155 university students in Salisbury after a stone-throwing riot. In this suddenly heightened atmosphere Erroll Barrow, the Barbados prime minister, spoke somewhat emotionally about raising a Commonwealth 'occupation force'. Later speakers softened the concept of such a force and, although Heath said it would prejudice progress in any discussions between the Smith regime and African leaders, most others including Trudeau thought the idea of a peacekeeping force was practical and could at the right time have appeal for both sides. The idea waited for implementation more than six years; but the dispatch in December 1979 of a 1300-strong Commonwealth military observer group had its origins in Barrow's impatient call in Ottawa. The Heads of Government in 1973 also took a significant step in agreeing on the need to give 'every humanitarian assistance' to all the indigenous people of southern Africa engaged in trying to achieve self-determination.

The following year, bringing the change of government in Portugal, was a landmark in the Rhodesian saga although it was not until 1976 that ZANU's guerilla forces began operating in any numbers across the Mozambique border. For other reasons, as well, the political background to the next HGM – in Kingston, Jamaica, in May 1975 – was confusing. Although Ian Smith had released the leading detainees – Nkomo, Ndabaningi Sithole, Mugabe – and although the first two had signed a unity agreement accepting Bishop Muzorewa as leader, there were signs of cracks inside the nationalist movement, the most ominous being the murder of Herbert Chitepo.

The chairman, Michael Manley, invited several Zimbabwean leaders to Jamaica and announced at a press conference that he would be proposing to the meeting that they hear a statement from Bishop Muzorewa. Surprisingly, Pierre Trudeau was strongly opposed. He suggested to me that it was comparable to the UN General Assembly's action in voting to hear Yasser Arafat, the PLO leader, and would create a Commonwealth precedent for hearing a Quebec secessionist. I told him I saw no such analogy, if we agreed unanimously to hear the Bishop. If Britain, which had formal sovereignty over Rhodesia, did not object, there was surely no need for anyone else to do so. But Trudeau continued lobbying against the idea, and upset Nyerere and Kaunda who could see no conceivable analogy with Quebec separatism, until we all agreed on a face-saving compromise, by which the Bishop would address the heads at an informal gathering. Manley was to vacate the chairmanship, and I was to take over, introducing the Bishop and thanking him afterwards. Further to emphasize the informal nature, Trudeau left the chair designated 'Canada' and moved round to sit beside Harry Lee.

Muzorewa made some interesting points: he suggested that the rich Commonwealth countries should take white Rhodesians as immigrants, and thus provide a safety-valve. He also argued in support of my proposal that the Commonwealth should help Mozambique to apply sanctions fully and stop the transit trade to Rhodesia, on which the rebel colony depended for most of its imports and exports. The heads accepted this proposal, and stated so in the communiqué, with the result that a special Commonwealth Fund for Mozambique was set up in March 1976, immediately after the border was closed. The £1 million subscribed to this fund was used for developmental purposes, such as studies to expand the port facilities of Beira.

Dr Henry Kissinger entered the Rhodesian scene in 1976, anxious to avoid repeating the débâcle of Angola. He had not been at all interested in African affairs until Cuban troops appeared in Angola. Now he hastened to make up time with some shuttle-diplomacy over Rhodesia. The pressure which he put on the South African prime minister, John Vorster, to lean in turn on Ian Smith helped in the end to break the political log-jam. For he persuaded the Rhodesian leader to face what had been a taboo before, to concede majority rule in principle, and to talk about implementing it in two years.

This was a time, I thought, for a bold British initiative while the Rhodesians were off balance. I was out of office by then and back in Canada; but through Canadian officials and British diplomats I informally urged that the British Government should send into Rhodesia a new Governor to chair all-party negotiations, that British and Canadian paratroops land in his support, and that the Queen broadcast an appeal to the Rhodesians. With the Rhodesians off balance, I did not think their forces would fire on the British or Canadian troops. It was the same formula that I had suggested would work in 1965. At this stage it seemed an opportunity to move quickly into a constitutional conference with the important advantage for Britain of a military presence and authority in the country.

The opportunity, however, was not seized. It took Ian Smith a further two years to begin to accept the implication of his commitment to majority rule, but it was still a psychological breakthrough. The Geneva conference, which opened in October 1976, concentrated upon the structure of an interim government and eventually collapsed in January 1977 when Smith would not accept the scheme for a British commissioner and an African majority in the Council of Ministers.

The Commonwealth Secretariat was busily involved in the Geneva conference, for by then there were four African delegations (headed by Muzorewa, Nkomo, Sithole and Mugabe). At the 1975 HGM Commonwealth leaders had 'pledged to concert their efforts for the speedy attainment of . . . independence on the basis of majority rule' and, acting in this spirit, the Secretariat provided legal advice to the (still united) nationalists at the Victoria Falls talks in August 1975, and later during the negotiations Nkomo held with Smith. At Geneva the assistance was greatly increased to the point of providing a team of six experts to support each of the African delegations, while Emeka Anyaoku remained there throughout the conference to assist all of them.

Early in 1977 Britain's new Foreign Secretary, David Owen, took a different course from the line pursued at Geneva. He involved the Carter administration and its roving ambassador, Andy Young, in a joint initiative and concentrated as much on the independence constitution itself as on the transitional arrangements, which had been the preoccupation at Geneva. But the Anglo-American proposals, finally published in September 1977, also involved a toughening of the British line over the transition. The Smith regime would have to surrender power to a British Resident Commissioner (Owen's predecessor, Anthony Crosland, had only suggested an Interim Commissioner with reserve powers, working with a Council of Ministers). The Resident Commissioner would organise elections before independence, aided by a United Nations Zimbabwe Force to supervise the ceasefire and by a Special Representative of the UN Secretary-General. The police forces would keep law and order during the transition to independence, which might last a year since a period of up to six months was suggested between elections and independence. During this time a Zimbabwe National Army would be formed to replace the existing armed forces.

At the London HGM in June 1977 the Tanzanian Vice-President, Aboud Jumbe, was particularly insistent on the disbanding of the Rhodesian forces and this concern was reflected in the communiqué. Field Marshal Lord Carver, who was appointed Resident Commissioner-designate, worked out a plan for an integrated army of no more than 24,000 troops,* with those from the two warring sides balanced by a large number of fresh recruits. The proposals also promised a Zimbabwe Development Fund, jointly sponsored by the British and United States governments, with a target of between US $1000 million and $1500 million.

Why did the Anglo-American proposals not carry the day? One obvious reason is that Ian Smith began to undermine them, as soon as they were made public in September, and within a few weeks had managed to enrol African 'internal leaders' in settlement talks that led to the 'March 3rd Agreement' in 1978. But it is also significant that the momentum behind the proposals was already starting to slow. For this Kenneth Kaunda must take at least some of the blame.

The Zambian President accepted the Anglo-American proposals in principle, as had the other 'Front-Line Presidents' and Nkomo

---

*Later, in September 1979, he said he thought Zimbabwe could afford no more than 10,000 troops. Source: Gemini News Service.

and Mugabe. But Kaunda questioned some basic points. In particular, he argued against holding general elections before independence, for fear that the campaigning would spark tribal fighting between Nkomo's Matabele supporters in ZAPU and Mugabe's Mashona followers in ZANU, and end with full-scale intervention by their opposing armies. Realizing that this could be misconstrued as promoting the interests of an old friend, Kaunda nevertheless began quietly pressing for the formation of a government of national unity under Joshua Nkomo, somewhat after the pattern in India in 1947.

He was persuaded to abandon this scheme after talks with various people, but not before it had caused a split with Nyerere who maintained that they could not discard the principle of independence on the basis of 'one man one vote' for which they had fought so long; this principle, he argued, assumed elections before independence. The coolness between these veteran colleagues took a long time to vanish.

The truth is, Kaunda who has too often believed the best of people, fell victim to the wiles of Ian Smith, whose greatest talent lay in dividing his African adversaries to destroy them piecemeal. In his secret visit to Lusaka in September 1977, Smith sowed distrust between Kaunda and Nyerere and between the leaders of the flimsy Patriotic Front, Nkomo and Mugabe. By August 1978 Smith had decided that his main partners in the 'internal settlement' – Muzorewa and Sithole – were unable to wind down the guerilla war with their appeals to 'the boys in the bush', and went behind their backs to negotiate again with Nkomo in Lusaka. His negotiations also entangled the Nigerian Commissioner for External Affairs, Colonel Garba, as well as Kaunda; and though they fell apart after Nkomo's forces shot down a Rhodesian Viscount full of civilians, he was less harmed than his adversaries who were scattered in mutual distrust. Smith went back to his strained partnership with the internal leaders through the general elections of April 1979, which brought Bishop Muzorewa to the ambiguous post of Prime Minister of 'Zimbabwe Rhodesia'.

It was difficult for other Commonwealth countries, and the Commonwealth Secretariat, to chart a course through all these cross-currents. My successor, Sonny Ramphal, consistently put his weight behind the Anglo-American proposals as the best basis for a settlement, and behind holding elections before independence. What he was most concerned for was that the four Front-Line Presidents worked together, and that the two parts of the Patriotic Front did the same. When the PF leaders met British and United States representatives in Malta in January 1978, with delegates from front-line states present, the Secretariat provided technical and other advisers. And when Bishop Muzorewa flew to London immediately after signing the March 3 agreement, Ramphal questioned him closely on how the war could be ended without the involvement of the PF in the negotiated settlement, and urged him to work for greater unity among Zimbabwean leaders.

There was also the question of evasion of oil sanctions. At the 1977 HGM this was the main area on which leaders, especially Kaunda, focussed when discussing Rhodesia. As a result, the Commonwealth Sanctions Committee formed an eleven-nation working group to re-examine legislation in their respective countries with a view to strengthening the enforcement of oil sanctions and (in the words of the HGM directive) 'to persuade other countries to take similar steps'. The group in turn commissioned a study by Martin Bailey and Bernard Rivers, who later received an award as 'Investigative Reporters of the Year in Britain' for their work on this subject. The group's report in October 1977 pointed out that Rhodesia had managed to acquire up to 18,000 barrels a day 'with comparative ease' and cited allegations against the South African subsidiaries of Mobil, Shell and BP. The committee (comprising representatives of all Commonwealth countries, including Britain) made two recommendations. The first was that countries whose companies supplied oil to South Africa should tell the government there that it faced 'a stark choice'; either it must show it was cutting supplies to Rhodesia, or it must face equivalent cuts itself. The second was to seek from the UN Security Council a mandatory embargo on the supply of oil to South Africa, if that country failed to give adequate guarantees. The catch was that no time-limit was set down for South Africa's compliance, and British officials thereafter always argued that the time was not opportune for concerted action against the Republic. It was a Damocles sword suspended from a thick rope.

The critical moment came in May 1979. Margaret Thatcher's Conservatives won an impressive election victory in Britain only two weeks after Bishop Muzorewa's UANC had taken fifty-one of the seventy-two 'open' seats in the elections organised under the internal settlement. The Anglo-American proposals had finally foundered after Lord Carver's resignation as Commissioner-designate in November 1978, and Callaghan's emissary Cledwyn Hughes had recently reported there was no prospect of holding all-party talks.

233

There was an understandably big temptation for Mrs Thatcher to maintain that the internal settlement fulfilled the six principles, to offer her blessing to the Bishop, to legalise the country's independence and lift sanctions, and to pull Britannia's skirts aside if the blood flowed afterwards.

Fortunately, she did not rush at the situation. Her ministers made speeches about the 'fundamental change' brought about by the elections in Rhodesia, and senior Foreign Office men began commuting to Salisbury. But she did not commit herself to irreversible actions, and this restraint allowed time for knowledgeable advisers to call on her and her Foreign Secretary. The one key action she had taken – and a very wise one – was to appoint Lord Carrington as Foreign and Commonwealth Secretary. Carrington had been a good influence on Heath during the arms sales issue of 1970, and had kept in realistic touch with the Rhodesian situation through talks with Lord Carver and others.

Although Carrington on May 22 said the British Government would be guided by the conclusions on the Rhodesian elections made by Lord Boyd, he was careful not to say that would be the only guidance. Lord Boyd, whose heyday in Africa was as Colonial Secretary twenty years earlier, duly reported favourably, that the elections had been 'free and fair'. But much the more solid question was whether the constitution under which they were held was a basis for real independence. The Thatcher government began heeding authoritative arguments disputing its validity. Dr Claire Palley, who in 1966 wrote the definitive work on Southern Rhodesia's constitutional history, argued forcefully in a booklet 'Should the Present Government be Recognised?' that the constitution complied with none of the six principles. And the small but superb Legal Division at the Commonwealth Secretariat, headed by Kutlu Fuad and Jeremy Pope, wrote a devastating analysis of the constitution exposing the interlocking machinery by which the twenty-eight white MPs could perpetuate white control of the police, army, judiciary and key civil service posts, and concluded:

'Virtually every lever of institutional power has been retained in white hands; those few surrendered have been effectively emasculated. . . . The people are bequeathed a government bereft of the power to govern effectively, and a Legislature denuded of all means either to change the status quo, or to advance the legitimate aspirations of the nation as a whole. . . . (The constitution) is revealed as a carefully contrived subterfuge for sustaining a wholly anti-democratic regime.'

The Secretariat's analysis was endorsed in the report to Heads of Government of the Commonwealth Committee on Southern Africa (the old Sanctions Committee renamed), which said it justified their own conclusion that 'the elections could not, and indeed were not intended to, produce majority rule'. With some dissent from the British representative, the rest of the committee added:

'The present situation holds little prospect for an end to the mounting suffering and bloodshed in Rhodesia; indeed, recent developments may intensify the conflict. If an acceptable solution is to come to Zimbabwe through negotiations, it is self-evident that it must be by a process involving all parties to the conflict. To proceed on any other assumption is to accept the inevitability of a military solution alone – and one that could dangerously internationalise the conflict.'

A delegation of Commonwealth High Commissioners (including Australia, Canada, and Trinidad as well as African states) went with Sonny Ramphal to call on Carrington and express such concerns about Rhodesia. He had several other knowledgeable callers including Cyrus Vance. The UN Security Council (with Britain, France and the United States abstaining) and the Organisation of African Unity passed resolutions calling on states not to recognise the new Rhodesian administration. There could have been little doubt of the opposition building up against any British action to anoint the Bishop's government.

There were other restraining influences. Lord Harlech, who had a good grounding in Rhodesian affairs when he was a deputy chairman of the Pearce Commission in 1972, was named Mrs Thatcher's special envoy to Africa. In June he visited seven independent states (including Nigeria), met Mugabe and Nkomo and in early July went to Salisbury. And then at the end of June Mrs Thatcher found herself receiving strong cautionary advice from the Australian Prime Minister, Malcolm Fraser.

Until 1979 Australia had played a role in African affairs that was either unquestioningly supportive of Britain (as with Menzies always, and with Gorton at Singapore) or else relatively minor. Fraser was attending his first HGM in 1977, and had some inhibitions about playing a major role in the most controversial issue that year, the subject of apartheid in sport; for his neighbour, New Zealand's Muldoon, was the main target for African criticism. But away from the London limelight, he stepped forward to help engineer the Gleneagles Agreement and, in the process, he formed a friendship with Michael Manley. By 1979 he had firmly established links

235

beyond his region: with Manley through attending an 'economic summit' in Jamaica, with Julius Nyerere through a lively High Commission in Dar. He also could exert unique influence upon Margaret Thatcher, since the federal director of his Liberal Party, Tony Eggleton, had lent his remarkable talents as an election manager to the British Conservatives for two periods that year – and with effective results. Finally when in May Pierre Trudeau was defeated in Canada's general election by Joe Clark, a novice in international affairs, Australia and Malcolm Fraser became unquestionably a key factor in the balance over Rhodesia.

It seems clear that Fraser was influential in persuading Mrs Thatcher, on the morrow of her election victory, to hold off any action on Rhodesia; he may even have helped persuade her to choose Carrington (whom he knew as a former British High Commissioner in Canberra) as Foreign Secretary. For he dispatched two senior assistants at once to London to confer with top Conservatives on international affairs. Late in June she in turn visited Australia, and surprised a Canberra press conference and set the doves fluttering again by suggesting that she would not act to continue economic sanctions, when the parliamentary order expired in November; extending recognition to the Muzorewa regime would, she said, 'take a little longer'. But during her visit she received some useful advice from Fraser.

She caused a further stir by speaking of the 'final advice' she would give to the Queen on whether it was safe for her to visit Zambia around the time of the HGM, and implied that it would be negative advice. I was shocked at her ineptness. It was, after all, not the job of the British Prime Minister to advise the Head of the Commonwealth on this matter: it was the responsibility of Sonny Ramphal as Secretary-General or of all the Heads of Government collectively, for the Queen was planning to visit Lusaka as Head of the Commonwealth. In any case, the Palace did not wait for Mrs Thatcher to return to London and offer advice. The following day it issued a statement saying the Queen had 'every intention' of fulfilling her plans to visit Tanzania, Malawi, Botswana – and Zambia.

There had been speculation for weeks in Britain's Conservative press that the HGM might have to be moved to Nairobi because of the fighting across the Zambezi and the Rhodesian raids into Lusaka itself. Bishop Muzorewa added to the speculation in mid-June when he said, 'No one can guarantee the conference can go on peacefully without some disruption. I think they are taking a risk having it in Zambia.' This was a mild way of threatening disruptive raids, which would presumably be justified as retaliation for ZAPU attacks out of Zambia. So Ramphal and Anyaoku foreclosed that dangerous possiblity by persuading Joshua Nkomo to offer a suspension of cross-border activity for seventeen days, from the day before the Queen's visit began. The flavour of some British comment at that emotional time can be tasted in the following tidbit from John Junor's column in the London *Sunday Express*:

'Mr Joshua Nkomo graciously promises a two-week cease-fire during the Queen's visit to Africa. He should be told to go to hell. The Queen does not need, nor does she seek, any safe-conduct from that fat bladder of terrorist lard. . . .'

Doubts were removed about whether the HGM would go on in Lusaka, but they remained about Mrs Thatcher's approach to the conference. In a statement to the House of Commons on July 25, she signalled that her views were beginning to change when she said that the British Government was 'wholly committed to genuine black majority rule in Rhodesia'. But she had some distance still to go. The Australians began to build up their influence. The preliminary visit Malcolm Fraser made to Lagos was crucial in giving him credentials in African eyes. Meanwhile his Foreign Minister, Andrew Peacock, visited Kenya and Tanzania; in the latter country he felt the good atmosphere the Queen had created earlier in July in her first visit to that republic, a warmth that induced a mellowing of feeling towards Britain at a crucial moment before the HGM. They arrived in Lusaka optimistic about the outcome on the Rhodesian issue, and conscious that Australia had the confidence of both the British and African governments.

Ramphal and Kaunda, as chairman, had arranged that Fraser make one of the first speeches on the opening day, August 1, in Mulungushi Hall to an invited public – and to television cameras. In a strong speech he remained evenhanded on the Rhodesian issue but injected confidence in a solution being found that week. The election, he said, had settled nothing but it had

'created new facts and disturbed a stalemate. . . . There will have to be further changes. As to what happens next, that . . . is, to a very large extent, in our laps. Much depends on whether we can seize . . . the opportunity provided by the comparative fluidity which now exists. . . . Time is running out and we may not have such an opportunity again.'

Another weighty influence was brought to bear. The Nigerian

Government not only nationalised British Petroleum installations in its country on the eve of the HGM, but more privately had earlier made it known to British companies that, while the Rhodesian situation remained unsatisfactory, their bids for several lucrative contracts Lagos had put or was putting out to tender would not be considered. When they complained, it was suggested they take it up with their MPs!

The conversion of Mrs Thatcher to the need for Britain to call an all-party constitutional conference went through two further stages at the HGM.

The first came on the Friday morning, the third day of the meeting, after speakers had warmed up on a general political discussion (much of it about South East Asia and the flight and plight of the boat-people) and on world economic trends. The debate on Southern Africa, effectively on Rhodesia, began with Kaunda as chairman turning to Nyerere beside him, addressing him as Mwalimu (Swahili for 'teacher') and adding, 'Teacher, give us some lessons.' Nyerere's speech was a lesson in moderation, calling simply for a democratic constitution and internationally supervised elections ('It is not possible just . . . to coopt representatives of the external nationalists. For we have to make everyone feel involved', he said in gentle reference to his much earlier difference with Kaunda over Nkomo). Disregarding the advice from his own delegation, he held out both an offer of reserved seats for minorities and the suggestion of a resettlement fund for those Rhodesian whites who would rather leave the country than work under an African government.

For her part, Mrs Thatcher, who had been conciliatory but warm in her opening statement on Wednesday, acknowledged for the first time that the constitution under which Bishop Muzorewa had come to power was 'defective in certain important respects' and enumerated them: the power of white MPs to block constitutional change, and the government's lack of control over senior appointments. She also accepted that the British Government had to take responsibility to bring 'genuine black majority rule' on the basis of a constitution comparable with ones Britain had agreed with other countries.

She had said a good deal, but there was still areas of uncertainty. Would she call an all-party conference, or try patching a constitution together through shuttle diplomacy by her ministers? Would she try to do running repairs on the internal settlement, cutting out the rotten parts, or scrap it altogether? Would she try to impose a cease-fire before talks on a settlement began? Would Britain lift sanctions unilaterally or do it as part of a Commonwealth move? And what part would the Commonwealth or United Nations play – to what extent would elections be internationally supervised?

So a second stage of meeting was needed, and this took place during the weekend 'retreat'. By 1979 the pattern of having a relaxed weekend during which heads of government alone with the Secretary-General could meet informally in little groups to work out details of an important agreement was well marked. The 'retreat' this time took place not in some rural hideaway, for game park lodges could not cope with the numbers and Victoria Falls was too close to Rhodesia for comfort, but in the grounds of State House itself.

During Saturday afternoon a 'contact group' of eight worked out a basic agreement on Rhodesia. There were the veterans of Gleneagles – Manley, Fraser and Ramphal – together with Kaunda and Nyerere, and Mrs Thatcher with Lord Carrington. Interestingly, the eighth person was Nigeria's Adefope who on Friday had treated Mrs Thatcher's speech with scepticism, asserting that 'nothing had moved an inch' and threatening that, if something concrete did not come out of the HGM on Rhodesia, Nigeria would reassess the worth of the Commonwealth association. Once again, a neocolonialist attitude about the Commonwealth peeped out. But wisely he was included in the contact group, and he emerged satisfied.

A further meeting took place at Sunday noon, mainly to decide how much of the agreement should be put into the final communiqué. A draft was agreed early that afternoon, which was mainly the work of Ramphal and Sir Antony Duff, and it was to be shown to the other heads at the dinner that evening being hosted by Malcolm Fraser. While the British press was being blandly told by Carrington and other spokesmen that Mrs Thatcher had not changed her general line (a rather transparent smokescreen), the Australians were briefing their journalists positively at breakfast-time on Sunday. Peter Bowers, of the *Sydney Morning Herald*, rushed to start his story, 'Britain has agreed that Rhodesia should have fresh elections under a new constitution.'

But during the afternoon it began to seem that the agreement might come unstuck. Mrs Thatcher was upset about a remark from some briefing referring to her next Cabinet meeting, and she also had to endure a political sermon in the cathedral about the iniquities of the Rhodesian regime. If other irritations came later, everything might fall apart. There was a danger in leaving the agreement unpublished for two or three days. In these circumstances Kaunda,

Ramphal and Fraser decided to turn the barbecue supper briefly into an 'executive session'. The agreement was endorsed by all the other heads, and word that the Australians had already leaked the details to certain journalists happily led to acquiescence that it should be officially made public right then, before midnight. So the 'Barbecue Agreement' with nine short paragraphs opened the way for genuine majority rule.

Events after the HGM moved fast, with all the managerial drive on which British Conservative governments pride themselves. The Lancaster House Conference opened only five weeks after the delegates left Lusaka. Relations, however, between the British negotiating team and the Commonwealth Secretariat cooled. Carrington apparently believed that the Secretariat was too biased towards the Patriotic Front leaders. Ramphal maintained that his first concern was to help 'hold the ring' and to make sure no delegation walked out. He was not given observer status and had to operate from the periphery, although twice during the twelve-week conference he stepped in to save the talks when they were foundering.

The coolness persisted after the Lancaster House agreement was signed and plans for the election and its supervision were being made. During the HGM talks Mrs Thatcher had been flatly opposed to any United Nations involvement in the transition (such as was part of the 1977 Anglo-American proposals) and less than enthusiastic about Commonwealth participation. She had finally agreed to the phrase:

> 'The government formed under such an independence constitution must be chosen through free and fair elections properly supervised under British Government authority, and with Commonwealth observers.'

The ambiguity soon became obvious in December. It was not made clear, in the last four words, whether Commonwealth observers should consist of a collection of separate teams from various countries which could afford it, or an integrated group organised through the Commonwealth Secretariat. The British preference was for the first. Governor Soames and his British advisers (deputy governor, military adviser, police adviser, legal adviser and so on) were taking over the administration and running the elections, and a large Commonwealth unit (even though only of observers, not supervisors) might, they said, be seen by some in the country as an alternative authority. Australia and Canada were willing to send separate teams, and the Australians in the event did. But Sonny

Ramphal argued that only by having an integrated unit could there be a representative Commonwealth group, with small countries included. After some argument his view prevailed, although the Commonwealth Observer Group (COG) was smaller than he first planned: eleven Commissioners with twenty-two assistants in Rhodesia from January 24, and an additional thirty assistants who came a week before polling on February 27-29.*

Others will write more fully of the remarkable job the COG did, and of the extraordinary period of transition through these elections. What is important to underline here is how the COG helped to add a stabilising element of trust in an extremely volatile situation. When Rhodesian security forces did not disengage as expected, when South African troops remained in the country, when killings continued (about 150 a month, one-tenth of the level before the ceasefire) and when the ZANU election organizers in particular found a great number of administrative obstacles, the risks of explosion were high. The Commonwealth Ceasefire Monitoring Force of 1300 soldiers (from Britain, Australia, Fiji, New Zealand and Kenya) did an amazing and courageous job of befriending and restraining the 22,000 guerillas who gathered at assembly points. But the COG provided Zimbabweans with the assurance that the outside world was watching closely. COG commissioners were based in all eight administrative districts, travelled a total of 72,000 kilometres and visited 437 out of 647 polling stations. They were trusted to provide a balanced and informal view on whether the elections were 'free and fair' and on what part intimidation had played. So their interim report, published after polling but before the results were announced, was a crucial influence in the acceptance of those results.

There were some other influences at work, unofficial but by no means unimportant. Plans for a coup, code-named 'Operation Quartz', had been made by senior officers of the Rhodesian army in mid-February, in the middle of the election campaign.** These plans apparently involved a massive and concerted attack on Mugabe's ZANLA forces gathered in the assembly points, in the event of an indecisive election result in which Nkomo, Muzorewa and Smith

---

*The Commissioners and Assistants were drawn from Australia, Bangladesh, Barbados, Canada, Ghana, India, Jamaica, Nigeria, Papua New Guinea, Sierra Leone, and Sri Lanka. The chairman was Rajeshwar Dayal, of India.

**'Rhodesia's White Plot' by John Ellison, *Daily Express*, London, 14 August 1980, page 8.

might hope to form a coalition, although Mugabe held the largest single group of seats. The action was called off in the final hours just before the news of Mugabe's overwhelming election victory was announced (but was already known to the leaders).

This last-minute lowering of tension was, I am told, largely the result of two meetings, one between Mugabe and General Walls (the Rhodesian army commander) and another between Mugabe and Ian Smith. Among various individuals of goodwill and initiative who were working for reconciliation were members of three religious groups – Roman Catholic, Quaker and Moral Rearmament. Between them all they helped persuade Ian Smith to visit Mugabe for a talk between polling and the announcement of results. One of Smith's former ministers described to me, when I was in Salisbury for Zimbabwe's independence celebrations, how Smith told his caucus of MPs later that, to his surprise, he had ended the talk convinced that Mugabe could be trusted by the whites, that he was sincere in wanting most whites to stay and in his desire for a mixed economy and reconciliation between races and tribes. Ian Smith's son Alec and Stan O'Donnell, for many years the permanent head of his Foreign Ministry, both confirmed to me the reality of the cautious but genuine reconciliation. Allan Griffith, the Australian Government's election observer, ascribed these events to 'divine intervention'.

A glimpse of the tension in the assembly points and the flavour of the unusual assignment of the Commonwealth Observer Group are captured in this excerpt from a personal account by the Canadian Commissioner, Gordon Fairweather:

'I was urged by the Commonwealth Ceasefire Monitoring Force to go into an assembly point and speak to the armed and restless Zanla forces about the election process. I am not noted for being first off the mark to meet many challenges, yet this journey was indeed the first for a Commonwealth Observer inside such a camp. The journey made was in a landrover, driven at a furious pace on rutted roads by a young British subaltern. I sat beside him buckled in and choking with dust, and the rest of the convoy roared along behind us even dustier and more uncomfortable.

'We toured the camp and then a couple of hundred NCO's (or their equivalent, for there are no ranks in the people's army) squatted with AK automatic rifles across their thighs. I was just about to launch into my short election talk when I spotted one of the soldiers dressed in a tee shirt which bore the message "Patience My Ass". I begged him to give me just five minutes, and then he could do what he liked with his patience.'*

I was very happy to be invited to Zimbabwe's independence celebrations in April 1980. During my years as Secretary-General I had attended many such events. They are always moving. But this occasion, after the fifteen years of struggle, was particularly so.

It was my first time to meet Robert Mugabe, although we had corresponded and I had known many of his ZANU colleagues, including several in his Cabinet. With Joshua Nkomo I had a tearful reunion just before midnight at the independence stadium. This was not because he was upset at his ZAPU's winning only twenty seats, for he spoke loyally of Mugabe's leadership. Only 35,000 could be accommodated at the stadium and the police threw tear-gas at the crowd outside storming the gates to hear Bob Marley and his reggae band – and also to see the independence ceremony – at just the moment we arrived from the State Banquet. The tear-gas wafted over the stadium, and we stood greeting each other happily with eyes streaming.

I hope there will not be events to weep about in Zimbabwe's future. The years of UDI were appallingly divisive, so there are enormous problems ahead. The speed with which Thatcher and Carrington pushed through a new constitution and the transition period, once they had changed course at the Lusaka HGM, swept the country to independence with breathless euphoria. A more measured pace – covering about a year under the Anglo-American timetable, or in Mugabe's own suggested schedule – might have led to a faltering momentum. But in their haste to disengage within four months of signing the Lancaster House Agreement the British cut several corners. One was in the retraining of the army, and another in the gathering of donors of development assistance; for the $1,500 million Zimbabwe Development Fund promised in 1977 did not reappear in the agreement signed in December 1979. It would be fitting, for a start, if the British Government, as the controlling shareholder in British Petroleum, were to insist that BP make a substantial payment to the Zimbabwe Government as some recompense for the years during which the company contrived to evade oil sanctions. A much wider base of support has also to be laid. The

---

Rhodesia to Zimbabwe: Campaign '80, talk by Gordon Fairweather; Ottawa, May 1980.

British left a heavy weight of responsibility on Robert Mugabe and his government, and some of that weight should be shouldered by friends of Zimbabwe, and of peace, throughout the world.

In Fairweather's words: 'Independence came because people put their faith in the processes of peace. The new Prime Minister, erstwhile devil-incarnate, talks about "love and reconciliation" . . . He comes out of jail and exile, and talks about forgiveness. It matters a great deal that Zimbabwe should work after all.'

Chapter 11
TO AMIN AND BACK
What can one do about the
Bad Guys?

At the close of the Singapore Heads of Government Meeting in January 1971, Milton Obote of Uganda, who with two helpful speeches had helped ease tension on the issue of arms sales to South Africa, spoke enthusiastically to me of the conference: 'This has been an absolute triumph. We have all bought at least six months to extricate ourselves from various hooks on which we have impaled ourselves.'

But he never had his six months. The Singapore HGM closed on a Friday and on the following Monday (January 25), while Obote was still in Asia, General Idi Amin seized power in a midnight coup. Obote landed later that day in Nairobi, determined to rally his forces and re-enter Uganda; but he found hesitation among the Kenyans. The moment was lost, and he went into exile in Tanzania for more than eight years.

Obote in the 1960s was a true internationalist prepared to put great efforts into helping to solve other countries' problems (as with Nigeria in 1968), and a practical idealist in PanAfrican affairs. But at home he was beset by many problems which the British had left on his desk at independence in 1962: four kingdoms inside the single state; major land disputes between two kingdoms; the heart-land of the country – Buganda – with strong separatist inclinations; further divisions between the Nilotic tribes of the north (his own people, who furnished most of the soldiers) and the Bantu tribes of the south who were richer in coffee and cattle; divisions between religious groups, Muslim and Christian, Catholics and others; and a minority population of some 80,000 Asians.

Milton Obote not only relished the diversity of his country, but was even invigorated by the challenge of these problems, like a juggler keeping many balls in the air. The subtleties of practical politics fascinated him. Harold Macmillan he admired for his

245

smooth adroitness; and on the eve of the Kampala peace talks in 1968 he gave me a thoughtfully inscribed copy of *Macchiavelli 2000*, a book of tough-minded political essays just published for Ugandan students.

But by 1968 he had found the problems he had inherited not conducive to smooth management. Marrying a Muganda woman had not healed relations with the Kabaka's kingdom, any more than Trudeau's marriage in 1971 to a Vancouver girl had prevented western Canadian alienation. Obote found the Kabaka of Buganda, though installed as President of all Uganda, still putting tribal ahead of national concerns. He slipped into authoritarian decisions, sending troops (headed by Amin) against Buganda and, in an earlier crisis, arresting five of his own ministers.

In the last weeks of 1970 I did not know how fragile Obote's domestic position was; otherwise I would never have pressed him to leave home and come to Singapore. His reluctance was plain, but seemed based on pessimism about the conference, after the damage Heath had already done by his plan to sell arms to South Africa. So I telegraphed Obote, saying I still had hopes of persuading Britain to back off its strategic folly, and I badly needed his help. This message coincided with a strong anti-British protest by Makerere University students, and they combined to make him decide to play an active part in Singapore. But he left Uganda at a moment when Amin knew he had become prime suspect in the murder of Brigadier Okoya and in a complex plot involving Sudanese rebels – and so, because he felt threatened, was at his most dangerous. It was a fine gesture of Obote to travel abroad, but Macchiavelli failed him.

There were assertions later that Amin was helped to power by both Israeli and British intelligence agents.* There was a complicated conspiracy centred upon Uganda's neighbour, the Sudan, from which Amin took advantage. Israelis, the German mercenary leader Rolf Steiner and some British mercenaries were involved with southern Sudanese guerillas. Several days before Amin's coup, during a late night session with a few British journalists in Singapore, Edward Heath spoke resentfully of other heads of government and said he was not prepared to sit and be lectured at by people from regimes so immature and unstable that they could not even be sure if they would be able to return to their own country after the HGM. Several hours before the coup, a senior member of Britain's

---

Dirty Work 2: The CIA in Africa edited by Ellen Ray et al, Lyle Stuart Inc., 1979, pages 171-177.

246

defence staff telephoned his daughter in Uganda urging her, in guarded words, not to be worried by something which would soon take place.* This does not, in my view, add up to evidence that British intelligence – M16 – and thus the British Government were party to the coup conspiracy, although it seems likely that they had some advance knowledge of what was going to happen. Significantly, in the account which Obote wrote for Ivan-Smith's book he names the head of the Israeli military mission, Colonel Bar Lev, but makes no assertion about any British involvement.**

Why was a regime as evil as Amin's allowed to survive so long? George Ivan-Smith, a knowledgeable observer, has concluded that 'concerted, early international action against Amin's practices would have been effective'; effective, he implies, in restraining the brutality of the regime rather than unseating him entirely. Why, anyway, was there not international action at an early stage – at OAU, United Nations or Commonwealth level?

Part of the answer lies in the fact that for most of 1971 Amin behaved, as far as the outside world could tell, in a relatively reasonable way. The first comprehensive story of killings of Acholi and Langi soldiers, who were presumed loyal to Obote, by Amin's own Nubians was compiled by Colin Legum in *The Observer* in August 1971. By then, Idi Amin had won a credentials battle against Obote's envoys at the OAU summit in June and could insist, under Article III(2) of the OAU Charter, on other African governments respecting the principle of 'non-interference in the internal affairs of states'.***

Only two months after seizing power, Amin staged a clever if cynical scene which won him support among the Baganda and which was also intended to win him wider international recognition. King Freddie, the exiled Kabaka, had died in England in 1969. Amin sent two of his Ministers to Britain to have the Kabaka's body

---

Ghosts of Kampala: Rise and Fall of Idi Amin by George Ivan-Smith, Weidenfeld and Nicholson, 1980, page 76.

**Ibidem, pages 78-81.

***Britain had moved faster, offering recognition through the attendance of its High Commissioner at Amin's swearing-in ceremony on February 6, two weeks after the coup. But the British could argue that this was by no means the first military coup in Africa, and Britain's general policy was to move swiftly to recognise a government that exerts effective control: in Somalia it did so within five days.

disinterred and accompany it back to Buganda for a state funeral. The Ministers invited me to fly out with them. It was a highly political act by Amin. He was clearly hoping that my presence would be seen as Commonwealth recognition of his regime, even though most Commonwealth states had not yet recognised him. I made use once more of the ambiguities of the Secretariat. Yusuf Lule, my Assistant Secretary-General, was himself a Muganda and had been a personal friend of the Kabaka, so he it was who attended the funeral on April 4 and no one could say whether he was there in a personal role or a representational one.

I met Amin first when he visited London in July 1971, a few weeks after the OAU's act of recognition. He pressed me to fly back with him to Uganda and spend two days talking with his Cabinet. I avoided a commitment for several reasons, including the hope that a mediation mission might soon be launched in the Pakistan crisis. But, in a private talk with Amin in his London hotel, he told me he was so offended by the OAU's decision to change the venue of the Summit meeting that year from Kampala to Addis Ababa that he thought he would walk out of the organisation. I said that would be stupid: he would simply give a handle to his enemies, and he would do better to bide his time; they would recognise him in due course and no doubt an OAU Summit would take place later in Uganda. It was good advice, such as I felt bound to try to give to any head of a member state; but, if I had then known what an evil force he was shortly to become, I might have held my tongue.

After our morning meeting, Amin lunched with the Queen and shocked her by saying he wanted to cut a strip of territory from his landlocked country down to the Indian Ocean. (This would have involved grabbing a 700 km-long swathe of northern Tanzania down to the port of Tanga, and possibly a corridor also through Kenya's populous Nyanza province.) She quickly told Alec Home, the Foreign Secretary, who was asked that afternoon by Amin for British weapons, including armoured cars. At a reception given that evening, notes were compared between Alec and myself of these various conversations. It was obvious that Amin could be a very dangerous man, puffing out grandiose dreams.

I was alarmed after a border clash took place in August 1971, west of Lake Victoria, and after Amin had made threats to straighten the Uganda-Tanzania border-line in the Kagera Triangle area. So I sent telegrams to Amin and Nyerere proposing that I meet them separately for confidential mediation talks, and then possibly arrange a joint meeting. In a fashion that later became familiar,

Amin rushed to announce over Radio Uganda that he was accepting my proposal for a joint meeting with Nyerere under Commonwealth auspices. This, of course, made mediation more difficult; my idea of good offices needed postponing. But at least Amin stayed his hand, and took no action on his earlier threats of a land grab. On my way to the Third Commonwealth Medical Conference in Mauritius in November I talked with Julius Nyerere, who assured me that Tanzania did not plan any intervention and that there were no Ugandan guerillas in training in his country; and on the way back from Mauritius I visited Uganda.

By then the border had just been reopened, but the Foreign Minister Wanume Kibedi (who was Amin's brother-in-law) was complaining that Tanzanian police had refused entry into EAC headquarters in the Tanzanian town of Arusha to the Uganda appointee to the East African Community, Communications Minister Z. H. Bigirwenkya, (a very able man who had been Secretary of Obote's cabinet). For that reason Uganda was not prepared to approve the budget for the EAC common services. At the same time Kibedi and Bigirwenkya both told me they were worried by the way Amin would make provocative and threatening statements over Radio Uganda, against Tanzania and others, without consulting his Ministers and often after dropping into a Sergeants Mess for a drink. 'You should persuade him how unwise this is – he just won't listen to us,' they said.

I raised the matter with Amin during a private talk we had that day, saying that he must remember that, now he was a Head of State, whatever he said would be reported in many different parts of the world, and reactions would differ. While he was obviously familiar with the reactions of people near to him, he should also be prepared to take account of the probable reactions of people elsewhere. This meant, I said, that he would be wise to discuss his particular ideas with his experts and Ministers, and give them an opportunity to comment. I added: 'Of course, then, you'll take your own decision. It's up to you to decide, but you might as well decide in the light of probable reactions.'

He was visibly angry, but that evening he gave a formal dinner for me in the garden of State House, Kampala, and told me quietly that he had been thinking this matter over, and I was right. He promised, he said, that he would not rush into print or onto the radio with statements on which he had not consulted the appropriate Minister or adviser. He was pleased at having reopened the border, and he expected Nyerere to recognise his Community appointees in return. Sitting there under the stars, with lights twinkling on the seven hills of Kampala, it was possible to hope that a crisis was receding and the peoples of East Africa would know more settled times.

It was not until after February 1972 that the horrific nature of Amin's regime started to become plain to those of us in other parts of the world. In that month came newspaper reports of more killings of Acholi and Langi troops; and Amin also made his decisive move in turning away from Israeli advisers, whom he abruptly expelled, and starting to court Libya's Colonel Gadaffi for support in weapons and money. In deference to Gadaffi's pan-Islamic fervour, Amin undertook to convert Uganda into a Muslim state, a major task considering that only some five percent of the people were then of that faith.

Then in August came the inconsistent announcement that the country's 80,000 Asians (mainly Hindu, but a good number also of the Aga Khan's Muslim Ismaelis) had to leave Uganda within ninety days. A main motive seems to have been to provide loot for his Nubian soldiers. Taking advantage of the disruption of that period, a military group of Obote supporters attempted to invade in September. The attempt was badly botched, led only to more killings and terror, and opened the way to Libyan and Palestinian units who added to Amin's repressive machine.

I was invited by the OAU Secretary-General, Nzu Ekangaki, to represent the Commonwealth at the Organisation's Tenth Anniversary Summit meeting in Addis Ababa in May 1973, and so witnessed an extraordinary occasion in Uganda-Tanzania relations. Amin, dressed in his General's uniform and with more fullsized medals pinned on it than I had seen on anyone since receptions with Soviet Marshals at the Kremlin, made the most memorable speech of the meeting. It followed a fierce encounter between the Libyan and Ethiopian foreign ministers over an illjudged Libyan proposal to move the OAU headquarters from Addis Ababa to Cairo, which ended with the Ethiopian in a superb flight of anger saying: 'The issue is not whether to separate the OAU headquarters from Addis Ababa, but whether to separate Libya from the OAU. . . . Libya may be getting very rich, but it is time Libyans learnt that Africans are not for sale.' After that exchange, Idi Amin's speech satisfied his audience's wish for humorous relief.

He spoke without a single note, waving a brightly coloured baton in the air and saying with each new point, 'Mr Chairman, this is very important.' He said he agreed with Colonel Gadaffi that Israel was the enemy of all Africans, just as were the white racists in South Africa. But one could learn from one's enemies. Since Israel gained a lot of backing from Jews in the United States, he said, why shouldn't Africa do similarly? 'We have thirty-five million people of African descent in the United States, twenty million [*sic*] in the Caribbean, fifteen million in Brazil.'

Again, he said, 'African leaders should behave like Africans. Some even bring in table-water from Europe. What is the matter with African water? In East Africa we have water that is so sweet. You boil it thoroughly, put in a little chlorine, and it is marvellously sweet!' This barb at the 'black Frenchmen' among the assembled Heads of State had their neighbours convulsed in laughter.

Towards the end of his short speech Amin assured everyone that he loved all Africans, and that he particularly loved Julius Nyerere. 'In fact, if he were a woman, then despite the grey hairs I would marry him!' The Tanzanian President was sitting in the front row of delegates about twenty feet away from the podium where Amin stood; my seat, as one of the guests of honour, was beside the podium. I had a perfect view of a literal rapprochement. Nyerere clearly did not know what was coming next. In fact, it was Amin in person, for he strode over and put his arms around Nyerere, while photographers' flashbulbs exploded and Nyerere's bodyguard tried in vain to get between the two leaders.

As an afterthought Amin came back to his microphone and said how important it was to stand foursquare with Egypt against Israel and all her deeds. Just in time he had remembered what would please Gadaffi, his paymaster.

I recount this episode at some length to show how Amin could play on African humanity and the African sense of humour, and divert his audience in a double sense. As late as the 1977 OAU Summit in Gabon he was winning applause this way. But at the Addis summit he achieved more than applause. A letter from Obote to all African leaders, giving in horrible detail a description of many deaths and estimating that 80,000 Ugandans had been murdered under Amin's regime, failed to move them from their stand of non-interference. And the Emperor prevailed on Nyerere to sign an agreement with Amin under which both sides said they would not use their territory for subversion against the other. This agreement patently failed to get to the roots of the trouble.

From these three encounters I had an opportunity to assess Amin.

He was by no means the simple buffoon sometimes portrayed by British caricaturists and politicians. He had, I thought, a great native shrewdness and was an African populist demagogue of some genius. In the early days he possessed a revolutionary appeal, far beyond Uganda's borders, to the Africans for whom independence had not brought much change for the better. Among the African élite, young men in their thirties who had become Cabinet Ministers, professors, army officers, he stirred other emotions; they were, after all, the new tribe of Africa, a tribe which drove Mercedes cars and was nicknamed 'the waBenzi'. But for the non-élite and the deprived, Amin represented at first the Big Change they hoped would come with independence everywhere.

At Addis I had dinner one evening with Solomon Goodrich, a Jamaican from the New York office of the Congress of Racial Equality, and his colleague, Victor Solomon, whose visiting card said he was CORE's 'associate national director, working for the liberation of black people'. They were attached to Amin's delegation as foreign policy advisers (and seemed very able ones), while neither Paul Etiang nor any Foreign Ministry official had come to Addis at all.

These two clearly saw in Amin somebody who could be a significant leader of black political consciousness not only in Africa but beyond. He had not the skill to achieve that leadership and his revolution was to go wildly wrong through its terrible excesses, but the potential was there, and visible to other African leaders. This was, I believe, the main reason why they were so reluctant to attack him, even after the call of African solidarity had grown faint.

Before the OAU Summit took place, however, Amin's mass expulsion of Asians had caused major turmoil, and one effect was that Edward Heath began to talk about proposing the expulsion of Uganda from the Commonwealth at the next HGM, scheduled for Ottawa in August 1973. To put his notion in some context requires going back a few years to review the citizenship issue of Asians in East Africa.

Trade between India and East Africa reaches back many centuries before there was any British activity in the region, but large scale immigration began only with the recruitment of indentured labour, mainly from the Punjab, to build the Uganda-Kenya railway in the 1890s. The 'coolie' labour mostly returned to India, but their reports of East Africa stimulated others to emigrate. Small traders, artisans and administrative staff followed the trail of the railway. In

Kenya the Devonshire Declaration of 1923 on the paramountcy of African interests thwarted the aspirations of the more prosperous Indians to become farmers and landowners, and effectively confined them to commerce and manufacturing industry. In Tanzania and Uganda there was in any case little land available for alienation, but Indians were welcomed as traders and in Uganda they helped develop sugar plantations and the cotton ginning industry as well. They were entrepreneurs in many spheres; but they hardly mixed with the Africans, and did not train them or employ them in other than menial positions in their shops. As shopkeepers they also tended to be money-lenders.

Under the British Nationality Act 1948 all those born in her colonies were deemed to be of British nationality, but the Act did not spell out their rights of entry and residence in Britain. When the British Conservative Government came to negotiate Independence terms with Tanganyika in 1961, Uganda in 1962, and Kenya in 1963, the new African governments offered to give citizenship to those Asian residents (and also whites) who opted for it within a grace period of two years, rather than give it to them automatically; while the British Government also offered them passports. It seemed to me profoundly unwise of Duncan Sandys, the Minister who negotiated these arrangements, to give a community that was long settled in a country and making its livelihood there for more than one generation the option of *not* becoming citizens of that country. The option of becoming instead citizens of another country was an invitation and encouragement to them not to be loyal.

At the same time the British Government passed the first of its Commonwealth Immigration Acts in 1962, starting a system of controls after large-scale immigration had begun from the Caribbean. My own general view, expressed later to the Home Secretary, Reginald Maudling, was that Britain should base its immigration policy on the fact that it was a small, crowded island which could not afford significant increase in its population. It should not have a Commonwealth immigration act, but a general immigration act. On that basis it could offer small quotas to all regions of the world, to show that it was not refusing entry to nationals of any country. With that rider, it should operate on a principle of replacement: it would offer as many places in Britain to a particular country, say Australia, as that country had taken of British immigrants during the previous year.

The option of applying for citizenship in East Africa was not taken up with any speed, although the Ismaelis moved to do so under encouragement from the Aga Khan. During the first year of

Kenya's independence, less than 4000 Asians registered for Kenyan citizenship, out of a total of 182,000 Asians then in that country.

Both Kenya and Uganda passed new immigration acts in 1967, which affected non-citizens who now had to secure work permits. These acts, combined with trade licensing acts, deprived many Asians of their means of livelihood. Africanisation of the public service made thousands of other Asians jobless in Kenya. Predictably, Britain was faced by a great number of British Asians, many more from Kenya than from Uganda then, who demanded that they be allowed to cash in their 'insurance policies' and come to Britain. It was estimated there were possibly 200,000 Asians with British passports in all of East Africa.

During the Nigerian peace talks in Kampala in May 1968, Obote gave me a glimpse of the reason for his government's action. He pointed out of a window of the Parliament Buildings to the capital's main streets, where I could see a mosque, a Hindu temple and lines of Asian shops, and said: 'I don't want to do a Kenyatta; I am hoping not to squeeze my Asians. But I do have my problems.' For Africans to advance in commerce, and to realise some of the hopes of independence, they had somehow to break through this layer of almost monopolistic Asian ownership.

The Wilson government's reaction in February 1968 was to block the exodus from Kenya to Britain with a further Commonwealth Immigration Act, which restricted the entry to Britain of holders of British passports issued overseas. It began to admit British Asians on a voucher basis at the rate of 1500 a year (which could amount to 7,500 people in all, if there are on average four dependents). For the HGM in January 1969 the subject of migration and citizenship promised to be the most acrimonious issue. Britain was prepared to propose it as an agenda item but Australia was opposed; so it was arranged to hold discussions with interested governments under my chairmanship outside the formal sessions.

At the first meeting, Ministers and officials from seventeen governments (out of twenty-eight at the HGM) heard strong words exchanged between James Callaghan, then British Home Secretary and Tom Mboya, Kenya's Minister of Economic Planning. Resentment built up and the East African ministers took no further part in these general discussions. But in bilateral talks with the Kenya ministers, my colleagues and I managed to get them to slow down the squeeze upon the Asians in their country, and so make it easier for Britain to absorb those who applied to come. And the fourteen governments that persevered in these 'outside' discussions asked me (in the words of the communiqué) 'to examine general principles relating to short and long-term movement of people between their countries.' We drew up a questionnaire, concentrating on the facts of migration, and analysed the replies received from twenty-one governments during 1970.

The study, mainly carried out by consultants from the University of Sussex, concentrated on administrative aspects of migration. Among other matters it set out to clarify what the status of 'Commonwealth citizen' conferred in practical benefits, and concluded that although definitions of the status varied it 'usually conferred ... treatment on a most-favoured-nation basis'. However, where immigration for work was intended, work permits were required for every country except New Zealand (and, in some cases, Ceylon) and governments showed 'a common preference for skilled or professional immigrants, irrespective of alien or Commonwealth status.' It found very few countries (Britain and Canada were exceptions) had a system of appeals from decisions to extradite or refuse entry. It suggested there was scope for more detailed studies on appeal systems, on the rights of migrants' dependants and on the 'brain drain'. The study was submitted to governments before the Singapore HGM, but it was not discussed at that summit.* Later the question of 'brain drain' among doctors and nurses was studied for Health Ministers at the request of the government of Ceylon.

Amin's abrupt expulsion of Ugandan Asians in the last months of 1972 threw into disarray all schemes for phasing British Asians into Britain. The Heath government reacted as positively as it felt it could, and took 28,000 while appealing to other Commonwealth governments to help. I too appealed, not least to Ottawa. A Canadian immigration team was set up quickly in East Africa, and more than 7000 Ugandan Asians were settled in Canada by the time of the Ottawa HGM in 1973. They proved to be, on the whole, superb settlers: skilled, hardworking and often contributing capital. India also opened her doors wide in this emergency. I approached Forbes Burnham of Guyana, a sparsely populated and resource-rich country, where most of the population of East Indian origin supported the opposition party of Cheddi Jagan. I suggested that, if he took a group of Uganda Asians, there would be political spin-off for him in winning more multiracial support from these grateful immigrants. But he did not see the situation in this way, and refused to take any.

It was in this context that early in 1973 Edward Heath began talking to his officials about proposing the expulsion of Uganda

---

*The 35-page study was not subsequently made public.

255

from the Commonwealth, on the grounds of violating the Singapore Declaration of Commonwealth Principles. The mass evictions, the confiscation of property without compensation, the murders of the Chief Justice and the Vice-Chancellor of Makerere College and many other disappearances – all this had stirred British public opinion.

I thought this approach was exceedingly unwise, for several reasons. Heath and I had a tightlipped conversation about it, sitting in the garden of 10 Downing Street only a few weeks before the Ottawa HGM, and I also discussed it separately with Alec Home. I made my points. First, expelling Uganda would do nothing to help those most threatened by Amin's brutality, the people of Uganda itself. A time would surely come when the Commonwealth could truly help them. Secondly, if he proposed expulsion, Heath would find other African leaders taking up Amin's case, however unwillingly, because they would sense hypocrisy and racialism in the British attitude. I reminded him that there was an inconsistency in British views about expulsions of foreigners. Ghana had expelled far larger numbers – nearly 300,000 – in the months after Dr Busia came to power in 1970, but hardly a voice had been raised against this in Britain (in fact, one senior Cabinet minister had said to me revealingly, 'Oh, but those were other Africans'.) But, most of all, I emphasized the point that if he criticised Amin for his general domestic policies without putting exclusive emphasis on the Asians, Uganda would be isolated; if he proposed Uganda's expulsion, however, it would be Britain that would become isolated.

Heath as usual bridled against advice that ran contrary to his instincts, but was circumspect when he came to Ottawa for the 1973 HGM. He was haunted by General Amin, nevertheless, who claimed headlines and cartoons in British and Canadian papers with his request to the Queen to send one of her aircraft 'and the guards from Scotland' to bring him to Ottawa, and his promise to brief 'the Queen and her government' (presumably the British one) about how he had 'transformed Uganda into a truly black man's country'.* And Amin's unfortunate Acting Foreign Minister, Paul Etiang, had to gabble through the fifty-five minute text of the

---

*His request for aircraft did not end with the Queen, but extended to my own (non-existent) jet and to a current adversary. For, the day before the HGM opened, I received a cable from Amin which read: 'Mr Secretary-General, I have asked the Queen for a plane and asked Edward Heath for a plane and if neither of them can do so then Secretary-General please send me your plane because this is a very important conference and it is essential that I be there. If you don't send me your plane I will have no alternative but to ask Moshe Dayan.'

absent general's speech which had its hilarious passages (as when he described Africa as 'no longer a sleeping giant but an awakened black beauty with busting physique' – Etiang changed the text at the last minute to 'sustained physique') but also its barrage of charges that Britain had been 'undermining the Commonwealth' in at least three regions of the world.

Sensibly Edward Heath waited two days before making a full reply. Then he commented on 'the sheer callous inhumanity of expelling these people, at a moment's notice, in a penniless state and with little chance of compensation', and on the bad effect that the expulsions had had on race relations in Britain itself. He read out an extract from the Singapore Declaration ('We recognise . . . racial discrimination as an unmitigated evil of society. Each of us will vigorously combat this evil within our own nation') and said it was impossible to reconcile the Uganda Government's actions with that Declaration. But he stopped short of mentioning expulsion. He went precisely the right distance, I thought.

But, if Amin was not to be expelled, what action could Commonwealth countries take to show their disgust at what was reportedly happening in Uganda? What, in fact, can one do about the bad guys?

One difficulty was that there was no common front among Uganda's Commonwealth neighbours, to act together over Amin. The East African Community (EAC), established by treaty in 1967, was already under strain in 1971. It was a second post-independence attempt to draw the three countries into close collaboration. When the ambitious effort in 1964 to build upon the East African Common Services Organisation a fullscale political federation faltered, Nyerere suggested 'putting the plans on ice for ten years'. But countries cannot go into a deep freeze for a decade; and the Tanzanian President soon discovered the need to break up the common currency in order to control his own foreign exchange for national development. So there was a measure of desperation in the moves to arrest these centrifugal tendencies by forming the EAC. It was going to be more difficult in 1967 to coordinate economic planning, introduce a long-term agricultural policy, remove restrictions on trade, and so on, than it might have been in 1963-64; but the alternative was further separation, so it was worth the attempt. I was happy to be present in Kampala at the signing of the treaty, in June 1967.

In the event it failed, to a considerable extent because the leaders of Kenya and Tanzania had by then set off on different ideological paths, Kenyatta robustly pursuing private enterprise and Nyerere rigorously doing his best to put 'African socialism' into practice. Obote's proclamation of his own 'Common Man's Charter' put him closer to the Tanzanian camp; and since it involved the nationalisation of some eighty British companies, British businessmen and their political friends were shortsightedly not unhappy at Obote's replacement by Amin in January 1971.

In later years these countries did not switch attitudes back to the point of working for Obote's restoration. If they had, Kenya and Britain could have helped engineer Amin's swifter downfall provided there had been far more competence in mounting an invasion from Tanzania than was shown in 1972, and a foundation had been laid by effective propaganda to the people of Uganda. Britain could at least have cut off the weekly 'whisky run' from Stansted airport that helped sustain Amin's hold upon the soldiery, and Kenya – more basically – could have strangled supplies on which Uganda became increasingly dependent. Kenya did use its position astride the transit routes to Uganda several times to good effect: for example, Jomo Kenyatta threatened to hold up supplies in 1974 unless Amin gave safe conduct out of Uganda for a minister who had been arrested. And the Kenya Government allowed the Israeli aircraft carrying commandos on the Entebbe hostage rescue mission to refuel in Nairobi. But, for the most part, Kenyan authorities maintained a policy of neutrality towards Amin.

In 1974 Idi Amin made an effort to improve his international image, promising an inquiry into the disappearances of distinguished Ugandans such as the Chief Justice. He came spontaneously to swim in the pool of the British High Commissioner, James Hennessy, and to ask him to invite the Archbishop of Canterbury and the BBC to Uganda. With equally bizarre humour in June 1974, he telegraphed me that his nomination for the post of Commonwealth Secretary-General after my second term was completed in mid-1975 was – Milton Obote!

His first foreign minister, Wanume Kibedi, defected in 1973. Colonel Michael Ondoga, his successor, was grabbed by Amin's thugs one morning while driving his daughter to school and his stabbed body was pulled out of the Nile days later. But Amin floated over the carnage by the extraordinary act of appointing to this vacant post the stunningly beautiful Princess Elizabeth Bagaya, a former model for *Vogue* magazine. When she walked to the podium of the UN General Assembly that September clad in a golden gown, *The Guardian's* Jane Rosen reported that 'her speech was greeted with enormous enthusiasm by the non-aligned delegates, none of whom appeared to recollect the persecution that has characterised President Amin's regime'.*

By chance I had met Princess Elizabeth Bagaya at the very start of her career. A charity fashion show was organised at Marlborough House in 1965 for the Commonwealth Society for the Blind, for which various governments presented clothes and provided their own models. Uganda had no professional model, but they recruited a young woman studying law in Britain who had just been called to the Bar; a strikingly lovely figure with long Hamitic eyes and a graceful neck.

She was an instant hit that evening with photographers – and soon Elizabeth Bagaya was on the cover of *Vogue*, as well as appearing in films. She came again to Marlborough House in 1971 as Ambassador-at-large for Idi Amin, whom she was supporting because Obote had removed her father from the Toro kingship. Her job was to win recognition for Amin around African capitals, and she was much more effective in this role than Nnamdi Azikiwe had been for Biafra three years before.

In July 1974 Tanzania was celebrating Saba Saba Day with particular gusto, for it was the twentieth anniversary of the founding of the TANU party. On the platform under the awning I found myself placed next to Elizabeth, now the Foreign Minister, and beyond the special seats set a few places along the row for Nyerere and Kaunda I glimpsed another familiar figure, Milton Obote. While waiting for the Presidents to arrive at the parade-ground, I went over to talk to him and, on returning, told her whom I had seen. She said, 'Really, I must go and see him too'; and she did. When I asked her what they had said to each other, she told me Obote had said, 'You must not talk to me. That man will slit your throat!' and she had replied, 'Absolute nonsense, I know Amin better than you, and he's a very decent man.' The photographers meanwhile had been busy, and when the pictures of the Uganda Foreign Minister talking with the exiled former President arrived in Kampala, Amin was furious although publicly he used the incident to claim that Obote now recognised his government. Within five months Elizabeth was dismissed from her post and arrested, and Kenyatta's intervention was necessary to help save her life.

Amin meanwhile thrived. His time to be OAU chairman came in

---

* 'Beauty has good word for Amin', *The Guardian*, 28 September 1974.

1975, and he capitalised on that post to address the UN General Assembly that September – or rather, to sit grandly near the podium while his ambassador read out his speech. But he did not come to the HGM in Jamaica in May 1975, for he knew he would have been more vulnerable at a Commonwealth meeting where leaders discuss with each other rather than make set speeches; and there were at the 1975 Commonwealth Summit three African heads of state – Nyerere, Kaunda and Seretse Khama – who took their disapproval of his regime to the point of refusing to go to the OAU Summit in Kampala three months later.

Disapproval had turned to disgust by the time of the 1977 HGM, held in London during the Jubilee celebrations and the first to take place after Sonny Ramphal took over as Secretary-General. The breaking-point had been the cold-blooded murder in February of Archbishop Luwum and two Cabinet ministers, after they had been subjected to a kangaroo court trial in front of the whole diplomatic corps in the grounds of the Nile Mansions Hotel; but evidence was also widely available of the brutal killing of thousands of ordinary Ugandans. Amin went through his usual routine of seeking a sensational headline on the eve of the HGM by disappearing from Kampala ('Amin plane alert at Belfast'), but apparently without leaving Uganda. The thirty-three heads of delegation were not concerned with his pranks, but deeply concerned with his gruesome record. They took little time to set a precedent in the Commonwealth with an explicit and forceful condemnation of a member government. For an appreciation of the strength of their words, it is worth quoting the whole of paragraph 35 of the London Communiqué, under the heading of 'Human Rights';

> 'Cognisant of the accumulated evidence of sustained disregard for the sanctity of life and of massive violation of basic human rights in Uganda, it was the overwhelming view of Commonwealth leaders that these excesses were so gross as to warrant the world's concern and to evoke condemnation by Heads of Government in strong and unequivocal terms. Mindful that the people of Uganda were within the fraternity of Commonwealth membership, Heads of Government looked to the day when the people of Uganda would once more fully enjoy their basic human rights which now were being so cruelly denied.'

At the OAU Summit the following year, General Obasanjo of Nigeria gave a lead in that organisation by attacking Amin; but the body did not feel able even then to put its charter aside for a general condemnation. Nor did the United Nations ever condemn Amin while he was in power.

When finally Amin fled from Uganda in April 1979, after attacking Tanzania in the Kagera Triangle and crumbling in his retreat from Nyerere's footsoldiers, the Commonwealth was in a good position to help the new Ugandan leaders in their first steps towards national recovery. The wisdom of not expelling Uganda from the Commonwealth in 1973 because of Amin's excesses was clearly proved.

The man chosen to head the Uganda National Liberation Front, a coalition of exile groups, was Yusuf Lule who from 1970 to 1972 had worked at the Commonwealth Secretariat as Assistant Secretary-General. I had appointed him from his earlier post as Vice-Chancellor of Makerere University, and he went on to spend seven satisfying years running the Association of African Universities. When he was sworn into office as Uganda's President in April 1979, the burden seemed heavy for a sixty-seven-year-old academic, and he was replaced by Godfrey Binaisa within two months. But in that time he had rebuilt links with the Commonwealth. During Lule's second week in office Sonny Ramphal wrote him a letter recalling the phrases of the 1977 communiqué and adding: 'Now that the night is past and the day is here, we must make a reality of that commitment of fraternity. To that end we work with you.' CFTC managing director David Anderson flew to Kampala to discuss a programme of action.

Anderson was given an urgent request, to send a Commonwealth team 'to assess the task of rehabilitating the Uganda economy, and to recommend on priorities, with particular reference to immediate needs for technical and financial assistance'. Within three weeks a thirteen-member team had been gathered from eight Commonwealth countries, of economists and experts in administration, banking, industrial engineering, transport, health and communications, and were on their way to Uganda. Headed by British economist Dudley Seers, it included men like Sir Egerton Richardson of Jamaica and Sam Montsi of Lesotho who know well the international banking scene, and others whose jobs were at the grassroots level of needs that Uganda was facing in many sectors, such as Donald Peckham, a civil engineer who looks after country roads in Australia and has had six years' experience in northern Nigeria. I do not believe any other organisation could have assembled so quickly a team of such wide-ranging talents from countries with relevant experience.

The difficulties facing the team were daunting. The deterioration of administration during the Amin regime had meant a decline in the quantity and quality of statistics, and the spread of *magendo* (or 'black market') meant that a lot of exports and imports were unrecorded. Moreover, as Seers notes in his preface:

> 'Many key documents are missing, destroyed or dispersed in the war and the subsequent looting. Telephone communication is still poor, even between departments in Kampala and others in Entebbe, and road journeys often difficult. In the central ministries there is a scarcity of information about the current situation – the state of equipment, the size of inventories (and) whether estates, factories, offices, hospitals, trains, etc, are actually functioning.'

Nevertheless, in a hectic month of hard travelling and late-night writing, the team put together a comprehensive set of thirty-one sectoral papers, covering everything from the main export crops (which declined in Amin's time, as farmers retreated to subsistence agriculture) to cottage industries, and from tourism to the problems facing the University of Makerere. For the last twelve days the pool of Ugandan secretaries who were working on drafts of the report typed on average 30,000 words a day, and on the final day came to work through crowds of demonstrators and gunfire, for it was the day on which Lule was displaced by Godfrey Binaisa. But the two-volume report, *The Rehabilitation of the Economy of Uganda*, was handed to the new government in early July, and at the Lusaka HGM the next month President Binaisa told other heads of government it had been the main working paper put in front of a meeting of donor agencies the previous week.

The first, overview volume starts with the blunt sentences: 'The Government of the National Liberation Movement inherited a country in ruins. As a statement of physical damage this would be an exaggeration. It is the economy that has been ruined.' It put the case for external support strongly: 'The rehabilitation of Uganda will be impossible unless there is timely and effective support by many foreign governments. This support needs to be far more generous and flexible than is normally the case.' And it set out a two-year rehabilitation programme involving project aid of £650 million, but it put as an even more urgent priority the giving of massive balance-of-payments support to finance the import of consumer goods and thus bring down the appallingly inflated living costs.

The aid took much longer to start flowing than Ugandan leaders and the Commonwealth team had hoped; a year later, less than half the £650 million had been pledged. Meanwhile, in the middle of May 1980 Binaisa was removed from the presidency and held under house arrest by a Military Commission, whose chairman Paulo

Muwanga was an avowed supporter of Milton Obote. Two weeks later Obote returned from nine years of exile in Tanzania, and immediately Uganda moved into a high state of political excitement, with the promise of a general election before the end of the year.

Muwanga, perhaps prodded in this direction by President Nyerere, turned to the Commonwealth Secretariat to provide an election observer group similar to the one that had been so successful in Zimbabwe. Sonny Ramphal was understandably cautious, because this was the first time such a request had come from a sovereign state. He only accepted to gather such a group after Emeka Anyaoku had flown to Uganda to make sure that all four political parties agreed to such a group's coming to observe the elections and report whether they were 'free and fair'. A nine-member team* under the chairmanship of a veteran Ghanaian diplomat, Kojo Debrah, reached Kampala barely three weeks before election day on December 10, and just too late to witness the nomination of candidates.

Their assignment was quite as difficult as that of the Commonwealth Observer Group in Zimbabwe. Neither the team's interim report, published on December 11 before the results began to be announced, nor its final report completed a week later in London, minced words. In particular, the interim report recorded the team's 'deep unease' at the disqualification of a number of prospective candidates on or after nomination day, which resulted in the unopposed return of seventeen of Obote's Uganda People's Congress (UPC) candidates among a total of 126 constituencies.

At the root of a number of irregularities recorded in these reports lay the excessive anxiety of Muwanga to ensure a UPC victory. It seems clear that the UPC would have won the elections in any case (they would, for example, almost certainly have won at least half the seventeen uncontested seats if there had been polling in them). And there appears to have been remarkably little attempt to rig the results at constituency level. As the Canadian observer, Barney Danson (a former Minister of National Defence), later wrote:

> 'In some nine seats where the vote was close, only one went to the UPC, which to us testified to the legitimacy of the counting and reporting process.'**

---

*The team was composed of representatives of Australia, Barbados, Botswana, Britain, Canada, Cyprus, Ghana, India and Sierra Leone.

**Report written for publication.

The Commonwealth Observer Group achieved four main things in their three weeks of energetic travel, in which they visited nearly one-third of the country's 5000 polling stations and still managed to be on hand in Kampala to make speedy representations to Muwanga at moments of crisis. They provided a general reassurance to the country's 4.8 million voters that the election process was under international scrutiny, and they reinforced this by some vigorous investigation of irregularities; without doubt, they raised the level of honesty in the elections.

Finally, on two occasions their firm representations to Muwanga helped save the situation. Four days before polling, the group was 'astonished' to learn that the Electoral Commission had urged that counting take place at one central point in each constituency, instead of at the 5000 polling stations, as had been agreed with Muwanga. The carrying of 20,000 ballot boxes to central points obviously gave opportunity for 'losing' many en route, and the Democratic Party threatened to boycott the elections if this plan of centralising the count was carried out. The team managed to reverse it; they also persuaded Muwanga to order the removal of road blocks, and the confinement to barracks of Ugandan troops during polling, which greatly eased the atmosphere.

A second confrontation with Muwanga came on December 11, after he had extended polling into a second day and, by military proclamation, ordered the counting to take place at district headquarters and the results to be reported secretly to him, for him to judge on their validity before making them public. It seems that Muwanga panicked at rumours that the Democratic Party was heading for a landslide victory, not simply in Kampala and surrounding Buganda but in the country generally. Debrah acted swiftly in publishing the (quite critical) Interim Report, and in making clear in a letter to Muwanga that the team would leave Uganda forthwith if the proclamation was not withdrawn. There followed a meeting between the observers and Muwanga. This meeting, in Danson's words, was

'correct but tense ... He was sobered by our letter, our interim report, and our determination to depart if the situation was not rectified. He advised us that he had already issued another decree, but did not disclose its contents to us. When pressed, he sent an aide for it and, after some wait, it arrived, apparently freshly typed. In effect, it restored the agreed upon process.'

So the count, in the end, took place at the polling stations and results were verified by party agents. The intense yet remarkably peaceable participation of millions of Ugandans (the turnout at the polls was above ninety percent) was echoed by what the group's final report called the 'happy spirit of enterprise and cooperation between polling staff and party agents'. Considering the potential for a disastrous outcome, the elections were surprisingly successful.

Milton Obote, from several accounts, was embarrassed by Muwanga's partiality. Now back in the President's office, he has a formidable task ahead. The future of Uganda, a beautiful but devastated country of enterprising people, depends so much upon his ability to achieve political reconciliation, particularly with the people of Buganda; his immediate release of Binaisa was a wise first move. If he can make real advances in this task, he will at last be taking Uganda on the path to a harmonious plural society, the same hard journey on which Gowon led Nigeria and Mugabe has been leading Zimbabwe. He deserves all our understanding and support.

Chapter 12
THE QUEEN AND THE
COMMONWEALTH
A Silver Thread of Continuity

In the after-glow of the successful Heads of Government Meeting in 1979, which began with overt hostility to Mrs Thatcher from a Lusaka airport crowd and ended with her dancing with President Kaunda at the Lusaka Press Club to a new tune with sparkling words,* the *Zambian Daily Mail* had thoughts for the other remarkable woman who had flown out from Britain. The paper recalled how Queen Elizabeth had rejected advice from those who suggested she might cut Zambia out of her East African journey as being unsafe,** had put her trust in Zambians and by smiling her way through a round of visits in the days before the HGM had greatly eased the tension between Commonwealth countries. The *Zambian Daily Mail* concluded fervently: 'She can be elected Queen of all the world.' Not to be outdone, the *Weekend World* heralded a report of a Zambian priest's enthusiastic sermon with the startling page one headline 'The Second Coming: Queen as Jesus?'

How did it happen that Zambia, a Republic since its independence day in 1964, came to sound more royalist than any monarchy? I think the answer is fairly simple. What the Zambians were seeing for themselves, and warmly applauding, was the skilful job the Queen has been doing for years (in addition to being Queen of Great Britain and Northern Ireland, Queen of Canada, Queen of Jamaica and a dozen other independent states by 1979) as Head of the Commonwealth.

This title was adopted at a Prime Ministers' Meeting called in

---

*The refrain was: *Now come and dance, nice Maggie,*
You have nothing to fear.
Maggie's a good lady,
K K's a good man.

** See page 236.

April 1949 to deal with Nehru's request that India retain Commonwealth membership after becoming a republic. (Ireland had just withdrawn, assuming that republican status would be incompatible with membership.) A drafting committee including Mike Pearson worked out a formula which rejected any form of words that sounded like a constitutional agreement, in favour of a statement – to which India was pleased to subscribe – that all members recognised King George VI as 'the symbol of the free association of independent sovereign countries and, as such, Head of the Commonwealth.'*

The formula has worked well. The tradition that a country that wished to change from a monarchy to republican status was required to apply to retain Commonwealth membership has persisted because it was during this process in 1961 that South Africa was told that its apartheid policies were an abomination in a multiracial association. It became clear that, unless its policies were changed, its application would be rejected; so it withdrew the application instead. In effect, South Africa was expelled.

Later, when I was Secretary-General, several countries asked me to obtain the other members' agreement that they remain in the Commonwealth as republics, stating that they accepted the formula of the Queen as 'the symbol of the free association . . .' This went smoothly.

A few African cabinet ministers (but never Heads of State) asked me once or twice whether it might not be desirable to rotate the Headship of the Commonwealth, in the same way as the OAU chairmanship passed around (to Amin in 1975!). I always replied that I thought it would be profoundly unwise, for two reasons. First, because the continuity the Queen provided was valuable and the shared history that she represented was vitally important to the association as a whole. Secondly, because such a change would deeply upset British opinion at a time when Britain was still going through the neurosis of diminished relative power in the world. They should realise how useful it was to have a dedicated internationalist at the centre of British political life and how important a role the Queen was playing in helping take Britain (and the world) through this problem period.

For rather different reasons I have also been strongly in favour of

---

*For a full account of this early turning point in the Commonwealth, see *Mike*, Vol 2, the Memoirs of the Rt Hon Lester B. Pearson, University of Toronto Press, 1973, pages 98 to 106.

the Queen being monarch of several countries. It was long ago made clear that sharing a monarch involves not the slightest limitation on sovereignty. For example George VI was during World War II neutral as King of Ireland while belligerent as King of Britain and (a week later) as King of Canada. It is natural that a number of newly independent states, from India to Zambia, decide to become republics. But it is also good that a number of countries should share one monarch, as a community symbol which comes from the mists of pre-feudal history and yet points forward to an age of interdependence. As a Canadian I consider it mature, rather than irrational, to have a non-resident and shared monarch, someone who symbolises the transcendence of individual state sovereignty in the modern world. It is also important for countries such as Canada to have a reserve power, above political controversy, and above the head of the government of the day.

The Queen's reaction to a country's turning from a monarchy into a republic has always been a calm acceptance of the naturalness of change – in contrast to her grandfather, George V, who is said to have flown into a rage in 1923 on hearing that Canada had asserted its independence to the point of signing a halibut fisheries treaty with the United States. By 1981 the Commonwealth included twenty-five republics, and four countries with separate monarchs, as well as fifteen countries of which the Queen is Head of State.

During my first weeks as Secretary-General members of the Royal Family made what was clearly a concerted effort to give us a welcome and to impress upon Whitehall officials that I was to be considered one of the Queen's advisers. There were invitations to small lunches or dinners with the Queen's Secretary, the Lord Chamberlain, the Queen Mother, and the Duke of Gloucester as well as (my wife and I alone) with the Queen herself. It was made clear to me that the Palace recognised that it was important to be seen that the Queen was not primarily dependent for information on Commonwealth matters on the British Prime Minister, whom she received every week. As a matter of course, she saw all Commonwealth Heads of Government whenever they passed through London; but she was pleased that the Secretary-General should be seen as her principal informant and adviser on multilateral Commonwealth affairs. So whenever I sought it, four or five times a year, I was given an audience for a full briefing talk, often after I had been on a trip to a group of countries. I also began a practice of sending her copies of the more interesting Commonwealth docu-

268

ments, not simply key ones like the Minutes of the Heads of Government or other ministerial meetings but also detailed reports such as one on the employment problems of young people in Africa, and those of my circular messages to member governments that I considered interesting and important.

A few Whitehall officials needed some Royal prodding before they accepted the Commonwealth Secretary-General's position in the way the Queen saw it. Attending a Palace reception for the diplomatic corps Eve and I found ourselves placed in the line at the bottom of the chargés d'affaires. When Prince Philip eventually reached us, he asked 'What are you doing down here?' and Eve replied, 'It's your party, Sir. We go where we're told.' He answered: 'Yes, but you know who organises these things – the CRO.' A week later the Protocol man came to see me at Marlborough House and said he had had an idea and planned to put us in future before the line of ambassadors – together with the Papal representative. The whole little incident reminded me of the petty difficulties that the first Canadian High Commissioner, Sir Alexander Galt, encountered in establishing himself in London in 1880. Whitehall tried to insist that he be attached to the Home Office and, on the grounds that Galt had married his sister-in-law after his first wife's death, refused him an audience with Queen Victoria. In his case, also, a Prince came to the rescue; for the Prince of Wales befriended him and introduced him to his mother and many other people.*

The Queen has played an outstanding part in stimulating interest and spreading knowledge about the Commonwealth. Her journeys to various countries provide the opportunity for an intensive course of public education, not least in Britain, through newspaper articles, magazine and television coverage. Some of this coverage is inevitably superficial, but there is a cumulative effect upon the corner of the Commonwealth where it is most needed: for those in Britain who have been slow to accept the change from Empire to Commonwealth must still have been influenced for the wiser by seeing over many years the daughter of a King-Emperor taking such pleasure in building more equal relationships with the leaders of many independent countries.

She has a facility for drawing people out and making them be frank with her about their problems. I found that she was often better informed about the real views of various countries, through

---

Canada House, 1880 to 1980 by Nancy Gelber, Canadian High Commission, London, 1980.

269

having talked with visiting Heads, than Ministers in the British Government who receive diplomatic reports of events and thinking. I never felt inhibited from raising sensitive subjects with her on which my views differed from the British. At my first audience, after Rhodesia's UDI in 1965, I said it was a pity that Britain had never used its power to disallow discriminatory laws against the African majority, and told her I had proposed to Harold Wilson a plan for nipping UDI in the bud by sending in British paratroops and asking her to broadcast to the Rhodesian people. She did not comment directly on these points, but I had the impression that she would have willingly taken a more active role in the Rhodesian crisis, had Wilson asked her to do so.

The Commonwealth Secretariat benefitted greatly from her prompt action in generously offering one of her palaces as its headquarters. It had been used intermittently as a Commonwealth centre, for meetings and other activities, for two years before Nkrumah, Eric Williams and Obote proposed the establishment of a Secretariat during the Heads of Government Meeting in 1964. While this proposal was still being debated*, the Queen offered Marlborough House as the future Secretariat's home, thus showing her own enthusiasm for the proposal. Sir Alec Douglas-Home announced her offer to the conference, and it swung some of the more hesitant Prime Ministers around to support the scheme for a Secretariat.

Marlborough House was built in the early eighteenth century by Sir Christopher Wren for John Churchill, first Duke of Marlborough, and his wife Sarah. It is a place of modest splendour, whimsical charm – and some curiosities. Among its secret corners is the little cemetery in a shrubbery where seven of Queen Alexandra's pets – six dogs and one rabbit – are buried, tiny tombstones marking the graves. The most notable curiosities are the murals depicting the Duke's victorious battles across the breadth of Europe. It was the main distraction of Louis Laguerre, godson of Louis XIV, during four years of exile to paint around the main hall and up the staircases these gory scenes of French and English soldiers slaughtering each other at Blenheim and Malplaquet, and of farm women stripping the corpses. Stranger still is the library used for forty years by Edward VII whose residence it was while he was Prince of Wales – a library used more often, perhaps, as a trysting place than as a reading-room, for the 'books' along one wall which also conceal the door turn out to be simply bookspines with titles betraying a

*See Chapter 1.

schoolboy humour (five volumes of *Bacon's History of Greece*, six of *Boyle on Steam, Lamb on the Death of Wolfe, Spare the Tree* by Y. Hewett etc).

As my office I had a corner room that had been Queen Mary's bedroom, overlooking the Mall and St James' Park. On the walls hung a portrait of Arabella Stuart and some Gainsboroughs. The sense of history and grace in this room and the whole building was a delight.

During the Commonwealth Games in Edinburgh in July 1970, Eve and I were invited to stay overnight at Holyrood House, a very different royal palace. The ghost of Rizzio, the secretary of Mary Queen of Scots who was murdered in this converted abbey, is said to walk there. Certainly the visit began a little chillingly for us. Despite a sunny day, winds from Siberia cut through Eve's silk dress and coat and her teeth were chattering during the garden party for the athletes. ('The Queen no doubt has a little woollie on,' an aide explained comfortingly.) But the situation improved when we were led through echoing halls to our suite of rooms and to hot baths already drawn in huge wood-surrounded bath-tubs with steps up to them. We were given two bedrooms with a common sitting-room, but were somewhat surprised when scanning the telephone list to find that Eve appeared to be sharing bedroom number 57 and telephone extension 019 with Sir Robert Menzies, while I was promised the close company in room 56 of his wife, Dame Pattie. An unromantic explanation was soon apparent: in the cause of economy the staff had typed a single list for two days' visitors, and the Australian guests were coming on the morrow.

The Queen is a superb traveller, who always wants to gain the maximum value from any visit and consequently works her secretaries extremely hard. But there was one journey she wished to make, soon after those Games, which was denied her. This was to Singapore at the time of the Heads of Government Meeting in January 1971. It was made very clear to me by Whitehall that Heath was strongly opposed to her going. As I was already embroiled with the British Prime Minister over an issue – arms sales to South Africa – that was likely to dominate the conference, I did not want to open up another argument with him about her presence.* As well, I rationalised that her presence might make the Common-

---

*She has not, as some still believe, ever attended the conference itself or opened it but she has talks with each Head of Government individually, and gives a state banquet for all of them and the Secretary-General, with their wives.

271

wealth appear more anglocentric to Africans at a particularly sensitive time, when many of them were under domestic pressure to withdraw from the Commonwealth as a gesture against Britain, and she in turn might be embarrassed if some of them declined an invitation to dine aboard the Royal yacht. I underestimated their gallantry, I am sure. But I did not raise with the Singapore Prime Minister the desirability of inviting her. In retrospect I am sure I was wrong, for her presence might well have moderated Heath's behaviour and persuaded him to take a broader view; and the Commonwealth would not have come so close to collapse at that point.

At the Queen's request I called at the Palace afterwards to give her my impression of the Singapore HGM. I told her why in my view, unlike that of a number of British newspapers, it had been a great success.

I also suggested that the concern in Commonwealth countries about the implications of British entry into Europe was related to the fears about arms sales to South Africa: there was a general concern that a go-it-alone attitude was growing in Britain. The Queen expressed no views on Britain joining Europe but, when I said I saw no inconsistency between British membership of the EEC and her continued cooperation with the Commonwealth, she said with great feeling that it was unthinkable that Britain should turn her back on overseas links with other English-speaking peoples.

At one stage in our conversation there was a sudden, loud noise just outside the window of the little sitting-room at the back of the Palace where we were chatting. The Queen laughed, and said this often happened. It was Philip, she explained, coming down in his red helicopter, to get ready for lunch.

After Singapore I resolved, at any rate, to ensure that she was invited by the chairmen of all future Heads of Government Meetings. Heath had made clear to me that after the Singapore experience he did not want another summit for several years. 'Not in 1973 or 1974, possibly 1975 at the earliest,' Sir Denis Greenhill the Under Secretary of State told me on instructions. Naturally I made no commitment but I decided at once that we should have one in 1973. I also decided that one Head of Government whose invitation Heath and other leaders would find it hard to refuse was the Canadian; and in September 1972 I therefore cabled Pierre Trudeau asking him to offer to play host to an HGM in Ottawa in 1973.

With an election imminent, officials in Ottawa told me that I could not expect an early reply. But, to my delight, Trudeau made the offer publicly in a campaign speech, saying that he 'had been assured by the Commonwealth Secretary-General that such an invitation would be generally welcome'. I was in Canada later in the campaign, for a meeting of the Senior Officials from each Commonwealth country. Trudeau and I talked about arrangements. Perhaps remembering the heckling the Queen had encountered in Quebec City in 1964 (and forgetting the great welcome she received at Montreal's Expo in 1967), Trudeau was worried about criticism from Quebec, and asked me if he could (if need be) make clear publicly that it was the advice of the Secretary-General that the Queen must be invited on such a Commonwealth occasion. It most certainly was. I also spoke to the Conservative leader, Robert Stanfield, who said he would be delighted to host the meeting and invite the Queen, if he were to win the election.

The Queen placed a high priority on attending the Ottawa HGM and told me she would be available whenever it was held. The reluctant traveller to Ottawa was Edward Heath himself. Up to the last few days he would not say whether he would come or would send Alec Home as deputy. It was the Queen's firmness in showing that she at any rate would be in Canada that ended his sulky attitude; he could hardly stay away, if she were there. So he came; Trudeau, who had only just survived with a minority government that held 109 out of 264 seats, made an excellent chairman; and Heath to his surprise found the meeting useful and concurred readily with the proposal for a meeting in 1975 in Jamaica.

When I was in Kingston for the Commonwealth Education Ministers Meeting in June 1974, Manley and I discussed HGM plans, and he invited the Queen to visit during the 1975 meeting, whether in the meantime Jamaica became a republic or not (it did not). In Kingston she gave a banquet for Heads of Government aboard the *Britannia*, the comfortable and delightfully old-fashioned royal yacht with deck awnings and a handsome dining saloon embellished *inter alia* with two huge tusks of old narwhals from the Canadian Arctic. She asked my wife and me to arrive on board ten minutes early, and invested me as a Companion of Honour.

At the Kingston HGM Kenneth Kaunda spoke to me of his keenness to offer Lusaka as the site of the 1977 Summit, and to invite the Queen on her first visit to his republic. Harold Wilson then mentioned to me that the Queen had asked him to invite the Heads to meet in London in mid-1977 which would be the Silver

Jubilee of her accession. Wilson said that he did not want to oppose Kaunda and was therefore very hesitant to put in a counter-bid. So I spoke privately to Kaunda, and he immediately and generously agreed to postpone his invitation to 1979, so that the 1977 meeting could take place in London, to coincide with the Jubilee of the Queen as Head of the Commonwealth.

Closer to the time of that Summit, one or two people were concerned that the occasion, merging with the Jubilee celebrations, might be seen like an old-style Durbar. They need not have worried. The thanksgiving service in St Paul's Cathedral, on the day before the Commonwealth Conference, had its mediaeval elements: the Lord High Almoner and the Portcullis Poursuivant (in everyday life one Michael Maclagan) were prominent in the processions. But an onlooker could judge how greatly the world had changed, if he glanced along the pew where the Callaghans sat beside King Moshoeshoe of Lesotho, the Kaundas, Archbishop Makarios and Dr Banda.

I should particularly mention the Queen's role in establishing the multi-faith service, which now takes place in Westminster Abbey as an observance for Commonwealth Day, the second Monday in March. It is one of the most beautiful and profound religious occasions that I know. Yet in its first years the service caused great controversy in Anglican circles and I doubt it would ever have become established as a red-letter day in the calendar of both the Abbey and the Commonwealth without the Queen's active diplomatic support.

The first Commonwealth Day multi-faith service was held in June 1966 in St Martin-in-the-Fields by its vicar, the Rev Austen Williams. The original idea came from the executive secretary of the Royal Commonwealth Society, whose headquarters is nearby. Mr Williams adapted the form of service from one worked out by the Rev Joseph McCullagh for a ceremony the previous September during the 1965 Commonwealth Arts Festival. In 1966 Williams persuaded the Bishop of Kensington, the Rt Reverend Ronald Goodshild, to preside and introduce the service, which he did with these words:

> 'Our purpose in coming together this evening is to make common affirmation of faith. It is not primarily to make an act of worship. That would not be easy, since we start from widely differing conceptions of reality. We do well, however, to remember that God whom we all worship is not just the product of our history, tradition or imagination. He is not wholly within our understanding, yet He is the same yesterday, today and for ever. . . .'

The Queen and Prince Philip were present, and the service attracted attention. Complaints about it were made to the Bishop of London and the Archbishop of Canterbury. Certain sections of the Church of England pronounced themselves outraged at this service in a Christian church which had included a Bishop and some 'heathen'. The Archbishop's secretary let Austen Williams know that no further such services should take place at St Martins or indeed at any Anglican church. The matter was also discussed in the Synod of the Church. Many in the hierarchy and many laymen in the Synod were opposed to a multi-faith service, though Austen Williams had support from representatives of several churches.

The idea lapsed under this disapproval in 1967, but happily was revived in 1968, with a broad-based committee* lengthily negotiating which hymns and readings might be included that all faiths could accept. Called an act of witness, for four years it was held in the Guildhall, followed by a lunch given by the Lord Mayor in Mansion House. In the first year I sat at lunch beside the Chief Rabbi of England, who had been on the committee and confided to me, 'We all stretched ourselves to the very limits of our consciences – and some of us think rather beyond those limits.'

In 1972 the service was moved from the Guildhall to Westminster Abbey on the initiative of the Queen, and it has taken place there each year since. The point is that the Abbey does not come formally under the Bishop of London, or for that matter even under the Archbishop of Canterbury, but is termed (together with the chapels at Marlborough House and St James' Palace) 'a Royal Peculiar' and comes directly under the Queen as Head of the Church of England. It is an impressive service in the Abbey as the procession of religious leaders moves down the centre aisle followed by young people carrying all the flags of the Commonwealth to place them at the steps of the sacrarium, whereupon a fanfare of trumpets is sounded. The Dean leads the congregation in four affirmations (the second, for example: 'We affirm our common faith that the lives of all men are in the hand of God, and that He is wherever men are') and these are interwoven with readings by High Commissioners – the Hindu Mauritian, for example, reading from the Bhagavad Gita, the Malaysian from the Qur'an, the Bhuddhist Sri Lankan from the Samyutta-Nikaya. There have been sacred dances, and music from various cultures. Prayers are said in Sanskrit and Hebrew, Arabic and Punjabi, Pali and broad Scots. In 1979 the final prayer for the Commonwealth was said by the representative of the (Catholic)

---

*On which Emeka Anyaoku represented me.

Cardinal Archbishop of Westminster, and the reading from the New Testament – Christ's Sermon on the Mount – was given by the High Commissioner for Papua New Guinea with great dignity in his native Pidgin. It is a deeply moving experience, so many faiths and languages joined together for that hour in the Abbey, and worth a mighty fanfare.

I attach great importance to the multi-faith service at the Abbey – and to similar ones in other member countries on Commonwealth Day – because I do not believe that the great religions are in fundamental rivalry, even though at certain periods of history they have been the main support of rival civilisations. The real difference is rather between devotion to moral values and materialist egocentric faithlessness. In the battle to build one world an important step is to form an alliance between the faiths, and there is a natural alliance to be made among all those who profess moral values. So a multi-faith service, as part of man's progress to a global community, is also very much a political act – or, to express my point more accurately, political creativity is a moral and religious act.

The Prince of Wales began, during my time as Secretary-General, to speak out about the Commonwealth and showed that he was likely to become, in his individualistic way, every bit as good a public educator on this subject as his mother. In 1970 he made a memorable speech at the Albert Hall, 'an irreverent youth' (as he called himself) lecturing 5000 members of the Institute of Directors on 'Youth and the Commonwealth'.* Why don't young people, whose idealism reputedly knows no boundaries, become almost ecstatic about the possibilities the Commonwealth holds out? he asked. Because they have little or no personal experience of it, and they read only of disillusionment. More travel and exchanges and apprenticeships were part of the answer, he said, and he berated British Airways for its refusal to offer cheap air fares for young travellers. He told how he had gained some personal experience, sleeping in a hut in New Guinea 'occupied by man-eating spiders and acid-squirting caterpillars'. Why were there fewer than 2000 long-term volunteers from Britain then serving abroad? Partly, he

---

*Speech to the Annual Conference of the Institute of Directors, London, 5 November, 1970.

told the directors, because companies and industries would not release qualified young people for a year or two. It was a lively, challenging, necessary speech.

Earlier in 1970 Prince Charles had spent a full day at Marlborough House, visiting various divisions and lunching with a group of senior colleagues at my flat next door. I had noticed that he had been attending a day of briefings at some British Government department, and suggested to the Palace that he might wish similarly to learn about the Secretariat's work. He proved himself to be, already at twenty-one, an impressive questioner who went to the heart of all the subjects we discussed, whether it was the change of government in Britain, the attitude to the Commonwealth in India, or the difficulty of getting across to various publics what he saw as the good points of the Commonwealth – the easiness of communications between individuals, and the general understanding of each other's problems.

I remember a particularly moving moment in July 1969 connected with Prince Charles. When in the 700-year-old ceremony dated to Edward I he was presented to the people of Wales at Caernarfon Castle, he took as the newly inducted Prince of Wales his Oath of Allegiance to the Queen 'and her heirs and successors, Queens and Kings . . . Heads of the Commonwealth for ever!' The last six words hit me as a striking challenge at a time when the strains upon the Commonwealth were still daunting. But the castle walls about us were so sturdy, the young Prince so forthright, the ceremony so embedded in history, that one could not fail to feel strengthened in purpose.

Prince Philip has himself created special areas of Commonwealth cooperation, one with the agricultural societies and another with the Award Scheme for young people. He has also over twenty-five years sustained many people's enthusiasm for the Duke of Edinburgh's Commonwealth Study Conference on Problems of Industrial Society, a remarkable gathering every six years of some three hundred young 'high-flyer' managers, trade unionists and public servants from thirty or more countries who make well-prepared tours of one country's industrial communities, successes and problem areas alike, using the experience as background for intensive debate*. In a more controversial setting, the 'British

---

*The Conference Record of the Fifth Study Conference, *People in an Industrial Society*; Canada, 1980, is available from Lloyd Hemsworth, 'Tarnworth' R.R. 2, Rockwood, Ontario, N0B 2K0 at Canadian $10.00.

Commonwealth Games' at Christchurch in 1974, Prince Philip proved a vital ally. Violent feelings were expressed by Canadian, Australian and New Zealand committee members at the proposal, which I supported, to drop the word 'British' from the title of the games, while men like Nigeria's Chief Enaharo were adamant that it had to go. I was strongly attacked at a press conference, 'Isn't it the British Commonwealth?' and answered: 'Of course. But it's also the New Zealand Commonwealth, the Canadian Commonwealth, the Nigerian Commonwealth, the Indian Commonwealth. At the Governmental Summit level we long ago agreed just to call it the Commonwealth.' Prince Philip was less publicly taking the same line, and these veterans in their self-perpetuating committees respected him as a fellow sportsman and accepted the word from royalty; so the point was won.

The Secretariat has since 1965 shared Marlborough House with the Commonwealth Foundation which, as mentioned in Chapter 3, was set up at the same time as the Secretariat 'to administer a fund for increasing interchanges between Commonwealth organisations in professional fields throughout the Commonwealth'. Offering this accommodation to the Foundation was a further expression of the Queen's concern to improve Commonwealth links, in this case through non-governmental organisations (NGOs) in professional fields.

The Secretariat and Foundation are parts of the same package of plans made in 1965 for an increased content of activities for the Commonwealth, and for multilateral control of them. The Foundation is governed, and all its grants approved, by a Board of Trustees nominated by the various governments and filled in most cases by their High Commissioners in London, together with the Commonwealth Secretary-General ex officio. I enjoyed and valued my participation in its work.

For fifteen years the Foundation was directed by John Chadwick, a former FCO official with strong links to Newfoundland, of which he wrote an excellent history. The literary tradition is carried on by the second director, Ric Prichard Throssell, whose long career in the Australian foreign service, running the education and training part of their aid programme, has not hindered his becoming a prize-winning playwright.

While the Secretariat has expanded over the years with several new divisions and an enlarged budget, in response to the requests of

Heads of Government to become active in fields from youth training to food production and rural development, the Foundation has remained small in staff numbers and modest in budget. But the list of achievements during its first ten years is impressive.* Of the £2.6 million in grants made during the decade, almost half went to helping set up Commonwealth-wide professional associations (there were only two in 1966, covering medicine and architecture, and the number had grown to eighteen associations by 1976) and to establishing 'national professional centres' in thirteen countries. In Chadwick's phrase, a Professional Centre, either a selfcontained building or rented premises, 'provides one answer to mental professional isolation in the newer Commonwealth, and a dual bridge between the professions themselves and between them collectively and their communities.' There are good examples of how some of these centres have led professionals, who can be a self-satisfied élite, into community service: the Jamaican one running a counselling service for students, the Trinidad one organising a roster of engineers and doctors willing to give spare-time advice to community projects, the Singapore one actually undertaking such projects.

This is not the place to review the Foundation's work in any detail, ranging as it has done from special projects such as establishing a regional deaf-teacher training centre in Malawi to a long list of travel grants and exchanges. I should, however, note how the Secretariat and Foundation have worked in parallel in encouraging regional cooperation. For the Foundation this has meant a concentration on those areas of the Commonwealth – East and Central Africa, and the Caribbean – 'where the goals of Federation have been missed (and) efforts are now being made to retwine the functional threads.' Two regional organisations which the Foundation has helped into being are the Commonwealth Caribbean Bar Association and Nurses Association. And there are areas – in youth development, for example, and education – where the Foundation and CFTC have combined forces.

The Secretariat itself has had from the beginning a lively relationship with NGOs. The fact that it was set up by Heads of Government and is a servant of all Commonwealth governments in no way isolates it from the unofficial Commonwealth.' It was essential not to be isolated, especially in the years after the Secretar-

---

*A full account is available in the Fifth Report of the Commonwealth Foundation, 'The First Ten Years 1966-76', from which several phrases in this section are quoted.

iat developed its technical assistance programme and could promote functional cooperation in many directions. For direct links with many NGOs could multiply the effectiveness of many Secretariat activities. Again, in several developing countries the lines between a government department and an NGO are often blurred, and some talented and energetic person can be involved as a leader in both spheres. As a result, although the education and training assistance of the CFTC is based on government nominations, a great number of other contacts are directly with the nongovernmental (or sometimes quasi-government) worker. The Medical Adviser has his links with pharmacists and nursing associations; the Food Production and Rural Development division with appropriate technology centres; the Science Division with solar energy experts; the Youth Programme (through its regional training centres) with the YWCA and a range of community groups.

I was particularly concerned that communicators in the Commonwealth should be supported in their efforts to spread knowledge of the changing nature of the association. This was not an area strongly served by the Foundation with its concentration on professional associations and its inclination to categorise journalists and broadcasters as 'sub-professional'! Over the years, therefore, the Secretariat has supported the Commonwealth Broadcasting Association in the training courses and joint production plans worked out with African radio stations. And, when the Commonwealth Press Union took a leap forward from its old-fashioned clubbish character (it began as the Empire Press Union), we were happy to help finance the training courses it began to offer in African and Asian countries. Inevitably there are always other gaps to be filled, and the Secretariat itself has helped organise training courses in Britain for financial journalists, and has set up its own radio tapes service to a network of more than seventy stations in every part of the Commonwealth.

Parliamentarians and teachers are, of course, important parts of any communications system. The annual conference of the Commonwealth Parliamentary Association has always been an important date in the Secretary-General's calendar, and the attitudes of 'rich white' parliamentarians towards Secretariat activities soon changed from those described in Chapter 3. And, as well as the work which the Education Division did with teachers, I was concerned to help the Association of Commonwealth Universities (ACU), which among other tasks administers several exchange fellowship schemes among its 220 member universities and organises periodic conferences of their Vice-Chancellors. The ACU after about fifty-five years of service was faltering in the early 1970s when its newly elected president at the time, Tom Symons of Trent University in Ontario, approached me for advice and possible help. The ACU was modernised, its fee structure being made less difficult for developing country universities and travel grants offered to council meetings that had traditionally been held in Britain. I offered CFTC funding for exchanges and programmes. The changes he made, and the shot-in-the-arm which we were able to give, were timely and the ACU is in a healthy state today.

Many of the older NGOs have had to slough off a colonial skin before becoming active members in the modern Commonwealth. Several of the thirty-five branches of the Royal Commonwealth Society have managed this transformation with some elegance. In particular, the Canadian one has found its renaissance in an annual conference in which leading high school students from every province spend a colourful week in Ottawa in the role of delegates from all the different Commonwealth countries debating the issues that might arise at an HGM. The London headquarters of the RCS – almost a century old when the Secretariat was launched – has under vigorous leadership from such people as Betty Owen and Stephen Kemp, found several ways to shine in the modern world. One that leaves a lasting impression on participants is the Commonwealth Interchange Study Group Organisation (CISGO) scheme it operates for young people with a commercial or professional background, to make a month-long tour of another region of the Commonwealth. CISGO complements the Duke of Edinburgh's Study Conference on Problems of Industrial Society: much smaller (any CISGO group has fewer than twenty participants), it is more flexible, takes place more frequently and can be hosted by any country.

There is much vitality in so many Commonwealth NGOs* and they should be harnessed and coordinated for even better effect. Without them the Commonwealth would be a top-heavy association: they give it body and balance. If the Queen as its Head instils the Commonwealth with a special spirit, the NGOs give it much of its sustaining breath.

---

*Details of more than two hundred NGOs are given in a useful publication of the Commonwealth Secretariat: *Commonwealth Organisations* (second edition 1979).

Chapter 13

THE THREADS ENTWINED
. . . and the Greening of Australia

'Where there is no vision, the people perish.' This book has described several scenes in recent history, where leaders in key positions lacked vision and the result was massive suffering: for example, Pakistan in 1971, and Rhodesia during the years of UDI. Scores of thousands perished also during the Nigerian civil war, but that tragedy was significantly redeemed by the vision which Gowon and his immediate colleagues held to of reconciliation and forgiveness – a vision shared by Robert Mugabe in the transition to Zimbabwe's independence.

Many member countries have acted at times during the years surveyed by this book in a small-minded manner, whether it was with threats to leave the Commonwealth, with refusals to cooperate among neighbours, or with evictions and oppression of citizens and residents. All at times have shown some vision, and it is noteworthy that the shafts of light that illuminated the thinking and some subsequent actions of Commonwealth countries have come as often from the leaders of the smaller and newer states, as from the older and larger countries.

The most important function of the Commonwealth, as an association with the Secretariat as its central instrument, is enlarging the vision of its members – and, beyond them, of the world community. It is a cumulative process, rather than any dramatic revelation. Take the case of Canada. It has traditionally been an outward-looking country, though with some temporary isolationist lapses. Canada from its outset in 1867 thought in terms of a North Atlantic society as the minimum community in which it could feel prosperous and safe, and believed that a threat to democracy in Europe was also a threat to democracy in North America – and thus went to war in 1914 and 1939, in each case two and a half years before the United States came to share Canada's assessment of the common danger. But most Canadians before 1945 had no other horizons; its diplomatic missions were limited to London, Paris, Washington and an early one in Tokyo.

282

It was Commonwealth evolution that broadened Canada's horizons. Its first diplomatic missions in mainland Asia were opened in India and Pakistan when (and because) they became independent Commonwealth members. Canadian political leaders and officials began meeting Jawaharlal Nehru, his colleagues and officials shortly before John Foster Dulles began propounding his bipolar world outlook of western democracy versus communism. Although Canadians never played down the importance of Soviet-Western relations and indeed were the first to propose the creation of NATO, their contacts with India, Pakistan and Ceylon made them realise that bipolarity was grossly inadequate as a world view, and that the aspirations of colonial peoples for freedom and of poor peoples for development would be at least as important in the coming decades in shaping the future of us all. These missions in Asia began sending political reports to Ottawa; divisions in the Department of External Affairs began specialising in Asian affairs; Canada became involved in development assistance through the Commonwealth's Colombo Plan. The same cumulative process took place in black Africa, where the first Canadian mission was established in another new Commonwealth country, Kwame Nkrumah's Ghana, followed on their independence by others in Lagos, Dar es Salaam and Nairobi. In short, the Commonwealth was a crucial influence during the formative period on Canadian attitudes and horizons in the post-war world.

Much earlier, Canadians had pioneered a new road to freedom from colonial masters without the sort of all-out war that the Vietnamese or Algerians had to fight against France after World War II, or the people of Angola and Mozambique against Portugal. Marx and Lenin maintained that no 'class' voluntarily relinquishes domination. The history of the Commonwealth proves that this need not be true. The British were taught a lesson in the 1770s by their equally freedom-loving compatriots (including at least one of my ancestors) who had settled in the 13 American colonies. The Canadians therefore had to do only a little fighting – mainly in 1837 – and rather more demonstrating, organising and negotiating. Independence was gained by agreement in 1867. This path to independence which Canada pioneered with Britain has been followed by hundreds of millions of people in the South Pacific, Asia, Africa and the Caribbean.

The British learned early and relatively gracefully that a free people cannot maintain imperial control over another people once the latter is also determined to assert its freedom. The Russians have maintained their empire, and even expanded it since World War II; but they have not yet sought, much less gained, political freedom for themselves at home.

The British since World War II have had to grapple with a subtler lesson in international policy: that world politics is more, and other, than intergovernmental relations. This is becoming increasingly so as interdependence grows. But even as a student I realised that the future of my generation would depend on standing up early enough to Hitler; and that to do this it was at least as necessary to get rid of Chamberlain in Britain, and Daladier in France, and to change the isolationist thinking of United States senators, as it was to change the equally isolationist, if differently motivated, policies of Canada's Mackenzie King. The failure of most of our elders – Churchill was an outstanding exception – to see this before 1939 cost our generation some 30 million lives.

Throughout the thirty-five years when I was engaged as a practitioner in one or another field of world politics – whether as a national representative or later as an elected international politician – I have seen many disagreements on policy among various governments. But on the major issues these differences have seldom been between real national interests, much more often between differing perceptions of real common interests, or of how to deal with them.

Yet the British inherited the traditional European theory that the unit is the state, that the purpose of diplomacy is to protect or advance the interests of one's own state vis-à-vis those of others, and that only the most powerful states can be expected to interest themselves much in events beyond their own region – as if the chequebook and the big stick were the only instruments of diplomacy.

Canadians who thought about these things, as so many in smaller countries, have always known that they could never hope to be self-sufficient strategically, culturally, economically or politically. Hence the importance they have attached to instruments for collective consultation and decision-making. Britain's heritage as a former global power and the capital of a worldwide empire made it less difficult to continue to think in terms of the traditional but outmoded chessboard theory.

In the 1970s two major studies on Britain's representation in other countries – a 1972 Royal Commission chaired by Sir Val Duncan and a 1976 study of the Cabinet Office 'think tank' – recommended in effect that, *because* of the decline in Britain's relative power she should reduce her interest in, and attempts to influence thinking in, the Third World. The assumption that only the powerful and rich need to be concerned about the environment in which they and their children will live is almost the opposite of the truth. The idea that Canada or Britain should be less interested in the danger of alienation between the peoples of different races and continents than the USSR or the Americans is patent nonsense. The Commonwealth has helped them both see more profoundly.*

There are inevitable discontinuities in the Commonwealth association after changes of leadership; in Canada's case, after Pierre Trudeau took over from Mike Pearson in 1968. At the London HGM in January 1969 Trudeau was puzzled by the clubbish atmosphere and recoiled into a boyish insouciance, which had its lighter moments. After the state dinner at Buckingham Palace on the first evening, the guests were moving around for a short time before leaving and Eve was wondering to whom she might introduce the Canadian Prime Minister. Whom did he want to meet? Trudeau pointed to President Makarios of Cyprus. 'The Archbishop. I wonder if he's got hand-grenades under his robes. Let's go talk to him.' A few days later, he attended Harold Wilson's reception in the large upstairs rooms at Lancaster House, where Queen Victoria had heard Chopin play in 1848. When he wanted to leave, he asked Eve to show him the way out. She led him to the balcony, from which the double staircase curved down.

Trudeau started down the stairs, and Eve said after him, 'It's a beautiful banister.' He looked back over his shoulder for a moment, smiled and jumped on the banister, and with an 'Olé!' and a wave of his arm slid down into sight of the journalists in the hall below. It burnished his reputation as the 'swinging bachelor'.

Trudeau brought with him to the Prime Minister's Office some of the scepticism about the Commonwealth as a colonialist hang-over, and some of the isolationism, that typified many French-Canadian intellectuals of his generation. At the 1969 HGM he said virtually nothing. But he was observant, and he was clearly impressed by the informal, frank discussion. Within the next few months, during which he visited Singapore, Malaysia and other Asian countries, he became a genuine convert, partly by noting the incomparably greater ease of communication between Commonwealth members. At later conferences – at Singapore in 1971, and as chairman

---

*For a broader analysis of differences in Canadian and British approaches and policies towards the Commonwealth and the wider world, see a paper I wrote for an Anglo-Canadian colloquium at Leeds University, October 1979, in *Britain and Canada*, edited by David Dilks (Commonwealth Foundation Occasional Paper XLIX, 1980).

himself in 1973 – he showed how deeply he had come to value the association. He formed important friendships at it, and contributed greatly with his insistence on informal discussion and longer-range thought.

Trudeau later likened Commonwealth summits to 'graduate seminars for Heads of Government', stressing how much people in such a lonely role can learn from each other. He stimulated discussion about comparative techniques of government, which was a lively topic on the agenda at Ottawa in 1973 and Kingston in 1975. The day in 1975 that Saigon fell to Viet-Cong troops – to be renamed Ho Chi Minh City – I found myself sitting around a table in Kingston with Indira Gandhi, Lee Kuan Yew, Tun Razak, Harold Wilson, Gough Whitlam, Trudeau, Nyerere and the others, who naturally commented on the geopolitical implications as they saw them for South East Asia, for reassessments in US thinking about overseas problems, and other changes – a graduate seminar indeed. Discussions are, of course, not always so fascinatingly topical, but the educational value of bringing people together for frank talks can be enormous.

Learning from each other's experiences takes place through Commonwealth meetings at many levels, both official and non-governmental. To have lasting value, the educational ferment has to permeate several layers. In this book the floodlights may have focussed mainly upon the Heads of Government, and the particular kind of candid summit meeting which the Commonwealth developed. It is sometimes dismissively described as a 'club' atmosphere, but its techniques of off-the-record summit talks have been widely copied by leaders of the European Community, by the 'Industrialised Seven' and by various North-South groupings. Less floodlit by the news media, but warmed by the same atmosphere, hundreds of ministers, parliamentarians, officials, teachers, lawyers, agriculturalists, journalists, scientists, auditors-general, planners, foresters and sportsmen have gathered at some humbler Commonwealth occasions – and nearly always went home with an enlarged view, a wider vision.

Remarkable, too, has been the deepening of insights and understanding of various aspects of development (both its problems and processes) among participants of the periodic meetings of Commonwealth ministers responsible for such fields as education, health, law, food production and rural development. People have been able to learn from each others' successes and failures, difficulties and ideas; and these meetings have also increasingly given rise to decisions for cooperative action, both regional and inter-regional. Sometimes they have led to decisions to take collective, or harmonised, initiatives or positions in the United Nations or one of its Specialised Agencies.*

Ministers from developing countries, and their top officials, learn at these meetings a great deal from each other. What the representatives of the richer countries can learn – and on occasion contribute intellectually as well as materially – is not less significant; for their horizons, and their generosity, also need enlarging.

There are several bodies in which the world's rich caucus – notably the Group of Ten and the OECD – and many in which developing countries caucus among themselves, including the Non-Aligned conferences and the 'Group of 77'. And most regional organisations are mainly made up of rich or of developing countries. The Commonwealth is particularly valuable in providing occasions for frank and informal caucusing of a fairly representative cross-section of industrialised countries, poor countries, an important OPEC member (Nigeria) and some 'NICs' ('newly industrialising countries' such as Singapore and Hong Kong). As Sonny Ramphal has said, 'The Commonwealth cannot negotiate for the world, but it can help the world to negotiate.'

Commonwealth meetings educate key people in many fields – and they are increasingly action-oriented.

Among economically advanced countries one of the greatest changes and most important broadening of horizons through Commonwealth channels has come in Australia. The 'greening of Australia', from the antiquated and Anglocentric attitudes of Robert Menzies about the post-war world to the creative energy of Malcolm Fraser, determined (like a good farmer) to cultivate new relationships within and beyond the Asia-Pacific region (and to use the Commonwealth bridges to reach many of these new fields) is one of the triumphs of the whole Commonwealth operation over the last fifteen years.

Robert Menzies was an ebullient personality, who presided with verve over much of the impressive expansion that took place after World War II inside Australia. He considered himself a great

---

*See Davidson Nicol, *'Interregional Coordination within the United Nations: the role of the Commonwealth'* (UNITAR, 1979). The author is an Under Secretary-General of the UN and Executive Director of the UN Institute for Training and Research (UNITAR).

Commonwealth man – but his was a very different concept of the Commonwealth from that of recent decades. To Menzies and to colleagues like his Foreign Affairs Minister Paul Hasluck, Britain remained the mother country, the Commonwealth was a slightly amended version of Empire; and its new members, including men of world stature like Nehru, were gawky adolescents whom it was necessary to meet on Commonwealth occasions but never to treat as partners.

When Harold Holt succeeded Menzies in 1966, there were hopes of considerable change. When I visited Australia in April 1967, he reacted positively to ideas of increased Commonwealth cooperation and said he hoped he could win his Cabinet round to supporting a Commonwealth technical assistance programme, 'if you give me six to eight months'. But he did not have that amount of time, for he died in a drowning accident before the end of 1967.

With John Gorton as prime minister some attitudes returned to the Menzies mould. At the 1969 HGM he did not join in the discussions about citizenship and immigration that took place outside the formal sessions, and he opposed the subsequent migration study, giving journalists the curious explanation afterwards that, 'So far as I could see, all the countries were agreed that migration was an internal issue.' He also opposed reference in the communiqué to the People's Republic of China taking 'its rightful place in the international community'. And he opposed most suggestions for an extension of Commonwealth cooperation; although he was prepared to see a small Legal Section established at the Secretariat, he and Paul Hasluck argued for postponement of a Commonwealth information programme and a book development programme, and wanted youth matters left to UNESCO. 'After all, we have the United Nations. I see little point in duplicating UN operations,' was his refrain.

Gorton at least opened a window towards Indonesia after Sukarno's downfall, and was no doubt encouraged in that by his American-born wife Bettina, who learnt Bahasa Indonesia. But his views on the Commonwealth showed no advance at the Singapore HGM in January 1971, when he proved even more difficult than Ted Heath over the Declaration of Principles. His attitude towards the Commonwealth Fund for Technical cooperation, which was launched at that HGM with everybody else's blessing, was unyielding. He asserted that the Commonwealth was not an appropriate grouping for aid purposes; the four developed nations already gave eighty percent of their aid to Commonwealth countries, and could hardly give more multilaterally; they might only succeed in discouraging aid from non-Commonwealth sources; the CFTC would involve Australia in providing aid to Africa and the Caribbean, areas of limited interest; and it would encourage the expansionist tendencies of the Secretariat. The fact that one or two of these objections cancelled others out did not prevent his parading them all.

Nevertheless, there were sympathetic officials from the outset. Sir John Bunting, Permanent Head of the Prime Minister's department, did the Secretariat a great service by being one of those who recommended Yaw Adu to me as Deputy Secretary-General in 1965. Later, Allan Griffith who was always a convinced internationalist gave timely help from a strategic vantage point in the Prime Minister's department, not least during McMahon's administration in winning Australian support for the CFTC. And the Commonwealth benefitted enormously from the work of Tony Eggleton, both during his time (1971-74) as the Secretariat's first Director of Information and after his return to Australia.

While I was in Canberra in February 1971, for the Education Ministers Conference, I asked Gorton if I could steal Eggleton, who was then the Prime Minister's chief press secretary as he had been for Holt and Menzies. Gorton reluctantly agreed, but asked me to announce the appointment, which I did at a press conference in Canberra. After I did so, one hardheaded journalist paid an unusual compliment to Tony: 'Now you have made it inevitable that Gorton loses the next election.' (In fact, he never fought another election, being supplanted from within his own party soon afterwards by William McMahon.) Tony Eggleton had built up a remarkable reputation with Australia's press corps, a lively body at any time, and played an important part in restoring calm at the time of Holt's disappearance at sea. At the Secretariat he managed to produce good information material on a miserably small budget, help run the Ottawa HGM with aplomb and give me invaluable political advice, not only about Australia and Papua New Guinea, but in many other spheres.

It was during William McMahon's time as Prime Minister (1971-72) that Australia moved to support the CFTC. I waited six months after the Singapore HGM (which McMahon attended as Gorton's Foreign Affairs Minister) and then wrote him in July 1971, suggesting Australia might reconsider its earlier reservations since a meeting of senior trade officials had just recommended that the scope of the CFTC be expanded to help in the development of export markets. Wheels then began to turn, and the Department of Foreign Affairs did a study of CFTC projects in the South Pacific. When McMahon visited London in November, 1971, he was concerned about Australia's reputation as a 'reluctant partner' in the Commonwealth. That visit served to kindle enthusiasm for the Commonwealth in McMahon's large party, and happily the warmth has remained ever since. Australia began contributing to the CFTC in 1972 and has ever since been, with Nigeria, the Fund's third or fourth largest contributor.

Australia was changing much more than attitudes towards the CFTC. Before World War II Australians (and New Zealanders) tended to think of themselves as a Pacific outpost of Britain. In the shadow of the Vietnam war, Harold Holt swung towards the United States in search of an older brother in a lonely corner of the world, sent more than 6000 Australian troops to Vietnam, and during a visit by President Johnson declaimed, 'All the way with LBJ'. It was not a helpful service to be so unquestioning towards an ally, when the latter is intent on an unwise venture, any more than the automatic support that Menzies offered to Anthony Eden over Suez. Some fundamental rethinking had to begin when Nixon and Kissinger started opening a path to Peking. At the time it horrified Foreign Ministry officials in Canberra, but it led them to re-examine their whole attitude to their neighbourhood.

Gough Whitlam's internationalism was strongest in Asia, with a particular concern to build links with China. But Australia was also on the UN Security Council during his three years as Prime Minister, and took a leading part in proposing tighter sanctions against Rhodesia. At the 1975 HGM he spoke out strongly for special Commonwealth support for the training of Namibians.

It was however, after Fraser defeated Whitlam's Labor Party that Australia came to full bloom in the Commonwealth. The story has been told in an earlier chapter* of the crucial role that Malcolm Fraser and Andrew Peacock played over Rhodesia in 1979. Before that episode, Fraser had taken two other initiatives: the first was to pioneer regional meetings of Heads of Government in the Asia-Pacific region, and the second was to come out firmly in favour of the Common Fund for the stabilisation of commodity prices.

There were some misgivings when Fraser first suggested, during the 1977 HGM in London, the idea of holding an Asia-Pacific regional meeting. Was this the beginning of regional caucusing that

---

*Chapter 10.

might inhibit free discussion at full HGMs? What would Singapore's and Malaysia's partners in ASEAN – Indonesia, Thailand and the Philippines – think of this other regional initiative? Was it simply going to duplicate the talk and rehash the issues of the full HGMs? Fraser was firm in his argument that there were several subjects of common interest to the dozen Commonwealth governments in his region, for which there was insufficient discussion time at full HGMs, and that the 'CHGRM' would be seen to serve a complementary purpose – and not trespass on ASEAN ground, either.

So it proved, when the first CHGRM was held in Sydney in February 1978; and this view was reinforced by the second meeting which Mrs Gandhi enthusiastically chaired in Delhi in September 1980. All twelve regional Heads of Government attended the Sydney CHGRM, including the President of Nauru. Differences in size of population were more striking in the smaller grouping, where India sat alongside Nauru, and Bangladesh near Western Samoa. But in four days they not only explored areas of common concern, but set up two consultative groups under Indian and Australian chairmanship, on energy and trade. For they concluded, after hearing what India and Fiji had been doing with biogas units, Australia with solar energy and New Zealand in geothermal research, that there was valuable experience to be shared on alternative energy sources, and to be built upon in common.

As for trade, some leaders were shocked to discover how small was the amount of commerce within the region, India in particular neglecting the markets and the exports of its neighbours. Fraser, under pressure from the Prime Ministers of Singapore and Malaysia to relax restrictions on their manufactured exports, robustly answered that they should all combine to negotiate better deals with the 'Big Three' markets of Europe, the United States and Japan. Out of this lively discussion came agreement to form a study group that would certainly work to improve opportunities for their countries' goods in the major world markets, but would also examine specific measures to enlarge trade within the region – by improving travel and communications, by cutting transport costs, by simplifying procedures.

There was also a common mind on the Common Fund, and Fraser told the Sydney CHGRM how Australia had come to know the value of a buffer stock system after its experience in wool marketing, for the fluctuations of price and supply in earlier years had been levelled out to everyone's benefit. When the Secretariat convened a ministerial meeting on the Common Fund two months later, in April 1978, the Australian Minister for Special Trade Representations, Victor Garland, was among the most positive speakers. But raising the issue of the Common Fund has to take us back briefly to the 1975 HGM and to the broad approach that it launched to North-South issues.

A major issue discussed at length in the Jamaica HGM in May 1975 was world trade, finance and development in the context of what was already being called the 'new international economic order' or NIEO. The whole world had been jolted by the rise in oil prices after 1973, and a bad harvest in 1974 had also sent food prices soaring while the prices of raw materials were fluctuating wildly. Harold Wilson, referring to his own lifelong involvement with the problems of commodity trade (his first cabinet post was President of the Board of Trade), made a major speech suggesting the time had come to balance the GATT with a General Agreement on Commodities and setting out specific commitments and goals. Forbes Burnham, recalling the way the Commonwealth had pulled together the African, Caribbean and Pacific group to bargain effectively for the Lomé Convention, suggested forming a Commonwealth Group of Experts who could identify practical measures that could be taken without delay to create 'a rationale and equitable international economic order'. Pierre Trudeau, while acknowledging that the issues were complex, asked that the first report of the Expert Group be ready within three months, in time to help Commonwealth governments prepare themselves for the Seventh Special Session of the UN General Assembly, which was to be devoted exclusively to the NIEO.

So the task handed to the ten-member Expert Group which I was asked to appoint was to be swift as well as wise in its advice. The group was headed by Alister McIntyre, then Secretary-General of the Caribbean Community, and was chosen to represent a balance not only of regions but of kinds of experience. It went quickly to work, holding its first session with me in Marlborough House in June. Their Interim Report was formally presented at the United Nations Special Session and contributed substantially to the wide consensus achieved there. A Further Report, focussing on the issues of commodities, debt and industrial cooperation (Trudeau's particular concern), appeared in 1976, and their Final Report in March

1977. The exercise was a major operation of research and consultation, involving many technical studies as well as discussions between governments throughout the Commonwealth. It was carried out smoothly and without the adversarial pattern of many UN encounters; and the unanimity on detailed practical measures of its ten members, who were chosen as individuals rather than as government representatives, was heartening in a divided world.*

It encouraged the Heads of Government at their 1977 Meeting to ask my successor Sonny Ramphal to establish a technical group to examine the form and operation of a Common Fund for commodities. Again, the Commonwealth was taking the lead in picking up a global matter and, in its own less formal style, running the elements through practical tests to determine whether the formula was feasible. The report on the Common Fund,** written under the chairmanship of Lord (Jock) Campbell of Eskan, was not only effective in building some necessary political will among Commonwealth countries like Britain and Canada, but helped subsequently during the UNCTAD negotiating sessions of 1978-79 to produce the more positive atmosphere in which the Fund was finally established.

Of all the Heads of Government Meetings during my time as Secretary-General, one of the most significant was that held in Ottawa in August 1973. The Singapore meeting (starting the fund for technical assistance, youth work and the information programme as well as handling the arms sales issue) was no less important. But Ted Heath's truculence left emotional scars. The Ottawa meeting was a healing experience.

It is worth looking briefly at some of the practical elements of the successful Ottawa HGM.

After the Singapore HGM, we looked at ways to revise procedures for future HGMs, and before a meeting of Senior Officials in Ottawa in October 1972 the governments of thirteen countries from Britain to Tonga made detailed comments on a Secretariat paper. So the Senior Officials had solid material on which to base recommendations for improving HGMs. The two main questions they faced were: how informal did governments want HGMs to be? and how exactly could we restore the informality of past HGMs, since

---

Towards a New International Economic Order; first, second and final reports, Commonwealth Secretariat 1975-77.

**The Common Fund*; report of the Commonwealth technical group (Commonwealth Secretariat, 1977).

the number of delegations had grown from eight in the 1950s to more than thirty in 1972?

It was soon clear that governments wanted HGMs to be as informal as possible. We discussed with senior officials the gamut of arrangements to produce this result: the agenda, the types of session, the physical arrangements, the communiqué and press arrangements. And we took a lesson from Singapore, where a plenary session had been attended by up to 220 people and had involved a full and itemised agenda, a speakers' list, obtrusive voice-raising equipment and a battery of record takers producing an extended summary; several speeches were prepared in advance for that session, and the full texts handed to the press. The best discussion at Singapore, as at Lagos in 1966, was in the two days of secret sessions with Heads of Government and myself alone, and with no official record.

The number of people present at a particular session affects many of the other arrangements. In a post-mortem on the 1969 HGM, officials had taken the view that there should be space for each delegation to have seven members seated; lots of influential ministers and officials wanted to be in on 'the action'. The Singapore experience swung opinion back to wanting small numbers, and since then it has settled in favour of four seats per delegation ('one at the table, plus three') for ordinary sessions – and heads of delegation alone with the Secretary-General (and no record takers) for restricted sessions.

There are one or two tricks that can be used to encourage harmony as well as informality at an HGM. As well as the size of the room (it should not be too big), and the shape of the table (round or oval is preferred, but not a huge hollow oval as at Singapore), it is obviously not a trivial matter who sits next to whom. Before the Ottawa HGM, Heath was agitated that he might be placed beside Uganda for he had no desire to rub elbows with Amin, if he came. I was able to assure Heath that there was no possibility of this, not only because Idi Amin was unlikely to show up but because Heath would sit behind the nameplate of 'Britain' at Commonwealth meetings and not behind 'United Kingdom' as at the UN (where the British like to sit beside the USA and the USSR). But to avoid other awkward juxtapositions, I had long before 1973 developed a variety of seating systems, using alphabetical order but not necessarily in a simple clock-wise pattern. Some of my staff, with yearnings for orderliness, wanted a standard system; but I maintained that it was important to be able to use any version at any time, depending on which presidents and prime ministers were on cordial or choleric terms with each other.

I found it also important to get across to any newcomers (there were always one or two, what with an election here, or a coup there) that they must not treat other heads of government – or for that matter ministers of law, or health, finance or education) as a captive audience to which a written speech could be read. If anyone wanted to get a prepared speech in the minutes, or to release it to the press, it should merely be given to a Secretariat officer for circulation. But at the table there was discussion.

This distinction between procedures at Commonwealth and UN meetings is important. The UN practice is to make set speeches to the other delegates (or aimed over their heads at the press and public back home and, if possible, in other countries too). The UN technique is that used also by parliaments and congresses. It is a necessary part of the moulding of public opinion. Agreements are usually worked out 'in the corridor'. But heads of governments, or even foreign ministers, are naturally not prepared to be audiences for set speeches; they pay ambassadors to be 'permanent representatives', while they themselves may attend for a day or two to make a speech and meet a few opposite numbers. Commonwealth meetings, using what I called the 'smoke-filled room' technique, do attract prime ministers and presidents (and ministers of law, health, education, etc) precisely because of the informality of the discussions modelled originally on consultations within a cabinet.

The Ottawa HGM probably managed to achieve the greatest degree of informality. The agenda was brief and conformed to the officials' idea of time allocation (twenty percent for general topics, sixty percent for specific but mainly longer-range issues, twenty percent on Commonwealth functional cooperation). Trudeau's known dislike of set speeches helped keep contributions short and lively. Even the final communiqué was limited to thirty-six paragraphs and recorded only one case of a minority view (the communiqué's length has crept upwards since Ottawa, to fifty-six paragraphs in 1975 and to seventy paragraphs in both 1977 and 1979). Above all, the inspired move was Trudeau's invitation to Heads of Government and the Secretary-General, with their wives but no ministers or officials, to the weekend 'retreat' at Mont Tremblant, a time for relaxed and private conversations. There was a separate, parallel retreat for Foreign Ministers and my deputies a few miles away. The only links were telephones. This weekend retreat has now become standard.

The Ottawa HGM and the delightful meeting in Kingston in 1975 also benefitted from not being surrounded by the tension of one large political issue, as many other HGMs have been. HGMs may survive and even resolve crises, but they do not positively thrive on them. The prospects for the Melbourne HGM in September 1981 are that it can take place in the same favourable circumstances as the Ottawa HGM eight years earlier.

The Ottawa HGM, finally, established that these summits should take place regularly at two-year intervals, if possible between June and September (i.e. between the OAU summit and the UN General Assembly). Before 1973 the meetings had depended on ad hoc decisions each time; but when Heath made efforts after Singapore to avoid any further meeting for as long as he could, which might have broken the sequence altogether, I decided to propose to the next meeting the acceptance of regular biennial HGMs. This is now well established, with the Asia-Pacific CHGRM and a meeting of the top civil servant from each country occurring in intervening years.

It is time now to conclude by underlining what should have come through these pages as the three distinguishing attributes or activities of the Commonwealth association; consultation, functional cooperation, and what I have called 'working on the we-they frontier'.

Consultation: A great deal of this book has been about consultation to avert or diminish political crises. I have found, not totally to my surprise, that some of the larger countries (within and without the Commonwealth) are apt to be both the least enthusiastic about consultation and the most in need of it. A government of a rich strong country is more likely to feel comfortably self-sufficient, and therefore to be insensitive to the realities of the outside world in which foreign policy has to operate. A superb political early-warning system, the Commonwealth has provided one extra framework of consultation, or guard-rail, to prevent a government blundering too far.

There is a more positive side to Commonwealth consultation than the prevention or amelioration of crises. This is the consultation that has led to many forms of *functional cooperation*. At one stage it disturbed aid agencies in the rich governments that ideas for mutual cooperation and technical assistance programmes should emerge from ministerial meetings, law ministers calling for training courses for legislative draftsmen, health ministers wanting a feasibility study of the bulk procurement of drugs for smaller states and so on. In their view, it was not following the laid down channels of intergovernmental 'requests'. What it was doing, like a river rather than a canal, was following natural channels; it was being more truly functional. The technical assistance programmes of the Secretariat have never hesitated to use imagination and to move into fields still untrodden by bigger agencies – helping smaller states in mineral negotiations, for example, and helping manufacturers in developing countries to promote non-traditional exports in Europe and North America. Many of these efforts came from responding to the quiet ferment of consultation at so many levels that is a continuous part of the Commonwealth association.

Another part is what I call *working on the 'we-they frontier'*. The Charter of the United Nations starts promisingly with the words, 'We the peoples of the United Nations, determined . . . .'; but it long ago succumbed – I trust not permanently – to the divisiveness of ideological blocks with predictable voting patterns. The Commonwealth, working always by consensus rather than vote and veto, has managed to keep intact the unity behind the phrases starting 'We believe . . .' in the Declaration of the Commonwealth Principles.

Working on this frontier means, of course, more than declarations. It is the whole basis of CFTC activities. The Fund is not an aid agency of rich countries offering 'tied aid' of their own goods and services to poor countries. It is a programme of mutual assistance, predating by some seven years the official launching of the TCDC movement, of 'technical cooperation among developing countries', by the UN at the Buenos Aires conference in 1978. Every Commonwealth country contributes to the Fund; every country has a say in its operation; any country may provide experts or advisers or training places to another.

In August 1973 Canada made a generous multi-million dollar increase in its CFTC pledge, and offered to match all developing country contributions on a two-to-one basis up to this new ceiling and to consider raising the ceiling once reached. But by early 1974 there was a disturbing new attitude of stinginess among Canadian officials who told me they counted on our not reaching this ceiling for a few years! The explanation was that the Cabinet, reacting to the sudden increase in OPEC oil prices and its need to subsidise imported oil at increasing cost, had ordered an across-the-board cut in all previously authorised expenditures, including development assistance. It seemed outrageous that Canada should dream of cutting approved aid programmes to poor countries which would suffer far more than the West from OPEC's price increases. I visited Ottawa to press this point and was delighted that Mitchell Sharp, the minister responsible, took the same view and persuaded the cabinet to exempt Canada's aid programme from the cuts.

I also visited some developing countries, to activate this trigger on Canada's matching formula. In Lagos in August 1974, I managed to persuade Nigeria's Finance Minister, Shehu Shagari (who in 1979 became the country's President), of the value of the programme to the point that in September he pledged an unprecedented $1 million at the Finance Ministers Meeting in Ottawa; and John Turner, then Finance Minister of Canada, did not lose his chairman's calm as he remarked, 'You have just cost me $2 million.' Earlier in mid-1974, on visits to Trinidad and the Bahamas, I persuaded their governments to increase their CFTC contributions by some hundreds of thousands of dollars each, with similar multiplier effect. Some Canadian officials were not amused, but Commonwealth development was strengthened.

I could wish that the CFTC today was receiving support of the size it deserves. Its funding dropped from £11.3 million in 1978-79 to £9.3 million in 1979-80, and has recovered to some £11.8 million in 1980-81, partly due to Nigeria's doubling its subscription. But the total is still tiny, considering the potential in mutual assistance it can harness. To give the Commonwealth the sinews it needs, major donors should (I often urged and still believe) be channeling at least three percent of their total aid funds through the CFTC, instead of less than one percent.

The efforts in 1977-78 of a team of industrial specialists under Governor L. K. Jha of India on 'Cooperation for Accelerating Industrialisation'; and of the group of ten experts who in 1980 studied the constraints to economic growth in developing countries* are further examples of the Commonwealth working on this frontier. For these groups set out as a team to solve certain problems (and the Jha report led to the setting up of an Industrial Development Unit within the Secretariat) rather than as representatives from different blocs meeting to bargain for their own interests.

Further 'we-they frontiers' can lie inside national boundaries, between ethnic or other communal groups within a plural society.

---

*Their report *The World Economic Crisis: a Commonwealth Perspective* was published in 1980 by the Secretariat.

Most of the Commonwealth countries that have come to independence in the post-war world are plural societies, made up of several linguistic and cultural groups. The older countries in the Commonwealth have every reason to be humble, as well as to be heartened, by the quiet way in which many of the younger states have gone about building harmonious plural societies. The moments of discord are widely reported; the steady work of nation building is not. But, while Britain worries about coloured immigration or Canada is concerned (sometimes less constructively than it should be) over bilingualism or regionalism, a score of other countries are taking diversity in their stride. Several heads of government have told me that nation-building is their single most difficult but important task.

The art of successfully leading democratic plural societies is one of the key challenges of world politics in our age, and will become more so as we move towards a global society. There have been, inside and beyond the Commonwealth, many crises and a few spectacular failures. In the Commonwealth, federations have split, civil wars have been fought, an ethnic minority expelled. The Lebanon, until recently the most affluent society in the Arab world, has been tearing itself to pieces; Northern Ireland is sadly bogged down in communal conflict. (You don't need different languages to have a plural society.)

A main issue in both successes and failures is the question where people draw the line between those they generally think of as 'part of us' and those they think of as 'them'. The extent of acceptance and spiritual generosity, the breadth of horizons of understanding, fellow-feeling and goodwill, are crucial. Often in speeches I emphasized the importance of 'working on the we-they frontier' because I consider it the essence both of truly creative politics, and of the politics of disintegration – and the world is full of both today.

Another vital element for the coherence of democratic plural societies is to ensure adequately widespread participation in government and decision-making. Until recently at least, Canadian statesmen for example have known in their bones that government by majority is simply not good enough – you need at least the acquiescence of a working majority in each major group and region. Some form of proportional representation could make this easier, but Canada does not as yet have it. And it has been my impression that in recent years there has been a marked narrowing of Canadian horizons. In important sections of public opinion, of the bureaucracies, and among politicians, the narrowing of concern

299

has been not only from global to national, but from national to regional. It should be one of the goals of leadership to snap people out of this myopia.

Leaders can learn much about nation-building and how to govern plural societies from the good and bad experiences of other countries and societies. For this reason I suggested at a Senior Officials meeting in 1974 that this subject might be discussed at a Heads of Government Meeting under the item 'Comparative techniques of government', which Trudeau introduced. But it was considered too delicate a subject for discussion at that time! I still hope that Heads of Government will one year tackle this subject, and help each other in frank talk.

Towards the end of my years as Secretary-General I was sometimes asked whether I had found the scope of my job too circumscribed. My answer has been that, besides the constraints of a small budget (many things can be done with little money, but there is less leverage than with vast sums to allocate), there were few limits placed on my scope for action. There were no real constitutional limits set out in the Agreed Memorandum. The early sensitivity of the Australian and British governments about my exercise of executive functions faded, for I did not 'arrogate executive functions' to the Secretariat, in contravention of the Agreed Memorandum, but was straightforwardly asked to undertake them.

I took care never to play favourites among my many clients – I am sure that the Canadian Government never felt it was especially favoured. While my actions were sometimes controversial, I always felt they could not be successfully challenged at a top-level multilateral meeting. At the same time, I did not calculate on securing the consistent support of any particular majority of states. That could destroy cohesion. On each issue I tried to do what I thought right in the general interest. If politics is 'the art of the possible', this means trying to do as much good as you think you can get away with. So I faced the normal limits that would be imposed on anyone engaged in world politics.

If there were no constitutional limits, there was also no tangible power. The main lever was persuasion. The job of Secretary-General gives its holder the opportunity to talk, not to a single pair of governments as most ambassadors are confined to (that to which he is accredited and that back home, which may often prove the more obdurate), but to thirty or forty governments in every part of the world. It tests his ability to explain matters to governments, to advise and urge them to action; to talk to people all over the world, to key individuals and through press conferences and TV interviews to the public, and to get ideas across. Obviously my powers of persuasion were limited.

One of the occasions on which I deeply regretted that my powers of persuasion were ineffective was in July 1974, when President Makarios of Cyprus was overthrown by Nicos Sampson. Sampson was put in power after the palace at Nicosia was attacked by ten tanks two weeks after Makarios had demanded the withdrawal of 650 Greek officers from the Cypriot National Guard. Makarios' life was saved by his being whisked off the island by British forces. When I heard the news of the coup, I was in Ghana lunching with General Acheampong, and actually had an appointment to fly overnight to Cyprus for a working lunch with Makarios the next day. Instead, I flew back to London and at once urged the British Government to press a resolution in the UN Security Council calling for the immediate resignation of Sampson and restoration of Makarios, with a swift deadline for the UN peacekeeping forces already on the island to act in support. No UN peacekeeping operation could have been easier. The Soviet Union was opposed to the Greek junta, the US Sixth Fleet was nearby; the British also had bases on the island. The junta would have fallen, to the joy of the Greek people; the Turks would have been placated, Cyprus would have been restored to peace, and the West would have gained some credit. The British told me they would not act in the Security Council unless Kissinger agreed in advance. Instead, they hesitated while Kissinger sent his envoy to talk with the Greek colonels and the Turkish Government. The opportunity was lost, for within five days the Turkish army invaded Cyrpus. The Greek junta fell, Sampson resigned – and Makarios was eventually restored – but at the fearful cost of dividing Cyprus far more deeply than before, of leaving hostility simmering between Greece and Turkey, and of gravely weakening NATO on its southern flank.

The job of Secretary-General is exhausting and often frustrating. It is even at times hair-raising. But it was never dull, and on the whole it was a deeply satisfying job.

If it was so satisfying, why did I leave it in June 1975, at the age of sixty? In the early months of 1974 I was uncertain whether to seek a third term. Many of the hard battles had been fought and won. New programmes had been authorised in such interesting fields as youth, rural development, training in public administration. Above all, the Commonwealth post was a good base for continuing to try to persuade governments to face up to the problem of world development, of North-South relations, which (as I said in so many reports) is clearly the major problem of world politics in the final chapter of our century.

On the other hand, given the rich variety of the Commonwealth, it had occurred to me that there could be a case for a 'two-term' tradition for its chief executive. And there were a few interesting possibilities in Canada, that could provide an opportunity to get reestablished in my own country.

But I was surprised (perhaps naively) to learn from a variety of sources in May 1974 that a senior FCO official was spreading the word in Africa, the Caribbean and Asia that I was definitely not willing to accept a third term, and that he and his staff were trying to persuade West African governments at first (and others later) to nominate someone. At the same time FCO officials told Callaghan and Wilson that the Africans wanted to replace me; they told this also to Foreign Ministries of some other countries that did not have their own missions in African countries.

A number of African, Asian and other heads of government sent word, or told me directly, that they hoped I would stay on for another term. As well, Jim Callaghan said that he and Harold Wilson would like me to be re-elected; he also mentioned what his officials had been telling him about African views to the contrary. I guessed that the animus behind the intrigues by a few senior British civil servants may have arisen and festered as a result of earlier battles about proposed reverse trade preferences from developing countries in the EEC association, and other policy differences between the FCO and myself during the Heath administration.

At first, the discovery of these manoeuvres by some British officials, contrary to the policy of their current ministers, made me feel like fighting all-out for re-election. But I decided to take the matter coolly and recorded in my diary: 'I like having a fair hand in causing things to happen in politics, but where my own position is involved there is something satisfying in being relatively unconcerned.' So I decided to 'leave it to providence'.

Providence soon settled the matter. At the end of a trip to Canada, in October 1974, I suffered a heart attack, and I realised that I was not in shape to carry on for a third term with the energy the post deserved. The same month I notified Heads of Government of my decision, which was made easier by the fact that a first-class statesman, Sonny Ramphal, was available to replace me. For the rest of 1974 I had to work largely at home, and at half the normal pace; and I missed a meeting of Health Ministers in Sri Lanka. But in 1975 all went very well, with good meetings of Law Ministers in Lagos, Agriculture and Rural Development Ministers in London, and the Heads of Government in Kingston, Jamaica.

I was delighted that the very successful HGM in Jamaica elected Sonny Ramphal to take over on July 1. I could not have invented a better successor. There are evident differences in style between us, but that is to the advantage of the Commonwealth, which thrives on variety.

When I left Marlborough House at the end of June 1975, it was satisfying to know that the concepts our once small group had worked and fought for were becoming a reality; and it was reassuring to know that the continuing job was being left in such capable hands. I walked away in good spirits, my belief in the potentialities of the Commonwealth deepened by my decade of experience at its hub.

The modern Commonwealth is far more central and relevant to the international problems of the last quarter of this century than was the old six-nation Commonwealth – the white man's club – to the problems of the first part. The most dangerous issues of this century's first four decades were relations between the various states of Europe, which were mishandled and led to two world wars. The issues ahead are different. To be appreciated they are best seen in perspective, against the whole range of man's geography, history and spiritual imperative.

'Who is my neighbour?' a lawyer once asked a young rabbi, and instead of a definition got the tale of the Good Samaritan and then the question returned, creatively transposed into the timeless one about neighbourliness.

A straight definition of neighbourhood would be more prosaic: it is the area within which one can readily move about, converse, exchange or throw things. These limits are far from timeless. Once, as still in parts of New Guinea, they were measured by the distance one could walk, or throw a spear. Today, what with jet planes, short-wave radio, satellite television and intercontinental ballistic missiles, neighbourhood is already becoming for many purposes global. Unless a nuclear holocaust or some environmental disaster not only halts technological advance but reverses it, the interdependence will continue to accelerate in range and depth.

This growing scale of neighbourhood is simply a fact, for good or evil. The moral and political challenge of turning it into a neigh-

303

bourly community remains – and the stakes involved in success or failure increase with the growing technical power to help or to destroy. The Commonwealth is one of the world's most useful instruments to help its members meet this challenge.

To build a global community we must stretch the horizons of knowledge, understanding, and goodwill and develop habits of consultation and cooperation that transcend the limits of race, region, or economic level. This is precisely what the Commonwealth is about.

INDEX

union, 6-7; public's views on Commonwealth (1965), 34, 38; value of Commonwealth to, 38; Secretariat staff from, 46; technical cooperation, 48, 111, 112, 114, 119; Youth Programme, 123; Information Programme, 124, 125; Rhodesia: action at UN Security Council, 61, 67; aid to Zambia, 59; to Namibia, 225, 226; to Zimbabwe, 243; and Nigerian civil war, 83, 95; and Pakistan crisis (1971), 137, 141-6; and Uganda, 246, 247, 258, 263; and East African Asians, 253-5; and Caribbean Associated States, 115-6, 166; referendum in Gibraltar, 71, 172; role in Hong Kong, 173; and EEC: 182, 183, 185, 191, 201, 202, 210, 272; and EEC 'associables', 188, 194, 199, 200, 302; and world politics, 284-5; and Australia, 288, 290; see also, particularly, Rhodesia, South Africa (for arms sales issue), and Douglas-Home, Wilson, Heath

COLONIAL OFFICE, 7, 41

COMMONWEALTH RELATIONS OFFICE, reaction to Secretariat, 6, 13, 41, 42, 43; merger with Colonial Office, 41; handling of UDI, 41; Canadian comment on, 50; co-operation with Secretariat, 20, 21, 46; relations with Secretariat, 55, 109, 269; views on Commonwealth membership, 158

FOREIGN OFFICE, general, 1, 6, 47; Secretariat relations with, 40, 144, 200, 226, 302; amalgamation with CRO into FCO, sets up sanctions office, 71

OVERSEAS DEVELOPMENT MINISTRY, 110, 116

British Council of Churches, 46
British Labour Party, 6, 202
British Petroleum, sanctions breaking, 52, 71, 233; Nigerian operations, 79; nationalised in Nigeria, 54, 238, 243
Brown, Arthur, 9
Brown, Roland, 128
Bruce, S.M., 7
Bryce, Robert, 154
Bunting, Sir John, 289

Bureaucracies, problems of large, 45, 107, 109, 124, 225
Burma, 35
Burnham, Forbes, Rhodesia, 63; arms sales, 212; Uganda Asians, 255; economic order, 292
Busia, Dr K. A., 102, 210, 212, 256

Cadieux, Marcel, 176
Caffin, David, 159
Callaghan, James, Mozambique, 222; Namibia, 227; Rhodesia, 233; immigration, 254; for re-election of SG, 302
Cameroon, 78, 197
Campbell, Lord (Jock), 293
Canada, early views on 'imperial union', 6-8; inventor of Commonwealth, 30; views on Secretariat, 12; Commonwealth links, 4; vision enlarged by Commonwealth, 283-4; Rhodesia, 53, 58, 68, 230, 235, 240-1, 242; aid to Zambia, 29, 45, 59; to Namibians, 226; Nigerian war, 90, 100; reception of Uganda Asians, 255; Uganda election observer, 263; Indian Ocean study group, 218; in Pakistan crisis, 135-6; 137; 141, 143; aid to Bangladesh, 150; relations with Caribbean states, 166-7; views on technical cooperation, 111, 117; export promotion study, 112; technical assistance, 48, 111, 113, 114, 118, 297-8; CIDA, 116, 119; as plural society, 76, 299; monarchy in, 268; early attitude to L'Agence, 179, 180; aid to Francophone Africa, 175, 176, 178; and 'French Commonwealth', 203; Quebec: concerns about by Laurier, 7; and in Nigerian war, 90; and over aid, 117; and in Pakistan crisis, 139; Quebec and L'Agence, 177-181; and 'French Commonwealth', 203; the 1970 crisis in, 213; Trudeau's concerns, 229, 273; Newfoundland, 278; External Affairs Department, 20, 26, 45, 90, 117, 202; see also, Pearson, Trudeau, Arnold Smith

Harlech, Lord, 235
Harman, Nicholas, information director, 125
Hart, Dame Judith, 60, 61
Hasluck, Paul, 288
Hatch, John (later Lord), 213
Head, Ivan, 213
Heath, Edward, Rhodesia, 51, 52, 72; EEC and associates, 72, 183, 192, 201; Pakistan and Bangladesh, 135, 143; personality, 210, 215, 256; arms sales to South Africa, 205-207, 210-211, 213, 215; during Singapore summit (1971), 215, 217-220, 234; Uganda coup, 246, move against Amin, 252, 255-257; behaviour at summits, 293 (1971); 272-3 and 294 (1973)
Hemsworth, Lloyd, 277
Hensley, Gerald, as special assistant, 19, 30, 46, 83, 85
Heren, Louis, 182
Hicks, Douglas, 11
Hilaly, Aga, 22, 138
Hoare, Col Mike, in Nigerian war, 103
Holt, Harold, 288, 289, 290
Holyoake, Sir Keith, 6
Hong Kong, 173, 287
Howson, Peter, 50
Hughes, Cledwyn, 233
Hunt, Sir David, 83
Husain, Arshad, 135, 136
Husain, Azim, 135

Ikhtiar-ul-mulk, 113, 148
Immigration, Italians in Africa, 62; problem for Biafran, 89; Heath's view, into Britain, 253, 254, 299; Secretariat study, 255, Australian view, 288
India, as republic, 16, 267, 268; as plural society, 76; forgives colonial sins, 130; views on Secretariat, 45, 130; war with Pakistan (1965), 20, 24-25; relations in region, 22; SG's 1966 visit to, 49; war with Pakistan (1971), 139-140; increased influence in region, 149-150; relations with

EEC, 184, 191, 193; on arms sales issue, 209, 214, 218, 220; and Rhodesia, 68, 232, 241; and Nigerian war, 90; links with East Africa, 252; Uganda election observer, 263; on technical cooperation, 110, 118, 126; export promotion, 112, 131; Youth Program, 124, 171; cooperation in region, 291; general, 18, 41, 167; see also: Nehru, Gandhi
Indian Ocean, US warships in, 139, 140, 149; others in, 206, 207, 217; security of trade routes, 206, 208, 209, 213, 214, 218
Indo-China, 3, 63, 69, 78, 167, 238, 286, 290
Indonesia, 22, 288, 291
Industrial cooperation, 292, 298
Ingram, Derek, 125
Iran, 60
Iraq, 35
Ireland, 158, 267, 268
Ironsi, Maj-Gen Aguiyi, 80
Irvine, Dr Dennis, 162
Isle of Man, 168
Israel, general, 78; Biafran parallel, 97; and Amin, 246, 247, 250, 251; hostages rescued, 258
Ivory Coast, 95, 198

Jackson, Sir Robert, candidate for SG, 16
Jamaica, views on Secretariat, 9; Finance Ministers, 37, 42; and Queen of, 266, 273; on Rhodesian sanctions group, 66; and Indian Ocean Study, 218; relations in Caribbean, 163, 164, 165, 166; association with EEC, 186, 193; technical cooperation, 118, 162; buyers-sellers meet, 112; Gibraltar referendum, 172; aid to Namibians, 226; Zimbabwe election observer, 241; Uganda economic mission, 261; work with Commonwealth Foundation, 279; see also, Manley, Seaga;
Jamal, Amir, 168
James, Sir Morrice, on 1965 war, 25
Jardim, Jorge, 52
Jay, Douglas, 108

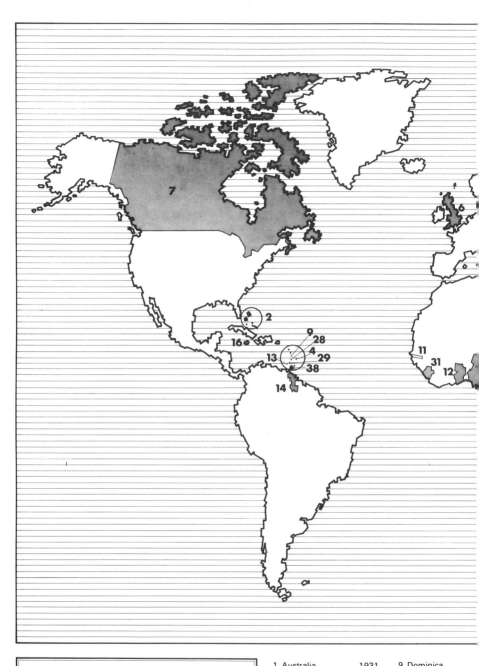

COUNTRIES
OF THE COMMONWEALTH
in the year 1981